Studia Fennica
Folkloristica 19

The Finnish Literature Society (SKS) was founded in 1831 and has, from the very beginning, engaged in publishing operations. It nowadays publishes literature in the fields of ethnology and folkloristics, linguistics, literary research and cultural history.

The first volume of the Studia Fennica series appeared in 1933. Since 1992, the series has been divided into three thematic subseries: Ethnologica, Folkloristica and Linguistica. Two additional subseries were formed in 2002, Historica and Litteraria. The subseries Anthropologica was formed in 2007.

In addition to its publishing activities, the Finnish Literature Society maintains research activities and infrastructures, an archive containing folklore and literary collections, a research library and promotes Finnish literature abroad.

EDITORIAL OFFICE
SKS
P.O. Box 259
FI-00171 Helsinki
www.finlit.fi

ANNA-LEENA SIIKALA
OLEG ULYASHEV

Hidden Rituals and Public Performances

Traditions and Belonging among the
Post-Soviet Khanty, Komi and Udmurts

Finnish Literature Society • Helsinki

Studia Fennica Folkloristica 19

The publication has undergone a peer review.

VERTAISARVIOITU
KOLLEGIALT GRANSKAD
PEER-REVIEWED
www.tsv.fi/tunnus

The open access publication of this volume has received part funding via
Helsinki University Library.

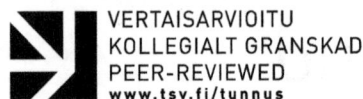

A digital edition of a printed book first published in 2011 by the Finnish Literature Society.
Cover Design: Timo Numminen
EPUB: eLibris Media Oy

ISBN 978-952-222-307-4 (Print)
ISBN 978-952-222-812-3 (PDF)
ISBN 978-952-222-813-0 (EPUB)

ISSN 0085-6835 (Studia Fennica)
ISSN 1235-1946 (Studia Fennica Folkloristica)

DOI: https://doi.org/10.21435/sff.19

Contents

II THE KHANTY: PRESERVING AND PERFORMING RELIGIOUS TRADITIONS

Acknowledgements

The great break in the structure of society in the early 1990s in Russia highlighted the cultural aspirations of indigenous and minority ethnic groups. The Finno-Ugric peoples wished to affirm their identities by cherishing their tradition and bringing it to the fore. Cultural festivals have a long history going back well into the Soviet period, but from the 1990s on they have been considered more important than hitherto. Both the normal experts in tradition and representatives of the state have participated in preserving and publicly supporting their own cultures. Foreign researchers have also been invited to the cultural festivals. The present volume arose as a result of field work conducted among many of the Finno-Ugric peoples. We began our systematic field work together among the Khanty of Shuryshkary in northern Siberia and the Komi of the Ust'-Kulomsk region of the Komi Republic in 2000, though we had both been to Shuryshkary among the Khanty in the 1990s. Because Oleg Ulyashev is Komi and Anna-Leena Siikala is also a representative of a related people, the Finns, the reception afforded us was positive. Oleg was at home in the Komi region, and the framework for the field work was hence excellent. Irina Il'ina from the Ethnographic Institute of the Komi Scientific Centre arranged many trips to the areas inhabited by the Komi, and spared no effort in equipping us for our journeys to Siberia too.

The collaboration between Finnish researchers and the ethnographic department of the Linguistic, Literary and Historical Institute of the Komi Scientific Centre has been sealed by the work on the Encyclopaedia of Uralic Mythologies series. The Encyclopaedia built up a strong network in the 1990s to bring together researchers interested in the religious traditions of the Finno-Ugric peoples. The researchers of the ethnographic section of the Komi Scientific Centre under the leadership of Dr Nikolaï D. Konakov were the first to prepare and publish, in Russian and English, a mythological work in the series, and collaboration between Finnish and Komi researchers has continued ever since. In Anna-Leena Siikala's first trip to Shuryshkary, Dimitriï Nesanelis and Valeriï Sharapov also took part, the latter being a travelling companion also in 2000. Thanks go to the Komi Scientific Centre and the leadership of the ethnographic section. Without the Centre's positive approach it would have been difficult to arrange trips.

The Academy of Finland funded several research trips during the project. Our research queries were formulated particularly during the projects Myth, History and Society: Ethno-nationalism in the Era of Globalisation, and The Other Russia: Cultural Multiplicity in the Making. In addition to the support of the Academy of Finland and the Komi Scientific Centre, the local official approval and the enthusiasm of the local bearers of tradition have helped bring about the publication of this work. We thank the cultural section of the Shuryshkary district government and the Regional Museum of Local Lore in Muzhi for help over many years. The professionals, intellectuals and culturally interested officials helped in the arrangements for our trips. Special thanks go to the head of Vosyakhovo village, Valeriĭ Ivanovich Konev, who made possible the trips to Vershina Voĭkar. The inhabitants of small Khanty villages, with whom we stayed during our field trips, took us into their families and gave us the information we needed. Our guide Nikolaĭ Nikitich Nakhrachëv showed himself over the years to be the finest expert on his own culture. His brother in Kazym-Mys welcomed us heartily. Time spent in Ovolyngort with reindeer-herder Pëtr Nikitich Longortov, his wife Varvara Petrovna and their children will always stay in our memory. The inhabitants of Ust'-Voĭkar, especially Yuriĭ Ozelov and his family and friends, and Martin Rebas' from Vershina Voĭkar offered their assistance and provided us with important information. Our Russian friends living in Muzhi, Alexander and Nina Balin, offered us help and friendship. We would like to thank them too and also all the inhabitants of Kazym-Mys, Lopkhari, Muzhi, Ovgort, Ust'-Voĭkar, Vershina Voĭkar and Vosyakhovo who helped us but are not named here. In the references, we only use the names of those informants who agreed to be mentioned in our publication; others are referred to by using initials or first names.

As Oleg Ulyashev is Komi, we received a warm welcome in all the Komi villages. In Vol'dino, we learned a great deal about the Komi song tradition at the home of Polina Alekseevna Ulyasheva and her singing companions. An important source of information was Yuliya Pavlovna Sergatova, who for many years led the Vol'dino folklore collective. In Bol'shelug, Bogorodsk, Izhma, Kortkeros, Nivshera, Pozheg, Troitsk, Vol'dino and Vyl'gort we got to know song groups and their leaders; thanks to them we were able to assemble some important materials.

Anna-Leena Siikala began field work among the Finno-Ugric peoples in 1991 in Udmurtia. The first field trip was organised by the National Museum of the Udmurt Republic; warm thanks to Serafima Lebedeva and her colleagues. Prof. Pekka Hakamies was a companion on many of these trips; with him, good relations were established with the inhabitants of Karamas Pel'ga, Kuzebaevo and many other villages. In particular the friendship of Lidiya Orekhova, the chair of the cultural society Kenesh, and Ol'ga Mazitova, her large family and the singers of Karamas Pel'ga, has warmed the heart over many years. Prof. Kaija Heikkinen and journalist Kirsikka Moring shared the unforgettable experiences of one culture trip. We wish to thank all, both institutions and individuals, who guided us in our research into the traditions of the Khanty, Komi and Udmurts, and their meanings.

The folklore department of Helsinki University provided working space and infrastructure for the project. It welcomed large numbers of foreign researchers into the project. The collaborative atmosphere and warm spirit of the institute's teachers and researchers was a good foundation for the research work. Research into folklore traditions of many peoples brings with it linguistic problems. Marja-Leea Hattuniemi's help on matters relating to the assembling of literature relating to the Finno-Ugric peoples, the perusal of materials and translating from Russian was irreplaceable. In transliterating Russian we have used the Standard English system (with ы marked by y). In addition to university courses, we received teaching in Northern Khanty from linguist Fedosiya Longortova, who originates from our research village of Ovolyngort. Prof. Vladimir Napol'skikh has also provided help in questions about the Khanty language, has translated various narratives and songs and provided Latin names for the Siberian birds and fishes. Merja Salo checked the transcription of the Khanty words and gave information on the dialectical variation of words, as well as providing Latin names for the Siberian fauna. The Komi researcher Galina Misharina has checked the English versions of the Komi songs. Clive Tolley has over the years translated our articles on the Khanty and Komi, has made many editorial comments and given help with the fonts. We thank all these people warmly.

11 April 2011
Anna-Leena Siikala   Oleg Ulyashev

Insights or parts of chapters have been published in:

Anna-Leena Siikala and Oleg Uljašev: Hantien monet maailmat – paikalliskulttuurit globaalistuvassa maailmassa ["The Many Worlds of the Khanty – Local Cultures in a Globalising World"]. In Sirkka Saarinen ja Eeva Herrala (eds.), *Murros. Suomalais-ugrilaiset kielet ja kulttuurit globalisaation paineissa*: 149–70. Uralica Helsingensia 3. Helsingin yliopiston suomalais-ugrilainen laitos, Suomalainen Tiedeakatemia. Helsinki: Suomalais-Ugrilainen Seura, 2008.

A.-L. Siikala and O. Ulyashev: Mir chelovecheskiĭ – mir dukhov, *Art: respublikanskiĭ literaturno-publisticheskiĭ, istoriko-kul'turologicheskiĭ, khudozhestvennyĭ zhurnal* 2 (2008): 126–44.

Anna-Leena Siikala and Oleg Ulyashev: Landscape of Spirits: Holy Places and Changing Rituals of the Northern Khanty, *Shaman. Journal of the International Society for Shamanistic Research* 12 (2003): 149–78.

Anna-Leena Siikala: Mythic Discourses: Questions of Finno-Ugric Studies on Myth, *Folklore Fellows' Network* 34 (June 2008): 3–13, 16.

Anna-Leena Siikala and Oleg Uljašev, "Sielulle ja itselleni". Komien folklorekollektiivit naiskulttuurina ["'For the Soul and the Self'. Komi Folklore Collectives as Women's Culture"]. In Tarja Kupiainen ja Sinikka Vakimo (eds.), *Välimatkoilla. Kirjoituksia etnisyydestä, kulttuurista ja sukupuolesta*: 85–102. Kultaneito 7. Joensuu: Suomen Kansantietouden Tutkijain Seura, 2006.

Anna-Leena Siikala and Oleg Ulyashev: Field Work in a Changing Culture: The Northern Khanty. In Art Leete (ed.), *The Northern Peoples and States. Changing Relationships*: 254–78. Studies in Folk Culture 5. Tartu: Tartu University Press, 2005.

Anna-Leena Siikala: Neotraditionalism and Ethnic Identity: Recreating Myths and Sacred Histories. In Eugen Helimski, Ulrike Kahrs und Monika Schötschel (eds.), *Mari und Mordwinen in heutigen Rußland. Sprache, Kulture, Identität*: 283–302. Veröffentlichungen der Societas Uralo-Altaica, ed. Klaus Röhrborn und Ingrid Schellbach-Kopra 66. Wiesbaden: Harrassowitz, 2005.

Anna-Leena Siikala: Sites of Belonging. Recreating Histories. In Anna-Leena Siikala, Barbro Klein and Stein Mathisen (eds.), *Creating Diversities. Folklore, Religion and the Politics of Heritage*: 139–52. Studia Fennica Folkloristica 14. Helsinki: Finnish Literature Society, 2004.

Anna-Leena Siikala ja Oleg Uljashev: Maailmojen rajoilla. Muuttuvaa hantiakulttuuria kohtaamassa ["At the Border of Worlds. Meeting a Changing Khanty Culture"]. In Pekka Laaksonen, Seppo Knuuttila and Ulla Piela (eds.), *Tutkijat kentällä. Kalevalaseuran vuosikirja* 82 (2003): 128–45.

Anna-Leena Siikala and Oleg Ulyashev: The Sacred Places of the Northern Khanty and their Rituals. In Ildikó Lehtinen (ed.), *Siberia. Life on the Taiga and Tundra*: 155–84. Helsinki: National Board of Antiquities, 2002.

Anna-Leena Siikala and Oleg Uljašev: Henkien maisema. Pohjoishantien pyhät paikat ja niiden rituaalit. ["The Sacred Places of the Northern Khanty and their Rituals"]. In Ildikó Lehtinen (ed.): *Siperia. Taigan ja tundran kansoja*: 155–84. Helsinki: Museovirasto, 2002.

Anna-Leena Siikala: From Sacrificial Rituals into National Festivals: Post-Soviet Transformations of Udmurt Tradition. In Pertti J. Anttonen *et al.* (eds.), *Folklore, Heritage Politics and Ethnic Diversity. A Festschrift for Barbro Klein*: 57–85. Botkyrka: Multicultural Centre, 2000.

Anna-Leena Siikala: Quest for Identity: Ethnic Traditions and Societies in Transition. In Heikki Kirkinen (ed.), *Protection and Development of our Intangible Heritage*: 77–83. Studia Carelica Humanistica 15. Joensuu: University of Joensuu, 1999.

Abbreviations

A.-L. S.   Anna-Leena Siikala
O. U.   Oleg Ulyashev
V. N.   Vladimir Napol'skikh
A. W.   Anna Widmer
rec.   recorded
b.   born

Representations of the
Russian Finno-Ugrians

I

1 Societies in transition

Since the collapse of the Soviet Union there have been noticeable economic and political changes in all the areas inhabited by Uralic peoples. The Western Siberian North, in particular, is changing rapidly and fundamentally: oil and gas exploration, the investment of foreign capital and the strengthening of international contacts are hallmarks of the era of globalisation. In the early 1990s, the infrastructure of transport, public healthcare and education built up by the Soviet authorities collapsed or suffered severe financial difficulties; state farms were transformed into co-operative enterprises. The process of transformation has been painful and long-lasting. More recently, after 2000, marketing problems have forced co-operative plants to close or find new means to sell their products. At the same time the financial benefits of oil and gas are accruing. The towns and areal centres are more prosperous than ever, while other centres of population nearby lack the means for people's subsistence, and distant villages are losing inhabitants.

The results of these changes can be seen on a social and cultural level. The simultaneous presence of different cultural elements and practices, both new and traditional, mark out economically stratified communities. The socio-economic processes affecting such European Russian minorities as the Udmurts and Komi are more subtle than in many other areas. Local rural communities suffer from typical problems: unemployment, decrease of inhabitants, high mortality rates and an aging population. On the other hand, rebuilding churches, schools and cultural centres are among today's enterprises. Local language, culture and religious activities give substance to life and help in coping with everyday problems. So, the developments in different areas proceed at different paces and in different directions. They do not lead to easily comprehensible cultural totalities, but to cultural domains in which different cultural elements are simultaneously present, to connections between phenomena which before were considered to be disparate and discrete. This is a typical feature of globalising culture.[1]

The introduction of new economic and social systems in the 1990s has led to an unstable society in which, besides the growing importance of the

1. See Marcus 1992: 321.

market economy, people turn to traditional practices of subsistence economy, barter and reciprocal networks of relatives and neighbours. The meaning and practice of "tradition" varies greatly in different areas depending on the economic and societal development. Tradition may be connected to everyday life: people turn to accustomed methods of livelihood and healing for economic reasons. "Tradition" is also a tool for the cultural policies of today. Caroline Humphrey, in her studies of economic and social changes in several regions of Russia, has paid attention to the emergence of new forms of traditional ritualism among ethnic groups.[2] In reaction to the internationalisation of economics and the flow of information, typical of globalisation, people strive to strengthen the local and marginal. During the process of change, ethnic groups are seeking to establish their self-awareness and self-respect, consciously constructing it by the bricoleur technique, exploiting and recreating their past and traditions.[3] Neo-traditionalism in Russia represents a global trend.[4] It is typical not only of the minorities of this huge state, but also of the majority: Russian nationalists, especially on the periphery, aim to revive their religious and imperial traditions. In the republics of the former Soviet Union the nature of neo-traditionalism depends on the historical, political and economic experiences of the people.[5]

Russian studies and research into Finno-Ugric cultures have a long and distinguished history. However, these two disciplines have traditionally been assigned different niches in academic debate, often isolated from another. It is also customary to examine Russia from the perspective of Moscow and St Petersburg, centres of the hierarchical state, and as a monolithic cultural empire. Ethnographic fieldwork in the various republics of Russia has demonstrated the need to approach the socio-cultural situation in post-Soviet Russia from a new perspective. The dichotomy between hegemonic state culture and minority "folk" cultures has to be deconstructed. If the perspective is turned upside down, from the margins to the centres, the great changes caused by the collapse of the Soviet Union and the new forms of globalisation, which resulted in an unstable society with simultaneous tendencies for rapid modernisation and the revival of traditions, can be seen even more clearly. The minorities of multicultural Northern Russia, such as the Finno-Ugric groups, should not be seen as islands isolated from one another but in relation to one another and to the main culture.

2. Humphrey 2002.
3. See Populenko 2000: 173–83.
4. Cf. Oracheva 1999.
5. Kappeler 1996; Huttenbach 1991.

2 Traditions in a globalised world

Are traditions dying?

The crisis in the nation-state in the 1990s has prompted sociologists such as Anthony Giddens and Scott Lash to forecast that traditions will vanish; as Giddens says, "the radical turn from tradition intrisic to modernity's reflexivity makes a break . . . with preceding eras".[1] The claim is founded on Western observations of the drop in esteem of such basic societal institutions as religion or marriage, and of the movements in the cultural mass markets, that appear to be vacant for the member of consumer society intent on the maximising of pleasure.

The evidence from the world as a whole does not, however, support this claim. The increasingly international economy and information exchange and changes in political regimes have raised problems of ethnic and national identity in various parts of the world. As Europe, with its long history of nation-states, moves towards closer integration, local identities are assuming greater importance, while in many other parts of the world the construction of nation-states and nations has been continuing of late. Historically, the world has reached a situation where nationalism, tribalism and neotribalism co-exist with various manifestations of international integration, and the cultural conflicts are forcing nations either to assimilate or to seek an identity of their own. As a result of population shifts caused by flight and evacuation, there are more and more displaced and multi-placed persons and multicultural communities.

Nation-building involves a search for identity through the use of simultaneously unifying and distinctive factors such as language, cultural traditions, values, religion, a shared experience of history and geographical location.[2] A national identity is not born of coincidence or of itself. Its creation requires the separation of self from the other and is thus a result of conscious action. Jean-Jacques Rousseau was already pointing out in 1762 that "Whoso would undertake to institute a People must . . . transform each individual . . . into a part of something greater than himself, from which, in a sense, he derives his

1. Giddens 1991: 175-176.
2. Anderson 1983; Hobsbawm and Ranger 1983; Gellner 1983; Abrahams 1993; Ehn, Frykman and Löfgren 1993; Honko 1988; Linde-Laursen 1995; P. Anttonen 1996.

life and his being", and, he argues, an essential feature of this whole is "some unity of origin, interest, or convention".[3] Identity is, however, far from being static; it may be described more accurately as a continuing process.[4] The "unity of origin, of interest and convention" help to consolidate a collective identity by calling attention to the group's uniqueness and difference from other groups. Groups without a written history have often looked into their own past by revitalising oral traditions and creating new forms of traditions. This activity is equally manifested in both myth and religion as well as in daily life and everyday routines. When it comes to identity, popular thought invests the past with symbolic authority. This popular notion is epitomised by the concept of tradition.

The Latin verb *tradere* means "pass something on", as from the past to the present. Tradition is "the past in the present", and is so understood in folklore studies.[5] Edward Shils, a sociologist, defined tradition with reference to inheritance: "the decisive criterion is that, having been created through human action, through thought and imagination, it is handed down from one generation to the next".[6] With the concept of tradition we allude to those expressions, modes of thought and action which are consciously seen to establish and maintain cultural continuity. Virtually any cultural process can attain traditional status and significance. Nevertheless, it must satisfy the requirements of a tradition, i.e. include the shared goals and activities of the ethnic group and nationality. Thus, though a single cultural pheno- menon plucked out of its daily context can assume the symbolic expression of cultural continuity. Labelling this expression as tradition is, however, a conscious act motivated by the need of a group for self-definition. Hence, the concept of tradition is actualised during periods of social upheaval and when cultural boundaries are being threatened. A tradition – the past within the present – turns into Tradition when the link between the present and a past invested with ethnic or national significance becomes topical.

Recent studies have focused on the way in which the past can be revived to validate the unique identity of a group.[7] Jocelyn Linnekin has also empha- sised that tradition "is not so much received as creatively and dynamically fashioned by the current generation".[8] She holds that the past is never an objective fact; instead, traditions are always the outcomes of choice. Using an expression such as "the invention of tradition", Eric Hobsbawm alludes to the same kind of process of revival, which includes the normalisation and ritualisation of phenomena referring to the past.[9] Whether chosen or

---

3. Rousseau 1993: 214, 223.
4. Friedman 1992a: 194–210; Friedman 1992b: 839–59.
5. See Ó Giolláin 2000: 8; Anttonen 2005: 11–12.
6. Shils 1981: 12.
7. Pertti Anttonen discusses ideas of the relationship of tradition and political identity: Anttonen 2005: 95–113.
8. Linnekin 1990: 151.
9. Hobsbawm and Ranger 1984: 4. The discussions concerning "intention", "authority", "authenticity" and "truth" of traditions are handled in Siikala and Siikala 2005: 38–45.

invented, the traditions deemed significant are hardly arbitrary.[10] To satisfy the shared goals of an ethnic group, an authority over the community and its individuals is needed. National symbols are fashioned from material which bears the prestige of the past and thus has a unifying power.

Tradition as a concept of introspective Western sociology

It is clear that the concept of tradition as an ideologically loaded element is not confined to the European nation-states alone. For it also appealed and appeals today to peoples who have never succeeded in their nation-forming projects or even entertained such ideas. Research of the early 1990s into globalisation and ethnic processes has come to focus on the way the cultural past is revived to validate the group's identity. The problems of this discussion, which has been popular among sociologists, historians and anthropologists during recent years, lie in three main domains: 1. how tradition and traditional society is understood; 2. the idea of basic cultural phases which allows the use of such concepts as pre-modern, modern, post-modern and post-traditional, based on the understanding of cultural development in the Western world; and 3. an implicit or open political stance in discussing the invention or revival of tradition among ethnic minorities or in multi-ethnic communities.

In the sociological debate on the modernisation and globalisation of the present world, the understanding of the concept of tradition is based on the ideas presented long ago by the eighteenth-century Romantics. The referential ground for arguing the "traditional community" is often found in the classical anthropological literature examining isolated cultural entities. The clearest example of this anachronistic definition of tradition was presented in 1994 by Anthony Giddens in his article "Living in a Post-Traditional Society". He states: "Tradition, I shall say, is bound up with memory, specially what Maurice Halbwachs terms 'collective memory': involves ritual; is connected with what I shall call a formulaic notion of truth; has 'guardians'; and unlike custom, has binding force which has a combined moral and emotional content."[11] The background of the formulation is provided by the knowledge produced by the British structuralist-functionalist school of social anthropology as well as the notions of Durkheimian thinking. Tradition is cut out of the everyday life of the people, its representations are rituals and "real" folklore. In its repetitive, backward-looking way, tradition maintains social cohesion, includes and expresses a formulaic truth guarded by specialists, elders, magicians, shamans and so forth. The guardians of tradition are deprived of all capability for rational thinking. Giddens excludes not only customs but also everyday folklore from the sphere of tradition. "Tradition" is – according to him – the expression of the common interest of a group or community. Its truth is not questioned or negotiated.

10. See Siikala and Siikala 2005: 45.
11. Giddens 1994: 63.

The main problem with this argumentation lies in the idea of *local knowledge* (pre-modern or traditionalist knowledge) which is maintained because of its mystical character and which is bound to mechanical repetition. Briefly, for Giddens tradition is a *thing* which can change, even die and be revived, but which nonetheless is a totality, a monolistic entity which leaves no room for discussion or negotiation. This kind of "cultural objectification" is not, of course, restricted to the usage of sociologists alone. As Richard Handler and others have argued, the objectifying vision has dominated Western theories of culture and society.[12] Empirical-style studies of folklore and oral tradition treating folklore as things to collect have followed the general lines of objectifying thinking.

Traditions, viewed as objects, will die, according to Giddens, unless tradition is, as he states, "discursively articulated and defended – in other words, justified as having value in a universe of plural competing values".[13] Here he points to the central role of tradition in the cultural processes of the post-colonial world, which indeed has been observed by many ethnographers.

The theorists on European detraditionalism see the development of culture as distinct periods in which traditional vs. modern, modern vs. post-modern or even post-traditional follow one another in sequence. The tendency to view issues in periods is an inherent feature of introspective Western sociology. Traditional cultures, both European folk cultures and non-European cultures, are regarded as static, closed systems characterised by the epithets cold, repetitive, ritualistic, predetermined, differentiated and organised, in contrast to the hot, experimental, reflexive, undifferentiated or unorganised modern/post-modern West.[14] A good example, again, is Anthony Giddens, who discusses the role of tradition in the building of modern European culture. He states that modernity destroys tradition even though a collaboration between modernity and tradition was characteristic of the earlier phases of modern social development.[15] He seeks tradition in Europe instead of Africa, and sees the monumental "great traditions" of Europe, associated with the rationalisation of religion, as interconnected with the small traditions of grass-roots communities. Even though this relationship did influence the lives of small communities through control by a central power and the resistance of the people, it did not (according to Giddens) penetrate the heart of social activity and change the auto-programmed life of small communities.

Locality, globalisation and identity-formation

The monolithic conception of tradition presented above has been anchored to the concept of local community, which was in the classic sense marked

12. Handler 1988: 14–15.
13. Giddens 1994: 100.
14. Heelas 1996: 3.
15. Giddens 1994.

by common space, shared values and shared identity and culture, and which formed one of the basic frames of reference orienting both anthropology and folkloristics.[16] But, as Arjun Appadurai, among many other scholars interested in modern identity processes, states: "the landscapes of group identity – the ethnoscapes – around the world are no longer familiar anthropological objects, insofar as groups are no longer tightly territorialized, spatially bounded, historically unselfconscious, or culturally homogenous".[17] In the world of dispersed groups and translocal cultures, we could speak of dispersed identities or multiple identities instead of locally bound coherent entities. For the identity of any person or group is produced simultaneously in many different locales and activities.[18]

Interconnections and dialogue between locality and global forces – administrative, economic, cultural, etc. – form a complex field of studies which we can here touch on only briefly. Appadurai has defined locality as primarily relational and contextual rather than as scalar or spatial.[19] He sees locality as a mental relational construction created using the symbolising power of both tangible and intangible devices (building constructions, cultured landscapes, folklore and oral memory) in interaction with different kinds of contexts. In seeing "local" as an actively produced and maintained construction, he reserves the concept of neighbourhood for concrete spatial units of social reproduction. Neighbourhoods themselves are, according to Appadurai, context-generating; the relationship between local and global opens up, he maintains, only in the context-generative dimension of neighbourhood.[20] It is possible to emphasise the nature of globalisation processes as economic and power relationships. Globalisation is basically a product of recent capitalism, which is at the moment a dominant force behind the economic life of most countries. Many scholars, such as Stuart Hall, see the new form of globalisation as essentially a spreading of mass culture. The processes of globalisation are complex, dealing with power relationships on the level of both government and economy, grey economy, culture, information exchange and technology.[21] The complexity of globalisation processes is obvious if we study cultural changes and transcultural processes determined or effected by multinational organisations, or in such gigantic and administratively hierarchic states as Russia or China, where globalisation happens on different levels and in different areal pockets of society, each influencing others both vertically and horizontally.

George Marcus points out that one of the paradoxes of world-wide integration is that it does not lead to an "easily comprehensible totality, but to an increasing diversity of connections among phenomena once thought

16. Marcus 1992: 315.
17. Appadurai 1996: 48; see Anttonen 2005: 121–2.
18. Marcus 1992: 315–22.
19. Appadurai 1996: 52.
20. Appadurai 1996: 184.
21. Hall 1991.

23

disparate and worlds apart".[22] It could be added that the experience of complexity is increased by a new notion of meaningful space. Areas which were seen as remote and peripheral enter into international transactions. A good example of these kinds of processes is the Republic of Sakha (Yakutia), which immediately after the collapse of the Soviet Union created – on the basis of the richness of its natural environment – good connections with the centres of the financial world in the United States and Japan. The improvement of information technology has contributed to the emergence of new spaces in marginal areas of the world. Speakers of Finno-Ugric languages live mostly in rural areas. The celebration of their own culture involves local traditions, and ideas for possible ways of changing their culture are learned from the media and television.

When locality has lost its former meaning we may have problems in defining our field of studies. How can we examine complex processes of tradition and identity-formation in diffuse networks of diverse interconnections, of ideological, economic and power relations? Many scholars agree that we cannot isolate parts of an integrated world, but that the articulation between the local and global is crucial for "the generation of specific social realities".[23]

One reaction to globalisation is the cultural empowerment of the marginal and the local.[24] This is most often achieved by recovering one's own officially non-existent, orally transmitted history.[25] In the Pacific countries, for example, the pre-colonial traditions and customs have been valuable as strategic resources in the struggles for independency of the post-colonial era.[26] Globalisation happens not only in the offices of international corporations, but in local communities. This is seen not only in the West but also all over the former Soviet area. We cannot understand recent social upheaval in the countries of Eastern Europe by mere analysis of the structural changes in government or society from the perspective of periodisation in Western social science. The way of life and world view of the Russian population – both the ethnic Russians and the minority groups – have been formed by Soviet culture. This culture pervades both ways of seeing and being in addition to a wide range of locally significant traditions. The changing governmental system poses a challenge to local and ethnic traditional thought in many ways and will affect virtually all areas of life. This encounter also affects the orientation to the future.

Co-existence of divergent traditions

Tradition and ethnic self-awareness must be viewed against the tendency towards globalisation within the framework of the interaction between

---

22. Marcus 1992: 321.
23. Ekholm-Friedman and Friedman 1995: 134; see also Friedman 1994.
24. See Mathisen 2004: 141–4.
25. Cf. Hall 1991: 34–5.
26. Siikala and Siikala 2005: 41–5.

nations, and not only as a national, local, ethnic, gender and social-class signifier. The minorities of Russia and Siberia belong to a multicultural society in which identity is formed in relationship to other nationalities. The ethnic religious traditions found in these regions cannot be seen as isolated cases separate from the whole, but must be examined in relationship to the corresponding traditions of other groups. The problem with early studies of Finno-Ugric religions was that they were described as forms of consciousness cut off from the mainstream culture. In the study of Finno-Ugric religions it is necessary to take note of the long historical processes of interaction and assimilation, the result of which is the formation of pockets of Finno-Ugric peoples practising an ethnic religion within a Russian context.

When discussing detraditionalisation, the invention of tradition or the authenticity of tradition, we should remember that the study of traditional cultures has, especially in the light of the *practice* and *action* theories, contested the staticism of "traditional cultures". Viewed from within, even the traditional culture has acted as an arena for differing motives and interests, for various survival strategies and the creative processing of tradition. The key question is: to what extent and in what way do people in different cultures depend on their traditions, or create their culture by constructing traditions? No one today describes the individual even in traditional cultures as being fettered by norms and rules in the manner of the interactionalism of the 1960s or the Parsons school. On the other hand, there is probably not a single culture that permits complete freedom of choice. Rather, different cultures generate different dialectic relationships in which the latitude of agency is determined under pressure from various conventions and social constraints.

Scholars emphasising the co-existence of divergent cultural processes claim that the processes of detraditionalisation do not take place in a vacuum but simultaneously with the processes of tradition-preservation: the construction or recreation of traditional ways of life.[27] Traditions are always open to human action, be they invented, revived or inherited. According to Timothy Luke and Barbara Adam, there is evidence that detraditionalisation really does take place. Instead of leading to the obliteration of all traditions, detraditionalisation can be seen as a trend either competing with the processes of preserving and constructing traditions or influencing and even permeating them.[28]

Traditions bound to crumbling institutions vanish, but in doing so they make room for new traditions to be created and preserved. In multicultural communities traditions serve as a means of creating a distinct self-awareness, of constructing and expressing the self of a person or a group. Revival of tradition is a mark of the battle of survival of small minorities. Traditions unite displaced communities and create significant differences within the consolidated urban masses. Tradition-processes nowadays represent the pursuit of identity in a world where economy, technology and flows of information change the interconnections between the local and global.

27. Heelas 1996: 7.
28. Luke 1996; Adam 1996.

An examination of traditions in a global context reveals that the periodising contrasts, such as traditionalism vs. modernism, modernism vs. postmodernism, employed by the Western social sciences and with a clear "before and after" mentality are incapable of handling the polyvocal complexity of the present day.[29] The social upheaval after the collapse of the Soviet Union and unification in Europe cannot be comprehended merely by examining changes in the political or social structures in the light of period thinking. The way of life and worldviews of the silent majority, which consists to an increasing extent of minorities and has always consisted of groups divided by social, economic and cultural borders, are moulded not only by shared "European" or national views and behavioural models but also by all manner of cultural traditions of local significance. The present-day restructuring of political regimes is encountering local, ethnic, gender, age-specific and other outlooks in different ways and in many walks of life. This encounter will also shape the orientation of the future.

29. Heelas 1996: 3.

3 Belonging and neo-traditionalism

Ethnic self-awareness

Research focusing on the ethnic awakening of minority groups has to take a stand on the concepts of "nationality", "nationalism", "ethnicity" and "identity". The limits of the concept of nationalism became visible when, in the 1980s and 1990s, the crisis of European nation-states led to debate on nationalism and the invention of traditions in the construction of national identities (see pp. 19–20). In this debate, the concept of nationalism seems to have become blurred, mixing national attitudes, the cultural and social programmes of the European nation-state processes which contributed to, for example, the establishment of education and health care systems, the political programmes of these processes, and the aggressive expansion politics of chauvinistic nationalism with its destructive results in the Second World War.[1]

David G. Anderson has observed the special usage of the term "nationality" and "nationalism" in Russian studies: "In analyses of Russia, 'nationalism' tends to apply to peoples whom the Soviet state had classified as nations (titular nations) while other social movements are described as 'ethno-nationalism', 'ethnic mobilisation', or even subgroupism. Some students of the former Union also use the term 'nationality' in their analyses, although in each of these cases their usage suggests that nationalities are diminutive forms of proper nations."[2] Because the dynamics of social life depend on the scale and organisation of society, the concepts of "nationality" and "nationalism" lead to problems in the study of minority groups and indigenous people. For this reason many ethnographers choose to use the concepts of ethnicity[3] and ethno-nationalism.[4]

Ethno-nationalism – like nationalism – has been given different values depending on whose ideology it represents. According to Stanley J. Tambiah, ethno-nationalism "refers to the generation of regional or subnational reactions and resistances to what is seen as an over-centralised and hegemonic state, and their drive to achieve their own regional and local socio-political

1. Kemiläinen 1999: 7.
2. Anderson 2002: 203.
3. Polyanskiĭ 1999.
4. Drobizheva 1996; Balzer 1999.

formations".[5] John L. Comaroff contrasts Euro-nationalism which, according to him, is characterised by universalist principles of citizenship and a social contract, and ethno-nationalism, celebrating cultural particularity and granting membership by ascription.[6] From this perspective ethno-nationalist ideas are seen as "primitive" and "irrational", and as a threat to the existing political order.

The concept of ethno-nationalism should be used very cautiously, if at all, because if the self-awareness of minority groups is regarded as falsely based on irrational primordialism and threatening separationism it might provide an excuse for state terrorism. The ideological fields of ethno-nationalism and nationalism should be examined in their concrete international and socio-economic contexts, in their relationships with the partner groups and nations that constitute the field of mutual action, not forgetting the historical past of these relationships or economic interests of partners often disguised in ideological rhetoric. Among the Uralic peoples, the cultural awakening has been peaceful and not given to separatist action. Some of the Uralic groups belong to the those small nationalities of Russia whose cultures are seen as being in need of special safeguarding.[7] Biculturalism is a visible feature of the life of these people and the saliency of multiple levels of identity is seen in, for instance, the term "Rossiany", meaning multi-ethnic citizens of Russia.[8]

It is customary to use the concept of identity in studies of ethnic self-awareness and self-construction. But the concept of identity is not by itself a sufficient conceptual tool for analysing the practices and meanings of ethnic and social relationships in face-to-face communities. When studying an Evenki group, David Anderson proceeds from vernacular usages and develops the conceptual idea of "belonging",[9] which leaves room for an understanding of the multiplicity of factors in people's self-definition. In referring to the interrelationship and reciprocity of face-to-face communities, which according to Anderson are evident in aboriginal representations of identity, the concept of *belonging* is anchored in the concrete practices of everyday life.[10]

Whereas Western research into society and culture has seen the invention of traditions as an instrument in the nation-building processes, the Marxist ideology formulated by Vladimir Il'ich Lenin saw national consciousness as a means used by the bourgeois state to improve its capitalistic competitiveness. The self-consciousness of minorities within Russia, the "ocean of peoples", and later in the Soviet Union, were seen as a by-product of bourgeois socio-economic imperatives which should fade away once the economic basis for class distinction had been removed. For this reason, Lenin's policy

5. Tambiah 1996: 128–9.
6. Comaroff 1996: 175.
7. Bagramov *et al.* 1993: 89–98.
8. Balzer 1999: 213; see also Grant 1995: 159 and Piirainen 2002: 158–9.
9. See also Siikala 2000a.
10. Anderson 2002: 208–10.

on ethnic groups was liberal during the first years of the new state. The Bolsheviks reorganised the territorial division along ethnic principles: the series of republics bearing the names of ethnic groups was a result of Lenin's will to safeguard other nationalities from the domination of Russians.[11] During the Stalinist regime of the 1930s, the nationality policy changed, leading to suppression, the forced resettling of whole ethnic groups to other parts of the vast country and to the extinction of intellectuals speaking languages other than Russian. Collectivisation and the crisis caused by the famine of the 1930s destroyed the social structures at the micro-level. The Stalinist language policy, in turn, limited the possibility of speaking minority languages.[12] In the 1960s, Russian was propagated as the native language of minorities, which weakened the position of the small languages.[13]

According to Henry R. Huttenbach, these historical experiences of ethnic groups contributed to the failure of the world's greatest social experiment. In the 1990s, people realised there was a multiplicity of histories, apart from the canonised Soviet understanding of the past in which they could not locate their personal or communal histories. The decade can be characterised as the decade of recalling and reinterpreting history. If we remember the traumatic past of many ethnic groups, we will understand better the emotional loadedness of ethnically relevant traditions and the striving for self-determination of minorities in the former Soviet territory.

The state, intellectuals and the construction of heritage

Since 1985 and the days of *perestroika*, national identity has raised a good deal of discussion in Finno-Ugric intellectual circles.[14] Because of the suppression of the Stalinist regime and the ensuing absence of the written culture of many Finno-Ugric groups, orally preserved traditions and ethnic religions seemed to provide the foundation for a national culture. Similar trends have been visible in Siberia, where drama, literature, fine arts and the construction of local culture have drawn inspiration from the traditional modes of shamanism.[15] These tendencies are typical not only of Siberian minorities or Finno-Ugric peoples; they are a global sign of the times.

In referring to folklore and ethnic religion as a source for constructing nationally relevant cultural capital, the above-mentioned intellectuals follow the models already being used in the nation-state projects of nineteenth-century Europe. Interest in the folklore of cultures lacking written history was based on the Romantic ideas presented by Johan Gottfried Herder at the end of the eighteenth century. The example *par excellence* is the creation of Finnishness and its symbol, the *Kalevala*. Kirsten Hastrup claims that where

---

11. Huttenbach 1996: 353; Williams 1999.
12. See Simon 1991: 99–100; Tishkov 1997: 35–43; Vdovin, Zorin and Nikonov 1998: 59–82.
13. Lallukka 1998: 94; see also Salve 1998 and Lallukka 1990.
14. Rasin 1993; Sanukov 1993 and 1996; Kraïnov 1996: 72–3; Pimenova 2009: 161–2.
15. See, for example, Balzer 1995: 18–19.

a shared history is absent, traditions may be invented for the purpose of distinction.[16] Traditions may be constructions, selections or inventions, but they are not just any constructions. In everyday life the feeling of belonging is born of common practices and important social relationships. The building of self-awareness within an ethnic group needs symbols greater than that. National symbols are sought in sources that have the authority and uniting power of the past. We should ask what kinds of "traditions" are selected for the construction of a nationally important heritage, and by whom and how these traditions are selected.

In the Nordic countries study of the politics of heritage has shown how organised work in the collection, preservation and publication of oral traditions modified the picture of nationally representative tradition.[17] Analogous heritage-building processes can be found in Russia and the Soviet Union, despite their different ideological backgrounds.[18] The role of Russian and Soviet ethnography, which depicted cultural forms of minorities, has been crucial in the self-understanding of these groups. Cultural portraits created by researchers were transmitted to local people through museums, folklore publications and exhibitions. The museum institution, for example, has been acting at different levels of the cultural administration of the republics from big towns to tiny villages.

The great influence of the state in the creation of locally visible representations of ethnicity is also evident in the central position of the "folklore collectives" in rural villages. During the 1930s, when the Soviet state wanted to promote the cultural development of the rural population, leading Russian folklorists recommended folklore as a basis for socialist folk art. In the 1940s centrally planned socialist folklorism acquired a strong organisational basis, including a network of cultural houses and clubs in all the socialist countries.[19] Soviet/Russian folklore collectives received their instructions from the representatives of the ministries of culture in the republics. Nowadays they form a tradition in themselves and are visible participants in all the cultural festivals.

Soviet culture workers fixed their gaze upon the present day in order to develop cultural expressions of rural populations, to create new socialist forms of folk art. Today the intellectuals of the minority groups are more clearly aiming at the construction of ethnic awareness. In their heritage-building processes they are seeking traditions bearing the authority of the past. It seems that different groups pick out different yet characteristic elements from the pool of past traditions. The main traditions symbolising the cultural unity of, say, the Eastern Khanty and Mansi are bear ceremonialism and shamanism.[20] The Volga Finns and Udmurts value their holy groves

16. Hastrup 1987: 258; see Hobsbawm and Ranger 1993.
17. Klein 2000: 33.
18. Harvilahti with Kazagačeva 2003; see also Hakamies 1998.
19. Kurkela 1989: 104; Suutari 2010: 321–3.
20. Gemuev 1990; Moldanov 1999; Moldanova 2001; Kulemzin 2000.

and sacrificial rituals,[21] whereas the symbolic focus of Russian Karelians is *Kalevala* poetry, which seems to bear the voice of the past in its mythic themes and images. An interesting topic for study is the relationship of the traditions chosen as ethnic symbols and the self-understanding of the people they are supposed to characterise.

Finno-Ugric ethnicities in the making

The present work examines the making of post-Soviet cultural multiplicity in local communities. Special attention is paid to the recreation of indigeneity. "Ethnic" in this connection does not refer to a homogeneous entity of a primordial nature. On the contrary, the cultural multiplicity of North Russian communities is a consequence of not only the multi-ethnicity of neighbourhoods, but the fact that ethnic groups are internally divided by many factors such as economic opportunities, politics, values, religion, dialect, everyday habits and the relocation of populations.

In our research we have aimed to identify the diverse mechanisms of societal and economic change in different Northern Russian areas and their relationship to the transformation of cultural practices. We have tried to illuminate the uses of oral and ritual traditions in the secret and public performances of the performers' own culture. What do people understand by "tradition" that is worth performing? Should we talk about neo-traditionalism or are there divergent ideas of tradition among the people? Why and at whose initiative is the "culture" performed? What are the political purposes of collecting and presenting tradition? How do the public performances affect people's self-awareness and self-respect? Are the processes similar among different Finno-Ugric cultures or are there differences in the dynamics of the processes of tradition?

These preliminary questions were formulated along the following principal lines of investigation, aimed at orienting the work in the field:

1. To examine the formulation of the cultural multiplicity of the post-Soviet era.
2. To trace oral and literal discourses, events and cultural processes expressing ethnic diversities in micro-level local communities and to examine them from the perspective of area, state and global cultural policies, and in the light of historical and socio-economic developments.
3. To see the pursuit of new socio-cultural activity by minorities as interaction in a multicultural situation instead of as a minority–majority dichotomy.
4. To trace the different "voices" of minorities in culture-making processes, for example seeing recreations of tradition as a topic for negotiation and even conflict among ethnic groups, not as cultural forms based on common consent.

21. Vladykin 1996; Tojdybekova 1997; Minniyakhmetova 2000, 2001; Shutova 2001.

31

5. To pay special attention to the gendered nature of these processes and the role of women in the making of the symbols of ethnicity.
6. To define the forms and items of culture (rituals, myths, local history and poetry, dress, food, etc.) which bear symbolic value in presenting ethnicity and the arenas and ways in which these symbolic representations are manifest.
7. To examine the role of politicians, intellectuals and the media in circulating different interpretations of recreated traditions.
8. To trace the political and economic implications of different manifestations of neo-traditionalism.

The research mainly deals with cultural changes of Northern Russia, where the economic mechanisms, regional policies and changing societal values have to be taken in consideration. Our views are based on long-term field work conducted by Anna-Leena Siikala from 1991 in Udmurtia and then from 1999 with Oleg Ulyashev in the northern areas of Russia. The target areas of field work were the Shuryshkary region in the Yamal-Nenets area (the Khanty, Nenets, Komi and Russians), the Upper Vychegda district in the Komi Republic (the Komi and Russians), and the Alnash district of the Udmurt Republic (the Udmurts, Mari and Tatars). These regions differ in their history, society, economy and culture, which had an impact on our work. The concrete research tasks and co-operation with local researchers varied according to the target area. Also the main principles and aims of the research were reformulated following on from discussions in the field. The present-day Khanty religion cannot be understood without a knowledge of past ideas and practices. We were also surprised at the amount of knowledge concerning religious beliefs and practices. The main concerns in different areas were as follows:

The Northern Khanty of Western Siberia live in a rapidly changing environment where the expansion of the oil industry and the multiculturality of society are transforming the living conditions and culture. The research topics address the private and public representations of Khanty beliefs and rituals, the interrelationships between local ethnic groups, and the role of the cultural administration and intellectuals in the performance of Khanty culture.

Among the *Komi*, women play a conspicuous part in maintaining and enlivening the rural culture and the work of the folklore collectives. The research material collected permits study of the meaning of "belonging" to women, and of the repertoires and song tradition preserved by the singing groups. Ethno-futurism is especially strong among Komi artists and provides an insight into the contemporary interpretation of the mythic world view.

In *Southern Udmurtia*, the ethnic religious cults have special meaning for the self-awareness of the Udmurts; they are also performed at national festivals. The research in Southern Udmurtia examines neo-traditionalism in the field of religion, the making of ethnic symbols by women and the role of politicians and journalists in building the national culture.

We deal with the above questions in four parts of this book. The first, "Representations of the Russian Finno-Ugrians" written mainly by Anna-Leena Siikala, presents our questions, the ethnographically important aspects of the research tradition concerning Finno-Ugric peoples and the principles of our field work. The second part, "The Khanty: Preserving and Performing Religious Traditions", describes the religion of the Khanty of Shuryshkary in detail, because the public reviving of the tradition cannot be understood without a knowledge of the beliefs and rituals in people's everyday life. The third part, "The Komi: Proliferating Singing Traditions", deals with Komi folklore collectives and their performances, and singing as part of women's culture. Because Oleg Ulyashev is an expert in Komi folklore and culture, his contribution has been vital. The fourth part, "Comparisons and Observations", discusses the topics under consideration among the Udmurts and presents a comparative overview of the revival of tradition among a number of Finno-Ugric cultures. We have dealt with the questions posed in this book in many articles; they are included in the bibliography as well as in references.

4 Interest in Finno-Ugric peoples

The images of Finno-Ugric peoples were created by scholars from a number of countries over a couple of centuries. In Finland, research into Uralic peoples and their folklore and religions has a long history. From the outset we should point to the early-nineteenth-century researcher into Finnish roots, and visitor to Siberia, Matthias Alexander Castrén, as well as to many other pioneer scholars of folk culture, such as August Ahlqvist, K. F. Karjalainen, Heikki Paasonen, Kai Donner, Uno Holmberg-Harva, Toivo Lehtisalo and U. T. Sirelius. Moreover, the folk-poetry collections published as a result of the work of the Finno-Ugric Society contain a great deal of the mythology of the Finno-Ugric linguistic area. Many generations of researchers in Russia and Finland, as well as Hungary and Estonia, have applied themselves to the collection, publication and investigation of materials. Hence investigation of Finno-Ugric mythology has a particularly good infrastructure with archives and libraries, which have a huge amount to offer scholars. During the Soviet period, the field work of Western researchers was very limited, even if a few did have some opportunities to carry it out. Most research was based in archive materials. For this reason the stimulation of the research tradition was felt to be both topical and necessary in the 1990s.

Language, myths and folklore as "evidence of history"

Castrén blazed a trail to the heart of the related peoples of Siberia and laid a foundation for Finno-Ugristics, which contributed to the construction of Finnishness and long offered a referential background for Finnish cultural research. But his work was a consequence of a broader and earlier interest. Once Finland was severed from its former mother country, Sweden, to become an autonomous grand duchy of the Russian Empire in 1809, the young intellectuals turned their attention to the construction of a culture that was inherently Finnish. The Russian state favoured this move, because it might cut the closeness of the relationship with Sweden. The national awakening was, to begin with, hesitant and did not aim at the establishment of an independent state. Rather, it sought to foster a nation with a language and culture of its own, and a history that would place it on a par with other nations. Among others the writings of Henrik Gabriel Porthan, a professor of rhetoric at the Åbo Academy, inspired the minds of young students. Porthan had already pointed out the importance of language as a nation's identifying factor and stressed the ability of folklore and folk customs to provide knowledge of ancient times.[1]

The ideas had European roots. In 1799 Porthan paid a five-week visit to Göttingen, where one of the professors was the German scholar August Ludwig Schlözer, who had spent some time in Sweden and had been professor of Russian history in St Petersburg. Schlözer's book on the history of Eastern Europe, the material for which had been collected by many scholars under the auspices of the Russian Imperial Academy of Sciences, gave a more thorough account of the Finno-Ugric peoples than any other to date. His stay in Göttingen strengthened Porthan's desire to seek the history of the Finns among the neighbouring peoples to the east.

Like the Göttingen scholars of the latter half of the eighteenth century, and above all August Schlözer, Porthan wanted to examine the history of nations using linguistic, ethnographic and folkloristic material.[2] This was in fact one of the most thriving disciplines in humanistic research and one of the strongest inter-disciplinary traditions, as was repeatedly manifest in German scholarship in the nineteenth century. One major figure of influence in the study of cultures was Wilhelm von Humboldt, in particular in his views on education; like Herder, he emphasised the special role of culture rather than the universalism of Immanuel Kant and the Enlightenment, and defined the principles of comparative anthropology (in the sense of the study of language and culture) in 1795–7.[3] The Humboldtian view of language, folklore and myths evolving in the nation's historical processes and thus reflecting the history of the nation and its inherent way of thinking was introduced into American cultural anthropology by Franz Boas at the end of the nineteenth century.[4] The ethnographic-folkloristic expeditions arranged by Boas to Siberia, his considerable collections of Indian folklore, and the large-scale collection of folk poetry carried out by the German Adolf Bastian in the Pacific in the 1870s are manifestations of this trend.[5]

In Finland, these ideas inspired Porthan, but he left the task to younger scholars. The Russian Imperial Academy of Sciences offered him an opportunity in 1795 to conduct an expedition among the Finno-Ugric peoples, but the sixty-six-year-old Porthan declined on grounds of age and health.[6] The expeditions were ultimately led by Anders Johan Sjögren, who directed and assisted Finnish scholars in their travels among the Finns' linguistic relatives.

1. Sihvo 1973: 53.
2. Sihvo 1973: 39.
3. Dumont 1994.
4. Bunzl 1996.
5. Jacknis 1996; Koepping 1983.
6. Branch 1973: 26.

The expeditions of Finns and Hungarians to their linguistic relatives in Russia

Anders Sjögren belonged to a group of students who wished to dedicate their lives to the creation of a Finnish literary culture. The visit of the famous Danish linguist Rasmus Rask to Finland in 1818 gave him an idea for the comparative study of Finnic peoples. He travelled in 1820 to St Petersburg and first got a position as librarian to Count Rumyantsev, who was interested in the study of the relationship between the Finnic languages in Russia. In 1821 Sjögren published an article, "Über die finnische Sprache und ihre Literatur", in which he referred to Porthan's ideas on Finnic peoples living in Russia. He then travelled around the European side of the areas inhabited by Finno-Ugric language-speakers, and in Kazan in 1828 wrote a work, *Die Syrjänen*, about the Komi. Even though he rose to an exalted position in the academic world of St Petersburg, his failing health prevented him travelling to Siberia. The man who fulfilled his dreams was Matthias Alexander Castrén.

Castrén, born in 1813, spent his student days in the company of those inspired by national romantic ideas. The publication in 1835 of the Finnish national epic, the *Kalevala*, acted as an enticement to study folklore and mythology. On the other hand, Castrén wished to apply the method Rasmus Rask had used in studying the Germanic languages to the study of Finnic languages. In 1841, Castrén made a journey to Lapland in the company of Elias Lönnrot, the compiler of the *Kalevala*. The trip was especially tiring: having been forced to spend a couple of weeks in a cold, uncomfortable Sámi hut, the two companions fell into an argument, sparked off by some minor dispute, and did not speak to each other for a considerable time, though they later became good friends, and Castrén travelled to Archangel with Lönnrot to learn Samoyed. Lönnrot had the intention of studying Samoyed, but on observing Castrén's ability to learn Yurak Samoyed (Nenets) he realised that Castrén would be a better man for the job. Castrén continued his trip in Northern Russia, studying Samoyed and Komi, and crossed the Urals and went to Obdorsk (the modern Salekhard) in the Northern Ob' area. He stayed in Obdorsk three months because of health problems and then travelled down to Berëzovo, where a doctor told him that he had tuberculosis. Even though his health worsened he did not return to Finland, but travelled still further, to Tobol'sk and Tyumen. The expedition lasted two and half years, and its most important outcome was the collection of materials which proved that Finnish and Samoyed are related languages. Castrén also collected a great deal of folklore material.

The second large-scale trip was undertaken with Johan Reinhold Bergstad and lasted from 1845 to 1849. This time Castrén used the southern route to Siberia, going first to Kazan and the Urals through Ekaterinburg and then to Tyumen and Tobol'sk. On the Irtysh river, Castrén studied Eastern Ostyak (Eastern Khanty) dialects and on the Eniseï river the non-Finno-Ugric Eniseï Ostyak (Ket) language. Castrén showed the connections of Uralic languages and became the first writer on the linguistic history of the Finns. His expeditions also have a great ethnographic value. He collected not only folklore and text materials but made notes on belief systems and described the places and people he met. Castrén's success as an ethnographic reporter was influenced by his linguistic training and his modest ways of contacting people in his field work. Castrén became the first professor in Finnish language, but the trips to Siberia had worsened his health, and by 1852 he was dead. His extensive accounts of journeys and his lectures were published later by academician Franz Anton von Schiefner in the twelve-volume work *Nordische Reisen und Forschungen von Dr. M. A. Castrén.*

Castrén's work opened a tempting field for Finnish researchers. The related languages in Russia needed to be studied more closely. After the establishment of the Finno-Ugric Society in 1883, a wave of expeditions began to European Finno-Ugric and related Siberian peoples, which continued to 1918, the time of the Russian Revolution.[7] Though the researchers undertook long expeditions, they specialised in their linguistic work on the study of previously agreed peoples. The text collections were published by themselves or later by other researchers in the *Memoires* of the Finno-Ugric Society. Some of the research expeditions were directed to the Volga Finns and Permians. In 1898–1902 Heikki Paasonen studied the Mordvins, Tatars, Chuvash, Cheremis (Mari) and Ostyaks (Khanty). He published two volumes of Mordvin folklore, and Paavo Ravila continued his work later. His descriptions of Mari and Khanty rituals are of interest to researchers of folk belief. In the 1980s Hungarian Edith Vértes published his text collection of the Khanty in four volumes. Yrjö Jooseppi Wichman concentrated on Permian peoples living in the European portion of Russia, though he also collected Mari texts. Besides his texts on the Komi and Udmurts, he published *Tietoja votjaakkien Mytoloogiasta*, a work on Udmurt mythology, in 1892.

Following in Castrén's tracks as scholars investigating the Samoyed groups were the Finnish researchers Kai Donner and T. V. Lehtisalo, who edited, among other things, Castrén's anthologies of shamanic songs *Samojedische Volksdichtung* (1940) and *Samojedische Sprachmaterialen gesammelt von M. A. Castrén und T. Lehtisalo* (1960). Lehtisalo travelled to Siberia through Tyumen and Berëzovo in 1911. His aim was to study Nenets in Obdorsk (Salekhard) and related areas in the gulfs of the Ob' and Tas. He stayed there the next winter, and in 1914 he came back to Siberia to study the Forest Nenets.[8] Lehtisalo's extensive works on Nenets (Yurak Samoyeds) are *Entwurf einer Mythologie der Jurak-Samojeden* (1924) and *Juraksamojedische Volksdichtung* (1949), which give a versatile account of the rite technique of the shaman, songs and knowledge on Nenets mythology. Donner concentrated on the Selkup Samoyeds and Eniseï Ostyaks (Kets) in particular and in his travel books (1915 and 1938) describes not only the material culture of these peoples but their shamanism and beliefs.

The most important researcher of Uralic religions was Uno Harva (originally Holmberg), whose work also related to other Siberian aboriginal peoples. Harva carried out field work among the Cheremis (Mari) and

---

7. Cf. Korhonen, Suhonen and Virtaranta 1983.
8. Korhonen, Suhonen and Virtaranta 1983: 140–54.

Votyaks (Udmurts) of the Perm, Ufa and Kazan areas in 1911. In 1913 he travelled again to research the Eastern Mari. He travelled to Siberia in 1917. During the short trip he conducted field work among the Tungus and Eniseï Ostyaks (Kets).[9] Harva used the results of his first-hand observations of rituals and photographs in writing a series of monographs on Finno-Ugric religions. The publications *The Mythology of All Races IV: Finno-Ugric, Siberian* (1927) and *Die religiöse Vorstellungen der altaischen Völker* (1938) were exhaustive works on the Siberian aboriginal religions, and they made their author world-famous.

The Finno-Ugric peoples of Western Siberia, the Mansi and Khanty (Voguls, Ostyaks), have been an object of particular interest to Finnish and Hungarian scholars.[10] At the turn of the century numerous expeditions were made to Western Siberia, the primary aim often being to collect linguistic material, but also produce information on popular beliefs. August Ahlqvist's work *Unter Wogulen und Ostjaken* (1883) was a result of research expeditions among the Finno-Ugric peoples of Siberia. The question of who might study the Khanty became a matter of significance in the Finno-Ugric Society in 1897–8. When three young researchers, Heikki Paasonen, U. T. Sirelius and Kustaa Fredrik Karjalainen, applied for a scholarship for a field trip to Siberia, the matter developed into a contest between the leaders of the Society.[11] However, all three candidates made their field expeditions. Though there were a lot of doubts and competition between Paasonen and Karjalainen in the beginning towards each other's work, they became friends in the field, and hunted and visited a long Khanty bear ceremony together. Reports of field journeys by Sirelius, Karjalainen and Artturi Kannisto, who studied Mansi, were published in the journals of the Finno-Ugric Society between 1900 and 1908, in other words immediately, whereas the publications of material had to wait decades before coming to light. Thus, for example, Kannisto's six-volume work *Wogulische Volksdichtung*, which also contains texts on shamanism and the cults of the Mansi, was edited by Martti Liimola and published between 1951 and 1963. Likewise Kannisto's material on Mansi mythology did not appear until 1958, edited by E. A. Virtanen and Martti Liimola.

Karjalainen made expeditions to Russian Karelia and later to the Khanty of Tobol'sk and Tomsk governments. He drew on his own observations and collections of material in writing his extensive study of the religious life of the Mansi and the Khanty.[12] The work has been published in Finnish, German and recently also in Russian. In his study of religion Karjalainen preferred empirically based work to theory. His descriptive texts are rich and detailed, which make his notions valuable even today. Due to the shortcomings of the note apparatus it is, however, difficult to say which facts are based on his own observations and which have been passed down from

---

9. Anttonen 1987: 47–77.
10. See information in Siikala 1987: 84–5.
11. Salminen 2008: 61–3.
12. Karjalainen 1918.

earlier travel reports – a problem of source criticism that places the reader in search of reliable information on guard in glancing through this otherwise commendable work.

The Finns were not alone in the Finno-Ugric and Siberian field work. The Hungarians were mostly interested in their closest linguistic relatives, the Mansi and Khanty. Antal Reguly had visited Finland and gained an idea of the importance of Finno-Ugric studies. After a while in St Petersburg, he travelled in 1843 to Siberia in order to study the Mansi and Khanty. Over two years, he collected a great amount of Mansi and Khanty folklore. Among the Hungarian scholars mention must above all be made of Bernát Munkácsi, who travelled in 1888 to Siberia in order to continue the work of Reguly. Munkácsi's publications, specially *Vogul népköltési gyűjtemény* ("Collection of Vogul folklore"), present information collected not only by him but also by the great Hungarian Finno-Ugrists working among the Ugric peoples in the first half of the nineteenth century.[13] Years later another Hungarian, József Pápay worked among the Siberian Finno-Ugrians. He translated the collections of Reguly and collected Khanty folklore, poems, chants and tales and ritual accounts. Pápay's collections of the two dialectical areas of Northern Khanty are both linguistically and ethnographically important. They give a rich picture of the heroic epic of the Northern Khanty, which István Erdélyi published later in Khanty and German.[14] The work of the Hungarian linguist and folklorist Eva Schmidt on Khanty language, folklore and rituals is representative of Hungarian research in the last decades. She founded an archive for Khanty materials in Khanty-Mansiïsk after the Soviet collapse, but died herself in the early 2000s.

The aims of the Russian Academy of Sciences

The Russian Imperial Academy of Sciences, A. J. Sjögren's employer, began the study of the Finno-Ugric peoples by sending researchers and students to collect ethnographical material in Siberia. The research intentions of the scholars coincided with the political and economical interests of the Russian state in subjugating the Asiatic, Uralic and Siberian territories and the peoples inhabiting them. Grigoriï Novitskiï and Johan Bernhard Müller acquired ethnographic information about the Khanty in the early eighteenth century. The expeditions organised by the Imperial Academy of Sciences in the eighteenth century produced even more information.[15] The state was interested in the treasures of the soil, the possibilities and conditions for building mines, factories and transport and in the cheap labour resources. Naturally, it was important to become acquainted with the mode of life and thinking of the native population, who provided the markets with precious fur, fish from the Pechora and Ob', reindeer flesh and fowl, in order to evaluate how the

13. Munkácsi 1892–1921.
14. Erdélyi 1972.
15. Note the great number of researchers mentioned by Kulemzin *et al.* 2006: 30–1.

industrial development would interact with the traditional activities and values of the population. The Imperial Academy of Sciences organised a series of scientific, statistical, geographical and ethnographical expeditions, and one of their main tasks was "the description of the peoples and tribes inhabiting the Russian Empire".[16] In 1886, the Russian S. Patkanov went to Siberia; his collections on Southern Khanty folklore are of great value.

Thanks to the ideas of *narodniki* and to the popular literature beginning from Zasodimski and Kruglov, the method of collecting correspondents' materials on folk culture began to develop in Russia at the end of the nineteenth century. As a result, by the turn of the century some unique collections of folklore texts and ethnological descriptions had been gathered. Gradually among the country teachers, doctors, priests, merchants and literate peasants there grew up a local research staff. In particular, at this period representatives of the Permian peoples improved academically and began not only studying their own cultures but also comparing them with those of the neighbouring peoples. Interesting in this respect were K. Zhakov's work on the Komi and Samoyeds and V. Nalimov's on the Komi and Udmurts; a little later appeared G. Startsev's works on the Komi, Nenets and Northern Khanty and K. Gerd's on the Udmurts with references to Komi culture. Vereshchagin's works on the Udmurts belong to this group, though he was not an Udmurt.

After the Revolution, field work was done mainly by Soviet scholars. V. I. Chernetsov, for example, carried out repeated field work among the Mansi and Khanty from 1930 to 1940.[17] Other important scholars of the Khanty were Zoya P. Sokolova, who worked among the Northern groups, and Vladislav M. Kulemzin, a specialist in the Eastern Khanty; both writers published their materials in the 1970s. Izmail Nukhovich Gemuev and Arkadiï Viktorovich Baulo from Novosibirsk are well-known scholars of the Mansi, who have published important work on the basis of their field experiences.

The basic model of ethnographic field work in the eighteenth and nineteenth centuries

Research carried out in distant areas of Siberia became familiar to readers through travel books. Besides material and other research reports, ethnographers and linguists published diaries, memoires and collections of letters. Castrén (1852, 1855), Donner (1915, 1919) and Lehtisalo (1933) published ethnographic accounts of their experiences among Uralic peoples in a literary style. The same can be said of the books of Sakari Pälsi, who travelled in north-west Siberia.[18] These books became very popular among ordinary readers.

16. Gondatti 1888.
17. Olle Sundström (2008) has studied the work of Soviet ethnographers, focusing on the study of Nganasan Samoyeds.
18. See Louheranta 2006: 354–5.

Travel books and memoires of ethnographers opened new worlds and made unknown peoples familiar.[19] Even Castrén had his models in describing the Samoyeds and Khanty.[20] The earliest European and Arab sources gave a grim and terrifying picture of the inhabitants of the Siberian North.[21] Earlier Russian writers characterised Samoyeds and Khanty à la Rousseau as people who lived happily and naturally before civilisation.[22] Khanty were pleasant people, but impulsive, and could not resist alcohol. These stereotypes have been passed from one publication to another, and formed the common notions of these people.

Travel books also revealed the model of field work common to students of different disciplines. The model is old, found already in the scientific travel books of the eighteenth and nineteenth centuries. The report titled *Vaeltaja* ("Wanderer") of Elias Lönnrot, the compiler of the *Kalevala*, written after his first field trip in 1828, demonstrates the travel-book tradition and the model of field work. Written in the form of a diary, it consists of thumbnail sketches describing the course of his journey, his own impressions, and the people he met, but it also contains elements of standard nineteenth-century ethnography: observations on the landscape, vegetation, occupations, people, folk customs, buildings, dress, religion, language and poetry. A good work for comparison in this respect is the travel reports of Pehr Kalm, a botanist. Kalm spent three-and-a-half years in the mid-eighteenth century travelling in North America on behalf of the Royal Swedish Academy of Sciences. The first volume of his travel diary appeared in 1753 and follows the model prescribed by Carl von Linné: "a diary in which observations and reflections follow one another as Kalm encountered them or as they occurred to him".[23] The purpose of his expedition was to assemble first-hand observations, facts and samples; these not only provided substance for his travel reports but later, at his desk, were arranged and interpreted in the light of comparative material to form scientific data.

This basic model for ethnographical fieldwork in the eighteenth and nineteenth centuries had its origins in the natural sciences but also lent itself well to the needs of the human sciences. The objects of these observations, nowadays so sharply differentiated, did in fact constitute a natural entity in the exploration of alien cultures. Thus a natural scientist who, like Darwin, was interested in the geographical distribution of species might equally well collect ethnographic data.[24] Geographers tended to take for granted the observation of nature, culture and customs, as the many expeditions to Siberia by German and Russian scientists prove. All-round observation was one of the primary objectives of these travellers. In addition to natural samples, members of the expedition sought information on human

19. Art Leete has analysed their representations of the Northern peoples.
20. Leete 2000.
21. Leete 1999a.
22. Leete 1999b: 41.
23. Leikola 1991: 7.
24. Stocking 1992: 21.

customs and language and used it to form conclusions on the characteristics of peoples and cultures.

Field work after the collapse of the Soviet Union

The interest in field work among Finno-Ugric peoples has depended on the historical times and social processes of countries involved. The motivation to find out more about the Finno-Ugric groups has varied from the geopolitical interest of the Russian state to the national romantic ideas of Finns, Hungarians and Estonians, and from purely scientific interest to cultural revival and identity-building among the ethnic groups in question. These motivations influenced the materials observed and published and their interpretation. Hence, it is important to see whose knowledge we rely on and how their results or the knowledge produced in field work should be interpreted.

After the collapse of the Soviet Union, field work among the Finno-Ugric peoples became more topical than for decades. During the Soviet period outsiders were not allowed to work in villages or among aboriginal people without special permission, which was almost impossible to obtain. When in 1991 the borders opened, Western researchers who had dreamed about field work among the peoples of Russia made use of the new possibilities, though some of them, like Marjorie Mandelstam Balzer, had already begun the work in the Soviet period. In this fresh move towards conducting field work in Siberia the contribution of Estonian researchers has been important. Art Leete, Anzori Barkalaya and others have studied the Northern and Eastern Khanty. The new interest in the Finno-Ugric peoples has in part been linked to their demands for a visible presence in the world, and for establishing their own identity. References to the new phase of work are given later in this book.

Our trips to the Finno-Ugric peoples of Russia belong to this new phase of field work. Anna-Leena Siikala had collected materials for her dissertation in the Asian sector of the Russian Academy of Sciences in St Petersburg in the autumns of 1972 and 1973. She had also learned that some of the cults in holy groves were still performed secretly in Soviet Udmurtia. When it proved possible to do field work in Russia, she travelled with two young Estonian researchers, Tiina Tael and Arp Karm, to Udmurtia in July 1991 to video the rituals. In 1992 she invited an Udmurt folklore group to Finland to perform in the Joensuu folklore festivals. Later, in 1993, 1996, 1997 and 1998, after some other field trips to Russia, she turned again to Udmurtia, now with Pekka Hakamies.

The main field work for this book was, however, carried out with Oleg Ulyashev, the other writer of this book. Both researchers had visited Shuryshkary in the Lower Ob' in 1996. Now, the work was more goal-oriented and concentrated on the religious rituals and their public performances. The first trip was done in 2000 with Valerii Sharapov. Thereafter the field work in Shuryshkary was undertaken only by the authors in 2001, 2002, 2003, 2004. The trips were short and made in summer time, but they were directed to the same settlements in Shuryshkary. The other research target was the folk singing of the Ust'-Kulom Komi; the authors worked there in the summers of 2000, 2001, 2002, 2004 and 2006. The last trip was organised by Irina Il'ina, who also took part in some of the other field trips in order to collect knowledge of folk medicine for her own project. Conversations were held in Russian or in Komi. In Shuryshkary, some older people, such as Varvara Pavlovna, did not speak Russian at all. We tried to learn Khanty, but most often we had to settle for using Russian. The songs were performed in the native language of the performer; the narratives were told either first in the native language and then in Russian or only in Russian, depending on the situation.

The above-mentioned linguists and ethnographers were able to take several years over their research, but we had to find another approach. The field trips were directed to the same villages and people one year after another, and they created close contacts with some of our informants. Letters and phone calls were also made during this time. The most important factor in becoming easily acquainted with people was Oleg's nationality. He is Komi and already knew beforehand many of the villages in which we have worked. Maybe for this reason we were allowed to discuss intimate matters and see rituals and objects which are not shown to outsiders. The other reason was our way of doing field work. Anna-Leena Siikala began her field trip projects in the usual way, through help from the administration, but saw that it limited the contacts with ordinary people in distant villages. With Oleg we made field trips in a modest way using trains and buses and fishermen's boats, carrying rucksacks and sleeping bags, which allowed us to sleep in all kinds of places, from the floors of the village elders' houses to various huts and conical tents. But mostly people invited us to their homes, especially Anna, an older woman. The hospitality of people in Komi, Udmurtia and in Shuryshkary has been a fine experience. Living with people provided us with a great deal of information about everyday life.

From moments to understanding

The recollections presented in this book of various moments experienced during field work are perhaps chance occurrences. Through frequent recollection, however, they have formed keys to the different types of truth encountered. Culture exists only as moments, and even millennia-old institutions live only in the chain of moments. Hence ethnography may be viewed as the grasping of evanescent moments. Moments change in the mind into memories, which are true from the experiencer's point of view, but possibly untrue in the mind of others who recollect them. Finding one's way in other sorts of cultures, in the border regions of the world order, has derived from our research objectives. Most moments and encounters thus belong among the commonplaces of ethnographic field research, although the intensity and duration of the work has varied according to the goals and possibilities.

How is one to depict a foreign culture when the foreignness clouds and dissipates the essential? Or to perceive in the passing of a moment, in chance encounters, the structures built up over ages? We observe the world according to scientific structures and feelings schooled by experience. It is not for nothing that those who have delved into field work have emphasised the importance of interest and enthusiasm, in the way that a cook sees and is in a position to describe analytically whatever is relevant to food, and a fashion designer whatever people wear. The ethnographer observing the moment is reminiscent of the journalist who, relying on her intuition, creates a picture from the essentials. There is a difference, however. The eye of the researcher has to be conscious of the direction it looks in and of where its predilections lead it. The eye must also be theoretically enlightened, systematic and the servant of a tenaciously seeking mind. It should be reflective and understand the value of chance, slips and mistakes in the process of analysis and interpretation. Often precisely a mistake teaches most about how something should be. Scientific analysis presupposes that interpretation and the reliability of interpretations depend on the certainty of the scientific viewpoint.

The examination of the countercurrents of the globalisation which has arrived in border regions necessitates an orientation in the midst of the chaos of existence, at which an ethnography which aims at universal applicability falls silent. Our moments of encounter with tradition are not merely mental pictures, but have also been recorded in diaries, hundreds of slides and a great number of taped discussions and interviews and videos of events. The voices and pictures awaken us, and bring to mind memories of the events and their interpretations. Most important perhaps are questions without preserved answers, which remain outside our understanding. They show where the boundaries of the mind and the world are found, and make it possible to cross them, if it ever proves possible.

Partial answers are recorded usually only in mental memoranda. Sometimes they are completed with a knowledge concerned with other worlds which flashes into memory. Perhaps ethnography should be written both experimentally and experientially, so that a text could be read as a narrative of a journey into "possible new worlds".[25]

Over the last couple of decades Western field-research methodology has involved deliberation continuing to the point of exhaustion for one's own emotions and physical experiences. The change in viewpoint will certainly enlighten those responsible for influencing the production of knowledge, but it will push the actual research objective into the background. Writing about the moment is a research process, a way to strive to understand people, traditions and cultures, and that interplay of influence from which ethnographical knowledge arises. Moments do not, however, tell us everything about people and cultures. They evaporate and reveal the interfaces of the participants' encounter, the chance flashes of illumination and the inevitable misconceptions, and never the whole picture. Only the web of moments in which the past and present, the self and the other, are knitted together can create fields of view in which the essentials stand out.

From whose point of view are the interpretations made? Actually, who

25. Ricoeur 1976.

are "we", the authors, in this work? We do not have one world view or one stand point of interpretations, because we have different cultural and linguistic backgrounds. Anna-Leena Siikala, called Anna by Russian friends and peoples in the field, was at the time an older professor of folklore studies in Helsinki University with the Western type of research schooling. She has worked in three institutions in Finland, done research in Australia and field work in South Polynesia. She has been active in UNESCO and talked of the importance of saving languages and cultures in danger in the Russian media, even on television and radio in Udmurtia, Komi and Shuryshkary. Her childhood after the Second World War, spent partly in town and partly in peasant homes in the countryside, where hunting and fishing were important, had, on the other hand, given her a knowledge of the everyday life of farmers, hunters and fishermen. Being an older woman with a fragile body and bad health give some advantages in the field: usually nobody is afraid of the older woman and it is easy to get close to people. But this does not apply to everyone. Especially in a male-dominated culture like the Khanty, the women are not allowed to see the most important offering-places of the men. At the least it would take some time to get the permission.

Oleg Ulyashev is a senior Russian-educated researcher of the Komi Scientic Centre in Syktyvkar. Anna describes him as a young, strong and healthy man who is used to doing what a man must do in the Finno-Ugric villages or any other Northern settlements. He is from the Komi village of Vol'dino, and not only speaks Komi but knows several dialects of the language and sings their songs. He is a good storyteller, taught by his aunt, and the skill was important sometimes in the evenings and when holding conversations during field work. Oleg is also a Komi activist, and a well-known poet and play-writer whose plays had been performed in the Komi folklore theatre; some of his friends are painters labelled "ethno-futurists" and many represent the intellectual generation of the Komi of today. As a young student, Oleg had to work in a forest work camp in 1983–4, and he learnt much of the darker aspects of life. Hence he is street-wise, which was helpful at some moments during our field trips, especially in towns, trains and railway stations. He is also a masseur and helped many people during the field work.

As a field-work group we worked well together. For example among the Khanty it is important that the researchers represent both genders. We had both done much field work before and did not complain about long journeys or the changing circumstances of life. The division of work was easy: if Anna took photos, Oleg used the video camera. Oleg has a better ear than Anna, who is not musically or linguistically very able, and Oleg is capable of writing fine field reports. His knowledge has been vital also in the transcription of the texts. In writing we have had to discuss the points of the text, but after working together for ten years it was not difficult to find common ideas, though the basic academic educations represent two different traditions. The co-operation has taught a lot to each other. Oleg has worked for some months every year in Finland and knows Finnish well, and Anna has lived with his family and relatives enough to learn their life style and social habits and the principles of the Russian world.

Between cultures: dialogues, monologues and silences

Writing about other cultures on the basis of records of touch, feelings, smells and tastes, of conversations, taped or not, and of presentations recorded as mental images continues the journey between cultures. Every encounter alters the mind and the concept of the world. Thus new experiences lend new significances to moments that live in the memory. In one way the ability to understand previously unknown people and their way of life depends on the experiences of other times and places which belong to one's own past. The pursuit of academic knowledge is not the least among these.

During the 1970s and 1980s there was a lot of discussion about the dialogical model for ethnographic work.[26] Dennis Tedlock demanded that "talking across" or "alternately" describing the dialogical field situation should not be replaced by discourse imitating the objectivity of the natural sciences.[27] It is clear that in circumstances where the researcher is in the position of a non-competent child in strange surroundings trying to learn proper ways to behave and express himself, the interactive communication with the masters of the culture creates a ladder to ever-better competence. Observation and recording need an exchange of illuminating knowledge, of explanations given in conversations. Another matter is how and to what degree this dialogue between representatives of two cultural worlds creates the basis for interpretations and how the reciprocal process of procuring the knowledge can best be described. This question is especially important in studying religion. David J. Hufford notes that reflexivity in belief studies helps to fill the gap between the "scholarly voice" and the "personal voice" of the researcher.[28]

Maybe the most crucial feature of ethnographic dialogue is the "between-ness of the world of dialogue" mentioned by Tedlock. He points to something important when he writes "the anthropological dialogue creates a world, or an understanding of the differences between two worlds, that exists between persons" who are apart in many ways at the beginning of their conversations.[29] The result of the meeting of cultures is at least the notion of differences in the newly created common world. The reactions in facing these differences depend on many personal factors difficult to anticipate or to identity. Mixed feelings in a mixed world! And yet we should recognise and sort out the emotions and intentions which guide the representation of field experiences in order to understand why we write what we write about.

The involvement in local life causes personal ethical problems. How should the culture be interpreted without hurting the feelings of people who have trusted us by telling their private views and feelings? What should be made public from the information gathered in friendly relationships and mutual confidence? Ethical questions in ethnography were a favourite topic

26. Dwyer 1977, 1979, 1982; Tedlock 1979, 1983; Rabinow 1977; Vasenkari and Pekkala 2000: 248–53.
27. Tedlock 1979: 388–9.
28. Hufford 1995.
29. Tedlock 1979: 388.

of the discussion about writing ethnography during the 1970s, and there is no reason to handle that topic on a larger scale here. It is not merely a question of safeguarding the intimacy of individual persons. Even more important than the individual right to be handled in a decent and honourable way is a correct understanding of the differences in the ways of thinking characteristic of them and us. Writing ethnography demands an ethical treatment of field experiences, and calls for an understanding and respect for how the cultures concerned see themselves. The Khanty have a notion of other people's understanding of their culture and they do not always agree with these assumed ideas. From a Khanty perspective not all that is interesting from the perspective of Western ethnography is something to be told.

During the field work in Shuryshkary and in Komi we lived with people in their homes. The spatial closeness created easy contacts with all people around and presented the possibility of talking about many important things during work and leisure time in everyday situations. Living as a guest in a Khanty household opened a new window on the world. When we look out of that window different things matter: new notions appear, old ones take on new meanings or they evaporate in the air of indifference.

The field work was recorded by video and photography. However, dozens of videotapes and audiotapes and hundreds of photographs do not tell everything about the work. Many topics were so personal or intimate that it was not possible to talk of them with an audiotape on. The Khanty especially do not like the Western type of "interviews",[30] though they were willing to perform their rituals with us. In these cases field notes, the best of which were written by Oleg, were important means of recording the knowledge. The discussions could be published as such, as for example Kevin Dwyer proposes. He wanted to preserve the creative nature of the field interaction by "attentiveness to the dialogical and temporal character of the event" in opposition to the "monological, atemporal form" of ethnographic writing.[31] But the notes of past discussions would not make sense for those who were not present at the events. James Clifford refers to Paul Ricoeur's argument that "you had to have been there" in order to understand the discourse when speaking of the translation of research experiences into ethnographic texts.[32] The events of discussion in the field cannot be interpreted as autonomous texts. All the participants transform the information passed according to their frames of reference into meaningful packages of knowledge. This concerns the ethnographer, whose task is to make sense of what is heard, even more than others. To remember and to reproduce experiences or sequences of speech requires an organisation of information. Writing of past experiences, "the translation" of field discourses separates them from the original moments of production. As James Clifford puts it, "Data constituted in discursive, dialogical conditions are appropriated only in textualized forms".[33]

30. See Barkalaja 2001: 144.
31. Dwyer 1977: 146.
32. Clifford 1988: 39.
33. Clifford 1988: 39.

The selection of discussions to be referred to and those not to be mentioned, as well as the framing and modes of expression, recreate the field conversations. If the knowledge of the other cultures must be seen as "the problematic outcome of intersubjective dialogue"[34] there must be other ways to show that contingency than mere repetition. Instead of naively believing that it is possible to eschew the responsibility of the writer in an ethnographic work, it is wiser to realise that in writing we are "giving form, making, transforming" our subject. That does not mean that we try to eschew the model of dialogue in producing the text. J. Fabian has stressed that "to preserve the dialogue with our interlocutors, to assure the Other's presence against the distancing devices of anthropological discourse, is to continue conversing with the Other on all levels of writing, not just to reproduce dialogues".[35] To him the main question is how the "praxis of writing relates to the praxis of written about".[36] In transforming the knowledge and experiences gained in the betweenness of worlds created by dialogues with people, we are interested in differences in thinking and viewing the world.

34. Clifford 1986: 109.
35. Fabian 1991: 218–19.
36. Fabian 1991: 215.

The Khanty: Preserving and Performing Religious Traditions

II

5 The land of the white crane

Behind the Urals

It is a long way to the village of Ust'-Voĭkar on the northern Ob'. The route to Vorkuta has to be followed through European Russia, and then the Ural Mountains traversed, to reach Labytnangi, and from there by road and by ferry to Salekhard, and thence by boat to the district centre, Muzhi, and from there by Khanty fishing-boat along the tributaries of the Ob', past the larger villages. Finally, on the banks of the river rise the silhouettes of grey timber huts and reindeer enclosures, one of the northernmost of the Khanty villages, where, with a few others, lives the fisher Yuriĭ Ozelov.

We stayed in the small cottage of the Ozelovs in the summer of 2000. In the evenings the baby Yuliya rocked in a cradle fastened from the ceiling, the children returned home from their games, the dogs settled down, and a place was found for the night for grandmother. Grandmother, or rather a picture of the dead grandmother, *ittərma*, a puppet dressed in fur and made without recourse to sharp-edged weapons and untouched by iron, partakes for four years in the meals and the company. She is put to sleep for the night in her safe-keeping box in some free corner of the cottage. The house spirits reside on the entrance shelf behind a curtain, the ancestors in the loft and in the forest in a four-legged hut. Once the children have gone to sleep the cottage fills with neighbours, the men chat amongst themselves and the women sit on their own side, whisper and rock the leather-strapped cradle. The cottage is over a hundred years old; in it gather both departed generations and the present-day inhabitants of the village. So it has been for as long as anyone can remember – and no doubt longer.

In the village of Ovolyngort, on the headwaters of the blue Synya, another of the Ob''s tributaries, the past feels even closer. Women's and men's cycles of existence are kept clearly distinct; there is no going into the other sex's area or into buildings inhabited by its spirits. Men's and women's sacrificial sites in the nearby forest are still in use. The harmoniously beautiful village of Ovolyngort might be called a dream of the folk researcher, and its calm lifestyle, concentrated solely on the essential, the last Paradise. Th electricity which was brought to the village in the Soviet period, and the television broadcasts which came along with it, have disappeared some time ago under the harsh forces of nature. The vain news of the outside world does not break the village's peace. "We live here like bears", our host Pëtr Nikitich Longortov declared, "there is fish and reindeer meat – what else do we need?" Seen from Ovolyngort, the rest of the world is a long way off: in the pathless wilderness the 40 km to the central village is a long journey, if there happens to be no boat and above all the petrol necessary to undertake the trip – as we came to realise some years ago as we waited in vain for a lift by boat.

As a result of the nature of the object of research many researchers into culture walk, in the words of a Finnish singer, Joel Hallikainen, "on the edges of the world, along narrow lanes, where good fortune is distributed", but along with it also deprivation. Research into foreign cultures is in many senses a surmounting of boundaries: geographical and cultural, but also the researcher's own physical and mental boundaries. Boundaries not only separate, they also unite. Cultural boundaries are bridges, places where different cultural presences begin.[1] So the "edges of the world" are not edges of culture. Places experienced as otherwise peripheral are centres of their own life. The Urals are considered a boundary between Europe and Asia. In northern Siberia the River Ob' acts as a boundary, from the deserted quay-side on whose eastern side a road sets off in the direction of Salekhard, and along which there is passage by water to the Khanty villages of the Shuryshkary to the south and to the lands of the Nenets to the north.

Worlds flowing into each other

The Shuryshkary Khanty living on the northern Ob' and in the Ural region belong among the easternmost Finno-Ugric peoples. Not, however, to the most easterly of all. The Eastern Khanty, differing from them in both living circumstances and in dialect, dwell along the tributaries of the Upper Ob', in the regions of the oil fields. The area of Khanty habitation is extraordinarily wide and its linguistic and cultural differences significant. The Khanty cannot be examined as a culturally unified group, nor can information gathered from one Khanty group be considered to give a picture of the Khanty over all. The same is clear even more forcibly as far as Russia's Finno-Ugric peoples are concerned, discussion of whom was kindled during perestroika by interested parties, both local and external. Despite the linguistic affinity, the Finno-Ugric peoples differ from each other in history, socio-economic and governmental situation, ecological circumstances and culture.

In speaking of minority cultures and original peoples, the initial concept is one of an "original, pure" culture. No single ethnic group's culture has developed without contacts with other peoples, however. Historical, economic and social changes have moulded the cultures of the different Khanty groups over the centuries. The northern Khanty have preserved their own culture tenaciously, but as a pocket among the Nenets, the Russians and the Komi who have migrated from the Izhma area. Holy places have been hidden from the eyes of treasure-thieving outsiders, but also from Orthodox

---

1. Bhaba 1994: 5.

priests, traders and later Soviet officials. Today's cultural phenomena are to be examined as a mirror of social and cultural change.

Shuryshkary, consisting of 62 square kilometres of land and water, is situated in the area between the Northern Ob' and the Urals.[2] In Shuryshkary the taiga turns to tundra and most of the land is flood-plain between the Bol'shaya and Malaya Ob'. The big rivers and their tributaries are known for Siberian white fish and other valuable fish. Water birds nest in the flood-plain of the Ob' and its tributaries. The Siberian white crane, rare in other areas, has its nesting spots in Kunovat; the Kunovat state reserve was established for it in 1964.

According to a resolution of the All-Russia Central Executive Committee, Shuryshkary was founded in 1930. In 1937 it was accepted as a part of the Yamal-Nenets National Area. Though the region is large, the number of people is small, 9800 inhabitants. At first, the centre of the area was in the village of Shuryshkary. Nowadays the centre is in Muzhi, where there are about 3000 inhabitants.

The Soviet regime brought to the Shuryshkary region a better infrastructure, communication routes, health services, libraries and schools in the central villages, and collective farms, which have made possible the marketing of products. At the same time the ethnic map of the region has become patchier than hitherto, with the Khanty language withering as education has taken place in intern schools, and their own belief systems have sunk into oblivion. The great social upheaval of the last decade has affected the region in many different ways. In the mid-1990s, it was getting over the consequences of the collapse of the Soviet Union: the end of the sovkhozes and disruption of the economy, lack of infrastructure, the huge distances, difficulties of marketing goods.

The infrastructure is now recovering. In addition to schools, kindergartens and libraries, there are centres for creative activites in Muzhi. The local museum gives information about areal history and culture. For more knowledge of the area, there are a new information centre, TRV-Muzhi, which uses internet pages, a local television-centre and a journal, *Severnaya Panorama*.

Fishing, hunting and reindeer-breeding are the traditional livelihoods of the Khanty. Though reindeer-breeding is diminishing, there are more than 30,000 reindeer in Shuryshkary. Fishing has recovered through the activities of commercial firms. The immigrants – Russians, Komi, Finns, Germans and Kalmyks – who founded villages such as Pitlyar and Gorki, have long invigorated the area and brought new industrial enterprises to it: for example, a fish plant has subdivisions in nearly all the villages of the area. The economy of Shuryshkary is many-sided – for example the municipal agriculture enterprises of Gorki and Muzhi are important in food production. Need is the mother of invention, and the struggle in the face of difficult circumstances has encouraged the development of survival strategies. Valerii Ivanovich Konev, the head of Vosyakhovo, a village of a hundred inhabitants,

---

2. Information on Shuryshkary: official site of the Yamal-Nenets Autonomous District (http://www.adm.yanao.ru/145).

has founded a school with a class equipped with twelve computers, where Khanty and Komi children are taught the basics of information technology. In the manner of Archangel Karelians, he is moulding the region's life-line out of cultural and exotic tourism. In the village of Ust'-Voïkar too fishing trips for tourists are being planned as a means of sustenance for the future.

Nearby Salekhard, situated in a pocket of the Yamal peninsula at the mouth of the Ob' near the Arctic Ocean, was, in the mid-1990s, a ramshackle and forgotten small town. Now its commercial palaces, castles of the nouveau riche, shops sparkling with wares and cash-dispensing machines working with visa cards contrast with the ornate Nenets and Khanty folk costumes and the centuries-old way of life in the neighbouring villages. Oil and gas have brought an international economy and a feverish information-exchange to the north. New are the Turkish guest-workers building the towns, but also the shady sides of so-called civilisation, the prostitutes and drugs.

The northern Ob' has long been a multilingual and multicultural area. In addition to the Khanty, Nenets, Komi and Russians, the region has been inhabited by speakers of German and Tatar, and even the odd Finn. North-west Siberia is now living through the most violent cultural upheaval in its history, where the native and the foreign, the past and the future are found alongside each other. The funerary obsequies at the cemeteries hidden in the woods gather together educated and urbanised relatives along with the inhabitants of the nearby villages. The shaman Vasiliĭ Petrovich makes a welcome appearance both at Khanty ceremonies hidden from outsiders and at performances arranged by the cultural centre.

A similar simultaneous presence of different ways of life, cultural phenomena, values and interpretations is characteristic of border regions the world over and – in many respects – of Western cultures too, which are seemingly well organised in social and economic terms. In globalised Western cultures, permeated by free-trade liberalism, a previously unnoticed multitude of phenomena are in fact present simultaneously. The truth of the matter, however, is hidden from view, because everything has its place, its own compartment. In the suddenly changing culture of the northern Ob' matters which from our viewpoint fit ill together are visible together, and settle to become parts of one and the same circle of existence. The multifaceted nature of culture affects our awareness. Worlds flow into each other in so many ways and with such force that we do not know how best to navigate the different currents.

Experience of locality: rivers and settlements like layers of an onion

With the development of technology, the speed of information exchange has brought about a simultaneity of events which is destroying the concept of time and place, and which is forecast to be one of the greatest challenges in the future. Innovations are disseminated immediately and ideas and thoughts spread with hitherto unseen speed. In a coalescing world our mental maps are broadening, our collaborators and working surroundings are altering.

The development of media technology with its sky channels and information superhighways has in the past few years blown apart the thresholds of inter-cultural communication. The media bring another world to the northern Ob'. For example, even in the Ovgort Khanty village club in August 2002 we saw the American film *Terminator*, dubbed in Russian, whose violent action and technological solutions we tried – perhaps in vain – to explain to an old Khanty woman.

The swift spread of consumer goods and commercial propaganda from country to country has resulted in a situation where the cultural phenomena of every region feel as if they are multiplying. One of the paradoxes of world-wide integration is that it does not lead to a single whole, a unified "world village", but to the increase of regional multiforms and the co-existence or merging of such cultural phenomena as were previously thought to be by their nature incohesive and to represent differing ways of life.[3] The world feels as if it is becoming more complex, and the ever-increasing displacement of people adds to this impression.

It must be remembered that globalisation does not take place only under the agency of international corporations or companies, but also and especially in local communities. The relationships and dialogue between local and global powers (we might also say "transnational" if we wish to avoid including the whole world as embracing the concept of globalisation)[4] form a complex research field. The American Arjun Appadurai (1996) has empha-sised that localness is in the first place relative and defined by the context, rather than being a concept of size or area. It is essential that our experiences of localness and globalisation are mental constructs. In practice, however, globalisation always realises itself in a place or more precisely in the relation-ships between local events.

On the northern Ob', space is divided by the waterways which make travel possible, which in the cold season function as winter roads. In a cul-ture which practises fishing, hunting and reindeer-herding, space, landscape and the possibilities of travelling in it are divided up differently from in an agricultural culture based on land ownership and which emphasises land borders. Village settlement is noticeably a late feature in northern Siberia. Life was apportioned into migrations from place to place, determined by the natural means of sustenance. The spheres and areas of activity were envis-aged loosely. Instead of boundaries, directions were emphasised, along with significant places and the connections between them: above all waterways, which for the maintenance of life are routes from one important place to another. The Ob', the great mother, and its tributaries are the most important routes in summer as well as winter. The boat is the most important tool of the fishing Khanty; the possibility of using it these days is determined by the price of petrol.

The logic of the landscape and of moving within it also determines the experience of localness. The continuum of localities does not follow the

3. Marcus 1992: 321.
4. Hannerz 1996: 6.

principle of geographical proximity, but the water routes constituted by the streams. There are thirty-nine settlements in Shuryshkary. Eight of them, Muzhi, Gorki, Ovgort, Shuryshkary, Pitlyar, Vosyakhovo, Azovy and Lopkhari, are centres of village areas. Smaller villages, *gort*-settlements, are situated on the banks of rivers and their inhabitants are usually Khanty. The Bol'shaya Ob', the Malaya Ob' and their tributaries shape the area in the manner of the layers of an onion: from the innermost, remote villages like Ovolyngort which represent the traditional Khanty culture one passes to the local centre, Ovgort, and thence again to the regional centre, Muzhi, and from there to the town of Salekhard. On from there lie the other regions of the nation.

Fishermen and reindeer-breeders live in different places during the year according their economic activities. Fishermen live in winter in villages, and in summer they move to the family fishing grounds, living in *chums* (Komi, conical tents) or in a simple log hut. Reindeer-breeders move with their herds into the Urals. When asked where they are from, people speak of their home districts, defined by rivers: we are from Synya, Kunovat, Voïkar and so forth. Sometimes they also add the name of the village to the information. When we were seeking a known shaman, we heard often that he might be in the winter village or fishing on the Ob', in Muzhi, or in some other place. For people who are yearly moving around, the place is not so important as for people living an agrarian existence.

A good example is the family of Rusmilenko from Kunovat. We met the family on a small island near Lopkhari, where they were fishing during the summer. Ėmel'yan and Fila Rusmilenko live with their family during the winter in Poshtygort, Kunovat, where they usually go at the beginning of September. Ėmel'yan worked for fifteen years for a fish plant and had to catch four tonnes every year for it. After that, he tended a herd of a hundred reindeer, of which forty were his. The work was hard. The reindeer fled from the mosquitoes, and bears and wolves caused trouble, so he had to leave the occupation. Nowadays the family lives by fishing and hunting. The good fish are given to a company which loaned a boat to fish with. The family gets a few dozen fish a day, being paid 12 rubles per kilo. The three older sons, aged thirteen, sixteen and seventeen, fish during the day and hunt at night. The younger children (seven and four) help mother at home. The fishing quota for the company was being completed in August and the family was already drying fish for themselves and for the dogs over winter.

Fila said that they had a potato field in Kunovat, but because they were moving around the whole time, they could not take care of it. Kunovat is in the forest 5 km from the river. All the fishing has to be done during the summer. Luckily, elks like the the sandy land of Kunovat; last year, said Fila, they survived by hunting elks. The family avoids Lopkhari and other central villages: "Ėmel'yan has many relatives there and they are always asking for help or money. Here everything is peaceful." Ėmel'yan has three dogs and they are very well fed. The oldest is a reindeer dog, but already retired, sleeping during the day. At night it guards the boats on the beach, and Ėmel'yan is proud of the old dog: "Nobody can take our boats or fishing tackle." The two younger dogs "do not understand reindeer" but "they are good in the forest [at hunting]".

The life of the family reflects the economic and social problems after the crisis of the state. The economic changes in the area have forced people to alter their main sources of living. But this does not happen haphazardly. Èmel'yan uses his own inherited skills, becoming, after a long period of work in the big Soviet-style fish plant, a reindeer-breeder, and again after the severe problems in this job, he returned to the old ways of life, fishing and hunting. His two oldest sons will continue his work. Seventeen-year-old Denis wants to be a fisherman and sixteen-year-old Anton loves to hunt. The family does not wish to move to any central village or town. They are happy in their distant village and fishing camps.

Although the change caused by globalisation is great, it has not brought about a cultural levelling. The change affects places of diverse culture in different ways, or more precisely local cultures put store by different things. This is evident in people's everyday lives: in the small, tradition-bound village of Ovolyngort all the women wear Khanty costume and "close off" their faces when they need to with a scarf. The Khanty costume represents far more than a piece of clothing. It actualises the sexually organised social rules which affect the use of space. This we encountered with the twenty-four-year-old Galina and her friend Ol'ga, of the same age, who hid their faces when Ol'ga's husband's male relatives and friends were present, as young women who meticulously observed the traditional Khanty culture. Later we met Galina in Ovgort's grocery store. As a sales assistant Galina's bearing was quite different, following the general Russian pattern. In moving from place to place people adapt, and actualise the set of values of the particular place. Place with its culture takes all under its wing.

The cross-draught in inter-ethnic relations

Shuryshkary is a multicultural area, in which people of different nationalities have been living for a couple of hundred years in or near the same settlements. The Khanty live mostly in their villages, where the traditional means of livelihood remain important. The Russian population has concentrated in the local centres for administrative reasons, but they inhabit the smaller settlements too. The settlements of the Komi and other immigrants, for example Pitlyar and Gorki, have increased livelihood opportunities by bringing cattle-breeding and farming to the area. The Komi who came to Shuryshkary in the middle of the nineteenth century were reindeer-breeders and worked together with the Khanty and Nenets. Though the Khanty were converted early to Christianity, they preserved their rituals and shamanic practices in secret. Therefore, the life of two parallel cultures continued for a long time in the area: the Russians and Komi were Christian and the Khanty and Nenets had their own religious customs. The difference between the groups can be seen for example in marital relations, though today marriages between members of the various ethnic groups have increased.

The ethnic boundaries are reflected most clearly in burial customs. There are graveyards for the Khanty and others for the Russians and Komi. On the basis of the grave symbolism it is possible to draw the conclusion that in the graveyard of Muzhi all ethnic groups may have their last resting place. However, the shift to the common graveyard has not passed without pain. Comments on the burial customs of the other ethnic groups can be quite bitter. Once a Khanty acquaintance of ours from Ust'-Voïkar intercepted Oleg as he was going to look at a Russian burial ritual, and asked him for money for a bottle he said he needed. When nothing came of the request, the man looked at the burial procession, spat and said: "People are buried like dogs, dug down in the earth." Burying on or in the earth brings about disputes even among the Khanty. In the northern villages, to which Ust'-Voïkar belongs, the corpse is buried in a small hut of the dead above the earth, whereas in the south a hole is dug for the hut of the dead. In the latter case the huts are shallow, nearly level with the earth. Similar suspicion hovers over the part that Russians have in the Otherworld. When we asked: "What will happen when a Khanty dies?", the answer was: "When a Khanty dies the souls fly to heaven, and the corpse will be on the earth, maybe with *Kŭl-ilpi-iki*, the Spirit of the Lower World. But the Russians fly up in some kind of coffer."[5]

A similar contempt for the burials of the other ethnic group was heard from the Russians too. One of our Russian friends recommended the continuation of the old burial practice. Graveyards should be separate because the burial customs are different:

> Last year a Khanty was buried in the Muzhi Orthodox cemetery. Nearby Komi and Russians came to make the funeral repast for their relatives. But the wind blew straight from Yugan. And they say there was such a stink. Well, the corpse decomposed, and it was not buried [covered by the earth]. They cursed horribly then. And rightfully. If you bury in an Orthodox cemetery, do it according to the Orthodox way, not after your pagan rites. And if you want to do it in a pagan way, you have your own Khanty cemetery there. You have nothing to do with the Orthodox one. People cannot come for the funeral repast to their graves. A stench and completely insanitary.[6]

Resentment against the government population policy culminated in this outburst. The commentator regarded indigenous people as getting finance for no reason for their businesses, in the form of loans without interest, and other advantages missed out on by the Russians and Komi. According to him the businesses established by the loan money do not last long, because "the owners drink and will be left with nothing at all". The fish companies are not profitable because swindlers buy fish from Khanty for the price of a bottle. Besides, a Russian cannot understand the catching of large spawning fish with nets made for small fish. That destroys the species.

Views, not only on religious rites, but also on the use of natural resources

5. Rec. in Muzhi, 2000.
6. Rec. in Muzhi, 2000.

for fishing and hunting, differ between the ethnic groups. The Khanty do not directly blame the Russians, but the different values are clearly seen in their ideas about fish and water birds. Khanty do not eat flat fish. Their fish are "white fish" or "Khanty fish", for example *mŏχsəŋ* (Russian *mukšun*, Siberian white fish), *nel'ma* (Russian, white salmon) and white fish. They view "black fish" as belonging to Russians; such fish are ones such as pike and perch. In practice the idea is not followed through; thus in Synya the black fish was eaten in the autumn even though it was called "Russian trash fish". The water birds are similarly divided into grey or Khanty ducks (*χănti vasi̯t*) and black or Russian ducks (*ruś vasi̯t*). To the former belong *χenši*, teal (*Anas crecca*), *vŭjəv*, wigeon (*Anas penelope*) and *kŭrek*, pin-tailed duck (*Anas acuta*).

The relationship of the Khanty to the Komi is closer than to the Russians. The binding link between them has been reindeer-herding; Khanty men worked with Komi and Nenets in reindeer brigades. In these brigades bi- or even multilingualism was a common feature. For example, a couple born in the 1930s in Soïyakh, Filip Alekseevich Ozelov (a Khanty) and Anna Nikitichna Khunzy (a Nenets), speak Russian, Khanty, Nenets and Komi. Accordingly a shaman from Synya speaks, besides Khanty and Russian, also Komi and Nenets; the latter languages he learned in reindeer brigades, because the Izhma Komi men who worked there could not speak Russian. He spoke about shamanism to Oleg in Komi, because he could not recount such things in Russian.

The inhabitants of Kazym-Mys are Khanty and Komi nowadays. The first occupants of the village were Komi, who had a good relationship with the aboriginals living nearby. The "local historian" of the village is Komi; he showed us the common graveyard of the Khanty and Komi and spoke about the birth of the village in the 1920s:

> At first to Kazym-Mys came two Konev families and they settled at a place near the Holy Peninsula. Khanty lived in the neighbouring villages, but their attitude was good, because they knew their customs and language and did not much want to penetrate into places which were not theirs. Before that our ancestors lived in Muzhi, which they moved to from Bol'shezemel'skaya tundra after the death of thousands of heads of cattle. The reason was potato blight. Before the move the family of Konev had twelve head of cattle: the horses and cows which they took with them. Before, the graveyards of the Khanty and Komi were separate, but they are buried in the same place now.[7]

Sometimes people identity themselves with another group in everyday discussions. A reindeer herder from Vosyakhovo continually called himself Khanty, though his appearance and the testimony of his Komi wife revealed that he was a Komi with Izhma roots. Also the head of Vosyakhovo, a Komi, learned Khanty in childhood and can understand the Khanty points of view. Hence, he is a local leader valued by all the ethnic groups. The multilingualism smooths the relationships between ethnic groups; the same can be said also

7. Konstantin N. Konev, Kazym-Mys, 2003.

of the global markets with new consumption habits. Khanty have adapted Russian customs, but at the same time they value their own culture. Nowadays it is possible to publicly show rituals, the hidden side of Khanty culture.

Division of space and practices of avoidance

The Synya, a tributary of the Malaya Ob', gets its water from the Urals. It is a river abundant in valuable fish and an old fishing land of the Khanty families. The route to the upper Synya river villages leaves from Ovgort, a central village with six hundred inhabitants. Many of the villages near Ovgort are nowadays increasingly used only during the summer time, when people who move to the centres come back for the summer holiday. In the villages further away there are still some families even during the winter time. One of them is Ovolyngort, 40 km from Ovgort, where the paths through the forest to the Urals begin.

Ovolyngort is a traditional Khanty village on the upper reaches of the Synya. People leave the village, but also return to it. The young move to the centre of the settlement, Ovgort, or further afield in search of work and return when there is need, in the summer, to help the aged or for some other reason. Those who have left long since return in their retirement and build their cottage, as has been the custom. The village has preserved its traditional way of life. During the summer, the reindeer are in the Urals and the majority of the population fishing in the mighty Ob', at the immemorial fishing places of the family group. Those left in the village make hay for horses, gather lichen and mushrooms for the reindeer at home, visit the woods, go berrying and make do with the fish brought by the shallow water: occasional white-fleshed Khanty fish and pike, "Russian fish". When autumn begins, the time of high water, the fish and people return. The village belongs to the general workspace of the fishers, where the yearly fishing quotas which they have to give to the company are large, but the means of living are secured because they also get fish themselves. The products are put on the market.

The upper part of the village is situated on a hillside some 200–300 metres from the river. The beautiful scenery with birches and other deciduous trees fascinates the incomer, but paths leading uphill to the village are hard for those who have to carry heavy things. Hence, women use another, easier path to the river when bringing water for everyday use. Ovolyngort's dwellings are small timber cottages, surrounded by fences and small wooden storehouses and wooden *chums* for keeping food. In some of the houses there are small beds for vegetables and flowers, though these are difficult to grow in the semi-arctic climate of Shuryshkary. The head of the village, Ermil Petrovich, who lives himself in Ovgort, built a sauna in 2002 in the upper part of the village. It offered the opportunity to wash in private and was often used by us. Before the building of the sauna, Anna was urged to wash in a brook between the parts of the village. The area was peaceful and people assumed that "the Mishka [a bear] will not cause a problem". On the other hand, the "Mishka" had just killed a horse near the village.

The Synya river. – Photograph by A.-L. Siikala 2001

In the upper part of the village, the houses are in a row facing the river, though that is not seen from the village. The village is divided into three parts for different families. In the area of the Longortov family, there are four houses. In the centre of the green is the closed house of the grandfather, which is forbidden to women. It is a *jemaŋ χot* (sacred house). Galina Petrovna related that women cannot pick berries, though they can eat them, from bushes behind the house, because the ashes from the forbidden house were put there. She remembered that the grandfather's wife also had her own small house, a private *chum*, for the times when she was not considered to be pure.

Everything in the village has its place, both holy and profane. As the village has expanded, men's and women's old sacrificial trees have remained in its centre, but new offerings are no longer hung on their branches. Near the house of Pëtr Nikitich there stands a holy tree from an old male holy place. In the tree, at a height of 8–10 metres, rests the skull of an elk. If the tree falls down, it will be set up again in its place. It is not permitted to burn the tree. Using it as a log for warming a house would be dangerous.

The unused sacrificial trees show also the gap between the sexes: the one is situated beside the path leading to the latrine reserved for men, the other near the corresponding place for women. Men's and women's universes within the circles of the village are visible, and at the same time distinct from each other.

The village holy places are in the forest. Men's and women's ritual places are situated near the village but cannot be found by outsiders without help. The graveyard is a little further away, downstream on the other side. Two *ura*

The path to Ovolyngort. – Photograph by A.-L. Siikala 2001

groves for commemorating the drowned or otherwise vanished dead are in the forest (see pp. 172 ff.). One is 700 metres from the village, the other even further away. In the forest, there are also other holy places and trees. These can be identified by the gifts of cloths hanging on their branches.

The visitor has to know where to walk in a Khanty village or camp. Many of the paths are forbidden to outsiders and especially to women. According to the old system, the forest on one side of the village was reserved as a latrine area for women and on the other for men. In the same way, the paths leading to holy places have to be known. Near Lopkhari, a fishing camp was divided according to strict rules. A family with many members lived in summer in a small *chum* or *χot* (a conical tent), which was situated on a tiny waterway joining a tributary of the Malaya Ob'. The path to the boat harbour was about 100 metres long. Outside, in front of the *χot*, was a hearth, because the summer was warm and the *χot* was not heated. The door opened to the south and the latrine paths led east (for men) and west (for women); the use of these paths was regulated by gender rules. A path used by everybody went north-west, to the inner part of a small island. A short path to the north led to the platform called *nŏrəm*, where the home spirit, *ʌuχ*, was kept in its box under a cloth. The *nŏrəm* were quite small, one metre long and half a metre wide. The legs of the platform were 1.3 m high. To the right of the *χot* was a narrow pole, called *jir jŭx*, for offerings. This ritual place, consisting of the platform of the spirit and the offering pole, was used only by men. Thus the area was divided into three sectors, an area for men, one for women and a common area for everybody.

The male side of the house of Konstantin Sergeevich Longortov, Ovolyngort.
– Photograph by A.-L. Siikala 2001

In Soïyakh, an old reindeer-breeding couple (mentioned above) lived during the summer in a *chum*. The division of space here followed the old Khanty tradition. The left side of the hut was for men, and women could not stay there. The right side was for women and the mistress made a table for visitors on that side. At the back of the hut, opposite to the door, was the sacred place, where an Orthodox icon was hanging and where the offering was performed before drinking and eating. The box of kitchen utensils and food was under the icon.

The division of the space and avoidance practices also mark the use of the χot. In the small gort villages, the houses are small, consisting of one room and a vestibule and perhaps a porch. Russian-type houses with many rooms are common in larger settlements. The timber cottages and conical tents of the Northern Khanty, which are nowadays used at the summer fishing places or while herding reindeer, are places of close co-existence. The model of how space is used in traditional Ovolyngort houses resembles what was found with the Yugan Khanty houses described by Peter Jordan. The most important part of the house is the back part, on the far side; there is a low table and bench, and the oven is near the door.[8] Jordan also mentions that men have the privilege of using this space: they eat first at the table and occupy the area of the holy objects. Still, it seems that the traditional rule system is not very strong in the Yugan area. He writes: "Informants talked

8. See figure 7.2 in Jordan 2003; also pp. 194–200.

Ol'ga Philippovna (the wife of Konstantin), her friend Galina Petrovna and children. Ovolyngort. – Photograph by A.-L. Siikala 2001

of more formal ordering of space in the past when women were not allowed to cross the area of the sleeping bench under which the black cloth . . . was laid out lengthways, as a body lies in sleep."[9] In Ovolyngort, the house space is divided traditionally and in strict accordance with sex and age group. In the front part of the cottage is the oven and food bench, on the back wall the sleeping platform and on the right in the back corner the holy shelf. The oven area is mostly for women, the middle part of the room for everybody as they work, play or just sit on low stools in the room. The area immediately around the holy shelf is forbidden to children and young women. On the bench beneath it the honoured elder folk, and above all the men, sleep and sit while eating. The left-hand corner part of the sleeping platform is in Ovolyngort separated by a side wall from the "better" part. It is for the use of women, children and young couples. Everyone who moves in the cramped space knows or soon learns their place. The female researcher sat generally on the left, on the women's side, but was also invited over to the festive table set up in front of the men's sleeping platform; around it were set low stools as seats. The male field workers sat, naturally, in the place of honour while dining, on the men's sleeping platform. During the night, the sleeping platform is covered by mosquito tents. "The bench should be covered, otherwise devils will go there", joked Arkasha, Pëtr Nikitich's son.

9. Jordan 2003: 198.

The same type of space division can be noticed in conical tents. In Lop-khari, a *chum* where we lived with a large family faced south. The tent was divided, according to the usual local model, into two sides. On the right and left side, there were bed furs and over them mosquito curtains during the night. The family members slept on the right side of the *χot*, the visitors on the left side. The number of mosquito curtains differed according to the number of people from three to four. In the middle of the *chum*, there was a wooden platform with a hearth in the middle leading to the back, the northern side of the *chum*. At the back of the tent were the holy corner, the food storage, the kitchen utensils and a small table, which were put near the right-hand beds used as a bench at meal times. The fireplace in the middle of the *chum* was not used, but the fire was lit in a bucket. The bucket usually stood in the middle of the open door, or sometimes in the centre of the tent, repelling mosquitoes. Almost all of the activities happened outside, in front of the *chum*, where the summer fire site, washing place, fish-drying area, and tool store were to be found.

Gender: together but apart

The precise division of space and limitations on movement, the breaking of which is *śohma* (translated into Russian as "sin"), presents a picture of the gender organisation peculiar to the Khanty culture and of the evasion and honour behaviour connected with it. The prohibitions and aversion rules connected with women's behaviour apply to holy places but also to other areas of life. In Ust'-Voĭkar we saw in one house the images of departed ancestors preserved in travel trunks set up as a room in the upper part of the dwelling on the unfurnished space of the back wall. Women could not step into the area in question, because women may not walk over a man or his clothes. A young man explained the reason: "Since it can happen that a woman can be over a man, things will turn out badly for him."[10] Town houses might be a problem. Our friend, a Khanty, told us in Muzhi that he has a good apartment:

> There is only one imperfection in it. A woman lives in the second floor, above me. It is a real nuisance. Everyday she treads on me. *Śohma*! But of course there are iron and wires and lines there [in the floor between the apartments], and – I have also something else [a magic protection]. Maybe nothing comes of that. The iron does not let through anything impure. Iron is pure.[11]

For the same reason a woman's death doll is not preserved in the loft. Women may not step over fences, the support posts of houses or dogs. They may not sit in the forward direction in a sled drawn by dogs, but cross-wise.

Anna was guilty of breaking the purity rules in the home of Pëtr Nikitich

10. A. A. S., b. 1983, Ust'-Voĭkar, 2000.
11. Rec. in Muzhi, 2003.

when she climbed onto the bed platform; when Varvara Petrovna asked to look more closely at an icon in the holy corner Pëtr moaned, "Now you're stepping into my bed, Anna. My legs will start hurting." It emerged that in the night the hostess changed the men's mattress unbeknowns to us, and Pëtr's legs were saved.

According to field work undertaken in 1976 among the Khanty by Marjorie Balzer a woman's misbehaviour is a threat not only in religious life but also in the preparation of food and in social contacts. In particular the physiological changes which take place during pregnancy, child-birth and menstruation make a woman impure and subject to the laws of aversion and purging in her relationships with her spouse's male relatives.[12] For that reason, for example in Ovolyngort the wife of the grandfather had her own small *χot* for "impure times". In practice, separate houses offer a place for women to wash themselves and take care of their private needs. Classification as impure affects not only relationships between the sexes, but also the organisation of the socially controlled space.[13] Ethnographers noticed the weak position of women in a patriarchal Khanty family at the end of the nineteenth century. K. F. Karjalainen described the life of Konda Khanty women as difficult. The husband had to pay for his wife and could treat her as he wanted. Domestic arguments were usual.[14] Some of the so called "fate-songs", which tell of people's life experiences, describe the stressful situation of women. Some Shuryshkary men still said that a Khanty woman has to be content with modest living, though many women seemed to be strong and determined in household and public matters.

Although the Soviet era brought equality to the sexual organisation of the northern peoples, in remote villages which stick fast to tradition the laws of aversion behaviour are still followed. For example, the shading of the face with a corner of the scarf is an honourable gesture, which belongs to the behaviour not only of the old but also of young women. Thus the scarf is an obligatory part of everyday dress. Even young girls learn to cover their faces. In the pictures taken by Anna the method of covering is not observed, since they did not cover up in the presence of a woman. When Oleg tried to capture women with the camera they would "close" their face. Face-covering is an effective means of determining social distance and proximity. In Marjorie Balzer's view, beside the dominance of men in Khanty culture, the solidarity among women and their independence are evident. Thus women do not emphasise the aversion behaviour as a limitation, but as a sign of their separate existence.[15]

The rules of gender organisation create a field-work situation in which a researcher's sex takes on greater than normal significance. Thus a man–woman team is essential for the formation of a whole picture. Rules may be broken when need arises. Once when the men left to go bird-hunting, they

---

12. Balzer 1981; cf. also Balzer 1987, Jääsalmi-Krüger 1996, 2001.
13. Anttonen 1996: 146.
14. Karjalainen 1983: 67–9.
15. Balzer 1981; 1987: 139–40.

asked Anna to gather blueberries in the woods, where a bear had just torn open a horse. Wandering alone she clattered the berry basket from time to time and frightened a flock of black grouse into flight. When the men returned almost empty-handed and heard about the black grouse, Anna had to go along the next day on the hunting trip, to show the way. Impurity rules are subject to negotiation: their interpretation and circumvention, and the seriousness of their infringement, may be adapted at need. As a last resort the shaman explains unclear situations, and he is resorted to whenever an infringement of the rules has resulted in sickness or some other misfortune.

6 Dual organisation, totemic ancestors and kin groups

In forests near the Synya river are to be found sites of archaeological interest: groups of hollows in the earth. The holes, which are over a metre deep, were perhaps bases of the dwellings of ancient inhabitants. In Yamgort, there is a site consisting of more than ten similar clearly visible holes. The inhabitants living in the village believe that the spirits of ancestors live there. Hence the graveyard, χăλaś, was established nearby. In Ovolyngort, Pëtr Nikitich showed us a similar *mŭv-χot-раул*, "earth village". He told us that the inhabitants were "ancient people", probably Khanty, but nobody knows. He added: "Maybe our old people knew who they were. The Khanty do not feed the spirits of these people." When we asked, "Who does feed them?", he answered: "They feed themselves. They fish and hunt wild animals. That's how they live." Feeding, or, in other words, making offerings to the spirits of ancient people, is not necessary, because they are not relatives. There is no need to remember them. They take care of themselves.

The local identity of the Northern Khanty is rooted in rivers and dwellings, the villages, fishing grounds, reindeer routes and other places important in seasonal activities, but the kinship and family are crucial factors in situating oneself within the realm of social networks. Kinship and family also represent a person's roots, and thus the history of the people. The past, the ancestors, takes care of the present, the descendants. Hence, it is necessary in reciprocation to take care of ancestors.

Moś- and Por-people

After a memorial ceremony in the Ovolyngort graveyard in 2001, we drank tea with Pëtr Nikitich and Varvara Pavlovna. Varvara, who had been active in the memorial ceremony, seldom talked when we discussed beliefs or rituals. But after visiting the graveyard she had something on her mind: "I am a *Por-ne*", she said, and then, making faces, in Russian: "*Baba-Yaga*" (witch). And Pëtr is a *Moś-χu*, Moś-man. *Por-ne* means a woman from the *Por (pur)*-phratry, but it is also a name for a mistress of the forest. People even today can usually tell which group their parents belong or belonged to. For example, the father of Nikolaĭ Nikitich was a *Moś* and his mother a *Por*.

Who are *Moś*- and *Por*-people? The nature of the Khanty kinship and family system has been a topic of discussion for a long time.[1] Among the Northern Khanty, kin groups (*rod*[2] in Russian) were organised in a moiety system,[3] which contained two exogamous phratries, *Por* and *Moś*.[4] Marriage between members of same phratry is forbidden, because the people are considered to be blood relatives. They also have a common mythical ancestor. The ancestor of the *Por*-phratry is a bear, but the ancestor of the *Moś* is *Kaltaś*, which appears in the form of a hare or a female goose. Another mythical ancestor and the protector of the *Moś* is *Mir sawittə χu* (equivalent to *Mir-susne-χum*, "World-watching Man", among the Mansi). The horse cult of the *Moś* is connected to this deity. The phratries have other symbols besides: the Siberian pine (*Pinus cembra ssp. Sibirica*) is a plant of the *Por* and the birch that of the *Moś*. Both phratries had their main ritual places, the *Por* in Vezhakory and the *Moś* in Belogor'e, where their mythical ancestor was believed to live.[5]

The moiety-system is not found among the Eastern Khanty, who divided themselves into territorial groups. They have three exogamous clans or kins (*sir*; Russian *rod*): of the Bear, the Elk and the Beaver.[6] The kin organisation of the Eastern Khanty resembles that of the Kets and some other Siberian ethnic groups. Though there is no knowledge about the phratries among the Southern Khanty, the Northern Khanty moiety organisation is not unique. It is found among the Mansi, near relatives of the Khanty, who also have *Por* and *Moś*-phratries.[7]

E. V. Perevalova conducted field work in Shuryshkary in the 1990s when studying the ethnic history of the Northern Khanty. She claims that the idea of the *Por* and *Moś* as exogamic phratries is characteristic of the Khanty in Synya, Kunovat, Berëzovo and Kazym. In Salekhard, people do not admit such categories.[8] Synya tales relate that *Por joχ*, *Por* people, and *Moś joχ*, *Moś* people, talked different languages. They were believed to be always fighting with each other. The *Por joχ*, who were also called *poslan joχ* (people of ducts or channels) or *poχrən joχ* (island people), were stronger than the *Moś* phratry, because they were more numerous.[9] The following information, given by Pëtr Nikitich, refers to these fights:

> In the old times when the Khanty hunters met one another, they never came close to each other. Everything they needed they passed from a distance. For example, if one wanted to give another person *šar* (tobacco for chewing), he put

1. See Chernetsov 1947; Steinitz 1980; Sokolova 1983.
2. Russian *rod* is translated into English as family, clan, kin; we use "kin".
3. Kulemzin *et al.* 2006: 19.
4. Steinitz 1980.
5. Kulemzin *et al.* 2006: 19 and 126–7.
6. Jordan 2003: 69–79.
7. Gemuev *et al.* 2008: 99–100, 116–17.
8. Perevalova 2004: 131.
9. Perevalova 2004: 130.

*Pëtr Nikitich Longortov.
– Photograph by A.-L.
Siikala 2001*

it on the end of the hunter's staff (*suvsər*) and stretched it out to the other person. The other one took [the share] he needed and gave the thing back in the same way, so afraid were they of each other. Well, they were always at war. Here, not far away there is *mŭv-χot-pauʌ*, "a settlement of earth-houses" – we do not even know who lived there. And our grandfathers did not know. But some people must have lived there. Maybe they were at war, too, and were driven out or murdered. The pits there are already old.[10]

After Varvara Pavlovna revealed that she is a *Por*-woman, Pëtr Nikitich became amused. He said that his father had a *Por-ne-kŭškar* (a nail of the forest woman) in the attic. It was used to stop sores bleeding. Later they found that the *pŏrton*, medicine, was alum. Then Pëtr Nikitich began a story of *Por-ne* (*Por*-woman) and *Moś-ne* (*Moś*-woman). The story describes the different characters of women belonging to the two phratries:

Two hunters married, one a *Moś-ne*, the other a *Por-ne*. They went to the forest to hunt. They were away for a long time. The women had no food any more. The *Por-ne* killed a child, and brought the meat to entertain the *Moś-ne*. The *Moś-ne* did not eat, only the *Por-ne* ate. Then she said: "I've entertained you, now you entertain me. Kill your child." The *Moś-ne* did not want to eat her child, so she

10. Pëtr Nikitich Longortov, b. 1929, Ovolyngort 2001.

*Varvara Pavlovna
Longortova.
– Photograph by
A.-L. Siikala 2003*

cut a rotten stump, cooked a rotten birch and gave to the *Por-ne*. The *Por-ne* said: "Your child is not tasty, mine was tasty." The hunters came, brought meat, brought fish. The *Moś-ne* brought her child to greet the father. The *Por-ne* put some wood into the cradle. The *Moś-ne* had her child. The *Por-ne* had no child.[11]

Narratives about conflicts and competition between a *Por*-woman and a *Moś*-woman seem to be common in Synya. A. V. Val'gamova told a short tale of a similar type to E. V. Perevalova's in Ovgort in 1989.[12] The narratives were previously longer stories with several parts. Wolfgang Steinitz published a long folk tale containing several episodes about *Por*- and *Moś*-women. It was told by Prokof Ermolovich Pyrysev, a young Khanty student from Yamgort, Synya river, in St Petersburg in 1934–7.[13]

According to the Synya folk tales the *Por*-woman is "wild" and "raw". She represents the backward people of the forest. *Por-ne* is also a name for an evil spirit who lives in hollows of trees and on the edges of marshlands. She tries to inveigle herself into human society. Sometimes malevolent and

11. Pëtr Nikitich Longortov, Ovolyngort 2001.
12. Perevalova 2004: 131–2.
13. Steinitz 1939: 80–8.

quarrelsome women are called by this name. In Vakh and Vasyugan she is an evil spirit, the spouse of *Səwəs*; she and her children have six fingers and toes.[14] The *Moś*-woman is more "civilised" and acts in an acceptable way. According to the narrator, all people today live in the *Por*-way, badly. Varvara Pavlovna was punning when saying that she is a *Por-ne*: she was a very intelligent and active woman with many children and grandchildren.[15] Yet she was also proud to belong to her phratry, to be a *Por-ne*.

The origin of the phratries reveals the ethnic history of the Khanty according to the local understanding. Perevalova noted that the *Moś*-people are believed to be "pure" Khanty in Synya. According to the ethnic memory told for example in narratives, they came from the west, from the Ural area. Originally, the *Moś* people lived on reindeer-breeding and used conical tents. The *Por*-people were fishermen and came from the south. The earth houses belonged to them and they lived on fish and fish fat.[16]

The different kins of a phratry were considered to be related. To the *Moś-joχ*, who were considered to be the "local" or "pure" Khanty, belonged five Synya families. Three of them, Longortov, Valgamov and Kurtyamov, were originally Komi (*Săran rut*), but they were totally assimilated with the Khanty.[17] To the group *Por* or as it is known in Synya, *Poslan joχ*, belonged eight families.[18] The Synya *Moś* people called *Śańa joχ* (*Senja joχ* according to Perevalova) had a common spirit-protector, *Kev-ur-χu-akem-iki* ("Stone Nenets Uncle Old Man"). On the Kunovat river among the *Kun avət joχ* group of the *Moś* phratry there were tree spirit-protector (*loŋχa*) brothers: *Un-moś-χu* ("Big *Moś* Man"), *Kütəp-moś-χu* ("Middle *Moś* Man") and *Aj-moś-χu* ("Little *Moś* Man"). All the spirit-protectors were kept in their own sacred store house. There had been a common sacred place, where three brother-*loŋχa* stood near each other. The Big *Moś* Man "wooed and fought with the Nenets and Komi".[19] The best-known spirit-protector of the *Moś* group is *Kasum-naj-imi*, the Great Kazym Woman, which was worshipped by several families in the Kazym area.

Perevalova also gives information about the the various *Por* groups' spirit protectors and their sacred places. The information shows that the *Moś* and *Por* phratries were divided into family groups known by the river names. Some of the big families lived in several villages. However, the members of a kin group came together to the sacred places of their common spirit-protector.[20] E. V. Perevalova claims, on the basis of ethnic history, narratives, sacred places and their spirits and historical knowledge, that the *Por* and *Moś* people represent two different ethnic populations, the first coming from the south along the Ob' and the second from the west. In the Shuryshkary

14. Kulemzin *et al.* 2006: 127.
15. Varvara Pavlovna Longortova, b. 1930, died in 2007.
16. Perevalova 2004: 128–31.
17. Martynova 1998: 95–6.
18. Perevalova 2004: 133.
19. Perevalova 2004: 134.
20. See for example Perevalova 2004: 140.

area they merged with each other. Some of the later immigrants assimilated with them.

The animal protector

The animal protector of the kin was often mentioned during our field work. Kolya Nakhrachëv told of the totemic protector of his family in the following way:

> The goose is the bird of our family, of the Nakhrachëvs. Every family has its own protector. Our family has the goose. And the cedar-tree, too [*Pinus sibirica* is not actually a cedar but a kind of pine-tree]: *noχr* "(cedar) cone" and *aś* or *aśi* "father" – *noχraś* "cone's father" is cedar. *Aj-lut-iki*, "White-Cheeked Brent-Goose Old Man", is a protector only of the Nakhrachëv kin; other kins have other protectors; *ʌuχ* are spirits in general, not only the protectors of a house or a kin; the spirits in the *kŭrəŋ lapǎs* [sacred store house] are also called *ʌuχ*. And the ones in the sacred corner are the kin spirits or the things sanctified by one of them. The kin's protector spirit is kept by one person and some things are sanctified by it: like a cloth with coins sewn into its corners; it can be also a kerchief or a bear paw. We also have a bear paw. And otherwise our kin spirit is *Aj-lut-iki*. The sanctified cloth given to a family from a protector spirit is called *ašin*.[21]

Kolya Nakhrachëv is from Kazym-Mys. His father is a *Moś*-man and mother a *Por*-woman. The totemic bird of the Nakhrachëv family which represents *Moś*-people is a white cheeked brent goose (*Branta bernicla*). *Aj-lut-iki* protects the members of his kin group. On the Lower Ob', the protector spirit of a kin group takes care of all its members. But only one member of the kin group keeps the *ʌuχ χŏr*, the image of the protector spirit and things given to him. The protector is kept in the sacred corner of the house. All sacred things of the members of the kin group are made sacred by the totem animal: a small piece of cloth with coins, a scarf or a bear paw, which the family of Nakhrachëv also had. The sacred piece of cloth is called *ašin*. According to Nakhrachëv, the keeper of the family spirit is Vasiliĭ Petrovich, a shaman. "He is the oldest of the Pugurchins and he has a strong spirit. In addition, he can do magic acts with the drum. That is a gift which is not given to everybody."[22] There is also a human protector or guardian of the locality, the river area. We heard that in Synya, the protector of the local area is Kulak Mishka.

The Longortov family of Ovolyngort represents the *Moś*-phratry and belongs to *Śăńa joχ*, the Synya kin. The spirit-protector bird of the family is *śak-voj* (a hammer-animal), a goose with red throat. The bird is called a hammer-bird, because it migrates late in the autumn and has to find its food from the frozen earth. The spirit-protector of Rusmilenko from Kunovat

---

21. Nikolaĭ Nikitich Nakhrachëv, Ovolyngort, 2002.
22. Nikolaĭ Nikitich Nakhrachëv, Ovolyngort, 2002.

is "Man from Pike River". His *ʌuχ χŏr*, the image of the spirit, is a pike. Rusmilenko also showed the *pos* (Russian *tamga*, "symbol") of his family.[23] According to Perevalova, the family of Rusmilenko belongs to people who migrated to the Lower Ob' from Northern Sos'va and Lyapin. The family represents the *Sort jugan joχ* (or *Kuš avət joχ*) and belongs to the Shchuch'eĭ river people.[24] The wife of Ėmel'yan Rusmilenko said that she belonged to the family of Toyarov. Their spirit protector is *ŭli portị voj*, "a terrible mauling beast". The name refers to the wolf and its image; *ʌuχ χŏr* is wolf. The Toyarov family belongs to *Poslan joχ* or *Por*-people of Kunovat river, who had an image of *jevri iki*, Old Wolf.[25]

A young man, born in 1983, said that in Ust'-Voĭkar the dead can come to their relatives and those close to them in the form of an animal, but not in the form of such dangerous animals as the wolf and bear. Only shamans can turn themselves into these beasts:

> They can be *ʌoʌmaχ* (wolverine), *ŏχsar* (fox) or *ʌaŋki* (squirrel). Usually they come in the form of the animal which is described in the surname. But they cannot come in forms of *ŭli letị voj* (wolf = a beast which eats reindeer) or *tojpər* (bear). Only strong shamans, which we do not have any more, or spirits can take these forms. But if you want to turn yourself into a bear, you have to cross a bent tree, the top of which is falling to earth, but a normal man cannot turn himself into a bear.[26]

In mentioning the animals, he referred to the spirit animals of the Ust'-Voĭkar families. There are special sacred store houses called *kŭrəŋ lapăs* (store houses on "legs", poles, see pp. 124–5) in Khanty villages, where spirits are kept. Each family also keeps their furs there: the Ozelov family has a wolverine fur, the Alyaba family has one of fox and the Sevli family has a squirrel fur. The narrator did not remember what kind of fur belonged to the Rebas' family. There is a similar kind of store house in Ovolyngort, but we were not allowed to look inside it, because the keeper was fishing and "had taken the spirit with him and there is nothing but furs".

All *χŏr* (appearance, form, image) images of spirit protectors were made ritually. The inner part is made of metal – gold, silver, zink, tin or lead. Then they have clothes: "they were small pieces of cloth". Destroying the *χŏr*, image, of a spirit protector is dangerous:

> After the Revolution, when the police began to search out shamans and put them in gaol, a big family in Kievat gave their *χŏr* to the police and threw all the clothes around. After that, their family disappeared: they shot and killed each other. One of them was put in gaol. In Khanty-Muzhi too there was a strong family. They treated their deities badly. They began to disappear and it was the end of

---

23. Ėmel'yan Rusmilenko (Kunovat), Lopkhari, 2003.
24. Perevalova 2004: 139.
25. See Perevalova 2004: 134.
26. A. A. S., Ust'-Voĭkar, 2000.

the family. Only Kolya was left, and P. N. T. But he was an outsider, not from the same family. But he puts everything right, and follows all the regulations. That's why everything in his family is in order. But everything was not OK with Kolya. He had to sit in gaol on top of everything else that had happened.[27]

These kinds of beliefs and memorate narratives remind us of the importance of the holy places, the idols and their equipment. They are symbols of kin groups and their prosperous future, which should not be forgotten. For that reason, the images of spirits and their ritual practices were preserved despite the pressure from the Orthodox Church and then the Soviet authorities.

L'aksas, reincarnation of a person

One day four-year-old Semën brought some wood for the fire. He was working eagerly and his father Yuriĭ Semënovich laughed heartily and said "It is good to see my dad working so much. He has returned. At first he fed me, now I feed him." The father had died some years ago and his name was given to his son's first son. Yuriĭ Semënovich said that the belief was that the father was reincarnated, *l'aksas*. The name of the grandmother, who died two or three years ago, was given to a granddaughter. Yuriĭ Semënovich described the naming of a child in the following way:

> The names are given in different ways. Sometimes after the relatives. The old people gave a name in that way. When a child is crying, they ask: "Who you are going to?" And then they listed to the names of relatives. And then, when a child stopped crying when one of the names was said, they gave that name to him. That means that he goes to that person.[28]

People liked to refer to the idea of *l'aksas*. When in Ovolyngort Anna asked a neighbour working at the door of her house if she knew a Khanty linguist named Fenya born in Ovolyngort, she went inside and came back with an old photo. "This is Fenya." When Anna hesitated and said that in the photo there is a young girl, she laughed and said: "This is my aunt. Your friend got her name and she is Fenya nowadays."

The rules of exogamy are applied to persons who might be remotely related but who have *l'aksum* relationship. Then they are considered to be near relatives. According to Nikolaĭ Nikitich, a man can be born again as *l'aksas* five times, a woman four times. He is the *l'aksum* of his father's brother, who died in 1942. The idea of *l'aksas* is connected with the beliefs in the several personal souls (see pp. 154–6). On the other hand, because the incarnation takes place within the family, it emphasises the kin relationship.

27. Rec. in Ovolyngort, 2002.
28. Yuriĭ Semënovich Ozelov, Ust'Voĭkar, 2000.

The kinship system

The Khanty kinship system is complicated if studied only in linguistic terms, because it contains a large number of terms which have a variety of meanings. Wolfgang Steinitz studied the meanings of kinship terms on the basis of the social reality and the relations of different terms in his article "Das System der finnisch-ugrischen Verwandtschaftstermini".[29] He notes that the meaning of each term (for example *jaj*, "older brother, younger brother of father, stepfather" etc.) is a representation of a meaning of a defined group of people who are classified as opposites: male/female, older/younger, related/unrelated by procreation, natural-born/matrimonial, directly/indirectly related by marriage.[30] The classification of kin terms made by Steinitz facilitates an understanding of the social world behind the Khanty kin concepts. It points to the distinctive levels of a Khanty kin model in practice.

Migrations, assimilations with other ethnicities and especially the long shared life with Russians and the practices of the Orthodox Church have affected Khanty understandings of kinship. In speaking Russian, the Russian models may hide the Khanty meanings. There are cases when the surnames have been changed. Yuriĭ Ozelov said that the Vozelovs are related to his family. "When their ancestors had a disagreement with some family members, they moved to Utsyl'gort and added one letter to the name and wrote it as Vozelov. But nobody knows how it really happened."[31]

There has been disagreement over the nature of the kinship system of the Khanty. V. G. Chernetsov views the distinctive features of Khanty kins (Russian *rod*) as exogamy, a family name, the totemic animal of the kin group or a protector or ancestral hero, the symbol of the kin group (*tamga*), and the shared cemetery and the blood feud.[32] Chernetsov based his ideas on his knowledge of Mansi and Northern Khanty material. Zoya P. Sokolova, who has carried out field work in Synya, has claimed that among the Northern Khanty the exogamy kin unit cannot be separated from the dual system: the Khanty have local and totemic or genealogical groups instead of kin groups.[33] E. P. Martynova, a specialist in the Eastern Khanty, in turn argues that exogamous Khanty groups show characteristics of the kin (Khanty *sir*, Russian *rod*); though it is possible to draw borders around the area where kins reside, yet the kins are non-localised.[34] People who belong to the same kin are considered to be brothers and sisters and they share a communal territory, worship a general group of spirits and practise exogamy.[35] The dispute over the kin system of the Khanty derived partly from the field-work areas; researchers have specialised in culturally and socially different people, the

---

29. Steinitz 1980.
30. Steinitz 1980: 368.
31. Yuriĭ Semënovich Ozelov, Ust'-Voĭkar, 2000.
32. Kulemzin *et al.* 2006: 19–20; Chernetsov 1947.
33. Kulemzin *et al.* 2006: 20; Sokolova 1983: 156–60.
34. Martynova 1995: 99–100; Kulemzin *et al.* 2006: 20.
35. Jordan 2003: 70–1; Kulemzin and Lukina 1977: 192–3, Martynova 1995: 100.

Northern and Eastern Khanty, and draw general considerations depending on their own field materials.

The characterisation of the kin group presented by Chernetsov suits the situation in Shuryshkary. The local and totemic connections are important factors in describing people's affiliation to a kin. According to our observations, in the middle areas of Shuryshkary, the exogamic phratries include kins with the same surname, totemic animal and kin progenitor and *tamga*. The kin groups which represent the same phratry and live in the same locality, usually a river area, for example *Šăńa joχ* in Synya, again have their own spirits and human protectors. Also, every family has its own spirit protector. But the large kin groups belonging to the same phratry which can live in the same area or be non-local have their common spirit protector or ancestor, which is worshipped by all the families involved but kept in one family house or village. The uniting feature of the kin groups forming a kin is the ancestral hero and traditions connected with that figure. Hence Sokolova's analysis also describes well the kinship practices of the Northern Khanty. But still we should remember that the Northern Khanty also have a kin system with patrilineal heritage. The *l'aksas* system, which is based on an idea of inherited soul testifies to this.

The nature of the Khanty totemic system has been a matter of debate. K. F. Karjalainen refers to totemism, but notes that the animal progenitor tends to be a spirit.[36] Chernetsov and Wolfgang Steinitz in his "Totemismus bei den Ostjaken in Sibirien"[37] saw the Khanty kin system as totemic. Josef Haekel, in turn, evaluates the relationship of the kin group and protector animal from several points of view. He argues that the ancestors, except the bear ancestor of *Por*-people, are humans, heroes or local people. They may turn themselves into animals, use animal form in a shamanic way as a means of transport or appear in the form of animal. The spirits in animal form are in a lower position; they are helpers of the kin spirits. Tabu regulations do not concern all the animal spirit protectors of the kin. Hence, Haekel does not find "true" group totemism among the Khanty.[38] It seems that the problem of Khanty totemism is a problem with the concept and definition of the term totemism. The Khanty kin had a special relationship to a defined animal or bird species. The kin system of the Eastern Khanty and the *Por*-phratry were also determined by an animal relationship. This relationship is expressed in the Khanty mythic narratives, heroic epic and folklore.

36. Karjalainen 1918, vol. 3: 43–44.
37. Steinitz 1938.
38. Haekel 1946: 119–22.

7 Discussions about myths and tales

Myths written in the heavens

In primordial times before the time of man with cut navel, deities and divine heroes ruled over the world. The Khanty tell of this mythical time in songs and tales, the best of which were recorded in the nineteenth century.

THE SMALL *MOŚ* OLD MAN

One such song was that of Small *Moś* Man, which tells of the hunting of an elk in the sky. The song was performed in bear ceremonies by the Kazym Khanty even in the 1990s. V. I. Kil, Tat'yana Moldanova and O. V. Mazur recorded it in 1988 from Kuz'ma Semënovich Moldanov (1890–1990), who lived on a tributary of the Kazym.[1]

> My many men of the full sitting-house,[2] behold,
> do listen here!
> With a bow of smooth bird cherry [wood], a hero with the bow,
> the small *Moś* old man, now
> into this merry house of the bog-beast[3]
> from my nameless deep land[4]
> so I came in.
> I speak to every one of those:
> "[Like a] crow-bill-patterned rock,
> behind the patterned rock[5]
> [in] a house covered with the hide of a [large-]toothed beast[6]

1. Timofeï Moldanov transliterated the song and Tat'yana Moldanova translated it into Russian. The English version and comments are produced by Nadezhda Lukina, Anna Widmer [A. W.] and Vladimir Napol'skikh [V. N.]. Kulemzin *et al.* 2000: 243; for the poem in Khanty and German, see Kulemzin *et al.* 2006: 153–7.
2. The festive house of the bear ceremony [A. W.].
3. The bear [A. W.].
4. The *Moś* old man was active on the earth in primordial times, before the other good spirits came down from the sky, and life was put in order. Therefore his land (i.e. primeval earth) is called "deep" (also "low") and "nameless" [V. N.].
5. The Urals [A. W.].
6. Probably the bear. T. Moldanova and N. V. Lukina suggested the meaning "walrus" in their Russian translation, which is hardly acceptable. The meaning "bear" for the

[I,] the old man, sit down.
My many dear days of my heavens,[7]
the sleep [as deep] as if my head has been cut off
[I,] the old man sleep.
However, on the wide place of my sleep
[I] toss and turn.
My long childish [?] thought,
What does it think?
Behind my village with the back end[8]
[there] stood beasts.
Numerous woody hills [covered with] sappy aspen,
I have many.
On the tracks of a fleeing beast
if I hunt, why is it bad?
My head rich in many plaits
I raised high.[9]
From the corner of my house with sacred corner
two good boots made from fish skin,
the two top-boots with toes like merganser[10] bills
[I,] the old man put on.
The full dress of a clothed man
I put on.
In the corner of my house with sacred corner
a fish-scale[-covered] quiver[11] packed full with a hundred arrows
to the dear place between [my] shoulder-blades
with clinking sounds of ice pieces
[I,] the old man put.
The bow pasted with red birch-bark
[I,] the old man took.
From the corner of my house with sacred corner
the waning-moon-shaped sabre
I took.
Out of my house with door
when I went out,
at the back side of my house with back side
two wood [pieces] [soled with fur] of water-beast[12] with hems

expression "large-toothed beast" is also given in [*DEWOS*: 1189] [A. W.].

7. Khanty *torəm*, "heaven, God, weather", so: "the days made by God" [A. W.].
8. Lit. "at the back end of my village with back end". Such constructions with reduplication of an attributive as the adjective (before the noun) and as postposition (after the noun) is a standard formula widely used in Khanty poetry. See also, for example, line 46: "at the back side of my house with back side". To save the original essence of the text this is also as a rule kept in the translation, though actually a simple expression like "at the back side of my house" would suffice to give the sense in such cases [A. W., V. N.].
9. The hero decides to go hunting, is up and prepares himself for the hunt [V. N.].
10. *Mergus albellus* [A. W.] – a small species of the duck family specialised in fishing [V. N.].
11. Covered with metal scales [A. W.].
12. The beaver; the period describes skis soled with bear-fur [V. N.].

to the motley toes of my shining feet
[I,] the old man fastened.
The motley ski-stick of a man of the cedar forest[13]
in my fingered hand with five fingers
[I,] the old man take.
On the back side of my village with back side
by the skiing feet's place
[I,] the old man walked.
Many stretches of sweating back[14]
although I ran,
[left by] any kind of beast
the end of an icy track
I have not noticed.
To the numerous woody hills [covered with] sappy aspen
I came.
In some place of this sort
[with] six arms [and] legs[15]
heavenly young elk, a son of an old man,
at his place of a strong bull
it was scared.
Then he [the *Mos* man] said:
"The good end of the icy track
with the end of the icy [skiing] stick
if you stab,[16]
to an unknown land,
to the land of good Komi,
to the land of good Mansi
it [the elk] would run [by] the marshy way."
The small *Mos* man, the old one,
the good end of the icy track
with the end of the icy [skiing] stick
now, let me stab!
The heavenly sacred holy beast, lo!
To an unknown land,
to an unfamiliar land
[it] is chased.
The good end of the icy track
following I pursue.
In some place of this sort
heavenly young elk, a son of an old man,
at his place of strong bull
it was scared.

13. Probably a skiing stick made from cedar [V. N.].
14. Long and hard enough to make the back sweat; a stretch one can run without a rest [A. W., V. N.].
15. Actually "six legs" – the arms are mentioned for poetic parallelism. The mythical elk was believed to have had six legs in primordial times [V. N.].
16. Touching and damaging the tracks of an animal is normally banned for the hunters: according to a widespread (not only Khanty) belief, in this case the game would be frightened and run away [V. N.].

The many mossy peat bogs
so it reached,
in a place of reindeer-moss
in the ends of fir twigs
it was entangled.
The many lichen-grown hill forests
when it reached,
in a place of many reindeer-lichen
in the ends of fir twigs
it was entangled hard.
And so 1,
the small *Moś* old man,
on the two quick feet of a spring ptarmigan
did chase it.
On the places of rugged soil
the back ends of my skis with back ends
do not stick into the snow
like the ends of the tail-feathers of a spring ptarmigan.
On a place of rugged soil
the ends of the pen-feathers of a spring ptarmigan
[empty]
do stick a bit into the snow.
Many stretches of sweating back
I walked a lot.
[And] as I [once] simply checked –
to the land of good Komi,
to the land of good Mansi
I had already come!
I, the small *Moś* old man,
at a certain moment
to the sandy sea,
to the sea of fine sand
came.
The good end of my sweating
came out.
At a certain moment
my many-seeing two eyes,
what have [they] seen?
The heavenly young elk, a son of an old man,
lay down there.
On the two quick feet of a spring ptarmigan
[I] pursued it.
To the side of the beast with side
[I] rush.
At its poor back legs
with the waning moon-shaped sabre
[I] did strike.
The legged beast[17] with four legs
ran further on.

17. The elk [A. W.].

The heavenly sacred holy beast,
so may you live in this form hereafter!
By a Khanty man with cut navel,[18]
by his iron arrow, down,
so will you be slain.[19]
[For] hundred[s] of ages of your coming life
as a legged beast with four legs
so you will live on.
In your legged form of six legs
you will live hereafter
beside your great heavenly father
on the side of the sparkling morning star.[20]
To the many men travelling in the morning
on the side of the sparkling morning star
as a bright star shining in the sky
may it appear!
By a Khanty man with cut navel,
in the sex-legged form[21]
beside its great heavenly father,
may it be seen!
So on, my, the *Moś* old man's
good end of the icy track[22]
beside my great heavenly father
may it appear!
By a Khanty man with cut navel
may it be seen there.
So I have been seated
in my house covered with the hide of a [large-]toothed beast.
On the side of the sparkling morning star
as a bright star shining in the sky[23]
may it appear!
To a Khanty man with cut navel
my house covered with the hide of a [large-]toothed beast
may be visible!"
About the small *Moś* old man
with my good news of the news-bringing beasts
over the good hunting ground
into this merry house of the bog-beast
I have come in.

18. That is, by those born to women – at the time of the Great Elk-hunt human beings were not yet present in the world [V. N.].
19. Since the elk has thereafter only four legs, it can be hunted and killed by ordinary people [V. N.].
20. Here are introduced some of the numerous names of constellations connected with the myth of *Moś* old man hunting the Great Elk (see examples in [*DEWOS*: 943]) [V. N.].
21. Probably: *Arcta maior*, called "elk" in Khanty dialects [*DEWOS*: 1563] [V. N.].
22. The Milky Way [A. W.].
23. The star called "Star of the *Moś* old man" [A. W.] (not identified [V. N.]).

The Small Old *Moś* Man is an ancestral hero, the forefather of the *Moś*-phratry. His deeds are told in epic songs. The song describes how the elk-hunting myth is performed in a festival house. The Small Old *Moś* Man wakes up, with an awareness that behind his house stood "beasts". He takes his hunting attire, arrows, bow and sabre and goes to hunt in unknown lands, those of the Komi and Mansi. He slays the "sacred heavenly holy beast", the elk, and cuts off two of its legs. Now it has four legs and can be slain by a man with cut navel, an ordinary Khanty.

The myth was performed with singing, but today myths are usually told as narratives. Besides narrated myths, *moś*, (*mońś*), folk tales (*Märchen*), are still a living tradition among the Shuryshkary Khanty. The Khanty genre system has its own features and it cannot be compared directly to European genre practices, though the Khanty have adopted and recreated according to their own taste some Russian folk tales. The mythic songs can seldom be heard today; bear wakes were their last vestiges. On the other hand, there are different types of new songs, some of them created in the Soviet period.[24] The epic songs, *ar* (*arə*), telling of deities and heroes were traditionally performed in sacrificial rituals and bear wakes or in other marked situations by people who had specially learnt the tradition with its stylistic features and great numbers of lines. K. F. Karjalainen notes that the sacrificial ceremonies were not limited to prayers, the killing of the animals and the common meal but contained also entertainment, play contests, the singing of epic songs and dances. Singers told of the living conditions of the spirits, events in their lives and the renown of old heroes. The songs were accompanied on a string instrument, a five-stringed *dombra*, or with a nine-stringed harp, which was called a crane.[25] The term *ar* (*ärəχ*) and the Mansi term *ēriy* has been borrowed from Central Iranian languages (cf. Ossetian *arğáw*, "folk tale"; *arğawyn*, "to perform a church service").[26] According to Nadezhda V. Lukina Khanty folklore includes a conception of "the origin of the earth, constellations, natural phenomena, animals, man, gods and spirits".[27] In addition to astral myths, bear rites, heroic and spirit verses, the Khanty and Mansi also sang about the life of "those with navels cut", that is ordinary people. These songs depicted among other things the turns of fate in women's lives and their difficult position in a male-dominated culture. Tales of fate, named according to the personage of the song, are still heard, and Nikolaĭ Nakhrachëv from Muzhi was happy in 2002 to perform examples in Ovolyngort learned from his mother.

THE ELK HUNT AS ASTRAL MYTH

The Northern Khanty culture was close to that of the neighbouring Mansi. Old *Moś* Man was a divine hero of the Mansi too. In 1888, a century before the recording of the above song, the Hungarian linguist Bernát Munkácsi set

24. Schmidt 1981.
25. Karjalainen 1918: 474–5.
26. Kulemzin *et al.* 2006: 75.
27. Kulemzin *et al.* 2006: 24.

out to research the Mansi language in Siberia. He gathered a broad collection of folk poetry, including a mythic song depicting the hunting of the elk.[28] After the long and detailed poem there is the following comment:

> In the times of the creation of the earth the star elk was created first six-legged on this lower earth by our father *Numi-Torem*. It had two more forelegs in the middle of its belly. It was not possible for ordinary mortal people to chase it, to kill it. For mortal people to chase it, the *Moś* [a heroic ancestor] man was prayed to. The *Moś* man had chased it, overtook it, and cut off its two superfluous legs and then said: "In the future, with the establishment of the world of the human beings' time, with the establishment of the world of the human beings' life, it will be possible to kill you, four-legged. With six legs mortal people would not be able [to kill you]." That elk was depicted as the Elk-Star up in the sky. The *Moś* man's ski-path was also reflected in the sky. The *Moś* man's family in the house is also seen in the sky.[29]

The songs relate how a hunting trip which took place in the earth's primordial time changed the six-legged elk into a four-legged animal, a suitable prey for hunting. The myth is known to many Siberian peoples. It also belongs to the central body of myth of many Finno-Ugric peoples. The Finnish *Kalevala*-metre "Elk of Hiisi" recounts how a hunter prepares his skis and how he pursues the elk he is hunting to a mythic place, Hiisi. The corresponding Komi mythic narrative describes how the hero Jirkap hunts a blue elk, using magical skis. With these he is able to pursue the elk on a long journey to the east, as far as the Urals. The myth concerns a theme of importance to people who relied for sustenance on the hunting of the elk.

The myths are astral: the events in them are depicted, according to the singers, in the sky. In Sámi tradition the constellations of Orion, the Pleiades and Arcturus belong to the cosmic elk-hunt.[30] The Evenki, Kets, Selkups, Buryats, Mongols and Mari interpreted the Great Bear as an elk being hunted, along with its pursuers.[31] The Khanty regard the Milky Way as the tracks of the skis of the mythic elk-hunter, the *Moś* man. Nikolaï Nakhrachëv explained the matter thoroughly to us in the summer of 2002, pointing to the special skis needed for winter hunting:

> For us the Milky Way is not the way of birds [cf. Finnish *linnunrata*, "way of birds"], but *nimləŋ juš*, "the ski track". *Niməl* means "skis covered in the skin of a reindeer's forefeet" and *juš* is "way". We had a hero, Moś man. He was not so strong as other giants, but similar. He beat spirits and heroes. He was able to change into all sorts of beings. When he had changed into one and you looked at him, he became another. On skis he sped as if flying, and ran across the sky. The Khanty did not like unsoled skis. When you go on those unsoled skis, the

28. Anna Widmer and Vladimir Napol'skikh have commented on and translated the text into English for *Mansi Mythology* (Gemuev *et al.* 2008) along with an interpretation.
29. Gemuev *et al.* 2008.
30. Pentikäinen 1995: 135.
31. Cf. Harva 1993: 190–6.

track is obvious and it lasted for three weeks. If you go hunting with them, very soon the hunting place will be rutted all over by tracks. What wild animal is going to come there then? But when you go on fur skis, the track disappears quickly, the snow scatters and the track becomes unclear. It is the same with the Milky Way: there are two parts like bands and the stars are scattered like snow, unevenly and unclearly.

Astral myths, judging by their wide distribution, represent a very ancient mythological tradition. In northern Eurasia, astral myths are connected with large animals. In addition to the elk, the bear is also widely found as a mythic subject. Kolya Nakhrachëv's comments and the explanation for the use of skin-bottomed skis show that ancient tradition is still worth investigating and assessing. We may also ask what significance these old mythic tales have in the life of modern people. Is there any significance to the investigation of myth in today's folklore research?

Myths of Uralic hunting cultures

The great myth-theories created by the German romantics and evolutionary theoreticians in the nineteenth century, and by many well-known researchers in the twentieth, have guided the manner in which folklorists have understood the nature of myth and also identified myths of the Uralic tradition. Classical theories of myth basically present five main directions. These are: 1. Intellectual examination methods which consider myths as an explanation of the world and an expression of the world view (the nineteenth-century evolutionists, James G. Frazer and E. B. Tylor); 2. Viewpoints which emphasise mythopoetic thought (Max Müller, Ernst Cassirer); 3. Psychological interpretations (Sigmund Freud and C. G. Jung); 4. Theories which emphasise the bonds to society, among which belong the basically functionalist viewpoint of myths as texts of a rite (Émile Durkheim and Bronisław Malinowski); and 5. Structuralist interpretations (Claude Lévi-Strauss).[32] Although classical theories of myth are sometimes represented as in opposition to each other, it is characteristic of them that they are partly overlapping and complement each other.[33] Myths are in fact many-dimensional and may be approached from many angles, whose appropriateness depends on the object of research and the given material.

Myths are narratives, poetry, but not merely poetry. Mythology recounts how the world order began, and what sort of forces are behind it. It does not, however, contain a fully fledged religious philosophy or normative dogmatic system. Although myths deal with problems and preconditions of existence, they do not necessarily offer explanations, nor do they require explanation. In the manner of poetry they are open to various possible interpretations. For this reason myth and fantasy readily merge with each other. The particularity

32. Cf. Cohen 1969: seven main theories; Dundes 1984: 1–3.
33. Honko 1984: 46.

of myths lies in their ability to contain within themselves both the eternal and transcendent, temporally bound and immediately present.[34]

Instead of logically related concepts, mythic consciousness works in the form of metaphors and images welling up from symbolism common to cultures. Thus religious symbols and ones which express human and societal organisation generate a network of images and metaphors, which delineates a different, but nonetheless fundamental, truth.[35] Mythic expression is characterised on the one hand by the persistence and long age of the fundamental symbolism, and on the other by the kaleidoscope, in perpetual motion, of images deriving their force from the implicit significance of these symbols. Fundamental mythic images are so widespread that they have been considered universal manifestations of the workings of the psyche. Eternal and universal mythic images are, however, culturally determined and handed down within a culture. Their meanings emerge from a process of interpretation in which the symbolism of the cosmos, and the nature of the otherworld and human kind, is filtered through an individual culture, the reality subsisting within the consciousness of the community and of the person, and its flip-side, a second reality. Mythic images are based on the logic of the impossible. It is precisely in their contradiction that they are able to form world images which have proven comprehensive and thus influential. They are both ancient and continually reborn.

In codifying the structures of a world view, myths carry the thought patterns of the past.[36] The structures of cultural consciousness which maintain the world view and values and strive to solve conflicts within them are more deep-rooted and conservative than superficial cultural phenomena. Hence mythology belongs among those slowly changing mental representations, those "long-term prisons" (to borrow from Fernand Braudel), which live on tenaciously even in transformed circumstances and carry the memory of the past. As culture is renewed, old themes take on new historical forms. They are interpreted within the frame of reference of each culture in a way appropriate to the social context and contemporary world concept.[37] Thus conservatism in the central structures and even central materials, motifs and images, and also a continuously renewed interpretation of these structures and materials, are characteristic of the life of a mythology borne as a tradition from one generation to another.

Researchers of comparative religion have shown that mythic materials woven into the mythic poems and narratives of the Finno-Ugric peoples, motifs depicting the birth and structure of the world and the creation of cultural phenomena, belong to a widespread international tradition,[38] with parallels among Indo-European-speaking cultures and also further afield in Asia and America. Thus the astral myth of the cosmic hunt is known not only

---

34. See Gaster 1984: 113.
35. Cassirer 1946; Ricoeur 1976: 54–5; Siikala 2002a: 53–6.
36. Siikala 2002b.
37. Vernant 1992: 279.
38. Napol'skikh 1989.

among the Khanty and other Finno-Ugric peoples, but among north-east Asian aboriginals and among the native peoples of North America.[39] What these common points tell of the mental atmosphere of pre-Christian cultures is a fascinating but difficult research task. However, the mythology gathered from narrative motifs, mythic images, metaphors, symbols and significant concepts reveal cultural contacts. By means of comparative research into the mythic materials, mythic images and vocabulary it is then possible to trace in the mythic heritage similar levels of tradition inherited from different cultural contacts, which linguists have confirmed by examining the history of native and borrowed vocabulary.

Although many basic questions are still a matter of debate, for example where and in how wide a region the Uralic languages were spoken at different historical stages, the common lexicon indicates quite clearly what the culture of the population groups who spoke Uralic and Finno-Ugric languages was like. As Kaisa Häkkinen has shown, the common Uralic lexical fragments point to a language of a community "living in a relatively northern region and practising hunting and fishing".[40] Characteristic of the religious traditions of the known hunting cultures of northern Eurasia was a great variety in points of detail, and a striking similarity in the fundamental structures. The former derives from the oral nature of the tradition and the lack of codified doctrines, the latter relates to the similarity in systems of sustenance and living conditions, but also goes back to very ancient patterns of thought. As the cultures which spoke Uralic and Finno-Ugric languages are believed to have been northern hunting cultures, the conclusion may be drawn that the distinguishing structural features of their mythologies were connected with the demands of their nature-based lifestyle and with their observations of the revolving firmament. We may assume that the early Uralic hunting culture possessed fairly consistent mental models relating to the structure of the cosmos, the Otherworld, human existence and relationships with nature, as well as shamanistic and animal-ceremonial practices.

Analogues are found to many of the documented cosmological images and myths of the Uralic peoples so widely that the tradition has been regarded as very ancient, even palaeolithic.[41] Over all, Uralic mythology appears to form an integrated world view reflecting the fisher/hunter world view and constructed on the basis of interconnected complexes of images. Among its cosmographic features are the world image centred upon the North Star, the model of the universe in which horizontal and vertical merge, the emphasis upon the north–south axis and the centrality of water courses as links between this world and the Otherworld. The north–south axis is emphasised also in the depiction of powers representing death and maintenance of life. The centrality of the (water) bird, reflecting astral mythology, is connected to the cult of the sun and the life-giver in female form, whose attribute is

---

39. Berezkin 2005: map on p. 91.
40. Häkkinen 1990: 176.
41. Napol'skikh 1992; Ajkhenvald *et al.* 1989; Siikala 2002b.

the birch, a variant of the world tree.[42] Uralic peoples also shared the astral mythology centred upon animals and the complex concept of the soul characteristic of Eurasian hunting cultures, concepts which formed a basis for animal ceremonialism and the institution of shamanism.[43]

Patterns of thought which go back to the early hunting culture were best preserved in those cultures where hunting and fishing have been continuously significant as a means of sustenance. The most important break in thought patterns took place in many Finno-Ugric cultures at an early date with the move to agriculture. However, the move was so gradual and deferent to sustenance by hunting that the mythology long preserved its millennia-old materials and images.

We know that cultural contacts and dominant religions change the mythic tradition by destroying the old and bringing in the new. The patterns of thought rooted in the past offer a conceptual framework within which new elements can be accommodated. Assimilation takes place therefore within the conscious terms set by the existing culture. This is evident in particular in the case of concepts of the higher divinities and the realm of the dead, where alternatives presented by the stronger cultures and high religions have continuously displaced native material. A noticeable feature in mythology is the existence side by side of ideas and images which, although contradictory in their background, are effective and complementary. The more important and deeply rooted the values, stances and beliefs are, the more thorough are the cultural shifts needed to change them. The elements of religion and the mythic world picture were able to survive changing cultural systems. Yet their meanings did not necessarily stay the same: motifs and images have been interpreted and formed anew as they have been accommodated to transformed contexts.

Mythic corpus

Eva Schmidt has shown in analysing present-day Ob-Ugrian poetry that the Khanty and Mansi poetry consisted of different genres and subgenres. For example, men and women divided songs recounting the fate of the singer between songs of men and women.[44] The genres and subgenres are linked with each other in many ways. It is encumbent on the researcher of their mythology to investigate the song poetry as a whole, rather than gathering separate mythological fragments as an object of investigation.[45] Edmund Leach has also presented a consideration of the myths of a small community as a corpus which forms an entity reflecting a common world view, where the understanding of the parts demands an understanding of the whole corpus. Although mythic elements follow each other in the narrative, they

---

42. Napol'skikh 1992: 11–14.
43. Siikala 2002b.
44. Schmidt 1981: 151.
45. Cf. Siikala 1995.

contain cross-references irrespective of the course of events.[46] William G. Doty portrays the mythic corpus thus in his work *Mythography. The Study of Myths and Rituals* (2000 [1986]):

> A mythological corpus consists of a usually complex network of myths that are culturally important, imaginal stories, conveying by means of metaphoric and symbolic diction, graphic imagery, and emotional conviction and participation the primal, foundational accounts of aspects of the real, experienced world and humankind's roles and relative statuses within it. Mythologies may convey the political and moral values of a culture and provide systems of interpreting individual experience with a universal perspective, which may include the intervention of supranormal entities as well as aspects of the natural and cultural orders. Myths may be enacted or reflected in rituals, ceremonies and dramas, and they may provide materials for secondary elaboration, the constituent mythemes (mythic units) having become merely images or reference points for a subsequent story, such as folk tale, historical legend, novella, or prophecy.[47]

The central point of value in Doty's characterisation is the conditionality of the catalogue of features of mythologies. All features are not always present at one time on account of the cultural ties of mythological corpuses, although they may be observed repeatedly when viewed from a comparative perspective. Gregory Nagy considers the identification of mythical corpuses and research focusing on them as a reflection of the whole concept of myth. He observes that as a corpus, myth must be read not only "vertically", on an axis of paradigmatic (metaphorical) choice, but also "horizontally", on an axis of syntagmatic (metonymic) combination.[48] Anna-Leena Siikala and Jukka Siikala have considered the manner of reading along both the vertical and horizontal at the same time as indispensable in the investigation of the Polynesian mythic-historical tradition.[49]

The intertextual relationships of myths are relevant equally to the field of ritual poems, charms, fairy tales and heroic epic. Because myths relate the events of the formative period of the world, they present, in the manner of a heroic epic, a reflection of history, although in a different sense. They present "holy history", but the individual and social interpretations of the events differ from each other, and myths become attached to different, even related genres.[50] In his work *The Destiny of the Warrior* (1970), Georges Dumézil has shown how the ideological structures of Indo-European myths are established in Roman historical narratives. Myths are thus worth examining not only as stylistically pure representatives of their own genre but also as a discourse which, while carrying indications of mythicality, crosses the narrow confines of genre.

46. Leach 1982: 5.
47. Doty 2000: 33–4.
48. Nagy 2002: 244.
49. Siikala 2000b: 352–3; Siikala and Siikala 2005.
50. Eliade 1984: 145–6.

When mythic narratives are approached as a *cultural discourse*, its meaning may be analysed on all the levels of text and performance of oral tradition. For example, epic poetry may then be treated as series of narrative entities performed in known circumstances, as narrative poems, and as mythic corpuses composed of these poems. In addition to mythic motifs, firstly those questions about the world, culture and mankind which are delved into in the narratives may be set out, secondly those oppositions through which these questions are posed, and thirdly the world of symbol, metaphor and image which forms the distinguishing mark of mythic poetry and by means of which the character of the discourse is defined even in performance situations.

A stumbling block to comparative research has been the separation of mythic materials from their cultural and social connections. We may also approach myths as the living culture of small communities, as integrated corpuses of oral tradition. When mythic tradition is investigated as a *cultural practice* and as a tool of people's social action, attention is fixed on the presentation of mythic tradition, on the *habitus* of performers, the modes adopted by singers and narrators, on the strategies and contexts of performance and selection of themes and poetic means. Singers and narrators interpret myths in their own way. The performer's bearing and choices relating to his performance influence the content of presentation, which varies – though within the framework determined by tradition – even in the same community because of the abundancy of strategic alternatives. The ideal of performance and the performer's *habitus* for their part determined the type of performance arena that was seen as best to appear in and what sort of bodily language and verbal register the singers chose for their performance of mythic poems.[51]

In tracing *mythic corpuses* it is natural to start from the community in whose network of internal interactions the myths circulated.[52] Mythic discourse is not, however, composed of clearly defined categories nor is it understood consistently in the same community. The genre relationships of myths belonging to the same corpus may break down, for example for the axis myth/fairy tale, myth/history, myth/ritual poem etc. Thus the specifying of corpuses is useful for the examination of the *intertextual relations of mythic discourse*.

Adapting Paul Ricoeur we may say that if we wish to know what a myth is talking about, we must first examine what it says.[53] Myths recount events and deeds of a fundamental type. They are built from episodes of activities in which the framing of the action, the actors, their central relationships, their deeds (among which belong also the dialogues) with their objectives, methods, targets and outcomes create the phenomemal world of mythic discourse, conflicting and illogical as the events of this world may feel. The *thematicisation of mythic narrative* as a consequence of

51. On the methodical model for myth study, see Siikala 2000c, Siikala and Siikala 2005.
52. See Urban 1996: 66–7.
53. Cf. Ricoeur 1976: 98.

repeated epithets, deeds or images and/or their opposites, for example in reference to inception/time/birth/sex/age, reveals central levels and connections of meaning.

Metaphor belongs among those characteristics which distinguish mythic discourse from other types of discourse. Thus mythic archetypes, crystallised motifs, *symbols, metaphors and images* are identifying marks of mythicality, whose special meaningfulness guarantees their preservation for long ages. Mythic meanings often present themselves in choices and forms of words, *keywords*, bearing archaic or symbolic meanings. Thus an analysis of poetic language and *poetic structures* may reveal crucial connections of meaning.

Myths of individuals and small communities

The collections of the nineteenth-century researchers of Finno-Ugric myth began to take on life for us when carrying out our field work among the Northern Khanty. We heard one important Khanty myth on a train as we ascended the Urals in July 2004. The myth recounted the origin of the Khanty holy lake *Num-to*. It was told by a man who by chance had landed up as our travelling companion, who wished to show that his people had an ancient and valuable culture.

As field work in the small Khanty villages in 2000–4 concentrated on the observation of local rituals observed in secret during the Soviet era, the myths were merely an evening entertainment whose value we appreciated later. We stayed in the village of Ovolyngort in 2002 in a forest cabin, whose only source of light was the hearth opening, with my folklorist colleague Oleg and the Khanty Nikolaï Nikitich Nakhrachëv or Kolya whom we had originally taken to be our guide. When by day we discussed matters with seventy-six-year-old Pëtr Nikitich Longortov, who arranged the village rituals, Kolya wished to relate his own view of the origins of the world, of the birth and essential nature of animals and of the most important deities. Through the long dark evenings and the depths of the night the men kept each other in happy company telling myths and tales. Oleg, apart from being a folklorist, is also a writer for the Komi folklore theatre and a poet, who as a child had learnt a great host of Komi tales from his aunt. He told these during our field trips, sometimes continuing the same tale for three nights running. Kolya had heard his myths and tales from his aunt Mariya Semënovna Nakhrachëva, who was born in 1930 on the far side of the Malaya Ob', in the village of Poslovat in Kunovat.

BEAR MYTHS
The rites related to the bear and the slaying of the bear have a part even today in the life of the Khanty. In Ovolyngort a bear had eaten a horse in the spring and done other harm in the mushroom and berry woods. Previously it had slashed up the holy sleigh at the village's ritual site. There was a lot of talk about bears and their wake ceremonies. One evening Kolya took up the topic:

*Two storytellers, Nikolaĭ Nikitich Nakhrachëv and Oleg Ulyashev, in Ovolyngort.
– Photograph by A.-L. Siikala 2002*

When it is said or written that the Khanty are sprung from the bear, it is not true. It is all a lie. The bear has always been small, he has always been a younger brother to the Khanty. He is God's son.

When he lived in heaven, he was still small, but he could already talk and walk. He began to vex his father. He looks down to the earth and says: "How beautiful it is down there below, how golden everything is there. Let me down, father!"

Father said: "Down below live people, and they hunt their food with their brow in a sweat. There you too will have to hunt your food. You cannot do that." But father got fed up, and he put his son in an iron cradle and let him down on a silver chain.

When God's little son came to earth he saw that it was only from above that it looked beautiful, thanks to the yellow lake flowers, *patʌəŋ-oχ-lipət*. Water lilies are called by this name in Khanty.

He was disappointed. He raised his head on high, but it was already too late. Father had decided, and it was his own will too.

Then he went to sit down and started to yell in fury. He began to look for something to eat, but did not know how to find food. Soon he was growling the whole time.

He began to walk on all fours and pick whatever he happened to come across. He began to grow a bit hairy. He grew bigger, and became the size he is now. But although he is very large, he is all the same the younger brother of mankind, because he was little when his father let him down onto earth. People had already appeared, in fact.

And nowadays, when he is slain, he is really being punished for his disobedience and crimes. Can't elder brothers punish a younger one if he doesn't obey? And then they ask forgiveness [in the bear wake] and say "It's not us, it's you who are guilty, you should have listened. It's not us killing you, but someone with a bayonet." A knife is called by that name, because the names of objects in ordinary life and in rituals are quite different.[54]

The structure of the myth is simple: the young bear sees the beautiful, golden land of people, and wants to go there. His father refuses, but then decides to let him down anyway. The young bear was disappointed, but had to stay on earth. He grows bigger and hairy, but he is still the younger brother of man. The myth of the bear's birth belongs to astral mythology and is connected with the bear ceremonies. The bear wake involves a multiform poetic corpus telling of the bear's origin, its sojourn on earth, the stages of its hunting and its return home. The Finns and Sámi also considered the bear to be a relative of humans. The myth of the bear's birth, which relates how God himself lets down his son onto the earth in a cradle on a silver and gold chain is known in *Kalevala*-metre poetry from the Finnic area, recited in connection with the rituals of the bear's wake, preserved in ceremonies similar to those of the Khanty and Mansi up to the nineteenth century. The myth of the bear's birth was sung in Finland with another purpose, as a protective charm for cattle, as in the following example, in which in the manner of the Khanty songs the bear is let down to earth in a cradle suspended from a silver chain:

Missä ohto synnytelty,	Where was the Bruin born
Mesikämmen kiännätelty?	the honey-paw turned over?
Tuolla ohto synnytelty,	There Bruin was born
Mesikämmen kiännätelty:	the honey-paw turned over –
Ylähällä taivosessa,	in the upper air
Otavaisen olkapäillä.	upon the Great' Bear's shoulders.
Missä se alas laskettiin?	Where was it let down?
Hihnassa alas laskettiin,	In a sling it was let down
Hihnassa hopiisessa,	in a silver sling
Kultaisessa kätkyyssä,	a golden cradle:
Sitte läks saloja samuumaan,	then it went to roam the woods
Pohjanmoata polokemaan.	to tread the North Land.
Elä sorra sontareittä,	Don't hurt the dung-shank
Koa maion kantajoa,	kill the milk-bearer:
Enemp' on emoilla työtä,	mother has more work
Suuri vaiva vanhemmalla,	the parent big trouble if
Jos poikonen pahan teköö.	the little boy is naughty.[55]

54. Nikolaï Nikitich Nakhrachëv, Ovolyngort, 2001.
55. Olli Tervonen, Kitee, North Karelia, O. A. F. Lönnbohm, 1894; Kuusi, Bosley and Branch 1977: 262.

Kolya wanted to dispute the generally agreed idea that the Khanty are the offspring of the bear. The denial is even more interesting because Kolya's father belongs to the *Por*-phratry, whose forefather is held to be a bear (as noted above, the Khanty are divided into two exogamous phratries, named the *Por* and the *Moś*). His mother, from whom he heard the folk tales, belonged to the other phratry according to her family: she was a *Moś*-woman. According to Kolya the bear is just a younger brother, so punishing him is possible because the bear has caused damage by coming to the earth inhabited already by people. The sentence "It is not us killing you, but someone with a bayonet" averts the blame for the killing from the hunter onto someone else. The same idea is found in the Finnish and Sámi bear-hunting tradition. The Finnish hunter might say that the bear caused the misfortune and the knife which killed him was made in Estonia or Germany. The Sámi in turn might say that hunters are "Swedish, German, English and from all the countries" other than the one they were actually from.[56]

Instead of a mythic theme suggesting that the bear is the ancestor of human kind, which is important in bear wakes, in everyday discussions people were more interested in damages caused by bears. Pëtr Nikitich said that bear is not a bear, if it is a wrongdoer. It cannot hunt well. Especially bad are the visits of bears to graveyards, nowadays a common thing, but known to happen also in old times:

> Once, long ago, in the old times, when the inhabitants of *Ovolynkur'* still used to fish on the Ob' river, behind Akanleim and Azova channel, such an event happened. When they were absent – all the families always go away [to fish] – a bear completely destroyed the cemetery. The people went to get food and the bear went to get food. Only they went to get food in a good way, whereas it did so in a bad way. Such bears are to be shot immediately, because if a bear begins to attack people, living or dead, it is not just a bear any more. This is a bear which cannot and will not hunt in a proper way any more. This is a sick bear, a freak. They looked for that bear for a long time and then caught it, finally.[57]

Kolya Nakhrachëv, however, returned to bear themes the next year, commenting now on the myth in another way, connected to himself:

> The bear is God's son. When he lived in heaven, he looked down and saw that *everything there was golden.* So he started asking his father if he would let him down there. Father says: "Down below *you have to search out food.* You do not know how." However, he made his father so fed-up that he put his son in *an iron cradle* and let him down *on a golden chain.*
>
> When the little son of God came to earth, he saw that it looked beautiful only from above because of the yellow colours of autumn. *He lifted his head on high, but it was already too late. Father had decided,* but still his thoughts turned to home. He sat down and began to groan, greatly upset. For the bear the most unpleasant of all things on earth were the mosquitoes; yes, and even

56. Kuusi 1963: 46–7.
57. Pëtr Nikitich Longortov, Ovolyngort, 2001.

food had to be searched out. He began looking for food, but did not know how. He began walking on all fours and to pick everything that came his way. *He began to grow a little hairy.* He was a beautiful youth, but he began to change into a wild animal. *He grew bigger until he became as big as he is now.* But *although he is large, he is still the yonger brother of mankind, because he was small when his father let him down to earth.* If he was once let down in a cradle, it means he was still small. *The nutcracker (noχr-leṭi-ne, "Siberian pine-cone-eating woman") is considered his elder.* Firstly, because she was already on the earth when the bear came down; secondly, because she made a lot of demands. *Among us small people are undemanding. But those who are older grumble, they are not satisfied and impose on others.* Thirdly, he does not quarrel with the nutcracker, she howls more. They usually have quarrels with the bear. They eat the same food. She howls that the bear is eating her cones. "Shar-shar!" she weeps the whole time.[58]

This time Kolya's comments are even more personal. The animal protector spirits of the kins and families are still important beings in people's lives. Sacrifices are made to them and their idols may be present on the walls of houses. Indicating his father's family, Kolya related that the goose (*Aj-lut-iki*, "White-Cheeked Brent-Goose Old Man" is the bird of the family Nakhrachëv and also, expressed in the family name, cedar (or rather Siberian fir) tree, *noχraś* (Siberian cembra), which is actually "Cone father", *noχr* meaning "cone" and *aś* or *aśi*, "father". And hence the last part of Kolya's tale, which concerns the relationship and quarrel between the bear and the cedar-tree-seed-eating nutcracker, is important to him. The structure of the narrative and sentences in italics show that he reproduced the most important parts of the myth nearly word for word. On the other hand, the point of the myth was now new. Instead of speaking about the special position of the bear he turns to the relationship of bear and nutcracker. The tiny bird is "elder", she has authority over the bear. Kolya, who has a schoolmaster's education, and is a helper of a strong shaman in public ritual, and an exceptionally good hunter, is small in stature. Hence "among us small people are undemanding" also might point to his personal experiences.

The nutcracker (*Nucifraga caryocatactes*) eating cembra cones appeared in another of Nakhrachëv's myths.

The bear brought home with a special ritual becomes a god and protector of the house. And, since he knows the character of *his sister*, he warns her.

In the very beginning the nutcracker was a big bird, like the wood grouse. Its flesh was white, like the hazel-grouse's. And the Khanty hunters considered it as good luck to catch it and to put it on the festive table. Since it ate cedar cones [nuts], its meat was white, tasty. And the bear's spirit senses misfortune, you know, and warns her: "Sister, do not fly to the Sacred Cedar Cape. Do not take cones from there. You have all the forest at your disposal."

And it was just the autumn time, the season for storing the cedar cones. First the nutcracker took a hold of herself, then could not stand it any longer and flew to the Sacred Cedar Cape.

58. Nikolaĭ Nikitich Nakhrachëv, Ovolyngort, 2002.

And again the bear's spirit spoke: "If you ever come there, do not shell it there, do not fly to the village."

But she tried to shell it on a tree. It was not comfortable. So she flew with the cone over the whole village. The people saw the nutcracker with the cone. The most skilled boy shot with his bow. He did not hit, but the nutcracker was afraid and dropped the cone. The most skilled boy came up first, running to the cone. Some nuts he gave to his friends, all the rest ate himself. And then a disaster happened. At night the boy's belly was swollen and by the morning he died.

The shaman came to find out from the house's protector why the boy had died and ordered the bear's spirit to punish the nutcracker.

The bear's spirit said: "Well, sister, you are guilty. A human being died because of you and I must punish you. Your white flesh will become blue. Your big body will dry out. And your blue dry body nobody will eat, even the hungry beasts. Your hungry stomach all the taiga dwellers will remember from your mournful scream, like weeping: *shar-shar-shar*! When anybody sees the nutcracker in the forest, remember my words."[59]

Kolya said that this myth is performed by singing and telling. He heard all the folk tales from his mother Mariya Semënovna Nakhrachëva[60] in the village of Kazym-Mys. The myth describes why the nutcracker is small, though she is an older sister of the bear. In the beginning everything is fine. The nutcracker is big like a wood grouse and a tasty bird, but it breaks the rule: it flies to the Sacred Cembra peninsula and eats the cones. People shoot it and it drops the cone, from which one of the boys became sick. The first sentence shows that this myth was sung or told in the bear-wake ceremony. After the bear is taken home, it will be a "god" and the "protector of the house". The bear gives right orders and the soul of the bear tells what will be the punishment for wrongdoing. In the course of the narrative, the shaman, who is a problem-solver in many Khanty myths, is consulted. He knows that the guilty one is the nutcracker.

In the whole process of ritually organised bear-hunting a great number of songs were performed among the northern hunters, Khanty, Mansi and even Finns. The bear wake was a culmination of the whole ritual process and the bear was entertained by performing songs to him. Some of the songs express the bear's view, some tell of heroes and deities.[61] At the end of the myth, the cry of the bird is imitated as at the end of many myths concerned with birds. The myths of the bear presented above tell of the relationship between the animal and people. The problems concern the moral order: what is the right way to behave? Myths also reveal why some animals or birds are valued and some are not.

---

59. Nikolaï Nikitch Nakhrachëv, Ovolyngort, 2002.
60. Mariya Sotrueva, b. 1930 on the river Kunovat, the village of Poslovat.
61. Khanty and Mansi bear songs are found in a number of folklore collections: Honko, Timonen and Branch 1994: 120–3, 675–8 . Some of the bear songs in the collection of Wolfgang Steinitz (1939), collected from the North Khanty, have been translated into English by Aado Lintrop (1998).

Kolya mends a grouse trap on the Ovolyngort hunting path.
– Photograph by A.-L. Siikala 2002

ATTITUDES TOWARDS BIRDS

When we once discussed yearly celebrations, Kolya Nakhrachëv mentioned the *vŏrŋa χătʌ* celebration, an important feast of the Northern Khanty. He said that when there was a *vŏrŋa χătʌ* feast in Muzhi, local papers wrote that the crow is a cunning and skilful bird, stealing everything. Hence, people cannot do anything to it, they are afraid of it and honour it, they are astonished because it is so skilful and they value it. "But it is not so. I heard one legend and printed it in the local paper." After that Nakhrachëv found that some other people published the text and claimed that they had created or discovered it. "But it is the case that I found the myth and published it. I should have the author's rights. But, on the other hand, I only polished it a little bit. The legend is a folk legend and not owned by the author."[62] Then Nakhrachëv told the myth:

> And that's why the *vŏrŋa*, crow, is honoured. She comes flying always at one and the same time. She comes back to us to bring up her nestlings. The 7 April was always her day, and at this time she comes flying.
>
> Once upon a time long ago, the crow came as always, and the people were sleeping. Everybody had fallen asleep and could not wake up. God sent this sleep upon them for some reason. The crow looked here and there. Everybody are sleeping. Everybody had fallen asleep.
>
> Then the crow sat down on a high tree, on the highest pine-tree. She gathered all its pain, all its strength. She croaked as loudly as ever she could.

62. Nikolaĭ Nikitich Nakhrachëv, Ovolyngort, 2001.

And one man got up. He woke up all the others. They say, just *at that time the Khanty people came into being*. It appears that the crow awoke the Khanty. It was as if *she gave life to them*. That's why the Khanty people respect her, and make a feast in her honour. And the crow brings the spring and the summer.[63]

The myth tells why the crow, which is not hunted, is honoured. It is a son of the Lord and wakes people up to celebrate the spring. It squawked so loud that someone woke up and after that all the people. The squawking introduced the Khanty to the world. The tale of the crow began a long discussion of birds, the meanings of their names and their values. Like the crow, the *savne*, magpie, has mythical meaning. A myth tells how it saved people from a terrible cold. Kolya Nakhrachëv said that the magpie is not so highly honoured as the crow. People say that it can bring messages and a hero can turn himself into a magpie. But the magpie is not really a good bird. His first variant of the tale of the magpie is as follows:

The magpie is not honoured so much as the crow is. The people view it as not so good, only so-so . . . They say she can bring some news and the epic heroes could turn into it. But not so good, she is not honoured. Although, *once it had rescued the life of human beings*, too.

The upper old man, well, this, you know, the head of the celestial chancellory began once upon a time to scrape away the clouds out of the sky. Well, just like the reindeer hides are scraped with a thing, with such an iron scraper, in the same way. Seeing a cloud from the window, he just rushes straight out and scrapes it away. And he began to collect the clouds at home in a sack. He began to gather them. There is not a single cloud in the sky. There is frost on the earth, the days are clear.

And the people began to freeze to death. Someone going out for water would freeze to the buckets, someone going out to the woods would freeze to the wood.

And there was a shaman in a camp. He looks: the people in his camp dwindled. But this is bad, for he is responsible for them. He must keep and guard them. He looks: there is a horrible frost outside. He thinks, whom should he send.

And at that very moment the magpie comes, rat-tat, to the window! "Oh, magpie!" he says, "I'll feed you very well and off you go, fly upwards, look why the weather is like this." He fed it full with reindeer fat.

She flew upwards, almost died from the frost, but came up. An old man and an old woman lived there. Rat-tat-tat! on the window it knocked. The old man and the old woman opened the door, saw the magpie, became glad. "Oh, oh," they say, "you have frozen so hard. Come in, we'll feed you." They fed her, gave her grain to eat. She pecked.

At that moment the old man saw a cloud from the window and rushed out to scrape the sky, just like the reindeer hides are cleaned of fat. And the magpie understood everything, found the sack and began to peck the sack with the clouds in while the old man was away. The old woman ran to the old man. "She," she said, "she's pecking your sack!" The old man stopped scraping, came running back: "Well, why are you doing this, magpie? We've taken you in and fed you, and you are damaging the sack."

63. Nikolaï Nikitich Nakhrachëv, Ovolyngort, 2001.

The magpie began to tell how all the people on the earth were freezing because of this. And from the worn-through sack the clouds flew out. They flew around the house and began to fly out from the door. The old man stood up in the doors but could not stop them, catch them, and all the clouds flew by. All the sky was covered by the clouds. Far from merely snowing, it even began to rain.

It became warmer on the earth. The people began to get warm, to thaw out. The one frozen to a bucket thawed free from the bucket, the one frozen to the woods thawed free from the wood.[64]

For some reason which is not told in the narrative, the Lord above began to collect clouds in a sack in his house. The earth became cold and all human beings were frozen. The problem is solved by a shaman of the camp, whose task it is to help people. He feeds the magpie and asks it to fly upwards to heaven and free the clouds. The magpie does it, and saves the people, who became warm and could live again. When we met Kolya next summer, he told another variant of the myth.

In the sky, above the white clouds *there is a very beautiful house. An old man and an old woman live there. The old man is a serious old man, Torəm old man (etər-iki, torəm-iki).*

The old man looked at the earth and saw *the people had become wicked*, and *he decided to punish them*. But how? He made up his mind: *the people should be punished by cold.*

And if there so much as appeared a cloud in the sky, the old man ran up to it and, holding a big scraper in his hands, he scraped the cloud off the sky very precisely and put it into a sack.

It got cold and the people became gloomy, and the beasts in the forests dug themselves into the earth; there was no game at all. And the firewood came to an end. When nobody could endure any more and went out for firewood, he would freeze to the wood. The women went out for water and froze to the buckets.

At the end of the village there lived a wise old man with his wife. He consulted with his old woman and said: "It cannot go on this way. Soon there will be no people at all in this village. We should change things. Here," he said to his old woman, "near our house I've seen a bird. This is a good sign. Catch this bird and bring it home."

The old woman caught the bird and brought her home. But the bird was completely frozen. The old man caressed her, warmed her, gave her frozen fat (*potəm vŏj*) to eat. And this happened to be an ordinary magpie, with round beak, long tail, all black and white. And the old man said to the magpie in the bird language: "Fly up to the sky to the white-bearded old man. He has a sack full of clouds in the corner of his house. Peck the sack. The clouds will come out and it will get warmer."

The magpie flew up onto the highest clouds and saw a very beautiful house there, and the white-bearded old man.

He said to his wife: "*iʌ ta mŭv χaŋšaŋ voj, iʌ ta mŭv eʌ'əŋ voj* '[It is] a motley beast of the lower earth, a beautiful beast of the lower earth' – granny, open the door, let her in here!"

64. Nikolaĭ Nikitich Nakhrachëv, Ovolyngort, 2001.

The old woman put the best meal on the table and led the magpie in. She pecked a bit at something. And at that moment a little cloud appeared in the sky again. The old man rushed out to scrape it away.

The magpie warmed up, and in the corner she saw a big black sack full of clouds. And she began to peck it and to tear it with her claws.

The old woman shouted: "The sack of clouds! The sack of clouds!"

The old man came running up with the little cloud, and stumbled. And the clouds flew out of the sack and scattered across the sky.

At that moment it began raining. The women who had frozen near the ice-holes thawed out, the women frozen near the wood thawed out. In gladness they ran home, and revelry began, shared by all. Glory to the bird![65]

The myth now has literary features. The motive for the scraping of clouds and cold weather is clear. The Old Man is *Torəm* (*etər-iki, torəm-iki*) who punishes people for their wickedness and lack of adherence to rules. The man who helps is not a shaman, but an old man from the village. Seeing the magpie is a "good sign". It is also frozen, but the old man cures it with a special frozen grease and he talks to the magpie in the language of birds. A line from a poem, in which form the narrative is performed, "*iʌ ta mŭv χaŋšaŋ voj, iʌ ta mŭv eʌ'əŋ voj*", is added to the narrative in order to show that the narrator is well-informed. The line shows also that this myth has been a poem which was performed by singing. The end of the story is happy and the magpie is honoured by everybody. It seems that Kolya had remembered or heard the story and "polished" it a bit.

The fate of the *kŭśt̩i voj* ("whistling beast, whistler", the hazel-grouse, *Bonaso bonasia / Tetrao bonasia*) was sorrowful:

Hazel-grouse long ago was a big bird, flying in the sky. When flying to the upper-most sky she touched God's eye with her wing. Then she was caught and torn into several pieces, and from the smallest piece they made the hazel-grouse as she is now. And other pieces scattered in different directions. One stuck to a black grouse [*Tetrao tetrix*], another to a wood grouse [*Tetrao urogallus*] and so on. So, then, the pieces of white meat which are found in these birds are the pieces of the hazel-grouse's flesh. I just do not understand why they were so cruel to the hazel-grouse. Well, anything can happen, and she just happened to touch [God's eye]. And this was not on purpose anyway.[66]

Kolya commented on this myth: "I do not know why the hazel hen was treated so severely. But it just happened that it touched God's eye. Nothing more than that."

In discussing birds, Kolya and Pëtr Nikitich pondered why some birds are sacred:

Raven (*χurəχ*). This is hardly a sacred bird among the Khanty. It is considered to be a messenger, an evil one, as a rule. It always lives here, does not fly away

---

65. Nikolaï Nikitich Nakhrachëv, Ovolyngort, 2002.
66. Nikolaï Nikitich Nakhrachëv, Ovolyngort, 2002.

anywhere like the crows, to say nothing about other birds. Like the magpie, it survives winter and cold together with the Khanty, and so they regard it, like the magpie, as their own, not as a stranger. It cries "*χurəχ!*", therefore it was named so.[67]

Kolya Nakhrachëv mentioned that the loon, *toχtəŋ*, is a sacred bird among the Khanty. It is a bird of the Lower World. The Nenets eat loons, but for the Khanty, at least Kolya, it is not permitted to eat it:

> Once we went hunting together with a Nenets. About ten ducks and loons were shot. We came home to his place. I saw: his mother straight away sat down and began to pluck the loon. I asked my comrade [the Nenets]: "Why does she pluck it?" The comrade said: "What do you mean, 'why'? She'll cook it for us now."
>
> I said: "Well, it is not allowed for me to eat a loon, you know." The old woman grinned in such a way, put the loon aside and took a duck.
>
> Among us one must not shoot a loon. And if it falls into a net, it must be released. But it nips, pecks, you know. It does not understand you would do it some good. It pecks till it bleeds. You should catch it by the beak and then untwine it. Then catch it and cast it away. If it dives straight away it is a good sign. If it swims, then for the one who released it there will be something bad happening.[68]

According to Kolya, the swan (*χŏtəŋ*) is not as mythically important a bird as among other Finno-Ugric peoples.

> The swan is not sacred among the Khanty; it is not respected as much as the goose is. The swans come flying first, before other birds, bringing the spring. Therefore they are esteemed. One may shoot them only before other birds come. After that one must not.
>
> A sacred bird is one which is clever. Well, among the human beings it is the same. They treat a clever person well, a stupid one only so-so. The swan is a stupid bird, it comes itself into shooting range. What kind of mind could it have? Look, to hunt a goose, one has to think. It does not let you to come close. To get it, you creep a lot, sweat and slave.[69]

After narrating this Kolya revealed that the spirit protector of his family is the goose. He and Pëtr Nikitich were both interested in birds. It was natural at hunting time – we discussed birds in August; but both also had birds as their family protector. The position of birds in the mythic discourse is connected to the seasonal round: birds which come north in spring are valued. If a bird is connected to the events at the beginning of the earth or deities and divine heroes, it may be sacred. For example, the diver belongs to the Lower World. It is a bird of the lord of the Lower World and therefore it cannot be eaten.

---

67. Nikolaĭ Nikitich Nakhrachëv, Ovolyngort, 2001.
68. Nikolaĭ Nikitich Nakhrachëv, Ovolyngort, 2001.
69. Nikolaĭ Nikitich Nakhrachëv, Ovolyngort, 2001.

The hunting season brings ducks for the evening meal. Lyuba Rusmilenko helps her mother in Lopkhari. – Photograph by A.-L. Siikala 2003

THE HEROIC TRADITION

The nineteenth-century collectors showed that the most impressive epic songs of the Northern Khanty told of their heroes. The princes of the heroic poems, the "cities", the weaponry of the warriors and so forth point to the Yugra culture and social organisation of the thirteenth to fifteenth centuries, known from historical sources. The first sources to mention the Yugra princes are medieval: Novgorodians were making trading and tax trips to Yugra by the eleventh century.[70] The Muscovites overpowered forty Yugra cities in 1499 and imprisoned fifty princes and a thousand other inhabitants. Although thereafter the Khanty rebelled, they remained subject to Moscow.

The Khanty heroic epics, poems hundreds of lines long, are "holy songs", and are performed only by men. They do not tell of warrior raids; the hero leaves on his journey for reasons of revenge and to gain himself a wife. Both Khanty and Mansi called heroic poems "songs of war, of destruction". The common name is thought to point to the great age of the songs. The poetic figures of the epic songs, which are retained in their memory, as well as the great quantity of verses show that they were performed only by professional

70. Bartens 1986: 15.

singers.[71] The songs are first-person narratives: the hero speaks through the mouth of a singer. The heroes lived in a heroic age, before the time of "man who has his navel cut". They are frequently compared, especially among the Mansi, with the deities and spirits, whose songs are likewise in the first person. The most important guest of the bear feast, the bear, also speaks through the mouth of the singer. In prose narratives heroes and deities no longer speak through a singer, but are indicated in the third person.[72]

The heroic tradition is nowadays related mostly in prose form. In 2004, we met Gennadiĭ Pavlovich Kelchin.[73] He recounted two heroic narratives, one of seven brothers and black *jik-ves* and another about *Tŏχʌəŋ-iki*, the Winged Man.

Seven brothers and black *jik-ves*, water monster
There were seven brothers. There were seven heroes. Among them *Otšam-iki* was a bit crazy. Thanks to him they all finally perished.

Choose a star: the one you choose he will hit, such a good archer he is. His bow was so big, that twenty *ort*-assistants (spirit assistants), carried it behind him, but he pulled it and shot so quickly that the second arrow hit the first in flight.

There was also *As-kŭr, pal-kŭr-iki*, another brother, the elder brother; the Ob' river was only up to his knees.[74]

Once the brothers went on a boat up the river to seek a bride for the second brother, to the Holy Lake, *jeməŋ lor*, from which seven rivers flowed forth. I think it was the lake *Num-to*. Very many rivers emanate from it, seven and yet more. It is just as sacred as Voĭkar Sor. It is thought the sacred water was brought there from Voĭkar Sor.

Well, then, the brothers forged anchors and chains the year long. They bound the boat's bottom round with iron six fingers thick, because in the river flowing out from the Sacred Lake, the Lake of Seven Rivers, there lived *jik-ves*. I think it was the Nadym river, this is what it seems to have been judging by the descriptions. One of the *jik-ves* was as long as the bends of seven rivers, the curves of seven rivers.

Fifty *ort*-assistants could hardly carry a *naχər*, iron shirt, for the younger brother on a pole thick as a pine-tree. The younger brother rode on a white horse around the earth, *ʌovən-χo*. They brought the hauberk. He put it on.

The seven brothers boarded the boat. Fifty times fifty *orts* struck with the oars. They started off. They looked: *Jik-ves-imi* lay there, the mother of all the *jik-ves*, seven river curves long, along the seven river curves she stretched.

One of the brothers threw the anchor into the water. Aha! Got it! Another brother threw, all the brothers threw the anchors. They hooked it. The oarsmen rowed to the bank, the boat stayed where it was. Two hundred and fifty oarsmen could not pull the *jik-ves* out.

Then *As-kŭr, pal-kŭr*, said: "Give me the chain, I'll jump!" They gave him it. Well, he jumped out. On the bank he held the chain; knee-deep he went down into the earth, waist-deep he pressed down into the earth.

71. Bartens 1986: 16–17.
72. Bartens 1986: 17.
73. Born in 1950 near Khanty-Mansiĭsk.
74. Heroes were like giants.

After him *Otšam-iki* jumped out and grasped the chain; knee-deep he went down into the earth, waist-deep he pressed down into the earth. The oarsmen came closer to the bank, too. They grasped the chain and the other brothers came too, hardly could they pull *Jik-ves-imi* onto the bank. Where there was flesh, they cut out flesh along the bones, where there were bones, they disjointed the bones along the joints.

This was the mother, but the father was still left. Four river bends long, four river curves long [he is]. They pulled out the father of all the *jik-ves* in the same way. Where there was flesh, they cut out flesh along the bones, where there were bones, they disjointed the bones along the joints.

Well, then. But there are many *jik-ves* left, their children. They covered all the river around, there is no way to go by boat, no way to walk above.

And *As-kŭr, pal-kŭr*, said to them: "Do not live here. Every one of you choose a river for your own, and live there, everyone on his own river." Now there are no *jik-ves*, but in every river, probably, there used to be. They were black, huge. Well, since they stretched along the river curves, they must be like snakes, or something . . .[75]

The Winged Man (*Tŏχʌəŋ-iki*)

There was Winged Man, *Tŏχʌəŋ-iki, Otšam-iki*. The seventh brother, the youngest brother, was a bit crazy.

The brothers started to go hunting, they went out to chase elks. And he was sleeping. He slept till the sun heated his navel, burnt his navel. He woke up: "Father, I'll go hunting with my brothers!" "Where are you going? They have already gone long ago, you'll never overtake them." "I'll overtake," he said.

There was a larch near the house. He cut the larch down, made a ski with knots looking backwards, split it into two, hewed it with a blunt axe, stood up on the ski: "Eh!" he said. "Father, you said they had gone long ago, but they have not yet hidden themselves behind three trees, have not hidden behind four trees." He started off on the larch ski, overtook the brothers. "I'll go forward, follow me."

He looks: there is a big elk herd, forty times forty heads. Once he ran around them, then a second time, a third time he ran around, chose the biggest one, drove it out of the herd, began to chase it. He chased, chased, overtook. He shot an arrow, killed it.

A woman came out from under the earth, a Nenets woman: "Why are you, my nephew, on my land, killing my animals?" The brothers' mother was Nenets, and hence she called him nephew.

"I was chasing my elk," he said, "from my land. I only managed to overtake it on yours. But I do not need meat," he said. "We'll eat together, I'll give you the meat, only the hide I'll take." They cooked the meat, ate, and he went back.

He was skiing, so, and heard: an arrow was coming level with his navel. He jumped higher than his navel and went further on.

He heard: an arrow was coming level with his heart. He jumped higher than his heart and went further on.

Again he heard: an arrow was coming level with his head. But he had no need to bend down: he was a hero! He jumped higher than his head.

He got angry, shot an arrow himself. He killed his uncle, *ur'-χo*. It was he who was running after.

75. Gennadiĭ Pavlovich Kel'chin, Salekhard, 2004.

He came back home, and said: "My uncle invited me to be his guest." The father said: "If he invited you, go on then."

They went out – and to meet them there came a huge army from *un-voš*, Big Town. *Otšam-iki* came to slay them. He killed all the army, half of the town, and started to kill his brothers. And the head of Big Town cried out: "Why are you killing your brothers, are you crazy?" He nearly murdered them all.

This I heard, but, I suppose, it was a long song. Here are just the pieces that I gathered and kept in mind.[76]

Kel'chin had heard the narrative in the form of a song, but knew it well. The description of heroes and their opponents is detailed and dialogues between characters vivacious. The heroes with fine arms, especially the youngest of them, *Otšam-iki*, are good fighters, qualified to attack monstrous opponents and even the worst of them, the mother of river snakes, seven river bends long. The youngest of seven brothers is connected to *Lovəŋ-χo* (*Ловəŋ-χu*), he rides on a white horse like him, the seventh of the sons of God. His other name *Tŏχləŋ-iki*, may also refer to mythic themes. Karjalainen mentions that in Dem'yanka Winged Man is the helper of the God of heaven and the same as *Päi-īka*, the Old Man of Thunder and Storm. He comes to help as a storm and can kill the evil spirit Kul with his arrow.[77] The mythic allusions show that the events of hero narratives relate to the time before ordinary men, "with cut navels". In the second narrative the opponent is related to the hero but married to a Nenets woman. At the end of the quarrel on the hunting lands, *Otšam-iki* slays the huge army and half the inhabitants of Big Town.

The wars with the Nenets also turned everyday discussions to the topic of historical legends. Nikolaĭ Nakhrachëv spoke about the last fight with the Nenets on the Polym headland (Salekhard). His father remembered the last member of an old Nenets warrior kin:

Before the peace was made with the Nenets on the Polym headland, warriors stood on the watchtowers. They did nothing: they did not go hunting or fishing, they only watched and waited for war. But when the Nenets army came, they noticed and gave the alarm. When the Nenets came closer, they were already met by an army. They were all black from the wind, not of great stature, but broad. They did not cut the hair but bound it in tails.

One last old man from this kin was left; my father still remembered him. He never cut his hair and always rode on a black horse. He harnessed it to a sledge [a Russian type of light horse sledge] and galloping entered Muzhi. And he never sat down, but always stood. There [in Muzhi] he drank heavily some days and galloped along the streets and then went away. And as long as he stayed in Muzhi, there was a mess. He lashed out with the whip, he never let it out of his hand – the horse would jerk like crazy. And he never would look to see if there was anybody in his way or not. He was trampled down in the same way himself. He stood near his sledge, sodden, in torn clothes. A merchant went galloping by in a troika. He probably thought it was some beggar who would jump away.

76. Gennadiĭ Pavlovich Kel'chin, Salekhard, 2004.
77. Karjalainen 1918: 327.

But that one did not jump. So he was dragged about 50 metres. He was a strong old man. He did not cut his hair or his horse's mane and tail, either; they even dangled along the earth. Nowadays there are no such warriors any more. This one was the last of that kin.[78]

The concepts and beliefs about warriorship live on in the Northern Khanty culture. The warrior's equipment, especially the sabre, are sacred objects used in rituals and kept in a holy corner of the house or in a sacred store house. A member of the family Sevli has such a sabre. He took the sabre to Muzhi with him, kept it in the holy corner and performed *porəʌətə*, sacrificial rituals with it. The iron shirt, *naχr*, is mentioned in place names, but sometimes confused with *noχr*, the cembra tree, as was evident when we discussed a local ritual place with the men of Vershina Voïkar. Martin Rebas' said:

In the middle of the river there is an island, seen from the house. Three spruces grew in the island. Three warriors, who were from the village behind the river, turned into them some time in the old days. Therefore the island is called Three Spruces.

Then one of the men gathered near Martin's house said that the island was called *Xŭʌəm noχr* or Three Larches. Martin rejected the claim in an authoritarian way:

What larches? There are no larches, and besides larches are something else in Khanty. What was it? Ah, larch is *naŋk*, *noχr* is cedar and not a larch. They call the place by another name too, but not *Xŭʌəm noχr* but *Xŭʌəm naχr* which means Three Warriors. When they fought there, the soldiers had iron clothes, so, such shirts. *Naχr* means iron in Khanty, then a warrior is also *naχr*. They did not want to give up, they destroyed all in their village. But three wounded solders escaped to the island. There they dug a turf house and began to live there. After their death they began to sacrifice there. The rites were performed on the island; only men went to the place and took children with them.[79]

After the discussion of local history we went to the island, performed a ritual, fed the spirits of the warriors, and took photos. We found a hole of an old turf house, but it was not ancient, built maybe forty to fifty years ago. Samuil Arkhipovich Alyaban said that the attackers killed the men and took the girls. Pavel Filippovich Rebas', a boat mechanic in Ust'-Voïkar, a neighbouring village, told Oleg that at that time people were always fighting. Sometimes the attackers took hostages:

Near Vershina Voïkar there is an island, which is called *Xŭʌəm-χul*, Three Spruces, or *Kăt-χul*, in Russian Two Spruces. Maybe it is after all Two Spruces. The old village was in Voshpaï; old people lived there. There is another old village,

---

78. Nikolaï Nikitich Nakhrachëv, Ovolyngort, 2001.
79. Martin Rebas', Vershina Voïkar, 2000.

Aïvosh, near the graveyard. Then they moved here and gave it the name Voïkar. But there in Voshpaï the old people lived. And they fought all the time with each other, all the time fought with each other. Like there [in the village] *Xŭʌem-χul* was attacked, all were killed and somebody was taken as a war prisoner. But two men were left. They jumped over the river and turned into two leafy trees. Hence, the place is called by the name *Kăt-χul*, Two Spruces.[80]

The historical legends do not speak about the wars with the Russians but fights with Nenets and between the locals. Kolya Nakhrachëv places the warrior zone in Salekhard, where Nenets were the opponents. In Vershina Voïkar, a small Khanty village near Salekhard, the fighting is more a local matter. Remembering warrior equipment, the iron shirts and the severity of fighting refer to historical war episodes. The attackers wanted to get the girls, which may relate to a real situation. The payment for a bride was large and a poor man might have had difficulties in finding a suitable wife. On the other hand, the narratives speak of the continuous fighting of "old people", which is typical in the situation of migrations when people had to find new land to live in. The island got its meaning from the heroic tradition. It is a holy place for men, who have organised their rituals to feed the souls of the warriors.

TALES OF DEITIES AND MYTHIC BEINGS

We learned from Pëtr and Kolya that Shuryshkary Khanty believed in four main deities: the Creator Master (*Num-torəm*), the Holy Mother Mistress *Jeməŋ-aŋki*, the Son of the Creator *Aovəŋ-χu*, the "man on the horse", and the Master of the Lower World, *Kŭl-ilpi-iki* or *Xiń-iki*. In addition, people honour the spirits of kin and family and local spirits (see pp. 123 ff.). In songs and narratives, the most popular divine personage is *Lovəŋ-χo* (lit.) or *Aovəŋ-χu* (Synya dialect), literally "horse man", a hero who has a winged horse and who wears *naχr*, armour, an iron shirt. His weapon is not a sword, but a sabre. On his back he has a shawl and on his head a cap of feathers. When he is needed, he is called, and he gallops to people's assistance on a cloud of down. According to Pëtr Nikitich *Lovəŋ-χo* appears as different personages: he can be a small child, an unhappy orphan boy, a snotty brat. His real character is revealed in his relationship with people:

> There are, as you know, such people who offend and annoy other people. There are also people who pass such miserable cripples by. But the third one feels pity, gives his shirt, if he has nothing else to give. In folk tales, *Aovəŋ-χu* appears as he is: he punishes people for wrong deeds, he is indifferent to indifferent people, he helps people who are pitiful.[81]

Pëtr Nikitich said that there are folk tales in which *Aovəŋ-χu* beats a mean *Jalań-iki*, a cannibal giant, which has three, seven or nine heads.[82]

80. P. V. Rebas', Ust'-Voïkar, 2000.
81. Nikolaï Nikitich Nakhrachëv, Ovolyngort, 2001.
82. The word comes from Turkic **jylan*, "snake" [V. N.].

The giant cannot look down because he has a bone sticking out under his throat. *Λovəŋ-χu* turns himself into *Imi-χiλi*, "aunt's nephew". He whirls at the feet of *Jalań-iki* and then nails him to a pine. The giant comes home to his wife with a pine on his back and groans that some little boy had done wicked things to him.[83]

In narratives *Jalań-iki* is a mean giant who likes to eat Khanty. Nikolaï Nikitich gave a description of him:

> *Jalań-iki* is such a tall fellow, his eyes are terrible, or maybe just the one eye he has. He is taller than the tallest pine-tree. There are seven brothers, the eldest with seven heads, the youngest with one head. They like very much to eat Khanty.
>
> And how do they eat? They eat meat, the guts they wind on the *pŭt-jŭχ* ["cauldron tree", a crossbar for the cauldron over the fire], the head they stick on the *maš-jŭχ* [the forks on both sides of the fire, on which the crossbar rests]. And if you see such a thing, this means *Jalań-iki* has had enough to eat.
>
> *Jalań-iki* is afraid of fire and of daylight; it strolls around only at night. Night is his *métier*. His eye glows like a star, with a dim light. He cannot look down: a bone under his neck hinders this. And sly hunters make him look down sharply. He stabs himself on the bone and dies from this, they say.

After that Nikolaï Nikitich went further in telling a story of *Jalań-iki* and a woman:

> And, besides, *Jalań-iki* is always hungry. It may be that he comes to a hunter's lodge. He cannot get in, opens the door and begs for a meal. If the woman has a strong heart . . . (Two women are staying there while the hunter is absent.) If the woman is weak, she faints and becomes his prey.
>
> And the strong women feed him with sheafs of dried fish, with cooked meals, call him "grandfather". *Jalań-iki* is thus satisfied. The woman would rake out everything from the storehouses. At the end she harnesses three dogs, and wraps the child in a kerchief. She gives the last crumbs to him and jumps onto the sledge: "purrr!"
>
> And before *Jalań-iki* succeeds in overtaking her, she reaches the village. And there are more people and the dogs and sparks fly out from the *śoχəλs* [open fireplace in the house corner covered by a wooden cover, *pŭλop*].
>
> *Jalań-iki* runs back to the lodge where the weak woman was staying. The next day the hunters come to the lodge and see that it has been destroyed and the second woman has been eaten by *Jalań-iki*.

The point of the folk tale is to show how a wise woman can take care of herself. A weak woman might perish, but a woman who has a strong will survives.

In a myth told in Kazym-mys, *Jalań-iki* appears in a local myth with *Λovəŋ-χu*. The myth relates how islands and a place called Stony Cape (*Kev ńoλ*) appeared near Kazym-mys.

---

83. Pëtr Nikitich Longortov, Ovolyngort, 2001.

Λονəŋ-χu flies in the sky on his winged mare and sees *Jalań-iki*. But this fellow always does harm to people. They (*jalań*) are few, human beings are many, therefore they are always looking for how they can make a mess, and eat people. *Jalań-ikis* are such giants; there used to be plenty of them.

Λονəŋ-χu looks around: *Jalań-iki* is busy with something. He is wearing a linen shirt, without trousers, and is running from Kazym Cape to the Stony Belt. He comes back with a hem full of stones and throws them into the Ob'. There is not much of the bed of the Ob' left free.

Λονəŋ-χu asks: "What are you doing?"

"There are plenty of people there," he says. "I want to block the Ob', so they will not be able to sail and fish." "No," says *Λονəŋ-χu*, "my fellow, it will not go this way. You will not bother people."

He struck his head once or twice with his fist, dragged him aside to the mainland, and *Jalań-iki's* toes carved out the two channels of the *Jalań-sojm* ("jalań's brook").

And *Λονəŋ-χu* is, you know, a god; he should probably drive him away with some words, he said, so that there should be fewer destroyers of people. He drove him to the mainland, cut his body into pieces and threw them all around. From the pieces of the *jalań-iki's* body appeared *ut puχər*, forest: cedar-tree islands among the swamps – "hands", "legs", "body". And opposite to Kazym Cape the Stony Cape appeared beside the Urals down by the middle of the Ob'.

The image of the stony belt refers to another myth of the Northern Khanty according to which *Num-torəm* fastened the land with his belts. From the first belt arose the iron ridge on the other side of the Ob', but the land did not hold fast. The belt of his shirt became the Urals and it chained the earth.[84] *Jalań-iki* tries to fill the Ob' with stones, but *Λονəŋ-χu* fights with him and prevents his mischievous work. The feet of the fallen giant dig out two tributaries of the Ob'. The island is made of the parts of his body. The motif of a body of an animal or a mythic being being torn to pieces to form new elements of the earth is common in the Northern Khanty folk tales. In a narrative collected by Wolfgang Steinitz a little *śiśki* bird is torn to pieces.[85] The same fate was suffered also by the hazel hen at the beginning of ages.

The forest spirit, *meŋk*, of Khanty legends and folk tales is a creature which resembles *Jalań-iki*.[86] Pëtr Nikitich told two Khanty folk tales in Ovolyngort in 2001. The one was about a cunning person and the other about *Kŭl'* of the forest (see pp. 119–20). *Kŭl'* and a connected name *Xul* have been understood in different ways among the Khanty and Mansi. The being has been compared to the Christian devil, or seen as a master of the Lower World or a bad spirit of water or woodlands. When the Lord created the earth, *Kŭl'* asked to be allowed to create animals. When God did not give him permission, he made a hole in the earth and snakes, frogs and lizards came from the hole onto the earth. *Kŭl'* also created the wolf.[87]

---

84. Karjalainen 1918: 306.
85. Steinitz 1939: 131–2.
86. Ahlqvist 1880: 6–12; Steinitz 1939: 107–15.
87. Karjalainen 1918: 355–6.

CHANGING INTEREST IN FOLKLORE

The intertextuality of narratives is a typical feature of Khanty tales: they cross genre boundaries and the difference between myth or folk tale and fantasy is vague. Epic poems telling of divine heroes and local spirits are called *ar-mońś (ar-moś)*. Nowadays people like to tell folk tales with fantasy themes and call them *skazka* (Russian; *Märchen*). Some of them are old Khanty stories, some are variants of Russian folk tales. Valerii Ivanovich Konev, a Komi from Vosyakhovo, said in 1994 that folk tales are told only on winter evenings. People do not tell folk tales in summer.[88]

The assimilation of Russian and Khanty narrative tradition does not happen only by selecting a Russian theme, but also by interpreting the narrative from a Russian point of view. Nikolaĭ Nikitich was very worried about the Russification of Khanty folklore. Thus he spoke about *ves*, a mythic being living in rivers in places where there are water circles; *Ves-iki*, Ves Man, is like a burbot. He said that some people think that Ves Man is a dragon or that *Ʌoŋ-verti̩-imi*, a local spirit, is a witch:

> Khanty do not have nor have ever had any dragons. Nobody talks about such things. Only people who know Russian folklore begin to compare everything to them and measure everything according to them. For example, about them *Ʌoŋ-verti̩-imi* (woman who ties blood vessels), who lives in the forest, people say she is Baba-Yaga. But Baba-Yaga is Russian, she is totally different. *Ʌoŋ-verti̩-imi* of course eats people and lives in the forest, but this is the only thing that connects her with Baba-Yaga.[89]

Baba-Yaga, a witch, is a very popular personage in Russian folk tales and even in everyday talk. Nikolaĭ Nikitich sees it as his task to collect original Khanty myths and publish them, if possible.[90] The interest in myths was the main reason for his willingness to accompany us in the Khanty villages. He thought that he might learn more about myths from old men, whom he also met by himself. Old myths in poetic form are still found in some areas, for example in Kazym,[91] where bear rituals are maintained. In Shuryshkary, it is the shamans who know the old mythic songs (see p. 188), but otherwise they are told in prose form. Folk tales are still told by some old Khanty. Our neighbour in Ovolyngort told three of them to Nakhrachëv. One of them resembled a narrative of Ershov, "The humpbacked horse", and the other was the tsarina of the sea, both originally Russian folk tales, but which had already acquired a local character. Pëtr Longortov told some folk tales, too, and S. J. Toyarov, who had been recorded many times by Eva Schmidt, presented in Lopkhari four Khanty *mońś*, and we recorded his performance on tape.

Because of his interest in folklore Nikolaĭ Nikitich was eager to discuss myths with Pëtr Nikitich. In the house of Longortov, we talked several times

---

88. Valerii Ivanovich Konev, Vershina Voĭkar. 1994.
89. Nikolaĭ Nikitich Nakhrachëv, Ovolyngort, 2001.
90. Nakhrachëv has published his own versions of Khanty tales in journals.
91. See Moldanov and Moldanova 2000.

about meanings of myths. Pëtr Nikitich Longortov, at seventy-six years of age, was an authority on religious knowledge. He belonged to a shamanic family. His father Nikita and Nikita's brothers Kuz'ma and Ivan ended up in prison for practising shamanism. Kuz'ma remained in jail for thirteen years. Pëtr Nikitich was the specialist on the rites of the holy place of Ovolyngort, and he gradually revealed his knowledge in the course of three years of conversations. Nikolaĭ Nikitich, in turn, was from Kazym-Mys, and an expert on Khanty tradition. The conversations demonstrated that each area has its own myths about ancestors and deities. Local myths concentrate on the deities, spirits and heroes who are valued and worshipped in the area. The astral myths and bear songs, in turn, are widely known. In the interpretations, social relationships were emphasised, and membership of a family or community, but also personal experiences and opinions.

8 Living with spirits

Religious worlds of the Northern Khanty

Christian beliefs and customs came to Siberia with the fur trade, missionaries and immigrants. Russian settlers brought the popularised Christianity and folk religion with pre-Christian elements, old believers their faith and practices. The Orthodox Church began its missionary activity early, a Christian centre already being founded in Tobol'sk in 1621. From Spaskiĭ Khutinskiĭ monastery, led by Kiprian, the first archbishop of Sibiria, priests with assistants were sent north to convert the Khanty to the Christian faith. The early phase of Christianisation was sporadic and achieved little. Native people did not understand the message of the priests and they were afraid of missionaries, who were linked with Russian Cossacks. The major Christianising campaign, begun in 1713 under the leadership of Metropolitan Filofeĭ of Tobol'sk, aimed at destroying the native idols and baptising the natives.[1] Two early writers on Khanty religion, Grigoriĭ Novitskiĭ[2] and Johan Bernar Müller, a Swedish prisoner, witnessed the baptism of the Khanty. The latter wrote:

> Accordingly he (Philotheus) went, attended by several clergymen, to the places where their chief idols stood . . . He represented to them the Vanity of their Idolatrous Worship of Wooden images and directed them how to adore the true living God . . . But those People . . . opposed all the Metropolitan's endeavours, alleging that their Ancestors had, Time Out of Mind, maintained the Worship of their Sheitans and fared well by it . . . Above five thousand Ostiaks were baptised, it happening by a Particular Providence that the greater Part of that Nation were then assembled.[3]

The Senate furthered the process by turning to a new policy: natives who became Christian were exempted from paying fur tribute for ten years. This led to a superficial "Christianising", with people gaining new Orthodox names.[4]

---

1. Balzer 1987: 428.
2. Novitskiĭ 1715, published in 1884.
3. Müller 1722 [1720]: 89–92; see Balzer 1987: 429.
4. Balzer 1987: 431.

Ethnic religion and its specialists, shamans, were not wiped out by this or later campaigns in the eighteenth century and even later. The result was syncretic ideas, especially on the concepts of deities. The Orthodox calendar affected the Khanty feasts.[5] The people of the north were most stubborn. While among the Eastern and Southern Khanty Christianity had a steady position in the nineteenth century, the Northern Khanty had their own religion besides Christianity, as is seen in some of the ethnographies of the time. One example is a young Khanty who became a priest's assistant. His Russian wife said that he made pagan sacrifices before ancestral idols, broke Christian fasts and behaved in an "unclean manner".[6] In Shuryshkary, the first native church of the northern Ob' was built in Kushevat in 1714.[7] Russian and Komi settlers improved the tactics of the missions. Muzhi became a religious centre of Shuryshkary when the church of St Michael was founded in 1840. The local activities of the Orthodox Church and later the cultural education of the Soviet authorities, in club houses and village reading rooms, affected people's religious ideas.

The Northern Khanty have now long been Christianised, but they still live with their spirits and make offerings to them. How are we to understand the multiform religious life and syncretic ideas and customs of the present-day Khanty? Can we talk about religion when we study rituals? Or are these forms of ritual behaviour only "tradition" or "culture"? For the answer, an evaluation of the concept of ethnic religion is necessary.

There are a great number of answers given to the question "What is religion?" One of the most popular definitions is that of Robert Bellah: religion is "a set of symbolic forms and acts that relate man to the ultimate conditions of his existence".[8] Instead of a definition, the family resemblance might be a better way to figure out the character of religion. Benson Saler lists features which form religion:[9] these are a set of features drawn from a prototype, none of which is alone necessary or sufficient to identify a religion. The prototype of religion for Western researchers is usually the Judaeo-Christian tradition.[10] Saler's idea of the cognitive approach has enlivened the old discussion on the relationship of the "emic" and "etic" concepts in the study of religion.[11] In particular the concept of "God", with its Judaeo-Christian background, has been a problem in comparative work.[12] Olle Sundström, who has studied Soviet ethnographers' interpretations of Nenets religion, deals with this discussion in depth.[13] He himself prefers the concept of *deity* instead of god. In this book, we follow the model of Sundström when it is possible. On the other hand, in referring to previous works or in citations

5. Balzer 1987: 403–4.
6. Polyakov 1877: 55; Balzer 1987: 435.
7. Shuryshkary region, official information.
8. Bellah 1970: 21.
9. Saler 2000.
10. See Guthrie 1996.
11. Jensen 2001.
12. Pyysiäinen and Ketola 1999.
13. Sundström 2008: 29–73.

we have also used the term *god*. The Khanty themselves see *Torəm*, the deity of of sky, as equivalent to the Christian God. When speaking about the Khanty religion, we use the terms of local dialects, because firstly it gives a better understanding of their religious ideas and secondly facilitates any later interpretations of the field-work material.

The sphere of religion is usually divided into strongly institutionalised religions with a written history and weakly institutionalised religions based on oral communication. Non-institutional religions existing in connection with authoritative Churches have in Europe been termed *folk religion, popular religion, vernacular religion, folk belief*. Religions of aboriginal people or ethnic groups, who do not have a clear connection to an institutional religion, are called *indigenous religions* or *ethnic religions*. We may ask why approaches to religion are conceptualised like this. The researcher's perspective is always determined by the times or the historical situation. The societal and cultural values of the Western world lie behind many terms and, additionally, the Christian heritage is a unifying element in Europe.

Folk religion is a concept which refers to weakly institutionalised religion. Dan Yoder tried to define it in the following way: "The totality of all those views and practices that exist among the people apart from and alongside the strictly theological and liturgical forms of the official religion."[14] Folk religion refers mainly to popular Christianity of (the European) "peasantry": the concept is historically loaded and suits the present-day situation only poorly. *Popular religion*, in turn, refers to "those informal, unofficial practices, beliefs, and styles of religious expression that lack the formal sanction of established church structures".[15] *Vernacular religion* has lately replaced the concept of folk religion and popular religion. It has a background in sociolinguistic thinking: like languages, religions have dialects, which depend on the speech community. Leonard Norman Primiano, who introduced the term, defines his ideas thus:

> Vernacular religion is, by definition, religion as it is lived: as human being encounter, understand, interpret, and practice it . . . Vernacular religious theory involves an interdisciplinary approach to the study of the religious lives of individuals with special attention to the process of religious belief, the verbal, behavioural, and material expressions of religious belief, and the ultimate object of religious belief.[16]

The habit of dividing religious fields into "real" religions and "folk/popular/vernacular" religions depends on what angle we view religion from, whether from the perspective of an institution or from that of religious life. The idea that we should study religion only on the level of individuals, as Primiano would have us do,[17] is naïve. For the study of religion both angles are

14. Yoder 1974: 2–15.
15. Badone 1990: 6.
16. Primiano 1995: 44.
17. Primiano 1995: 45.

important, because even oral religions of aboriginal peoples or ethnic groups are lived as social institutions. We could also ask, how well do "theoretical" descriptions based on Western religious thinking suit ethnic religions? In a community where people are living with spirits, these are not considered to be "supranormal". They are normal. It is only our point of view which makes such things "supranormal". For an oral community which is experiencing and practising its religion, it is difficult to conceptualise or explain it.

Ethnic religions do not live in a vacuum. State and hegemonic religions affect ethnic religious practices. Interaction, a dialogue with institutionally strong (world) religions leads to syncretic forms of religion. Instead of religions, be they denominations, ethnic religions or vernacular religions, we can look at the religious worlds in which people live. The notion of William E. Paden of religious systems as "worlds" opens the way. He writes: "*World* is here a descriptive word for what a community or individual deems is the 'reality' it inhabits, not a term for some single system objectively 'out there' that we all somehow share."[18] An important dimension of Paden's idea is the multiplicity of religious worlds. In the same society we find the religious worlds of individuals, of groups, of nations. Paden's ideas can be evaluated and reworked further when studying the oral religions of local and ethnic groups.

If we talk about religious worlds instead of "religions", we should remember that religious worlds are constructions of individuals or groups, not those of institutions. They can overlap and form a religious landscape, in which the historical roots of different elements have separate backgrounds. This concerns especially the concepts of deities and ideas, which have a long history. In the practice of religious life, one person can actualise different religious worlds in different situations. For ethnic groups living in the shadow of a hegemonic religious institution, temporarily actualised religious worlds present an opportunity to maintain their own tradition.

All concepts are theory-based, even descriptive ones. The level and theoretical background of abstraction varies. Researchers may talk about shamanism when they are interested in certain types of religious phenomena, but about shamanhood when studying people's religious practices. Hence, the focus of the field worker and the approach in constructing the religious world studied is a decisive factor. In defining other people's religions, we should first ask: What is our prototype of religion? In this study, we do not look at religion from a Western perspective, but try to understand Khanty religious ideas and practices as a part of their culture.

The cosmos

In northern Eurasia one encounters two different but often intermingling concepts of the structure of the cosmos. According to the vertical model the world is believed to be divided into several layers, upper worlds, a

18. Paden 1994: 7.

middle world for people, and lower worlds. The horizontal model pictures the world as flat, inhabited by people, over which the heavens curve like a *chum*. According to Vladislav Kulemzin (2006) the universe is called *torəm* in all the Khanty dialects. The word refers also to God, the god of the sky, the sky, weather and air.[19] Nikolaï Nakhrachëv said that his father described the difference between *Num-torəm* and the sky by saying: "God is *Torəm* and the sky is vice versa, *tərom*.[20] There has to be a difference between the sky and him to whom you can turn."[21] The North Star is situated in the midst of the Upper World.

The layers of the universe reflect the usual north Eurasian pattern. Vertically the world is divided into three parts: the Upper World that may consist of seven layers, the world of people (in Northern Khanty *mŭv*, "earth"), and the Lower World. The supreme deity and benevolent spirits live in the Upper World, the evil ones which cause sicknesses and misfortune in the Lower World. Izmail Gemuev has interpreted the conical tent with the central pole as being the model of the horizontal world structure.[22] In the microcosmos of the *chum*, the world tree is represented by the middle pole of the tent and the dome of the sky by the covering of the tent. The cardinal directions are represented in the parts of the tent. The meeting point of the cover and the bottom of the tent represents the boundary between this world and the Otherworld. Uno Harva assumed the horizontal model to be original in the northern regions. The stratified world view is, in his opinion, a borrowing from southern sources by the Turkic people of western Siberia.[23]

One of the crucial aspects of the Khanty world view is the idea that the centre of the world is the place where people are living at present.[24] Among the northern Siberian peoples, the cardinal points and directions of objects are carefully noticed. Varvara Pavlovna mentioned when we visited an *ura* grove in Ovolyngort that the Lower World is situated downstream, in the north. Anzori Barkalaya, who studied the orientation of space in settled Khanty areas, observes that in the world view of the Northern Khanty the north–south axis divides the world between two important directions. The north signifies the downward direction and is the oriented to the Lower World. The south marks the upward direction and points towards the Upper World.[25] The largest rivers represent the World River, which join the levels of the world. In the north the equivalent of the World River is the Ob'. Among most Finno-Ugric people living in the northern Eurasia, the north, towards which the great rivers flow, is a land of misery and hunger, whereas the south is the warm quarter. Vladislav Kulemzin notes that among the Khanty, east (where the sun rises) is a good direction, while the west is a bad one. The

19. Kulemzin *et al.* 2006: 141–2.
20. The explanation is not linguistically relevant.
21. Nikolaï Nikitich Nakrachov, Ovolyngort, 2001.
22. Gemuev 1990: 28–9.
23. Harva 1933: 39–40; cf. Kulemzin *et al.* 2006: 56–8.
24. Kulemzin 1984: 171–2; Kulemzin *et al.* 2006: 56.
25. Barkalaya 2002b: 5–7; Karjalainen 1918: 123; Schmidt 1989: 191.

Northern Khanty call the west *kev pelak*, "the stony side", referring to the Ural Mountains.[26] Though the houses seem to be built so that they face the river, the nature of the directions is taken into consideration in establishing settlements. The graveyards, for example, are usually situated downriver.[27]

The hierarchy of spirits

In a festival in Khanty-Muzhi the shaman Vasiliĭ Petrovich summoned all the main deities, holy heroes and spirits of the sacrificial place to take part in the ritual.

The four general deities of the Shuryshkary Khanty (see p. 107), the creator lord, the mistress, the creator's son and the Master of the Lower World, which are hierarchically higher or more important than the others, resemble the Christian God, St Mary, God's son, and the devil. *Num-torəm* is called also *Torəm-aśi*, *Torəm*-father.[28] The syncretic beliefs become apparent in the characterisation of *Num-torəm*; they have a long history with wide-reaching roots.[29] Vladislav Kulemzin notes that the Russians and Tatars have influenced Khanty ideas of the supreme deity and his attitude towards mankind.[30] The Mansi also call the deity of the sky *Num-torəm*, who in myths and tales is linked to the creation of the world and determines people's fates.[31] *Num-torəm* is active in the Khanty myths of creation too.

Among the present-day Northern Khanty, *Num-torəm* resembles the Christian God. He is the Father God, the lord and master of all the living. He lives in the sky and no images are made of him. The supreme deity does not usually deal with earthly matters, but gives orders to lower deities to take care of them. The number of female deities, who take care of birth and the well-being of living things, is quite large.[32] Many of the names refer to the same deities or those who have similar duties. Kolya Nakhrachëv explained the terms:

> The mistress *Jeməŋ-aŋki* guards everything born: grass, plants, shoots, wild animals, young birds and children – all that is born and grows. Hence she is the mistress, but she does not live with *Num-torəm* like a wife with a man. It's just simpler to say Master and Mistress, but they do not have this kind of concept.[33]

In discussing the deities, *Kăltəś-aŋki* was also mentioned. She is the wife of the supreme god. She is also called *Sorńi-naj*.[34] To the female deities

26. Kulemzin *et al.* 2006: 56–7.
27. Cf. also Jordan 2003: 191.
28. Pëtr Nikitich Longortov, Ovolyngort, 2002.
29. Karjalainen 1918: 296–9.
30. Kulemzin *et al.* 2006: 115–16.
31. Karjalainen 1918: 298–9; see Gemuev *et al.* 2008: 102–4.
32. Cf. A. V. Golovnëv's study of beliefs related to the birth rituals: Golovnëv 1995: 532 ff.
33. Nikolaĭ Nikitich Nakhrachëv, Ovolyngort, 2001.
34. Pëtr Nikitich Nakhrachëv, Ovolyngort, 2002.

connected to life and birth belongs also *Naj-aŋki*, Fire-Mother. Pavel Filippovich Rebas' noted that the Khanty previously honoured especially Sun-Fire.[35] Usually it refers to a woman, a mistress, but in a ritual connection means also fire. *Tiləś*, "Moon", is also important. They are like man and woman.[36] According to Pëtr Longortov and Nikolaï Nakhrachëv *Naj-aŋki* is the life-giver for people.[37] The earth-mother, *Moma-aŋki*, was also mentioned by Varvara Petrovna when we discussed Khanty beliefs. The earthworm, *mŭv-ʌer*, is a string of the clothes of earth mother, *săχ-kiŋenit*, "string of the coat of a forbidden lady". Hence it is not permitted to kill it.

> Now when we fish we use an earthworm, and it is permitted. But otherwise we cannot kill or harm it. But as we were saying, we can fish. We cannot kill any creepy-crawlies. It might be your brother, uncle or some other relative. The souls of the dead can place themselves in any living being.[38]

Ʌovəŋ-χu, "a man who sits on the horse", is also *mŭv-vanttị-χu*, "the man who looks at the earth", *mŭv-kerttị-χu*, "the man who goes round the earth", or *Torəm-pŏχ*, the son of *Torəm*.[39] He is parallel to *Mir-susne-χum* among the Mansi, and he is called among the Northern Khanty *Mir sawittə χu*. Kolya Nakhrachëv said that when people call him, they put out four silver plates for the legs of his horse, because they cannot touch the land. If he wants to help the poor, he puts men on his horse and women on a special swing under the belly of the horse. If he cannot offer help himself, he calls on other beings to assist him. These are helping spirits of the family, a bear, a diver and so forth.[40] Deities were above family spirits in the hierarchy of religious beings and could command them and give them tasks, if it was necessary.

Marianna Flinckenberg-Gluschkoff travelled in 1981 with Nikolaï Garin in the Urals, and they published a travel book relating their experiences. They saw many Russian icons in the holy corners of houses in mountain villages. The most popular were those of St Nicholas, St Mary and Christ. Christ, as Karjalainen mentioned, is associated with *Mir-susne-χum*, the son of the supreme god. The assimilation of Christ with the Khanty son of god has been easy because of the shared defining characteristic of both deities.[41] The popularity of icons of the Virgin Mary depends on the tendency to associate her with several Khanty female deities, for example *Kăltəś* (Kaltas), who was called *Bogoroditsa* (Russian, "birth-giver of God") by the Upper Lozva Mansi.[42]

35. *Naj* means "fire" in sacred and religious contexts: Kulemzin *et al.* 2006: 113. Karjalainen (1918: 416–17) claims that among the Yugra people sun and moon were not objects of worship.
36. P. V. Rebas', Ust'-Voïkar, 2000.
37. Nikolaï Nikitich Nahrachov, Ovolyngort, 2002.
38. Varvara Pavlovna Longortova, Nikolaï Nikitich Nakhrachëv, Ovolyngort, 2002.
39. Pëtr Nikitich Longortov, Ovolyngort, 2002.
40. Nikolaï Nikitich Nakhrachëv, Ovolyngort, 2001.
41. Flinckenberg-Gluschkoff and Garin 1992: 117–18.
42. Flinckenberg-Gluschkoff and Garin 1992: 118.

Xiń-iki, the Master of the Lower World, awaits a person's death. Sinful people have to go to him, but righteous people "go up". *Xiń-iki* likes to try people. He oppresses them as much as he can.[43] He sends a sickness for any offence a person commits. His *χŏr,* image, is a diver called *Toχtəŋ-iki,* "Diver Old Man". Black things and cloths are given to him in order to prevent sicknesses. The ideas and practices connected with *Kŭl-iʌpi-iki* are quite similar. In a ritual in Ovgort the former wife of the shaman Pugurtsin showed the gifts offered to *Kŭl-ilpi-iki,* black garments in the earth under a fir tree in a ritual place of the family. She said he is the Master of the Lower World and sends sicknesses to people.[44] Because he knows sicknesses, he is also the best protector against them if he is worshipped. Home spirits connected to him can often be seen in Khanty homes nowadays.

Pëtr Nikitich Longortov told a tale of *Kŭl',* and thereupon Varvara asserted that *Kŭl'* is a snow man living in the Urals. Snow-men are a popular theme in the Russian urban folklore of the Soviet and post-Soviet era. Similar references to modern urban stories were very rare in the small *gort*-type Khanty villages. Varvara spoke about an event when a person was taken by *Kŭl':*

> V. P.: More than ten years ago Pushkarev, an editor, went up the Yugan to search for *Kŭl'.* The Komi call *Kŭl'* also *yagmort* or *yamgort,* or something like that [laughs]. This Pushkarev went from Ovolyngort to the Urals. Then the tent was found in the Urals, on the upper part of the *Nak'jŏχan* river. He was not found; he had with him only a small knife and a small "tourist axe".
> N. N.: What a stupid man he was. Who goes to the forest without a gun?
> V. P.: He had left a message in the tent, saying that he was going somewhere. Where he went, nobody knows, but he had written it. But why did he write the message and leave the tent? And then disappeared. Maybe he found *Kŭl'.* And it did something to him.[45]

Nikolaĭ Nakhrachëv's comment is illuminating. Only a fool goes to the forest with a small knife and small tourist axe. A normal person would have a rifle. Anna Ivanovna, an expert on the graveyard of Vosyakhovo, thought that *Kul'* was a dead person.[46] Because the dead go to the Lower World, her interpretation comes close to the notion of the Master of Lower World.

Karjalainen takes *Kul* to be a Komi name mixed with the old Ugrian *Xul,* the Master of the Lower World.[47] Even in Shuryshkary, it seems that the nature and tasks of *Kŭl'* have been understood in different ways. The idea that *Kŭl'* lives like *Xul,* under the earth, or that he is the Master of the Lower World, can be understood from the Christian perspective. The devil does the same. On the other hand, *Kŭl'* also lives in forests and waters and sends sicknesses to people who have not behaved well. E. P. Martynova writes that in the Lower Ob' area the main deity of the Lower World is *Kul' iki.* Besides

43. Nikolaĭ Nikitich Nakhrachëv, Ovolyngort, 2001.
44. E. G. Pugurchina (b. 1931–3), Ovgort, 2002.
45. Varvara Pavlovna Longortova, Ovolyngort, 2001.
46. Vershina Voĭkar, 1994.
47. Karjalainen 1918: 357–9.

him the deities of the Lower World are *Xyn' iki*, known also as *Ilpi muv iki*, "Man under the Earth", *Kur ilpi iki*, "Man under Feet", and *Rušš iki*, "Russian Man". An image of him in a black coat was placed near every door, because it protected people from sicknesses.[48]

The god of the sky, who has no *χŏr*, image, determines life on earth and also people's fates. But he does so through different spirits. Even *Λovəŋ-χu* can give orders to lower spirits to help people. The world of spirits is large. In addition to spirits connected with nature, forest spirits, water spirits and so forth, or with special domains of life, such as sickness spirits, the most important as cult objects are local and kin and family spirits. They take care of the area or the kin group which makes offerings to them. Among the Khanty, the relationship of deities and lower spirits is usually described by using kin terms. *Λovəŋ-χu* is sometimes the seventh son of *Num-torəm* or sometimes the son of the latter's wife, *Kăltəś-aŋki*. Because the deities and spirits are called by different names, the connections between them are not always clear. *Śak-voj*, "hammer-animal", the goose with red neck, is the spirit protector of the family of Longortov, but the other spirit protector is *Sorńi-pŏχ*, "Golden Boy", who is also a spirit protector of the village of Ovolyngort, where many family members live. After an offering to *Sorńi-pŏχ*, we talked about his name. Nikolaï Nakhrachëv said that he knew of *Kăltəś-aŋki*, who is called *Sorńi-naj*, but he had never heard of *Sorńi-pŏχ*. Anton Longortov, a historian who took part in the ritual, assumed that in pagan times, when the first man who founded the village died, he was made a local god. This, according to Oleg, is a typical Marxist-Leninist explanation. Pëtr Nikitich agreed in seeing the *Sorńi-pŏχ* as a first inhabitant of the area. *Sorńi*, "golden", is an attribute of deities in mythic poetry. The latter part of the name, *pŏχ*, "boy", refers to the position of the god in the kin network of deities. The supreme god *Num-torəm* was *Torəm-aśi*, *Torəm*-father, and *Kăltəś-aŋki* his wife.[49] Golden Boy is possibly a son of the main deity, who had seven sons according to the myths. The Longortov family belonged to the *Moś* phratry, whose mythic ancestor was probably *Λovəŋ-χu*, also the son of *Torəm*. Hence, the name of *Sorńi-pŏχ*, the spirit protector of the Longortov family and Ovolyngort village, might refer to *Λovəŋ-χu*. Anzori Barkalaya noticed that among the Eastern Khanty *Sorńi-iki* or *Mir-susne-χum* is one of the main gods. His main seat of worship was near the confluence of the Ob' and Irtysh rivers near Khanty-Mansiïsk.[50] *Iki* refers to man or old man and *imi* to an old woman; according to Peter Jordan they mean among the Eastern Khanty "male elder" and "female elder" and refer to the time of sacred heroes when the land was populated.[51]

The spirit protectors of the kin, which have been discussed earlier (pp. 73–5), are not the only spirits worshipped by a community larger than the family. The spirits worshipped locally are even more important in the god/

---

48. Martynova 1998: 123.
49. Nikolaï Nikitich Nakhrachëv, Ovolyngort, 2002.
50. Barkalaya 2002a: 64.
51. Jordan 2003: 142–4, 154.

spirit hierarchy. Karjalainen mentions that local spirits, for example *Ort-iki*, *Pelym-tōrəm* and *Malaya-Ob'-tōrəm*, are the most important spirits of their place.[52] Nikolaï Nakhrachëv said that every place and every area had its deity. In Synya, it is *Jŏχan-iki*, "Old Man of the River", in Kazym, *Kasum-naj-imi*, the Great Kazym Woman. Kunovat, Polnovat and the Lower Ob' also have their deities. On the Lower Ob' it was *As-tij-iki*, the "Old Man of the Mouth of the Ob' River", whose *χŏr* is a gull, *χălev-iki*, "Gull Old Man".[53] Kuz'ma Nikitich Nakhrachëv, who lives in Kazym-Mys, remembered the history of the most important female deity of the Ob': "The daughter of *Sorńi-naj* stopped in some places and went up to Salekhard. She settled to live in *Jeməŋ-ńoʌ*, the Holy Cape. The other name of the headland is *Sorńi-ńoʌ*, "Golden Cape". She is the Mistress of the Ob' from Kazym to Salekhard, *Kasum-naj*."[54]

Kasum-naj lived on the same headland with another important female deity, *Λoŋ-vertị-imi*. A narrative about these two spirits tells how different their characters were. While the first is benevolent, the second was frightening:

On the *Lor-paj* there were two women: *Kasum-naj-imi* and *Λoŋ-vertị-imi*. It was said of *Λoŋ-vertị-imi* that she was like the Russian Baba-Yaga, that she eats people and so on. Actually she was a bit different. She is huddled up, wrinkled.

And *Kasum-naj-imi*, she just helps people from her good heart. It is all the same to her whom she helps: everyone who pleads to her will be helped. But *Λoŋ-vertị-imi* is not the same. She and *Kasum-naj-imi* are like two hands: *Λoŋ-vertị-imi* punishes the breakers of commonly accepted rules. She can punish anywhere: in the forest, at home – she will get you everywhere.

Once she took a child from a family. Well, a child was lost. They began to look for it. They came to the shamans. *Λoŋ-vertị-imi* said to the shamans: "Do not look for him. He is with me. He is my son's peer, they play well together, grow up together. And say to the parents not to worry about him. They'll get plenty of game, the animals will come to them by themselves."

But the parents did not believe: she was considered full of guile, and perhaps they were untrusting people.

They went to the *ura* storehouse where *Λoŋ-vertị-imi* lived. And there was that storehouse on legs: well, they set fire to it. And at the last moment she jumped out, amidst a cascade of sparks. Slowly she went to the forest, but looked back and wagged her finger as if to say: "Well, we'll see."

After that the people of the village began to die one after another. And finally the village became completely deserted. And in the *ura* were found two little hearts next to each other. It meant *Λoŋ-vertị-imi*'s son and the Khanty child really had lived well together. *Λoŋ-vertị-imi* can also send good luck, if a person obeys all the rules. Various coloured kerchiefs are donated to her, the better ones with tassels.[55]

52. Karjalainen 1918: 306.
53. Nikolaï Nikitich Nakhrachëv, Ovolyngort, 2002.
54. Kuz'ma Nikitich Nakhrachëv, Kazym-Mys, 2003.
55. Nikolaï Nikitich Nakhrachëv, Kazum Mys, 2003.

The holy place *Lor-paj* is about 5 km from Kazym-Mys on the river of *Šiẓiŋ-ʌor-jŏχan*. It is not permitted to fish near it. The story above noted also that *ʌoŋ-verṭi-imi* gives happiness to people who follow the rules correctly. For that reason she is also worshipped by the Khanty living in other areas. Konstantin Nikolaevich Konev, a Komi, who speaks Khanty, Komi and Russian, spoke about his own visit to the store house of *Lor-naj*, "Lor Woman":

> There is a holy place in *Sor*, the *lapăs* of *Lor-naj*. I have also visited the place. I asked if I can go there because it interested me. They said that it is possible. Some people said that they give furs, silk clothes and money to a woman. Then some strangers came, they maybe touched some things: the Khanty transported both the *lapăs* and its mistress. *Lor-naj* is the mistress of *Sor*. There is also *Kasum-naj*, she is also there, but I do not know what she is mistress of. Maybe she is the mistress of the same place: they just gave a different name to her. But the Khanty from all over converge on Lor-naj.

The store house mentioned here is a spirit house with four legs, *kŭreŋ χot*. Besides images of spirits, people also put gifts for them there and valuable things like sables. It is also possible to see spirit houses in villages (see p. 125), but the ones for important deities are often in the holy places outside the area used in everyday life. The spirit idol is dressed. The body is sometimes metallic, sometimes wooden, and the dress was made using cloths. Male spirits have *săχ*, a shirt made of broadcloth, similar to a woman's dress, *nuj săχ*. It was adorned with sacred embroidery, *jeməŋ-χănši*. Though spirits are hidden from sight when they move around on earth, they can be seen in dreams. They also appear as plants and animals in real life. In particular ancestral protector spirits appear as animals, whose designations are used as the basis of family names. The image of a spirit or deity is *ʌuχ χŏr*; it reflects the way it appears to people. For example, the *ʌuχ χŏr* of *Kasum-naj-imi*, the mistress of Kazym, is a cat.[56]

The fire spirit, *Tŭt-imi*, is on the same level of spirit hierarchy as home spirits. She is connected to the female sphere of life. A tale about the fire spirit describes this clearly:

> A woman in general must be kind by her nature. She must not demonstrate her anger. If she does not like anything, she should say so, but not throw things or, for example, poke roughly with iron in the stove.
>
> There is a Khanty tale about this. The fire gives light, you know. But everything that gives light has eyes. The fire has many eyes, so one must not strike it with iron, as the eyes are sensitive, and they can be injured.
>
> So, then. A woman was angry at something and began poking in the stove with iron (a poker). So roughly. And she hurt the fire's eye.
>
> The fire got angry and died down, and not only in this woman's stove, but in the whole village around. Well, everybody was related. They began to freeze, and there was nothing to eat, either. And this was before they had matches, so they say. They made fire either by friction or with a stone.

56. Nikolaï Nikitich Nakhrachëv, Ovolyngort, 2002.

They went to neighbouring villages to beg for fire. The fire was, you know, put to bed in the evening, was fed and was kindled anew in the morning. And in this case they had to beg in neighbouring villages. Well, nobody had a fire burning. Well, they took the fire, but could not bring it home: either it went out on the way or they dropped it.

They turned to a shaman. He shamanised and pointed that woman out: it's her fault, he said, she has insulted the fire. And the fire says it will burn again only after that woman has given her daughter. Well, what should one do?

The woman gave her daughter to the fire. And the fire burnt everywhere, in all the houses. But *Tüt-imi* said it would burn till the first misdeed was done.

If they were to insult it once more, it would never burn again.

Here, to tell the truth, is a trick: if, for example, one has to shut the stove down earlier, for example, in winter, to save the warmth, before breaking the live coals one should say: *"Tüt-imi, semʌən ʌavʌat"*, "Fire-Mother, take care of your eyes!"[57]

The narrative shows how necessary it is for women to be mild and good-natured in their house work. As in many narratives telling of problems caused by spirits, the shaman was asked to help. He solved the problem and life could continue.

Describing the Khanty pantheon is difficult because of the great number of spirits and their assumed relationships. In part the indistinctness of the picture is due to the immense size of the Khanty geographical area with its different environments, the many dialects and the contacts with other cultures. In part, problems arise from the way folklore and mythic poetry give a variety of names to the same deities and spirits. The understanding of the meanings of names or their relationships has suffered in the course of the process of syncretism, when the Christian God and Orthodox saints are compared to ethnic deities or fused with them. The hierarchical scheme can still be seen, however. The spirits of big rivers are more powerful than those of small rivers. Russian gods are felt to be more powerful than local ethnic ones. Anzori Barkalaya has explained this in quite a convincing way. The spirits of tributaries, such as the Pym, are weaker than *As-iki*, the Old Man of the Ob'. According to the myths the spirits of tributaries are younger and weaker than those of the big rivers. This represents the way the Khanty social world has developed: young people established their households upriver and thus new settlements were "younger" and "weaker" than the areas of their parents. This rule does not cover all the Khanty area: for example, *Kasum-imi* of the Kazym river is powerful in the Ob' area as well.[58]

Guardian spirits of home and family

Matthias Alexander Castrén travelled among the Khanty in the early 1840s. He worked for three years in Obdorsk (Salekhard) and continued further

---

57. Nikolaï Nikitich Nakhrachëv, Ovolyngort, 2002.
58. Barkalaya 2002c: 128.

to Berëzovo. Later he made another trip and got to know for example Irtysh Khanty. Castrén's description of Khanty spirits is illuminating:

> So when a Khanty for one reason or another needs the assistance of a higher being, he must turn to other, lower divinities. Some sort of image will have been made of these, and the images belong in part to the kin in general, in part to the families and individuals. All divine images are generally similar. For the most part they are constructed of wood in human form and represent sometimes male and sometimes female beings. The kin's divine images have, however, over the course of time been adorned more richly than others. On them are to be seen red clothes, necklaces and other jewellery. Their faces have usually been covered with iron sheetlets, and the male images sometimes have a sword on a belt and an iron byrnie on ... The Khanty personal and family gods are similar to those of the Samoyeds. Stones differing from the norm and other strange objects are considered as such; these are worshipped as they are, in the form shaped by nature. Most commonly the gods are small, human-faced, tapering wooden statues. Every family, and even individual, has one or more such statues, and a Khanty views them as protective spirits, which he takes along with him on all journeys. They are kept, as among the Samoyeds, in a special sledge, with a covering of ornate Khanty clothing, decorated with red ribbons and other baubles. Often, each such god is believed to have his own special task. Some protect the reindeer herd, others ensure luck in the hunt, maintain health, provide good fortune in marriage, and so on. In need, it is the custom to set them up in a hut, on the reindeer pasture or in hunting places. Then they are commemorated with offerings: fish oil and blood is rubbed on their lips and meat or fish is set before them to eat.[59]

In many details Castrén's observations are parallel to those we made in 2000 in Shuryshkary, though the tradition had weakened and it was hidden after the Revolution and the social stress caused by the authorities. Of all the spirits, the family spirits still maintain their value in the religious home life. The proper behaviour towards spirits is inculcated into every person; all know how to move and act so that spirits are not violated.

The main kin idol is kept in a hut called the *jeməŋ ura*, "the holy store house", whereas only rags and other objects which the shaman has asked the deities to bless remain in the holy corners of houses. Family spirits are kept in a holy corner of the house called *mŭʌ śuŋ*. The word *ʌuχ* is a general term for spirit but also refers to the guardian spirit of home and family. The *ʌuχ*-spirits in Shuryshkary were kept in storage bags called *appa*, which were then placed on a shelf behind a curtain or in a *kŭrəŋ χot* (storage house). One of the family members is a guardian of the spirits' house. Anzori Barkalaya heard recently among the Lyamin river Khanty that the spirits themselves select their keeper. The keeper takes care of the storehouse and dolls and organises offerings. He also distributes the offerings of people taking part in rituals to relatives as the gifts of the spirits. The decision of the spirits is proclaimed by a shaman serving the family. In one case the keeper was not

59. Castrén 1967: 214–15.

the oldest or most important member of family, but a young man. Barkalaya argues that the shifting of the responsibility onto a suitable young person is not surprising because they have a potential for re-envigorating the traditional world view.[60]

The duty to take care of the family spirits has to be taken account of all the time. When Anna in 1994 invited a friend who worked in Muzhi to Helsinki, he said that he could not travel. "Where would I put our family spirits? My brother cannot keep them and what would happen in customs, if I had a suitcase full of puppets?" The images of kin spirits and furs representing them are kept in the sacred storehouse of the village. Both men and women have their own *lapăs*. Our friend Andreĭ asked in 2000 in Ust'-Voĭkar if we had seen them, and gave a description of the male one:

> But did you not visit the hut when you came? There is a *kŭrəŋ lapăs* here, just behind the house, near it. A *labaz*, if we translate it [into Russian], on legs. The small store house of men is like that. Women have such a place too, which is called by the same name. Women are not allowed into the men's *lapăs*, but they can go near. There people put vodka before the spirits; the spirits have a box. They just pour a little on the floor. Sacred furs hang there. Every family has its furs . . . They praying to the spirits in the *lapăs*. When leaving they bow three times and three times they turn around. Sometimes they slaughter a reindeer, to remember the dead or something like that. They slaughter right there, near the *lapăs*. Around the neck of the sacrificial animal a bag is run, where there are spirits; it is run from head to tail and something is said. I do not know what is said, but they pray.[61]

People pray to spirits in the holy huts and make offerings during the feasts. Blood offerings are made nearby; sometimes a reindeer is killed in commemoration of the dead or for some important purpose. In front of the hut there is a holy tree for sacrificial cloths. Yuriĭ Ozelov took us to feed the *ʌuχ* in that *kŭrəŋ χot* – the party including only men; Oleg and Valeriĭ Sharapov went, but Anna had to stand outside and look at the storage hut from the open door like the other women. Two spirits were at the back of the small house, sitting on a white reindeer pelt near the wall. The scarves were opened and we saw a doll in a white fur coat embroidered on the cuffs and the hem. On the other walls were furs and clothes, for example the winter coat of Yuriĭ's son Semën. Yuriĭ had vodka and bread for the spirits and the men could join in the meal for the spirits.

According to Karjalainen, the home guardian spirits are imagined as having a human appearance; they are constructed by a relative, or, more often, an outsider. Cloth (to symbolise clothing or scarves) is wrapped around the body, which is carved from wood, bone, stone or metal.[62] According to our sources, a guardian spirit need not necessarily be anthropomorphic or zoomorphic, but is connected somehow to the person under its protection:

60. Barkalaya 2002c: 127–32.
61. A. A. S., Ust'-Voĭkar, 2000.
62. Karjalainen 1918: 140.

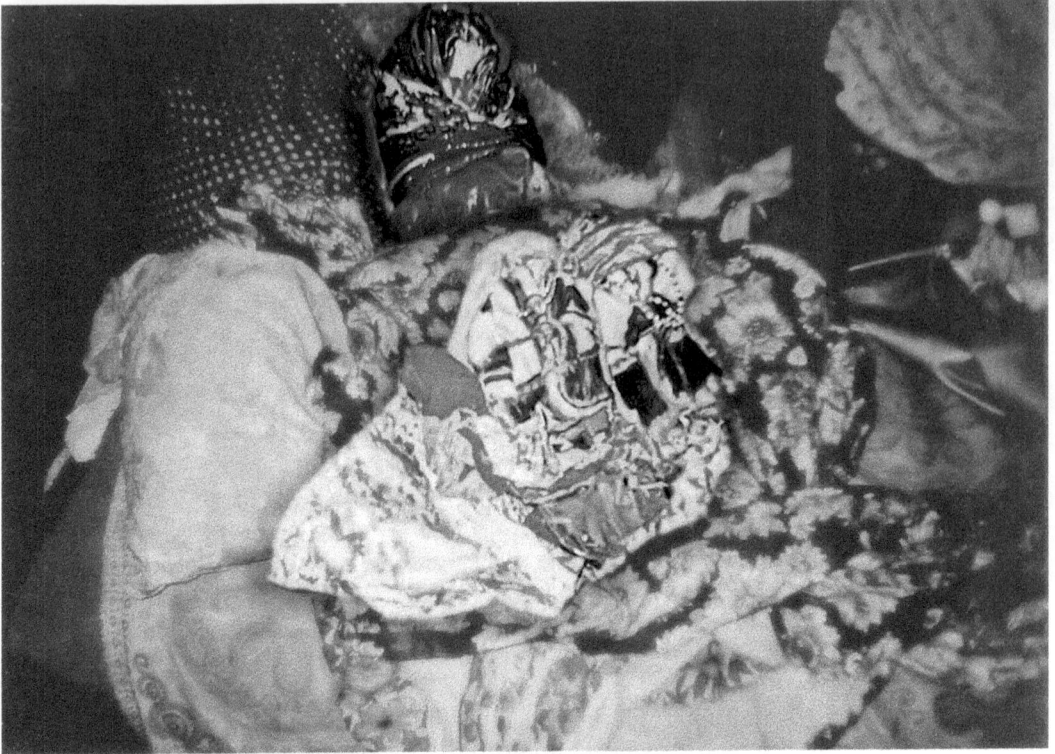

Guardian spirits of the home, Ust'-Voĭkar. – Photograph by Oleg Ulyashev 2000

the home guardian may be a goose beak, a bear claw, a small stone or even a button wrapped in a rag. The forty-three-year-old Nikolaĭ explained the relationship of the kin guardian spirit and objects consecrated by it:

> Objects kept in the holy corner of a home are kin spirits, or objects consecrated by them. The kin guardian spirit is kept by one member of the kin, and certain objects are consecrated by this spirit: rags with coins sewn in the corners, or scarves, or bear paws.[63]

After marriage, a girl takes the kin spirit for her own protection, provided the spirit sanctions this, after performing special magic rites. "If the spirits of these idols reject their new home, they cause illness in the household. Illness is removed by feeding the spirits, after which 'rags' are left in the holy corner."[64]

Z. P. Sokolova also wrote about this practice in the 1970s, basing her conclusions on evidence she collected among the Khanty and Mansi. A small object (coin, button, stick) wrapped in cloth was given to a girl before her marriage; this object personified the connection with her native home.[65] However, Sokolova does not mention the term лух in this context. We saw in

63. Ulyashev diary, 2001.
64. Nikolaĭ Nikitich Nakhrachëv, Ovolyngort, 2001.
65. Sokolova 1971: 231.

126

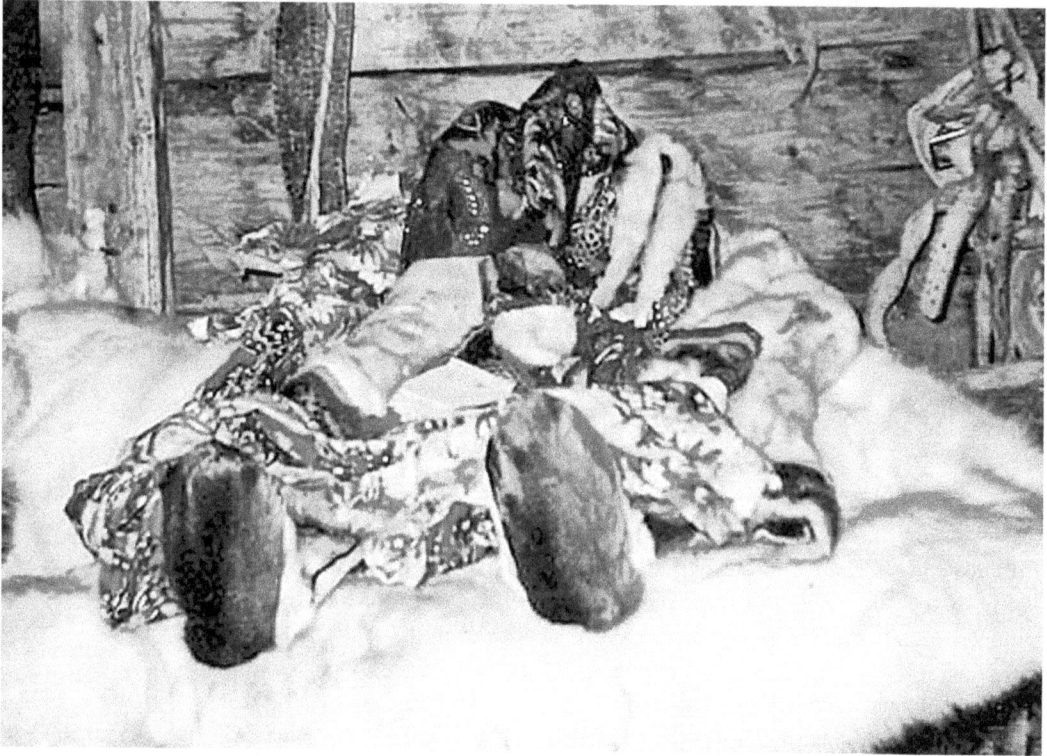

Guardian spirit in a lapăs, Ust'-Voĭkar. – Photograph by Oleg Ulyashev 2000

2000 a *лух* of this type in Ust'-Voĭkar; it was wrapped in nineteen scarves and kept in the holy corner of the house. Our neighbour Valentina then showed her mother's and aunt's *ittərma* (a death doll, see pp. 156–60), as well as the *лух* of the home and family, which they kept in separate bags in the holy (south-western) corner of the house.[66] The size of the death doll is 20 to 25 cm, and the *лух* is approximately 50 cm. In contrast to the *ittərma* in Yuriĭ's home, which was made of reindeer hides sewn together, Valentina's death dolls were made of cloth. The *лух* was wrapped in nine big scarves and ten small ones; old and new coins and a small iron bell were tied into the corners of the scarves. One twenty-kopek coin, dating from the nineteenth century, was so worn that the year was not clearly visible; the other coins were from the Soviet and post-Soviet eras. The scarves were bought by relatives who experienced some misfortune in life, either illness or unhappiness. Everyone exposed to a *лух* can tie on a coin, Valentina said, and "thus the spirit grows". One *лух* was made by Valentina's mother, Tamara Maksimova, when she was young. Then Valentina was brought to Ust'-Voĭkar (she was originally from Khanty-Mansiĭsk) when she married. Women, both the young and old, make spirits, at least those who know how to. Valentina herself does not know how to make one. The spirits are fed at festivals and also at the funeral meal; a bottle of vodka and food is put on the shelf or beside the stove. When a baby is born, the rite is also performed in the same way.

66. V. L. S., Ust'-Voĭkar, 2000.

127

We discussed spirits in Ovolyngort too. Varvara Petrovna mentioned that besides spirits they also have at home the *χotəŋ-imi*, "house wife", who protects the house. Pëtr's grandfather left the *χotəŋ-imi* behind when he died and she was then taken care of by the father's brother, Kuz'ma, under the *mŭʌ-taχa*, "the holy place of the house, holy corner". According to Varvara the protector of the home is *Kăltəś-imi*, but Pëtr objected to the idea:

> *Kăltəś-imi* is another deity, and only a few people have her at home. *Nŏrəm* is a shelf in the *mŭʌ-taχa* corner. We put there all the extra stuff [connected with the spirit]. Ten scarves I gave to *χotəŋ-imi*. Here are a lot of scarves. And they can dress the *ʌuχ* in this scarf as a shirt and keep it in the corner. Relatives bring the scarves; a brother can give them, also another brother and children and children of the brother. Outsiders cannot give scarves.[67]

According to Nikolaï Nakhrachëv, an outsider can also bring scarves and organise an offering. But that kind of scarf cannot be put on the spirit doll. It will be placed in the sack where the other extra stuff for the spirit is kept. All the gifts are kept in one place. "It is not proper to undo the wrapping, to open the *ʌuχ*. I never saw what my father put in his sacks, though I know what there might be."[68] When we said that we had seen spirit images in other villages, Pëtr Nikitich said that if people show you the *ʌuχ*, they are not real believers. He said that in Ovolyngort they did not see the spirits of other families. He said that he knows what his own *ʌuχ* looks like, but not those of his brothers. Actually, when we had fed the *ʌuχ* after a graveyard visit one day, we saw that it was kept on a small reindeer pelt in the bed under the *nŏrəm*-shelf at the holy corner of the house. Anna was naïve enough to suggest that Pëtr Nikitich might show the spirit to us, but he raised only the edge of the upper scarf and put the plate and the small glass full of vodka in front of the spirit. After that we had a common meal in the house.

Pëtr Longortov also said that his brother has similar spirits in the store house standing on four legs. We could not enter the house, because the keeper of spirits had taken puppets with him when we went to fish. When the keeper was away, there were only "furs", supposedly gifts to spirits in the storehouse. In the hut the family organised offerings and had a meal there. He had also visited the spirits's hut. "But I never saw the puppets, I have not opened the wrappings. My own doll I know, and what it looks like. Everybody knows their own doll, and what it looks like."[69]

There was also a *Sorńi-pŏχ* puppet in the holy place of the men in Ovolyngort. Once the men took it to the forest, put it into a sledge and went away, said Varvara Pavlovna. After that a bear came and tore apart everything and threw it all around, both the puppet and the scarves. Nothing was left unscathed. "Nobody can make a new doll. You have to know how it is done,

---

67. Varvara Pavlovna and Pëtr Nikitich Longortov, Ovolyngort, 2002.
68. Nikolaï Nikitich Nakhrachëv, Ovolyngort, 2002
69. Pëtr Nikitich Longortov, Ovolyngort, 2002.

how to make the face for it. That was that."[70] To this Varvara Pavlovna said: "But it was a *Ruś χŏr*, 'Russian image', not a doll." This indicates that a Russian icon was worshipped as the image of the Golden Boy.

Religious emblems based on syncretic ideas are seen in many Shury-shkary homes. In the holy corner of the house there might be Orthodox icons, St Nicholas being popular. Nikolaĭ Nakhrachëv said that in his father's house there was a silver icon. "Father said that it is God, but once when we came home, it was not there, it was lost. We never stayed at home, we moved around. Possibly it was stolen."[71] Anzori Barkalaya noted that St Nicholas was fused with *Sorńi-iki*, Golden Old Man, in the world view of a Lyamin informant.[72] According to him, hanging of Orthodox icons in the holy corner of houses is common among the Eastern Khanty, but the attitudes toward icons vary greatly. One head of a family from the Ai-Pim river explained their ideas about hanging icons: they are good on occasions when local gods fail. Icons keep malevolent spirits from the house.[73] In Barkalaya's informant's family the shamanic powers were given by St Nicholas, who undid the thread given by local spirits. While Margaret Balzer asserts that the Khanty turned to Christianity when it was beneficial for them in a material way, Anzori Barkalaya argues that in a state of crisis the new religion is seen as a powerful aid. Repressed people were seeking new power from a new religion.[74]

Feeding the spirits at home

Home spirits receive attention during feasts and when the family has visitors. It is customary to put a small glass of vodka by the holy shelf. If there is no shelf in the holy corner, for example in the new Russian type of houses, the glass might be put in the nearest possible place in the holy area. In Kazym-Mys we saw how the offering was made by putting the glass on a high wardrobe. When visiting some brothers living together, we sat in a kitchen. An open bottle was put on the oven "to avoid fire and for luck in the house". The second time the bottle was put on the *nŏrəm*-shelf "to feed the parents". After that the bottle was set on the table. The bottle was open and no vodka was poured in the glasses as an offering, as it usually is.

Near Lopkhari Oleg took part in an *ŏχ pontị* (lit. "putting down the head; bowing") behind the *chum*. Women could not come to the back and saw only of a part of the ritual. There was a short act for the remembrance of parents. Before sitting down at the table for the first time, Èmel'yan put a bottle on the far right corner (away from the door) onto *ʌaraś*, the chest of spirits, "to entertain the parents". Two hours later, before the dinner he carried out the ritual *ŏχ pontị* outdoors. The *chum* has its entrance to the south. Behind the

70. Pëtr Nikitich Longortov, Ovolyngort, 2002.
71. Nikolaĭ Nikitich Nakhrachëv, Ovolyngort, 2002.
72. Barkalaya 2002a: 64.
73. Barkalaya 2002a: 60.
74. Barkalaya 2002a: 65–7.

On the shelf of the house, gifts are presented to the home guardian spirit; the spirit under the blue scarf is being worshipped, Ovolyngoʁt. – Photograph by A.-L. Siikala 2003

chum, on the northern side some 20 metres away sits the *nŏrəm* with the *ʌuχ*: a shelf installed on four legs 1.3 m high, 50 cm wide, 1 m long. On the *nŏrəm* stays *ʌuχ ʌarăś*. On the right side if to look from the *chum* a bit sideways is stuck *jir jŭχ*, "sacrifice tree". It was stuck into the earth with its lower end and tied diagonally to the *nŏrəm*.

Oleg described his experience in the following way. The women are not allowed to come closer to the *nŏrəm*, so they stayed to the left of the *chum*. Ėmel'yan and I came to the shelf from the left side of the *chum* (with the sun, clockwise). Ėmel'yan moved the *ʌuχ ʌarăś* aside and put on the shelf a plate with bread, cakes, bagels and fruits. "If we'd had a *kevan*, 'bottle', it might be put here." When I gave him the bottle, he opened it, poured a bit into a glass cup and and put it near the plate. After waiting a bit he turned to the *nŏrəm*, bowed three times and turned around clockwise. Thus he made nine bows with three turns, took the plate and the bottle and went around the *chum* from the right side (with the sun, clockwise again). The women turned their right shoulders and went along the side from which we came. However, since they stood not so far away from the entrance, their move was straight, rather than with a left turn. The sanctified plate Ėmel'yan put closer, saying: "This is only for men." During the ritual Fila whispered to Anna, "That's our god", and then mentioned: "We do not wear black kerchiefs, we put them there, by the *nŏrəm*. It's not permitted to wear black ones." Whether this rule applied to all the rites or only this one, we did not hear. The black clothes are given

Home guardians are worshipped behind the chum, Lopkhari. – Photograph by A.-L. Siikala 2003

to *Kŭl-ilpi-iki* and spirits connected to him.

Another *ŏχ ponţi* ritual was organised when Fila's sister Masha with her daughter Katya and another Masha, daughter of Ėmel'yan's brother, visited. They made sacrifice near the *nŏrəm*. This time not only did the head of the family take part, but also his three sons. In the same way they bowed nine times in nine turns. They again went clockwise around the *chum*. Ėmel'yan went last, carrying the bottle and the cup, while the sons carried the food: fish, fruits, bread. The table was put outdoors to the left of the entrance (two tables: the women's one on the southern side and the men's one on the northern). The sanctified food was eaten only by men. They rebuked Anna, who was reaching for the men's plate.

The above-mentioned offerings were made for entertaining parents and the *лuχ* of the family. The fire spirit was also taken heed of. The third sacrifice Ėmel'yan did was after we came from Lopkhari with foodstuff and vodka, and it was performed for the fire. Before the fire he and his wife put the table with the bottle and foods. In deference to the *porə*, sacrificial ritual, in sacred places, in the forest, near a *nŏrəm*, or in the *лarăś* near the sacred sledge, it is not permissible to bow near the house and by the fire near the *chum*, because the status of fire and of the house spirit is lower than that of the outside deities. We could not record the situation, because this kind of offering is done without warning, as a normal routine of life. According to the rites of entertaining the fire or the house spirit or forefathers, the master

Fila, Arkasha and Èmel'yan eat after a feeding ritual, Lopkhari.
– Photograph by A.-L. Siikala 2001

of the house only speaks some words of good will. The sanctified meals are eaten together by men and women, unlike the meals sanctified by the higher protectors.

Why worship spirits?

People ask for help and success from the guardian spirit in the same way as they ask for help from the spirits that inhabit holy places. It is indeed customary to feed the home guardians every time there are guests in the house or a vodka bottle is opened. However, the sphere of influence of the guardian spirits of a larger kin group or society is greater, and thus they are imbued with more power. Therefore, people appeal to greater deities when they seek successful results in hunting or fishing, or success in general.

Today the attitude to spirits varies. The Soviet authorities were against all religious activities, both Christian and ethnic. Schools and institutions for education propagated a scientific, atheistic world view. People who have adopted the Russian way of life do not pay much attention to old deities and spirits. Most young people do not know much about the Khanty religion. Still, the fear of wrongdoing and punishment keeps the domains of spirits untouched. Stories of people who were punished after they offended spirits are common. The most typical punishment by spirits is sickness or even death. The most dangerous thing is to offend the holy place and its objects:

S. R. was a major in the police. He travelled, studied, came to Muzhi, came to work for the police and step by step followed his career up to major. And when he came he always asked his relatives: Where is it better to hunt? Where is it better to fish? And thereafter, as he came to know everything, he gradually drove everybody out, and put his hunting lodges here and there. If he saw somebody with a gun, he took the gun away. He wanted to be the only master himself. All his relatives, . . . he is himself from Voĭkar, he boasted. Somebody might have some wretched gun as his last tool, living by it, but he took it away. But there are sacred places, storehouses. He looked through and shook everything out. He took a sabre from a storehouse. It was an old sabre, ancient, with engraved handle, made with gold. But he took it, brought it home. And, evidently, for all these sins together he was punished "from the side": the god punished him. He became paralysed. Before, he did not recognise anything, but now he both took the sabre back and made sacrifices, made *porlam*. Now, it seems, he can go to the toilet himself, and is beginning to stand up a bit. They did warn him at that time: "Do not take it." He did not take the advice – in vain![75]

The fear of spirits is not a new phenomenon. Hence, these stories seem to belong to an old tradition. Nowadays the atmosphere has changed in society and interest in religion is approved. People can talk about superstitions and even value Khanty religion as an important part of Khanty culture. Marianna Flinckenberg-Gluschkoff has noticed the same tendency among the Nenets. The oldest brother of the well-known Nenets editor Anastasia Lapshuĭ takes part in family rituals, though he is an atheist, out of respect for his own culture.[76] In remote villages there are also people who are "believers", as Pëtr Nikitich put it. For them, rituals represent their own religion.

75. Pëtr Nikitich Longortov, Nikolaĭ Nikitich Nakhrachëv, Ovolyngort, 2002.
76. Flinckenberg-Gluschkoff and Garin 1992: 131.

9 Holy groves and common rituals

The landscape of the spirits

The Khanty, travelling by boat along the tributaries of the Ob', and beyond them the Komi, Tatars, Russians and other peoples make sacrifices of small change or drink a toast of vodka at particular places. We come across such places along the River Synya as we approach the village of Ovgort, the Holy Cape, and at the estuary of the River Voĭkar at Cape Kamennyĭ. These are holy places, whose spirits must be given their own gifts to guarantee a safe passage. "The offering has to be made, otherwise the spirit would be angry", Oleg was told in 2000 near Cape Kamennyĭ.

Karjalainen refers to a story from Dem'yanka in his description of Khanty ideas of nature: "Every swamp, every lake, every area of thick forest and every high bank or deep river access has its own spirit occupant, male or female; in some places there are even more than one, some powerful, some weak."[1] However, we must separate actual sacred locations from the general animistic beliefs characteristic of all northern peoples that Karjalainen describes. In addition to cemeteries, there are places defined in the Khanty language as *jeməŋ* or *pəsəŋ*,[2] which corresponds to the Finnish concept of *pyhä* (holy).[3] Karjalainen points out that in dialects of the Khanty language it is possible to find the stems of these attributes, *jem* and *pəs*. These probably refer to a certain entity's or object's inviolability, unassailability or sanctity with respect to other entities or objects. He compares these words with the concept of *tabu* in the religious sense. He also mentions that these words at this time (the beginning of the twentieth century) referred to everything that contravened propriety, i.e. anything unacceptable. Hence he translates these words into Russian as *grekh*, that is, sin.[4] The Khanty living in the Shuryshkary district today use the word *śohma* in the sense of sin or tabu.

On the other hand, Kulemzin regards the words *jəm* ("good") and *pəsəŋ* ("strong, holy") as meaning everything that is allowed in daily life in contrast to the term *atəm* ("bad, ill"), which means everything that is against the rules

---

1. Karjalainen 1918: 137.
2. In Synya: *păsəŋ*.
3. Karjalainen 1918: 188.
4. Karjalainen 1918: 188–9.

of religion, morality and law.[5] Like Karjalainen, Kulemzin discusses the ethical norms of Khanty social life and the attitude towards nature. These are in force not only in everyday life but also during ceremonies, bear festivals and funeral rituals; the breaking of these was strictly punished.[6] However, the northern Khanty word *jem* (the Eastern Khanty *jim*) is a different word from *jəm*, so the meanings do not become clear through the concepts of "good/bad". In the district of Surgut the female tradition of covering the face in front of her husband's "holy" relatives in situations that require avoidance and respect is referred to by the term *jimeʌtə*, a derivative of *jim*, which can be translated as "not to offend".[7] In the modern language the words *jem* and *jeməŋ* refer to the concept of "holy", which can be seen, for example, in the Eastern Khanty word *jiməŋ kåt* or Northern Khanty *jeməŋ χot*, which means a church.[8]

Veikko Anttonen, in his book *Ihmisen ja maan rajat. "Pyhä" kulttuurisena kategoriana* (1996), examines the concept of "holy" through cognitive study of religion. Basing his argument on Karjalainen's translation of the above-mentioned words with the concepts of "inviolability, unassailability/virginity", Anttonen believes that the expressions *jém* and *jémen* (Karjalainen's forms) were used for separating and limiting everything that belongs to deities, spirits, the deceased, bears, and so forth, and anything the Khanty regard with caution.[9] Beginning with the meanings connected with separation and limiting, he comes to the conclusion that the concept *jeməŋ* is a territorial category showing the border between the internal, populated territory and external sections of uninhabited woods and wilderness.

Anttonen finds additional evidence in the Samoyed concepts *jelpin* and *häebidje* found in Artturi Kannisto and Toivo Lehtisalo's collections, which he also considers to be connected with the concept of territoriality. Both in Ob-Ugrian and Samoyedic linguistic traditions, he argues, words are the element with which the boundary between the populated area and uninhabited wilderness is drawn, as well as the cultural rules with which the relationships between different categories are expressed (Anttonen 1996: 135). However, according to Lehtisalo the concept *häebidje jaa* in the tundra Nenets language means "sinful", and the concept *kajpla jaa* of the forest Nenets language means "sinful", "ill" and "poor".[10] Thus, the Russian translations of these words are nearly the same as the word "sin" recorded by Karjalainen, and probably reflect the evaluation of the Orthodox Church of the character of ethnic ceremonial areas and other things connected with ethnic rites.

Anttonen examined Finno-Ugric agricultural societies of Eastern Europe, where holy places are territorially defined with clearly marked boundaries,

5. Cf. Komi *jen(m)*, "god", and *pež*, "sacred filth", "dirtiness", "forbidden", or "sinful", and also the juxtaposition *jen/omöl*, "god/antigod", literally, "bad", "weak".
6. Kulemzin *et al.* 2000: 112–15, 134–5.
7. Interview from 15.11.2001 with Márta Csepregi, specialist in Khanty dialects.
8. Cf. the Komi word *jen-ko, jen-com*, lit. "divine hut", a god's hut, or *jen kola*, "chapel", lit. god's hut.
9. V. Anttonen 1996: 135.
10. Lehtisalo 1923: 192.

and it would be easy to agree with his interpretation if we confined ourselves to such areas. However, it is difficult to outline the borders of the Khanty sacred places. Already Karjalainen noted this detail: "Holy places do not have strictly defined borders. In some areas the border is a shore, the edge of a swamp or meadow, path, etc., but there are no clearly visible signs of a boundary."[11]

When we examine the models of thinking and behaviour connected to cult places, we must start with the general question of how people move in a certain space and how they use it, as for example Peter Jordan has done in his study *Material Culture and Sacred Landscape* (2003) on the Eastern Khanty. Memory of space develops during the target-oriented actions of innumerable generations. Maurice Merleau-Ponty has pointed out that man's acts in space require an ability to mark borders, directions, and – from the activity's reference – central places in the real world. In this way geographic space forms behavioural environments and value systems which externally express a subject's internal action.[12]

Cultures that subsist on hunting and fishing view topography differently from agricultural societies based on land ownership, which thereby regard land borders as important. We must remember that village settlement began rather recently in northern Siberia; thus, the Khanty view of landscape is connected to land use, which is characteristic of an indigenous non-agricultural source of livelihood.[13] The highlighting of territorial borders and the dividing of space into the internal sphere of inhabited areas and the external sphere of uninhabited forest and wilderness are not an apt description of the Khanty experience of the environment. Life is divided into periods of movement from one place to another in accordance with the seasons. When we wander along Khanty trapping paths or travel by boat from one settlement to the next, it is easy to notice that this logic of landscape is different from that of an agrarian society. Spheres of activity, and accordingly, space, are outlined rather broadly: directions and topographic landmarks such as roads, paths, water routes, heights, headlands and islands become important instead of borders. James Weiner met similar models of thinking that characterise hunting cultures among the Foi people of Papua New Guinea; here paths are the most central elements of scenery that outline space. The borders of areas are not important, but paths are, since they are ways from one place that sustains life to another. They shape and transform the ground, partition the earth, and create human space.[14] This logic of forming used territory and mental images of it characterises all northern Siberian hunters, fisherman and reindeer herders. This is especially noticeable in shamans' stories, where defining the cardinal directions and finding one's way to the hereafter is a condition for the shaman's spiritual development.[15]

11. Karjalainen 1918: 186; see also Balalaeva 1999.
12. Merleau-Ponty 1995: 112.
13. Jordan 2003: 249–74.
14. Weiner 1991: 37–8.
15. Siikala 2002a: 58, 158.

In Khanty culture holy places are not initially bordered territorially.[16] They are inviolate, forbidden places because of their third-dimensional aspect: they form an entrance to another reality. Thus, they become a meeting place with representatives of the Otherworld. Holy places are the residences of spirits, and therefore must not be violated by cutting down trees, clearing branches, or collecting berries.[17] The most important sign of holy places is the idol of the spirit; there can be many in one place including the spirit's family or servants. In Northern Khanty culture the number of spirit idols could be several dozen: it was said that one wooded area had over eighty idols. Near the idols were found wooden or lead images of zoomorphic spirit-servants.[18] Karjalainen, who examined Khanty cult ceremonies at the beginning of the twentieth century, pointed out that idols had already disappeared from many areas. However, even now spirit idols are both made and worshipped, though this practice occurs mostly in areas hidden from outsiders. The field notes from the year 2000 include interesting facts:

> There is a place called Elan' Pugor, a holy place, situated on an island 20 km from Ust'-Voĭkar; men made idols there some years ago. There were about thirty wooden idols there measuring 50–60 cm in height and made of spruce. If one does something unpropitious, a hand or foot may become withered. When men come to this place they make porridge, fish soup, and smear the idols' faces with the porridge.[19]

> Nine km from Vershina Voĭkar. There, on Kryzha Pogar island, I saw two *jalańs* (wooden idols with pointed heads), perhaps a little over 50–60 cm high.[20]

In addition to places guarded by spirits, forbidden places also include areas where heroic warriors met their death. Ritual meals are also organised in these places, as we witnessed in Vershina Voĭkar in 2000. Sacred islands once inhabited by ancestors provide topics for local narratives:

> In earlier times people often gathered together. They didn't have bottles with them, but they made tea and talked about how they should live. They sat together drinking tea. Today it's true that without a bottle people go nowhere. Before, people just gathered together. We have many such places where men gathered; men also gathered there on the island. They lived before on that shore, in the village, in the hills in Voshpaĭ. It was a long time ago. It was over girls that they all fought. Somehow this village was attacked. The girls were taken and all the men killed: only two remained. They swam wounded to the island and changed into spruces. They said, "Let them remember us". The *poraʌiti*, sacrifice ritual, was organised there. I still remember it; it happened in my lifetime. But only men remembered the warriors there.[21]

16. On the Eastern Khanty, see Jordan 2003: 146.
17. Karjalainen 1918: 189.
18. Karjalainen 1918: 91.
19. A .A. Rebas', b. 1943, Vershina Voĭkar, 2000.
20. A A. Nenzelov, b. 1976, rec. V. Sharapov, Vershina Voĭkar, 2000.
21. S. A. Alyaba, b. 1931, Vershina Voĭkar, 2000.

It is told that in those places lived warriors who had iron clothes. They fought, jumped through the island and once turned into three fir trees. Before, every spring and summer men gathered together and celebrated a *porəʌiti* under the trees: they slaughtered a reindeer cow. Only men could go there but they took some small children with them, even small girls. Men go to the men's holy place during the full moon. When the moon is waning, they do not organise the *porəʌiti*. Men can visit women's places, where women have their *porəʌiti*. When you come to this kind of place, you tie clothes to trees. But you tie coins to the clothes only when you will give an offering.[22]

Many holy places on the Voïkar river are situated on islands and headlands. The beliefs about an entrance to the next world via water as well as dangerous entities of the spirit world who impede or kill travellers are common among many northern peoples. Water routes played a significant role in choosing burial places among Finno-Ugric peoples from prehistoric times.[23] Potential dangers from the Otherworld forbid entry into sacred areas to those whom society considers to be weak or unprepared; visits to these places are also prohibited. Besides the holy residences of spirits, avoided places include areas where warriors of heroic times have died, abandoned villages, cemeteries and places where somebody has met a sudden death, for example by freezing or drowning. We should note that modern cemeteries are often situated on the sites of old settlements, i.e. in places where ancestors have lived and where they are considered to be still living: the villages of Yamgort (where rows of dugout ruins remain), Ust'-Voïkar (near Aïvosh), and the old cemetery of Vershina Voïkar (near Voshpaï) (see pp. 176–82). This tradition continues the Ugric or Samoyedic custom of transporting the dwelling place of someone who died, or even the transporting of an entire settlement where many people perished.[24]

According to Khanty belief the second of a deceased woman's four souls, or a man's five souls, called *urt* or *uras uj*, "wandering soul", lit. "soul animal", is especially dangerous because it can take a living person's soul either out of revenge because of offensive behaviour, or simply because of longing and missing someone. A relative's death, therefore, causes a dangerous situation for children.[25] In Ust'-Voïkar, for example, it was said that the children of a family could not swim after the disappearance and possible drowning of the grandmother. "When V.'s mother died, and her body was not found, the children were not allowed to go swimming because the drowned person whose body is not recovered can take their children or grandchildren with them, especially if they were much loved."[26]

It is forbidden to offend the peace of the holy place. We heard a warning story about a fisherman who did not follow the custom (see pp. 132–3): "Here in *jeməŋ ńoʌ* there was a fisherman. There on the hill is his hut. People told

22. M. S. Nenzelovna, b. 1916; A. M. Rebas', b. 1984, Vershina Voïkar, 2000.
23. Siikala 2002a: 126–7.
24. Sokolova 1971: 238.
25. Chernetsov 1963: 17–18; see also Chernetsov 1959.
26. Yuriĭ Semënovich Ozelov, b. 1973 in Ust'-Voïkar, Ust'-Voïkar, 2000.

him: 'Do not fish near the holy peninsula. There are many other places.' But they were modern people, they do not believe in anything. He did not obey. Then, relations in his family got worse. He shot himself.'

Lor-paj is a place where two of the Khanty local spirits have their seats. It is about 5 km from Kazym-Mys on the river of *Šiẑiŋ-ʌor*. It is not allowed to fish near the place of spirits. In *Lor-paj* there was a *lapǎś* containing the image of a spirit and his gifts. It was moved away because of people's undesirable actions . The holy places can have a Christian symbol or they may be hidden to outsiders. In Lopkhari we heard about a holy place in Kunovat:

> If you go upstream along the Kunovat river, there are three crosses. They are 2 to 3 metres high. You have to go a little further into the forest. The T. family have their holy place there. There they feed their spirits and drink tea. Not very far away, but if you do not know the place, you cannot find it.[27]

For fear of offending the spirits, even old and unused places of sacrifice retain an aura of sacredness and remain untouched; it is possible to see, from nearby villages, trees wrapped in faded cloth for ceremonial purposes. Trees in cemeteries are draped with the clothes of the deceased. This expresses the Khanty conception of souls and the avoidance of the deceased; according to these beliefs a dead person's third, external soul, or forest soul, moves outside the body and comes back to a person during sleep. If a person dies as this soul wanders then it will stay alive in the clothes of the deceased, according to V. N. Chernetsov. For this reason the clothes, in which the soul exists for a short time, are hung on trees either in or near cemeteries.[28] According to Sokolova, Mansi women hang old clothes, insoles and placentas on trees near women's holy places to guard against the creation of creatures that would pose a deadly threat to the community.[29] In Synya, women hang their clothes after childbirth on a tree near the village, or hang scarves on trees after bad dreams concerning relatives.[30] In Ovolyngort in the summer of 2001, next to an *ura* grove (special grove with small huts on poles for drowned or otherwise vanished people) we were shown a holy tree, *usǝŋ jŭχ*, "a tree full of holes", next to which blood sacrifices are performed on certain occasions. The tree is selected by a shaman and used as a preventative instrument against potential danger.

> If someone has a dream about a living man swimming upstream, then this is a good omen. If the person in the dream swims downstream [i.e. towards the Underworld], it is bad. If a relative begins to have these kinds of dreams often, then the person who has the dreams must inform the one seen in the dream. They then discuss their next course of action; in these situations, near an *usǝŋ jŭχ*, an animal is sacrificed to guarantee the safety of the person in the dream, to ensure that everything is in order. Some of his clothes are pulled through a

27. A. L. and U. L, Lopkhari, 2003.
28. Chernetsov 1963: 21–3.
29. Sokolova 1971: 238.
30. Sokolova 1975b: 386–7.

hole three times, then tied so that the holes can't be seen; in addition, a scarf is thrown over all of this.[31]

Places, especially holy places, are signs marking space for the needs of different social worlds. Cult places, cemeteries, deserted houses whose inhabitants have died, trees, or even the places where discarded ashes from houses are thrown and which must be avoided, transform the landscape into a network of meaningful sites. The dynamic forces implied in this network affect how people use their everyday environment. In fact, the spirits, the invisible inhabitants of certain areas, are part of the local topography. In these territories the separation between the supranormal and normal world can be overcome and an inevitable interaction between these two worlds can take place. Topography not only defines value categories and social groups, but also acts as a connector between these two, as Veikko Anttonen correctly observes.[32]

Men's and women's holy groves

The sacred grove of Khanty-Muzhi lies near the edge of the village, in a place where a meadow suited to gatherings and a forest meet. The grove reserved for the performance of rituals is small, about 20 metres in diameter. It differs from its surroundings only by the cloths that hang in narrow strips from the trees associated with sacrificial rituals. The symbols of ritual space are trees: the main tree in the middle, the men's tree to the right of the main tree, and the women's tree still further to the right. The first two (birches) are situated about 10 metres apart, the third (willow) is at the edge of the holy grove on the border of the meadow used in festivals. Near the men's area, on the left side of the grove, is a space reserved for the bonfire with stakes for pots over it. This area of sacrifice, which unites the Khanty people, is exposed to view. However, women enter the sacrificial area in a roundabout manner; for example, in August 2000 a local grandmother blocked immediate access to women, saying "Men may go where they wish, but women, go there and wait". As a result of this injunction women sat away from the area of sacrifice until the men had lit a fire and called them. The women then placed sacrificial gifts on branches and under the roots of the women's holy tree. They then sat beside the tree together and talked quietly while waiting for the meal. Khanty women especially avoid approaching the first two trees. A woman can only approach to place a plate of food under the women's tree, and this is done only in the context of a ritual performance.

The sacred grove of Khanty-Muzhi described above differs from similar areas of sacrifice in other Khanty villages nearby in that only here are rituals performed that local authorities officially sanction. Nikolaï Nakhrachëv, who acted as shaman's assistant in a publicly performed offering there, criticised the place severely. A holy place must be untouched and pure:

31. Varvara Pavlovna Longortova and Pëtr Nikitich Longortov, Ovolyngort, 2001.
32. Anttonen 1996: 135.

Holy groves are always selected from untouched pure places. The place selected at Khanty-Muzhi for a holy grove clearly violates all the rules. It is even more disastrous, because Khanty-Muzhi families have sold all their holy things. Pugurchin [the shaman who performed there], on the other hand, has done everything very seriously. He is not guilty of the fact that the administration and the museum under it selected that kind of place. He cannot reject it. And he agreed.[33]

The main mistake was that the authorities, who were responsible for cultural work, selected Khanty-Muzhi as the place of festivals and the public sacrificial ceremony. The reason may have been the site's easy access, as it is conveniently near Muzhi. The village people had sold their holy emblems and Nakhrachëv could not accept the place for that reason. But the shaman accepted the solution. Instead of the new place near Muzhi, Nakhrachëv would have preferred a traditional holy grove as a ritual site.

Zoya Sokolova recorded information regarding several areas of sacrifice along the Synya river in 1971–2.[34] In the summer of 2001 we noticed that several of these areas were still in use, although Sokolova, as well as the ethnographers who worked before the Revolution, wrote about these places of worship and religious rituals as if they were on the verge of disappearing. Conclusions of this sort were dictated in the beginning by the policies of the Orthodox Church, and later by Soviet authorities. Ethnographers, in order to please these two groups, were obliged to record conditions that describe the victory of Orthodoxy, and later of atheism, "over superstition and prejudices", although the field material could point to nearly the opposite conclusion. The reason for the researchers' hypotheses that certain cultural phenomena were on the verge of disappearing stemmed from the desire to protect their informants from persecution. Also, these early ethnographic descriptions, although commendable for their detailed description, often contain false information stemming from the realities of fieldwork. People did not show the hidden places. Thus, Karjalainen's material is very reliable, but it contains a number of remarkable errors. For example, he wrote that "the most noticeable feature in the attitudes towards holy places is, however, that in the old days women's access to those places seemed not to be allowed".[35]

It is true that even today women's access to men's holy places is forbidden, or at least restricted. Women participate in "feeding the spirits", which are kept in a *kŭrəŋ-χot* hut, but it is forbidden for them to go into the building. Food and wine are brought to women outside. Women are also not allowed to go to the attic of a house in which male spirits are kept. In 2000 only men participated in the "feeding of the spirits" ritual in the attic of Yuriĭ's home in Ust'-Voĭkar; the host did not permit the female researcher to go into the attic, but he did ask her to make food for the spirits. In Ovolyngort 2001, Oleg visited a men's worship area along with two Khanty men. When they had disappeared over a wooden path, a housewife in her seventies took Anna

---

33. Nikolaĭ Nikitich Nakhrachev, Ovolyngort, 2002.
34. Sokolova 1975b.
35. Karjalainen 1918: 190.

by the hand and said, "Let's go by another path to see the men's place". The women did not dare to approach closer than 50 metres to the men's sacred area; they did, however, receive a reprimand for even this behaviour. In the same village in 2001 the host did not allow the Khanty guests, who had come from the town, to gather currants where ashes had been thrown from a now abandoned house. Men were sent to collect the berries, although among the Khanty this is generally a task done by women.

Such behaviour among men is not proof of discrimination, because among the Khanty, at least in the Ob' area, there are female cult places near every village to which men are denied access. Women using those places are "young", of a fertile age, and married. In Vershina Voïkar male ethnographers were denied a visit to a women's place, because men are not allowed to visit them. Since it was impossible for Karjalainen to approach worship areas reserved for females, his conclusions regarding the Khanty religion became one-sided. Therefore, both ethnographers and others who research the Khanty religion err if, basing their studies on Karjalainen, they claim that Khanty women are excluded from cult life.[36] In fact, there exist gender-based parallel cults, which form a complementary but inter-exclusive unity. Another question regards the hierarchical relationship and significance of male and female cults from a general point of view, as well as the social importance of religious and magic beliefs connected to different spheres of activity. Male cults are based on the worship of the most important and powerful spirits. Thus it is in the central position, as far as the renewing of the society is concerned. The rituals a shaman performs in modern festivals that are "blessed by the authorities" continue traditions centred around men's cults.

In Ovolyngort, the male holy place and female holy place are clearly separated from each other, in line with the similar separation of the male and female in secular activities. Holy trees decorated with sacrificial cloths, camp-fire areas and sacrificial presents mark sacred areas. According to Sokolova, in the Synya region the tree that signifies female cult places is generally a birch, while spruce trees define male areas. People had different opinions about the value and meaning of trees. According to Nikolaï Nakhrachëv the birch cannot be a sacred tree among the Khanty:

> The birch is considered a weed tree by the Khanty. The Russians regard it as sacred and so on, but the Khanty as a weed. It grows in clearings and burnt places, therefore the birch cannot be a sacred tree. Well, maybe, only in the case where there are no other trees nearby. The women can hang cloths on a birch, but never the men. The men's trees are conifers: the pine-tree, larch, cedar, fir. And even if the women hang cloths on a birch, the tree still has to be sanctified: a coin needs hammering in, a prayer making. And in general, it is accepted that a Khanty woman must have only modest desires, praying for peace in their families, for their husbands' love. But the men ask for more important things.[37]

36. See for example Nenola 1992: 361.
37. Nikolaï Nikitich Nakhrachëv, Ovolyngort, 2002.

The statement associates the birch with women's offering places but at the same time denies their value. Women's prayers concern only family matters and the need of a husband's love. "Important things" in society are taken care of by men. Ėmel'yan Rusmilenko, in turn, when telling about celebrations on St Elijah's day, thought that the larch and birch are sacred trees.[38]

In the cult place of Khanty-Muzhi the birch symbolises both the male and female, while in a ritual in Ovgort on the Synya river women hung ribbons on a pine which held many similar past offerings. Oleg was asked to hang a ribbon onto a birch tree which held men's gifts. Naturally, there exist preferences as well as a well-developed symbolism regarding plants; however, the significance assigned to a certain tree depends not only on those who sacrifice, but also on local topography (swamp, hill, forest, lake or river) characterised by the predominance or absence of certain tree species as well as the hierarchical position of the spirit and of the phratry to which it belongs. In this way the rituals for the highest deities are performed under a birch, and spruce or cedar for divinities of the lower realm. The birch is a tree of the *Moś* phratry, while a fir tree and cembra belong to the *Por* phratry. Sacrificial animal skins are hung on the spruce and skulls from either birches or willows.[39]

The rules concerning activities regarding the inviolability of holy places are more strict, as Karjalainen already observed. In Ovolyngort the male area is situated at a distance of several dozen metres from any building in a rather gloomy pine forest that surrounds the village, whereas the female place, along a path that leads to the shore, is easily visible. The male area, it is believed, presents many dangers to women; conversely, women also endanger men's safety by allowing access for evil spirits. Rituals performed in male areas have blood sacrifices for local spirits: animal remains, bones and furs hang on nearby trees. However, on the scenic and well-lit female area multicoloured cloths hang on birch trees; an area reserved for campfires stands on the other side of the path.

Trees formerly used in both male and female rituals now stand within the village after its enlargement. According to the inhabitants, before the village enlargement the trees stood on the edge of the forest at a distance of 25–30 metres from the nearest house. No new offerings hang from their branches, but injunctions against using the trees for firewood are evidence of the honour and worship still accorded to them. The trees will be conveyed to the present sacred areas when they fall. The old trees still mark gender boundaries: one stands by the path leading to the men's lavatory, while the woman's tree stands by the lavatory reserved for women. The active use of sacred places reserved for females in Ovolyngort confirms the existence of parallel but separate rituals.

38. Ėmel'yan Mikhaĭlovich Rusmilenko, Lopkhari, 2003.
39. Sokolova 1971.

Offerings in holy groves

The concept reflected in sacrificial rituals of mutual giving and receiving is the basis for the existence and continued activity of holy groves. In addition to rites of public sacrifice, in which Khanty communities participate in large numbers, sacrifice takes place at other sites as well. Family and kin rituals are intimate in nature, hence participation in them requires a close relationship between host and guests. The following field notes describe the ritual of feeding the spirit in the kin place of sacrifice. The ritual was recorded on video.

> A.-L. S.: Ovgort, 6 August 2001. Galina walks at a quick pace along the path nearest to the village boundary. She stops at the gate and turns to the last house. The reason for this is clear: we are going to the kin place of sacrifice, and I must dress in the Khanty costume. Galina searches for a suitable *jernas*, a woman's dress, and a scarf that matches it.
>
> After we have left the village, we come to a pine forest. On the edge of the forest, hidden from view but still nearby, is a place for a campfire and two trees that stand close together, and on which hang pieces of cloth. We – Galina, her mother Evdokiya, who was the first wife of the shaman Vasiliĭ Petrovich, Svetlana, their daughters, and two dogs – soon arrive at our destination.
>
> The women light a campfire and bring out a low table and benches. Soon hot water for tea begins to boil, and Galina sets it on a bench at the table. This table lies close to the men's tree of sacrifice, which is decorated with cloths in which coins have been tied. It appears that this holy place has been in use frequently: people gather here for festivals, but also when a family group wishes to organise a sacrificial meal known as the *porə*. The participants place presents suitable for daily sacrifice on the table: fish, biscuits, sweets, tea and vodka.
>
> Grandmother Evdokiya ties light-coloured cloths on the men's and women's trees. The red ribbons, meant as sacrificial presents, are fumigated above the fire. Oleg hangs the ribbon on the men's tree, and grandmother on the women's tree nearby. Those who hang ribbons circle clockwise three times, bowing occasionally in the direction of the tree's spirit.
>
> The meal begins with the customary round of vodka; Oleg, who brought this gift, serves it to those present in small cups in the traditional manner. People converse, eat and smoke.
>
> When Evdokiya arrived, she placed a plastic bag under the men's tree of sacrifice. She now draws out from the bag a bundle of clothing that resembles the home spirits that are hidden in the corners of Khanty houses. That is what it is: a *лух*, a guardian spirit, has been brought to participate in this ceremony. Soon a cigarette lit for the spirit is placed on a box at the mouth of the bag.
>
> After finishing the meal, grandmother points out a nearby tree, under which offerings, *săχ*-robes, for the Master of the Underworld, *Kŭl-ilpi-iki*, have been buried. After digging up some soil she catches sight of some pieces of dark cloth with coins that have been placed between the roots of this spruce tree.
>
> Then the women wash the dishes and extinguish the fire. After the table and benches have been properly collected and stored under the tree we are ready to return.[40]

40. Siikala diary, 6.8.2001.

O. U.: Ovgort, 6 August 2001. Galina came already around 4 pm, saying "Let's go to the forest, the others have left already". We quickly dragged together everything that was needed. The food that was prepared in advance for the *porə* (treat) we managed to stuff into our rucksacks. I was very angry because I did not manage to shoot any video of our coming out of the house and carrying the *лух*. I came to the conclusion that they did not show it to us intentionally. Anna was dressed in *jernas* at Galina's home; moreover, they took so long dressing that I became even more suspicious.

However, it turned out that we were expected: Evdokiya, Svetlana, her younger daughter, Sveta, the eight-year-old daughter of Galina, Katya, Svetlana's six-year-old daughter, and we three arrived at our destination. The *put jŭχ* (a supporting beam for a pot) was stuck at an angle into the ground, although we had observed that it is usually fastened between a pine tree and a stake. A fire was burning in an iron container that held 20 litres. The table was set in our presence. Afterwards, Evdokiya gave everyone a piece of crimson cloth (measuring 50 x 20 cm); into the edges of the cloth two coins had been tied. Women hung the cloth on a pine, on which old ribbons were hanging as well; Evdokiya showed me a birch, the thickness of which was approximately that of a pole, and on which presents reserved for men were hanging. After this, having bowed three times toward the four directions, we sat down at the table.

This is a common holy place for the kin to come to feed the spirits; sometimes they pray to the highest god, *Torəm*, and his sons. They hang white and red cloths on trees, and have sown seven *săχs*, robes, of the same colour. If they pray to the old spirit of the Underworld, *Kŭl-ilpi-iki*, they bury seven black *săχs*, about 15–20 cm in length, under the roots of trees and beneath moss. Showing us an old *săχ*, Evdokiya took from a hole one white and one black piece of dilapidated cloth and said that the white one had fallen from the tree where it had been hung as a gift to the highest gods. However, she put it back in the hole: "It has fallen, that means that it is already with *Kŭl-ilpi-iki*, and must not be lifted up."

After the dinner of fish, known as *ńar*-fish, and tea, Evdokiya said that now it is permitted to smoke, and smoke we must. After lighting a cigarette, she set it on a half-open box where sat a *лух* on a box of matches in front of the idol. When the cigarette began to smoulder on the box of matches, she explained, "This means that the spirits are eager to smoke!" She buried the cigarette butt, after covering it with spit and crumpling it with her fingers to extinguish it, under the root of a pine and into a hole with a *săχ* for *Kŭl-ilpi-iki*.

After bowing three times to the four directions we went away.[41]

The stages of the intimate family rite described above follow the general scheme of the sacrificial ritual: 1. Preparation phase: dressing and gathering together to go to the place of sacrifice; 2. Building the ritual stage: chopping wood, lighting the fire, brewing tea, setting the table; 3. Purification rituals, the aim of which is to be freed from the profane: fumigating cloths with smoke; 4. Giving the gifts: hanging pieces of cloth on men's and women's trees; 5. Prayers; 6. Meals eaten in common, where both people and representatives of the spirit world participate by eating, conversing and smoking; and 7. Finishing the ceremony and preparing a place for the following ritual:

41. Ulyashev diary, 6.8.2001.

Gifts for spirits in Ovgort. – Photograph by A.-L. Siikala 2002

cleaning the table and putting out the fire, then ritually placing objects in their proper storage places.

Although Finno-Ugric rituals that take place in holy groves are quite similar schematically, they are endlessly variable in detail. The rituals we saw in Shuryshkary differed not only in their details and significance but also from the point of view of the actors and their actions. In the sacred area of Ovgort, the greatest attention was paid to the appeasement of the spirit who saw to the welfare of the extended family. The participants were female, except for the outside male researcher. In rituals of men's holy groves with blood sacrifice to the powerful spirits, the ritual practice is more formal. When the brother of Pëtr Nikitich came to Ovolyngort with his family in 2003, an offering in the men's holy grove was organised. Oleg had visited the place in previous summers, but Anna did not have a chance to see the place, because women may open the way for evil spirits and are not allowed to enter the area. Now Pëtr Nikitich came to a conclusion which was acceptable for everybody. Not only Oleg, but also Anna, who is not a Khanty woman and who studies folklore, could come so near the place that the holy tree and ritual activities were visible.

> We, the families of two Longortov brothers, Kolya and ethnographers, began preparations in the morning. Varvara Pavlovna made a fire on the right side of the house near a half-grown birch, which served as a holy tree for women. Varvara cooked fish and tea water. Our guest cut wood for the fire and we jointly laid the table. All kinds of food were found: fish, bread, blueberries, apples and tinned milk.

Offering to the Golden Boy, Ovolyngort. – Photograph by A.-L. Siikala 2003

When the fish was well done, the men walked in a line to the forest. The holy place is actually near, less than 100 metres from the house. But the path is narrow and the forest thick. Nobody could know that in a small clearing there is a holy place. However, the cloths hanging from the sacred tree and furs from animals in other trees reveal the character of the place. In the middle of the clearing there is a fire site. When the men left, women made their offerings, narrow strips of cloths in the corners which everybody tied coins into.

The men approached Golden Boy near his tree, put a couple of vodka bottles and the plate of fish under it. They put strings of cloths on the branch. When the food and drink were blessed, men drank a glass of vodka, bowed and made a circle according to the direction of the sun three times. After a while men came back to the table.

The low table was moved two times. At first it was near the fire. After the men came back, Anton raised the table, turned to the sun, and put the table in another place, where we had a meal.

Everybody offered drink from their bottle. Women got fish from their plate. They were not allowed to eat fish blessed at the men's place, but it was permitted to drink vodka which had been there.

After the meal the men went back to bow to Golden Boy. After coming back they sat, shared a bottle and talked a while. The women cleaned the table.

The ritual acts follow the pattern presented above. Only the purification of offerings was missing. The spirit of the men's place in Ovolyngort is *Sorńi-pŏχ*, "Golden Boy", seemingly an alternative name for Λοvəŋ-χu, a protector of the *Moś*-phratry to which the Longortov family belongs (see

p. 72). People are not sure of the character of their spirit, but they said that he is the protector spirit of the Longortovs and the village of Ovolyngort. The worn clearing with the fire and a *put jŭχ* near it, and the great number of cloths on the branches, testify to regular offering ceremonies. The ritual food was fish, but furs on the trees show that blood offerings are made to Golden Boy. As was mentioned before, there was a sledge with a spirit image, possible a Russian icon, in the place, but it was moved to the forest and a bear tore it apart.

In addition to rituals for kin and local protector spirits, the Khanty have made offerings during calendar rituals devoted to Orthodox saints. The most important Christian celebration is the day of St Elijah on 2 August. Together with a feast *Vŏrŋa χătʌ*, "Crow day", which celebrates the coming of spring, it has local roots. St Elijah's day is the summer feast of the Khanty. The year of the reindeer herders ends and a new one begins. They begin to eat meat again after the summer abstention and to pack for the next herding season. It is important to sacrifice to and ask protection from spirits. The fishermen also have a break in their seasonal variation. Good fish come to the rivers in August and fishermen gather in working groups for fishing. The families do the same.

> And the second important Khanty holiday [after *Vŏrŋa χătʌ*] is St Elijah's day. It is in the middle of the summer. It is the beginning of the bad time. It is like a boundary, then. So it is that the reindeer-breeders having packed their things up on the sledges did not touch them thereafter; they stayed closed in this way till St Elijah's day came. And when 2 August came, they looked: well, the reindeer are alive, safe and sound, the herd has been preserved, and they began to unpack the packs. They checked the harness, to see whether it is all in order, or a repair is needed. So it is that they did not eat meat in the summer. Only after 2 August did they begin to eat it. On this day they began to remember that they were in for a journey, that it would be hard during the wandering. They would need the help of spirits and the reindeer sacrificed to them for their assistance. And they began eating meat. And the fishermen celebrated St Elijah's day. Well, they used, of course, to fish before 2 August, but did not consider this to be real fishing. It was only so-so, just to get something to eat for a day. Only after 2 August did they gather into teams and start out. The women began to prepare fish for the winter: to dry-cure, to make fish oil, etc.[42]

As a day dividing the year into economic periods St Elijah's day is important for families. A blood offering belongs to St Elijah's day. Both Ėmel'yan and his wife Fila stressed the meaning of gender roles in St Elijah's feast and described the ritual from the practice they know best:

> E. M. R.: On St Elijah's day reindeer are slaughtered. One is slaughtered near the *nŏrəm*, for men, the other near the *chum* door, for the women. The second one is also slaughtered by the men, who thereafter go back to the *norəm*.[43]

42. Nikolaï Nikitich Nakhrachev, Ovolyngort, 2002.
43. Ėmel'yan Mikhaïlovich Rusmilenko, Lopkhari, 2003.

F. G. R.: The hide of the women's reindeer [lit. "women hide"] is thereafter put into the earth. Its head is hung over with glass beads, and it is put into the earth. And the bones are put into a basin, the guts are put above and then above this the hide from the head. It is decorated with glass beads and left. The men hides of the men's reindeer are hung on the tree, are lifted up.[44]

Fila Rusmilenko also said that they wanted so much to celebrate St Elijah's day in Khanty-Muzhi, but how could they in a Russian place? Everybody would come running there. Ėmel'yan Rusmilenko added to this comment that "*illa χătʌ*, St Elijah's day, is a family holiday. Where the people are, there they celebrate it." According to him, the sacred trees are larch and birch. He described the male ritual in a thorough way:

The sacrificed reindeer is first encircled clockwise with a kerchief, then covered with it for a moment. Having slaughtered the reindeer, they dip the kerchief into the blood and hang it on the sacred tree, a larch or a birch. First on the *jir jŭχ*, a sort of forked stick, they hang the tongue, heart, a rib and five thorax vertebrae, after they have been cooked. Then they hold a bit like this and bring it to the table. On the *jir jŭχ*, the tongue's tip is left, and all the rest is eaten by the men. The women are not allowed to eat from *jir jŭχ* or anything from near the sacred tree. Thereafter, having eaten everything, they hang up the hide. Together with the reindeer hide a fox hide is hung up. The fox hide is turned clockwise three times above the fire. Then they hang it up. They shout seven times. Seven times must one shout for everybody to hear.[45]

The dividing of the sacrificed animal and offerings to the sacred tree continue during the feast, as we saw in the St Elijah celebrations in Khanty-Muzhi in 2001 and 2002.

Fila described the ritual from the viewpoint of a woman, her husband from a male perspective. According to the theoretical thinking that underlies cultural practice, the ritual can be perceived as a situational strategy of action. In spite of the clear goals and means of the rite, which are known to everyone, many of its events remain in the subconscious of the participants. The nature of the rite also tends to produce a view about world order.[46] A ritual's strategy of action is based on prior knowledge of schemes and modes of behaviour, which in different situations can be applied creatively, and on negotiating each choice. Behaving according to rules is considered important. Pëtr Nikitich said that when they got the bear and just wanted to eat it, his uncle said: "As it is customary, as our grandfathers ate, just so shall we eat."[47] Keeping to rules makes rituals traditional. But rules can be evaded.

Thus, when rites are organised, specialists who both know the scheme of the ritual and have an idea of the possibilities and limits of proper

44. Fefina Grigor'evna Rusmilenko, Lopkhari, 2003.
45. Fefina Grigor'evna Rusmilenko, Lopkhari, 2003.
46. Bell 1992: 81.
47. Pëtr Nikitich Longortov, Ovolyngort, 2002.

performance are in a central position. Specialists differ in their ability to contact spirits. In the public rituals of Khanty-Muzhi in 2001 and 2002, which involved higher deities, a shaman acted as the specialist, whereas old women recognised as rite specialists were the principal actors in the kin's place of worship in Ovgort in 2001 as well as in the cemetery in the village of Vershina Voïkar and Vosyakhovo in 2000. The opening and closing of a graveyard so that the souls of the dead will not leave their residence needs knowledge of the proper behaviour. On the other hand, most people know well the rituals connected with the remembrance of the dead. In the cemetery of Ovolyngort an old man was the principal actor. Young men of twenty to twenty-five years of age acted as specialists in ancestor-feeding rituals in the *ura* of the village of Ust'-Voïkar in 2000 and in Ovolyngort in 2001: the prerequisite in these ceremonies was general knowledge rather than detailed knowledge, as is the case in other rituals.

A ritual begins at the moment when the participants come to a conclusion regarding its importance and prepare for it. Collecting clothes and other objects (and food as well) becomes the main attraction; these are actions that are important from the perspective of ritual symbolism. Dressing prepares the body for the ritual: symbolic decorations, covering or uncovering, and attention paid to symbolically significant details of the wardrobe. Among the Khanty of Shuryshkary, as well as in other Finno-Ugric areas, instructions concerning men's and women's ritual preparation differ significantly. Among men only active participants highlight their ritual functions with the traditional costume or belt (the most important symbol for men); however, dressing in traditional costume is not a requirement.

Women, in contrast to men, all dress in traditional costume. Thus, during the visit to the graveyard in the village of Vosyakhovo in 2000, one woman gave *jernas* for her friend on the rare occasion that she did not have the proper festive clothing. During the visit to the sacred area in Ovgort, as mentioned above, women searched for a suitable dress for Anna. In general, women wear the national costume even on weekdays much more frequently than men owing to their greater cultural conservatism, and also because, as is the case with appeals to ancestors, women in particular refer to the authority of the past, as in "old people acted in this way", or "we do not know, but old people tell it this way". Also, many rituals require women to dress in special clothing. Therefore, actions such as manipulating scarves during rituals, covering the face during lamentation, conversing with the soul of the deceased at the grave, undoing braids to sacrifice a lock of hair, changing scarves in return for those presented at funerals require not only the wearing of scarves but also knowledge of their special use.[48]

Fumigation is the most common purification rite among the Khanty, for example in bear ceremonies, in rites that take place after the birth of a child, and also in everyday life: if a woman steps on or over men's clothing,

48. The Khanty borrowed this feature from the Turkic Mongolians during the Middle Ages.

these items are then purified with smoke.[49] In the rites we observed, the participants, after circling around a bonfire three times, fumigated ribbons with coins attached before hanging these on holy trees. Also, participants fumigated the axe used in sacrifice as well as scarves given as gifts and the one used to cover the animal in a sacrificial ritual. The shaman fumigated his legs twice before he approached the holy tree. The colour red relates to several ritual meanings: it symbolises fire, blood and, consequently, life. For this reason red or white cloth is sacrificed to upper-world spirits, whereas lower-realm spirits receive black cloth. Additionally, although white is the main colour for gifts, people prefer cloths decorated with large red (orange or yellow as well) patterns called *χătʌ χănšə*, "the design of the sun".

The act of organising the area that contains the table and benches near the tree of sacrifice (or the grave in a cemetery), lighting the bonfire and setting the table creates a framework and central orientation for the ceremony: a sacred object, sacred area, fire and a table. According to our informants it is usually the spirits of the holy place who arrive at the kin worship area. However, it is possible to summon *Num-torəm* or other more powerful spirits. In situations such as these a more competent shaman performs the ceremonies. In the Shuryshkary region Vasiliĭ Petrovich, a seventy-year-old man, was the master of the shaman songs and prayers required to summon the highest spirits of both the Upper and Lower Worlds to the holy places. In Ovgort one festival participant was the family spirit, or *ʌuχ*, the idol of which the grandmother Evdokiya brought and placed under the holy tree. The conveyance of the family spirit to the kin's holy place during the *porəʌiti* ritual is customary.[50] Offering sacrificial gifts to the spirits, making a sacrifice, prayers and a common meal are the central phases of rites: they create connections with representatives of the Otherworld while simultaneously connecting and differentiating the participants of the event. In the men's cult in Khanty-Muzhi only a small number of the men present participated in slaughtering the sacrificial ram, reciting prayers and hanging the slaughtered animal's skin on the holy tree. However, both men and women ate the meat of the sacrificed animal and soup from common dishes at the table. It needs to be mentioned that during the performance of the women's rituals which contain blood sacrifice, the animal is slaughtered by a man specially called for the occasion. In most instances he departs after this act.

In Ovolyngort people visit the kin holy place quite often, especially during calendar festivals that are important in the promotion of the economic sphere. Concluding the rite and cleaning the sacred area to ensure that there will be a next time places the event in a continuity of ritual time. Just as the space of a landscape includes meaningful places, which make it possible to meet the supranormal, so too moments for encountering spirits are structured on a time axis. These places and moments are important for creating and renewing social order.

49. Kálmán 1968: 89.
50. Oral interview with Feodosiya Longortova, Helsinki, 17.11.2001.

Common rites, different meanings

Avoiding and honouring the holy places colours the everyday life of the small villages of the Shuryshkary Khanty even today. The environment of everyday actions consists of areas both for humans and spirits, the living and the dead. In the same way feeding the idols of the holy corners of the houses and the cult of the dead are a natural part of life, though the proper ways of acting may be a topic of negotiation and their meanings unconscious or forgotten. In the private sphere, the interest in traditional culture depends on the values and perspectives of individuals and the opinions of their relatives and friends. Public performances of common rituals need effort and acknowledgement of a larger group of people.

Many researchers, from Émile Durkheim onwards, have emphasised that a ritual gathers a society together as it also defines its boundaries. Rites happening in a family's sacred place or women's and men's cults gather the group with bonds to the holy place over and over again. This expresses kin unity, but also highlights differences connected with gender, age and values. At present not all Khanty have similar attitudes regarding rituals, and many refuse to participate. Thus, in Ovgort, Evdokiya's grandchildren considered as important their participation in the "feeding of the spirits" ritual, but the men of the family refused to take part in rites. Galina explained in simple terms, "Our men come here very seldom, and they don't like to come. They say, 'What should we do there? We could sit at home.' The time comes when they notice for themselves that they must come to the family's place . . . If someone must come, he comes, but you can't lead them there by force."[51]

On the other hand, it is not exactly proper to differentiate only between men and women. In this case we must examine the young men's unwillingness to participate in the ritual in light of tendencies that characterise contemporary young people who strive for modernity, often to the detriment of ethnic traditions. Most likely the scales, with modern comforts weighing on the one side, and on the other cultural spiritual fulfilment, at some time will be balanced. At the present time, among the young at any rate, illusions regarding modernity are gaining the upper hand compared to traditional beliefs. In this way the relationship to ritual aspects of Khanty life separate in many ways not only the male from the female but also the old from the young. Attitudes among the young, on the other hand, vary from rejection to keen interest and are often situational.

51. Galina N. Pugurchina, Ovgort, 2001.

10 Paths of souls, villages of the dead

Religious and ideological ideas are manifested in large graveyards, where members of different ethnic groups are buried. In the areal centre of Muzhi, there are Russian, Komi, Khanty and Tatar graves. The Soviet period left its marks, red stars, on the graves. Some graves have crosses as in modern Russian and Komi graveyards. Small statues, concrete or stone obelisks stand on new graves. We saw only a few traditional Khanty graves in Muzhi. Many Khanty families prefer their own old graveyards built in the traditional way even today. They are usually situated some kilometres from the village in a forest, often in a place separated by water from the living area. Keeping to tradition also means that Khanty graveyards in North and South Shuryshkary differ from each other. The right way to build a grave was a typical topic of discussion among those who came with us to visit graveyards. Symbols of the Orthodox Church and its faith are rarely seen in a Khanty graveyard. Today the relationship between ethnic groups is not so problematic as before, with those who value the Orthodox tradition, the Russians and Komi, using the same graveyards, while the Khanty and Nenets use their own. For the Khanty, graveyards are sites, or rather "villages", of the dead. The souls of ancestors can be met in graveyards. Hence, they give a feeling of history and continuity to their own way of life.

The Khanty χăлaś, "graveyard", is a place for remembering forefathers, relatives and those who were close and beloved when they lived. Belonging to family, to kin and even to ethnic and religious groups is expressed by burial and remembrance rites, the organisation of the graveyard, the structures of graves and their symbolic decorations. Marjorie Balzer (1980, 1987) and Edgar Saar (1998) have studied funeral processes among the Northern Khanty. Their detailed descriptions reveal the density of ritual language and the problems in understanding the ideological background of different ritual acts and events. Balzer refers to funeral rites as one form of crisis rites. But among the Khanty crisis rites are usually solved by shamans, the experts on the spirit world. Birth, marriage and death rites belong to the life of every person; they are rites of passages organised in the family sphere through the guidance of older persons who know the ritual details. The classical division of rites of passage into rites of separation, transition and incorporation[1] suits the overall pattern of the Khanty death ritual, but not the detailed schemes of the ritual phases, which have complicated religious backgrounds. In human life, rites of passages re-establish connections to the social world and visible nature, and recreate a person's place in the community. The burial rituals mark distinctions in the ethnic map of Shuryshkary, as was noted above (pp. 57–9). Catherine Bell has argued that just as strategic acts in ritual traditions can differentiate, ritualisation can also work to integrate societies.[2] Khanty burial rites can be viewed as the ritualisation of communication with the dead prescribed by religious ideas and rules for behaviour. A long transition period with many symbols and ritual acts which are recreated again and again distinguish the dead from the living but at the same time transform him or her into a part of a larger community of living and dead. Discussions over the right way of doing things and the best authorities on rites took place in connection with all of the rites we saw. For the Khanty, death is a major event in the transformation of the structure of family and kin. Communication with the dead cannot be done in any ordinary way, by using everyday rules, but only in a way which honours the special position of the dead as guardians of their living relatives.

In this chapter we discuss funeral rituals and their basic ideas, the situation of dead relatives and the rules for communicating with them. We also try to illuminate knowledge of tradition and the feelings of people who take part in funeral rites and remembrance ceremonies. Among the Khanty funeral rites form a long and multilevel process. The ritual acts in separate phases of the transition process seem to be explained by ideas and concepts concerning the soul and kin. Hence, it is important to understand the idea of the multiple-soul system of the human person. In order to familiarise ourselves with everyday practices in graveyards we visited several graveyards in Shuryshkary: in Muzhi, Vershina Voïkar, Vosyakhovo, Ovolyngort and Kazym-Mys. We were invited to funerals in Ovolyngort and took part of in a memorial ritual in Ust'-Voïkar. During visits to graveyards memorial rituals were usually organised by people who wished to remember their relatives. Local people do not go to graveyards without purpose. The dead should be remembered and treated well.

Concepts of souls

The soul, the essence of a person, ties him or her to family and kin. Pëtr Nikitich explained the concepts which determine a person's life: "*is* ('shadow') is soul, *ur'* the god who every day watches over you. Every person has a helper-protector and *nupət* is the life, the age, which is prescribed for you by the god."[3] However, Khanty concepts of the soul cannot be expressed by one word. Northern Eurasian shamanic cultures have an idea of multiple

1. Honko 1979: 374–5; van Gennep 1960: 10–11.
2. Bell 1992: 125.
3. Pëtr Nikitich Longortov, Ovolyngort, 2004.

souls or soul-parts. In sleep or in trance one of the souls can leave the body and visit different places. On the Lower Ob' we were told that men have five and women four souls, which have different characters and spheres of action. Chernetsov, who studied Northern Khanty and Mansi soul beliefs, described soul terminology by examining the appearance of each soul. The first and most material soul is *is* or *is-χŏr* ("soul-shadow", "aspect of a soul"). According to Chernetsov *χŏr* can be translated "aspect" or "form".[4] The word *is* and its parallels are found in all the Finno-Ugric groups. The Finnish word *itse*, "self", belongs here. A person without *itse*, who is *itsetön*, will be sick. The soul seen as a shadow is not only present in living but also in inanimate objects. It is tied to a person. If it gets lost, a person will be sick. A shaman has to find it and put it back.[5] After death it follows the person to the grave. The shadow-soul continues an existence in the graveyard similar to its earthly life.[6] There the shadow soul feels both cold and hunger and enjoys being taken care of. When it is treated to liquor, it may become drunk.[7] Anna had a good example of soul treatment when she visited the Vershina Voĭkar graveyard in 1994 with a woman whose sister's son had recently died. At that time vodka was not available as a result of the government's alcohol campaign. Visitors decided to buy beer for the remembrance feast and found a couple of bottles produced by a Dutch company in a small shop. Anna Ivanovna, the aunt, asked the deceased: "We could not buy vodka, but this is good beer. Would you like to try a new kind of drink? It might be an interesting experience."[8] The souls are not only talked to in the graveyard, they also talk to each other. They for example boast about the attention they get from relatives. The shadow souls are believed to be quite material and they can be dangerous for the living, because they may steal the souls from them.[9] After remembrance feasts in the graveyard apotropaic rituals are performed to keep the deceased in their right place.

The second soul, called *urt*, moves about in the form of a bird or man. After death it goes downriver to the realm of the dead. During sleep it can leave the body and meet other beings, good and terrible. If it fears the hostile spirits of the Lower World, it can run away, and a dream about this kind of experience indicates a death or sickness. If a person dreams about the soul of a relative, and does not let it home, the person will be sick or even die.[10] Varvara Pavlovna said that in this case, it is necessary to call a shaman to perform a magic ritual in a tree called *usəŋ jŭχ* (see pp. 179–80). The word *urt* is also used for wandering souls. A person who does not want to go to the realm of the dead can remain on the earth and visit relatives or children, or even take up residence in a stranger.[11]

4. Chernetsov 1963: 6.
5. Karjalainen 1918: 25–6.
6. Chernetsov 1963: 6–7; Paasonen 1909: 4.
7. Chernetsov 1963: 7.
8. A. I. Rebas', Vershina Voĭkar, 1994.
9. Chernetsov 1963: 11.
10. Chernetsov 1963: 14.
11. Chernetsov 1963: 17–18.

The third soul, *uləm-is*, "dreaming soul", may appear in the shape of a wood grouse. It lives in the forest and comes to a sleeping person. Because it moves out of the body, it is also called the external soul. The dreaming soul is sometimes believed to live in clothing. It dies when the human being dies. If it is harmed, for example by evil spirits, when it wanders around, the person dies.[12]

The fourth, little soul, is called ʌiʌ, the breath soul. Like *is*, shadow soul, the word ʌiʌ has counterparts meaning "soul", "spirit" or "courage" in most Finno-Ugric languages. It usually stays with the person, but if it leaves the person becomes powerless and feels fatigue. Chernetsov gives some ideas concerning the little soul: it is quick, connected to mind and most frequently represented by a bird. Because it lives in the head and especially in the hair, the cutting of the hair destroys it.[13] The ʌiʌ is reincarnated. It passes into the body of a new child in the family. This was noted already by Gondatti, who wrote that in every man there is a body and shadow, *is*, and the soul, *lili khelmkholas*; the latter passes into a child of the kin of the deceased.[14]

The soul of a deceased person is born into one of the offspring who has a similar character and appearance. In Kazym people guessed by the aid of *Kăltəś*, or by the afterbirth in a birch-bark vessel, whose soul is living in a new-born baby.[15] The Shuryshkary Khanty gave the name of the dead grand-father to the first grandchild to be born two to three years after the death of the grandfather. The grandmother's name was given to the first girl born after the death of the grandmother. It was believed that parents are reborn in off-spring, who were called *l'aksas*. The word means "formed from something".[16]

The ideas about the fifth soul are not as clear as those of the first four. Edgar Saar writes that some people assume that the fifth soul is the energy of the person, while some think that a person has two reincarnation souls.[17] Chernetsov says that it is impossible to see which one of the five souls is lacking in women.[18] At least the first soul, *is*, the second soul, *urt*, and the fourth, ʌiʌ, are also found in females.

Burial rituals

ITTƏRMA, THE DOLL IMAGE OF THE DEPARTED

After a person dies, the ʌiʌ has to have a place where it can be settled so that it has a chance to be reincarnated in a child of the family. Matthias Alexander Castrén noted how the Northern Khanty made death dolls in the middle of the nineteenth century:

12. Saar 1998: 35; Chernetsov 1993: 21–3.
13. Chernetsov 1963: 24.
14. Gondatti 1888: 39.
15. Voldina 2000: 192.
16. Yuriĭ Semënovich Ozelov, Ust'-Voĭkar, 2000.
17. Saar 1998: 36.
18. Chernetsov 1963: 5.

> After a death of an older and much appreciated person his nearest relatives produce an image, which is kept in his *chum* and which is honoured as much as the deceased was honoured in his life time. The image is brought to eat at every meal, every evening it is undressed and put to bed, every morning it is dressed and set in the usual place of the dead.[19]

The soul lives at home as a living person for four years if she is woman and five years if he is man. During this time the *laksas* can be born.[20] During these years the *ittərma* image is kept at home in a particular wooden vessel (*appa, лuχ-лarӓś*), the rims of which have been tied together by strings made of white tanned leather or cedar. Bread and vodka are given to the spirit (i.e. the soul), a knife and scissors are put near it and a wedding ring is tied on its back. Death dolls are made among the Northern Khanty, who probably got the custom from the Nenets.

We stayed in a house in Ust'-Voĭkar in which there was the *ittərma* of a grandmother. In the morning the box with the death doll was taken from the nocturnal place and put at the table. The image of grandmother was fed at the same time as the others. In the evening the image was put in a sleeping position, the box was covered with a kerchief and put in the corner near the bed. After four years the *ittərma* of a woman is put in a bag, which is kept on a shelf in the holy corner. The image of a man is put in the attic after five years.

> It is forbidden to put the *ittərma* of a woman in the attic, because she cannot be over man. A woman cannot go there, because then she would be over man. If she goes up and a man comes to the house, the man will be under her. It is *śohma* [a sin].[21]

Our friend, a fisherman, wanted to show us the "old ones" and home guardian spirits in the attic. The men climbed up to the attic to see the spirits of the family and planned to take photos and video of them. On a fur coat on the floor of the attic there were two boxes, covered by reindeer hides. The boxes were called simply *лarӓś* in order to differentiate them from the *лuχ-лarӓś* and *appa*, which were kept downstairs for the death doll of the grandmother. The two big boxes were fifty to seventy years old, and perhaps even older than that. Reindeer-keeping ancestors had transported them in a particular sledge when they herded the reindeer to the summer and winter places. The fisherman opened the smaller of the two boxes. He took from it a small box of the same size (20 x 30 cm) as the *appa*, in which the grandmother's *ittərma* was placed. He showed the death doll of the grandfather, which was dressed in clothes made from white reindeer fur. On the belt a silver ring and a seal ring were attached. Then our host opened a yellow copper box and showed a small image, saying that it was the spirit protector

19. Castrén 1967: 219.
20. Yuriĭ Semënovich Ozelov, Ust'-Voĭkar, 2000.
21. Ust'-Voĭkar, 2000.

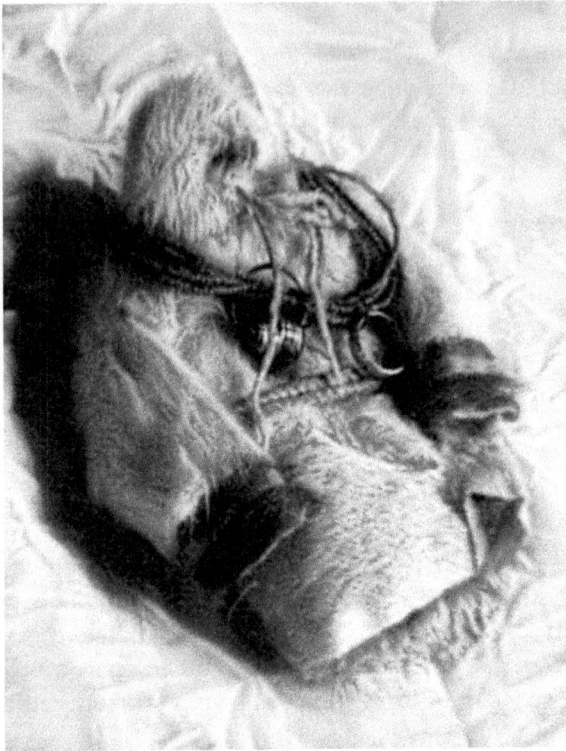

A grandfather's ittərma in an attic, Ust'-Voĭkar. – Photograph by Oleg Ulyashev 2000

of the home. "These are not the old ones, but they are holy. Well, that is just the same. At home we do not pray to spirits, we just feed them. We pray to those spirits which are in the sacred storehouse."[22]

Suddenly the fisherman's uncle came to the attic. He asked: "Are you feeding the old ones, or what?" And when the fisherman, accused of doing wrong, said that we had just come to see them, he shouted at him first in Khanty, then in Russian, and ended his heated arguments with swearing. Then he said to us: "If you want to take photos of the reindeer harness, I have lot of them at home. But you cannot come to the attic with empty hands." Then his anger was appeased and he said: "Do you not know, or what? You should tell the others, because they do not know." Later we went again to the attic and made up for our offence against the "old ones" with vodka. He did not let Anna go to the attic, because it would be *śohma*, but asked her to go to the cooking hut to make tea. After the event, our bewildered host repeated many times that without food it is not permitted to see or touch the spirits. But it is possible to feed them at any time.

A little later our neighbour and his wife Valentina L. invited us to their home. Valentina showed her mother's and aunt's death dolls and the spirit protector of the home. All the spirits were kept on the shelf of the holy corner of the house to the south-west (see pp. 127). The death dolls were about 20 to 25 cm long and the ʌuχ 50 cm. Not all death dolls have fur coats. Because

22. Ust'-Voĭkar, 2000.

A grandmother's ittərma at the parting feast of the soul on the fortieth day, Ust'-Voĭkar.
– Video picture by A.-L. Siikala 2000

Valentina does not belong to reindeer-herding people, her dolls were produced from cloth.[23]

In principle, near family members cannot make death dolls. Usually relatives who are not living together produce them. Pëtr Nikitich told us in Ovolyngort how a death doll can be made:

> Well, it is cut out of wood, like a human being: a head, arms, legs . . . then its head is poked for a short while into the fire, then a woman's shirt and *săχ* (coat) are put on it. Thereafter, when they go somewhere, they take it with them. A woman (the deceased's sister) made an *ittərma* on the fifth day, because for five days it is prohibited to work with a knife or to touch iron at all. After five years the death doll is brought up to the attic. For women it is hidden after four years.[24]

The death doll of Pëtr Nikitich's brother was made by his sister five days after his death. Before that time she could not make the doll, because for five days after the death scissors, needles or other iron tools cannot be handled.

Some of the male and female dolls are kept in a chest at the sacred store-

23. V. L. S., b. 1959, Ust'-Voĭkar, 2000.
24. Pëtr Nikitich Longortov, Ovolyngort, 2004.

house in Ust'-Voĭkar. Because women cannot enter the sacred hut only men are able to feed them. However, women can observe the feeding from an open door. During memorial rites a fire is lit near the door of the storehouse. The oldest man of the family first sprinkles vodka on the wall, which is over the shelf where the chest of dolls is kept. Near this shelf there are always towels and colourful kerchiefs, gifts for ancestors.

The funeral

Funeral rites are a long process ending in a parting ritual, the main rememberance feast being held fifty days (for a man) or forty (for a woman) after death. The door to the Otherworld is always partly open, but at the moment when a person goes from their home to the Lower World, the door is wide open. Hence in the transition time relatives have to be especially careful in their behaviour. When a person dies they perform protective rituals. If somebody dies at home, a metal box is turned upside down and scissors and a knife are put under it. The memorial fire is lit. It burns at the home of the dead for fifty or forty days (for a man or woman respectively).[25] The death doll is not only an image of the dead, but a place for their soul. People see that it is invited to table and put to sleep on time. The box of the death doll has to be covered with a kerchief when it is left at home. Open bottles of vodka are not taken out: "At night spirits think that the drink is for them."[26]

The brother of Pëtr Nikitich had died just before we came to Ovolyngort in 2004. We took part in the funeral meal though some of the relatives were annoyed at strangers being at the ceremony. Afterwards Pëtr Nikitich spoke about his brother's funeral and then generally about Khanty funeral customs:

Burying the dead
My brother was brought directly to the cemetery so that he would not rot. It was warm then. As soon as they came there, the grave pit was dug. They made the χăʌa (grave), from planks, which had been prepared beforehand.

Offering of reindeer
Before the coffin was put into the grave, they lifted it. Then it occurred to me and Tolya Artanzeev that he was begging us for reindeer. Except for him nobody has any idea of the proper customs now. Well, he used to go a lot with the reindeer, and there, in the herd, the old men know many things. But here there is nobody left. There were before, you know, the people who knew, but not now. We'll have to give the reindeer later, in the winter, when the herd comes. In general, it is permitted to do it after a year or two, or even later – when you're able to . . .

The parting ceremony forty/fifty days after death
The women cut a part of their plaits, and singe them a bit. The hair is then put together with the stick (*šumləŋ jŭχ*) where the days are marked up to the fiftieth into the box of the death doll. Now we made the funeral repast on the fifth day and then made the death doll . . . On the fiftieth day the stick calendar together with the women's hair and teal's feathers (head, wings and feet) are burnt on the

25. E. K. Rebas', b. 1942, Ust'-Voĭkar, 2000.
26. V. A. Sevli, Ust'-Voĭkar, 2000.

fire, near which a [tiny model of a] *chum* is made. For a man the *chum* is made from five sticks, for a woman from four. Fish oil and drink are sprinkled five times on the fire.

Getting the dead ready for the grave

At burial, drawings are made with coal on the deceased's boat of *tiləś* (moon), *χătʌ* (sun) and *śiśki* (a small bird). On the deceased's face they put a *veš lopəs* (mask), made from a cloth with beads instead of eyes. On every finger a ring is put. Then mittens are put on the hands. The dead is put on the plank bed, feet towards the door, in the middle. A table is put near the feet. It is kept in the house for three days. A woman is dressed by women, a man by men. The best clothes are put on. The clothes in which the person died are taken off and brought to a special place above a cliff. The dead is washed in the house. Everything the dead used to wear and carry is put into the grave. The bear tusks, the hone, some metal sheets are taken off the belt as keepsakes.

Objects put in the grave

The belt along with the knife and axe is put near the dead, the gun is cut up into pieces and the rifle butt is put into the grave. Nearby is put a cap with the deceased's initials or a notch, which is made when shouting out his name. The strings are tied, everyone is dressed in women's winter fur coats and covered over with a blind winter fur coat. Underneath is put a pair of hides. On the clothes some people make cuts: for example, the heel of fur boots is pierced through. For a reindeer-breeder the harness is left near the grave and two or three reindeer are slaughtered. The sledge is put above the grave, and the harness is put into the grave. Notches are made with an axe on the trees in the graveyard.

The meal in the graveyard

The meat is cooked and eaten at the grave, and given to those who helped, and the rest is brought home. The grave is not dug beforehand, only when the deceased has been brought there, for another relative would not "get" into the pit left open.[27]

Separation rites begin the funeral process. Pëtr Nikitich said in 2002 in Ovolyngort that a deceased person stayed at home for three days after death, lying in bed, feet towards the door. Women lay out a female corpse, and men take care of the men. When Pëtr Nikitich was once asked about washing facilities, he joked, saying: "A Khanty man is washed only twice, when he is born and after he dies."[28] He said that the clothes in which the person died are collected and put in a special place. "In every village there is such a place, for example on the beach. The clothes are taken and hung in a tree. They will stay there."[29] The deceased is dressed using his own clothes. Some of his clothes can be given to neighbours; men's shirts, for example, are given to men, but it is not allowed to give pants to anybody, to the living or dead. The best clothes of the deceased are selected for him before burial. He will have a new shirt, belt, knife sheath, gaiters and fur coat. A beautiful decorated woman's coat is put on a man. For big funerals a mask would be

27. Pëtr Nikitich Longortov, Ovolyngort, 2004.
28. Pëtr Nikitich Longortov, Ovolyngort, 2001.
29. Pëtr Nikitich Longortov, Ovolyngort, 2002.

made for the dead: a cloth in which eyes were marked out with embroidered pearls. A ring was put on every finger.

The deceased also gets tools and utensils, which are put in the grave. An axe and his cup with his initials will be given to him. Clothes may also have a mark put on for him. If he is a reindeer herder, a couple of reindeer are given to him and a sledge which is struck through with an axe.[30] According to Balzer the deceased might be carried from the house in a ritual order: through the window. A knife may be stuck in the threshold after the body is removed.[31] The grave should not be made earlier, because another person might die during the time when a grave is open. These kind of protective ritual acts are known among some other Finno-Ugric peoples. Edgar Saar describes the putting of clothes in the coffin, completing the grave house and the way the coffin is put into a grave in Azovy.[32] All phases were done according to ritual rules in order to please the deceased and spirits.

In Ust'-Voĭkar on the burial day of Yuriĭ Ozelov's grandmother a cow was slaughtered near the spirit hut. The skull of the cow was hung on the birch growing near the sacred storehouse at a height of a couple of metres or so. Blood was brushed inside and outside the walls of the family house. People explained the idea of the ritual: "When our grandmother died, that side was brushed, a corner of the house, and there [in west side of the house] a bit of blood was dropped. Then we also brushed the wall inside. I think that they dropped a bit on all the walls. They said that after that nightly spirits would not visit us."[33] In Vershina Voĭkar a cross is drawn on the back wall of the house in the blood of a sacrificed reindeer. It protects the house against visitation by the dead.

The reindeer, cow or ram offered at the fifty- or forty-day memorial ceremony, when the soul is conducted to the Otherworld, may be an offering to the deities to whom hierarchically weaker spirits cannot go without bringing something. But the memorial blood-offering is not only done for higher deities but for the dead too. Pëtr Nikitich mentions in his description of burial customs that the deceased wanted a reindeer to be offered in the graveyard. The dead need food, transport vehicles and reindeer, because they live in the Otherworld or in the graveyard, the village of the dead, as they did in this world. In a grave of a reindeer herder in Vershina Voĭkar, three reindeer, male and female, actually the whole team, were slaughtered along with the favourite dog of the departed.[34] All three reindeer were strangled with a lasso whilst being struck to death with a particular birch club designed for slaughtering reindeer. The hide, head with horns, and a piece of red cloth were hung on the birch near the grave. The first cervical vertebra was hung on the same tree along with the skull.[35]

30. Pëtr Nikitich Longortov, Ovolyngort, 2002.
31. Balzer 1980: 81.
32. Saar 1998: 32–3.
33. Yuriĭ Semënovich Ozelov, Ust'-Voĭkar, 2000.
34. Andreĭ A. Sevli, Vershina Voĭkar, 2000.
35. Martin Rebas', Vershina Voĭkar, 2000.

Relatives put the most important things for the dead in the Otherworld in the grave or near it: a wooden scoop and a wooden plate. For a reindeer herder a sledge is placed near the grave and a guide staff for the dog harness, for a hunter the end of a gun and for a fisherman an oar. Two signs must be made on all the objects. When a cloth is brought to the dead, it has to be hung on a four- or five-leaf-tree (for women and men respectively), for example on a birch branch before it is left in the graveyard.

In Vershina Voïkar people said that metal objects should not be given to the dead: only the back side of a gun can be left for them, and metal parts are taken away from a male belt, but bone parts left. We saw a metal bowl which was used all the time in a graveyard, but it did not belong among those things which were left for the dead. On the other hand, bicycles and parts of a moped, and even a wrecked motorcycle, were placed near some graves in Ust'-Voïkar and in Yamgort. The explanation was:

> All the time he drove a motorcycle. He bought it and never wanted to get off it. Well, where is there to drive in our village? From house to house he drove. Then he died and the motorcycle was brought here. It might be that he travels in the Otherworld. Here he could drive so little.[36]

Both the signs made on wooden objects and wrecking vehicles to make them unusable are simply explained by the fear of robberies. There has to be a sign which shows that spirits will take a person who tries to use the object or travel with the vehicle of a dead person. But the custom of making signs in things intended for the dead is inherited from old rituals. Tools and equipment of the dead are destroyed because the order of the Otherworld is opposite to the order of the human world. The things usable in this world would be useless in the other and vice versa.

BOAT BURIAL

Zoya Sokolova discovered twenty years ago that the Khanty buried their dead in boat-like coffins.[37] This tradition has not disappeared – the Khanty living in Shuryshkary often bury their dead in coffins resembling boats, called *kaldanka*, the bow and stern of which are sawn off. The boat is the main means of transport among the Khanty. One Khanty man joked that a Khanty is born with oar in hand, hence in the Otherworld a Khanty "sails" in his own boat fastened with the roots of a cedar tree. Myths relate that the river to the Otherworld is the world river, which among various Khanty groups is manifest as the main river of the area in question.[38] Among the Northern Khanty, the largest river is the Ob'. Though the coffin is used in many villages, the traditional boat funeral is valued:

---

36. V. A. Sevli, Ust'-Voïkar, 2000.
37. Sokolova 1975 (1974): 166.
38. Barkalaya 2002b: 6.

> A Khanty should not be left to be forgotten in a coffin like the Russians. They have to be put in a *kaldanka* boat, legs pointing to the prow of the boat and head to the aft. The dead will sail to the Otherworld with legs in the front of the boat.[39]

In recent years many have been buried in Voïkar by putting them in an open-board coffin:

> Now none of the dead are buried in *kaldanka* boats, because these boats are not made any more in Ust'-Voïkar, and, in general, nobody makes them in the villages nearby. For travelling or the burying of the dead the boats are ordered from Gorki village. Fishermen order *budarka*-boats from the same place.[40]

However, when Oleg was conversing in Vershina Voïkar with a Khanty who was making hay in a meadow near the river, he found two *kaldanka* boats, which were overturned on stakes made of poles. The boats were new, well tarred, untouched; it was clear that they would not be used soon. When Oleg asked if the man made boats to sell, he said that it was not his occupation. Nobody in Vershina Voïkar had made boats for at least thirty years.

> I bought these boats in Gorki. It is about 100 km from here. Well, it is more . . . They still make them there, there are masters there. In fact, I have one which I go to, over there, near the shore. But these boats are not for travelling. I bought and brought them for me and my brother, so that we would at least be buried in a respectable way. The fact is that we are already aged. My brother is even older than I am. Well, they also bury in those. Today, many are put in the grave this way. A coffin resembling a Russian one is knocked up, using boards, but it is not closed. I wish [to be buried] in the same way as our ancestors . . .[41]

The prow and back board of a *kaldanka* is cut in Ust'-Voïkar and Vershina Voïkar. After that it is left near the grave. A boat with a body is left on a special platform, which is 20 to 25 cm high. At burial, a little bird is drawn on the outside of the *kaldanka* coffin with soot or coal taken from a fire. The bird flies between the moon and sun in the direction of the sun. The sun is a guide for the dead and it is connected to the fifty- or forty-day memorial ceremony. The position of the dead in the graveyard is east–west; the head is towards the east and a window (*još-vŭs*) is made on the grave hut. If the dead died drowning, his hut is dug half into the earth and over it there will be his boat, which he used when he lived, upside down. The boat will have been cut in two pieces.

In Yamgort and Ovgort on the Synya river, the boat with its body is put into a half-metre deep hole. A couple of Khanty men discussed these kind of differences between burial customs with Oleg:

39. A. A. Rebas', Ust'-Voïkar, 2000.
40. Yuriĭ Semënovich Ozelov, Ust'-Voïkar, 2000.
41. S. A. Alyaba, Vershina Voïkar, 2000.

Y. S. O.: They do not bury like this in all places. They pray and bury in different ways. Where Aunt Fenya lives, a man was buried in a *kaldanka*, but it was done in the Russian graveyard. He came from some other place. He was a Khanty, but not local. Maybe from Kazym? There are different Khanty. How do we bury a person? We build a hut, but they dig it a little bit under the earth. But you visited Yamgort last time. Like there.

A. A. S.: Maybe Aunt Fenya's man was from Yamgort?

J. S. O.: No-o. Not from Yamgort. Maybe from Kazym. He was not local.[42]

These kinds of discussions show the need to maintain traditional ways of burial. Pëtr Nikitich emphasised that nowadays there are only a few people who know what to do and what it means. One of his relatives was a reindeer herder, and according to Pëtr among the herders there are still men who know old customs.

THE PARTING FEAST OF THE SOUL ON THE FIFTIETH OR FORTIETH DAY

Souls of the deceased are after death in a state of transition, which could be characterised as "not here, not there". At that time they have not left their home as they could not yet find their place in the Otherworld. On the fiftieth or fortieth day (for men and women, respectively), the soul is conducted to the Otherworld. The parting feast is the main remembrance ceremony for the deceased. Though the ritual is mentioned in the ethnographic literature, there are no thorough descriptions of it. Hence, we were glad to take part in a fortieth-day feast in Ust'-Voĭkar. In Vershina Voĭkar, Ust'-Voĭkar, Vosyakhovo and Muzhi, people said that on the fortieth or fiftieth day after death or during the funeral they slaughtered reindeer or other animals at the grave.

The parting feast of E. P. Penzelova, who had been buried in the graveyard of Ust'-Voĭkar, was at her home at 12.00–13.00 hours. On the table her *ittərma* lay in its box and partook of the generous meal for the relatives. Only the relatives come to the funeral repast. The oldest man or woman is the head of the ritual. On the fifth (fourth) day the death doll is made and put into an open box. The death doll is kept at home for five (four) years, and thereafter it is lifted up to the attic or brought to the forest. The days up to the fiftieth (fortieth) are marked on a special calendar stick, *šumʌəŋ jŭχ*, which is put in the box of the death doll to measure the time of mourning. The box should be put on the table so that the sunlight does not reach it: "Rays of sun should not touch the *appa*, because the *ittərma* already wants to go to the land of the dead."[43] A remembrance fire burns at home from the day of the funeral up to the fifty/forty-day ceremony. The remembrance fire, an oil lamp, is lit by one of the relatives by taking fire from the burial fire. If the oil runs out, the lamp is filled so that the fire is not quenched. The one who lit the fire extinguishes it at the end of the mourning phase.

---

42. Yuriĭ Semënovich Ozelov and Andreĭ A. Sevli, Ust'-Voĭkar, 2000.
43. E. I. Rebas', Ust'-Voĭkar, 2000.

From every relative a lock of hair is taken. If the person dies in winter, the hairs are kept till spring. In the spring a teal (*Anas querquedula* or *Anas crecca*), a wigeon (*Anas penelope*) or a pintail (*Anas acuta*) – i. e. a grey duck of the kinds which are called "Khanty ducks" – is shot down for the ritual.[44] It was said that female relatives of the dead do not tie their two plaits hanging on their back for forty/fifty days, because "the road for the dead is still open"; during normal times the two plaits are joined with hair ribbons, "fake plaits". All the women put on their scarves at home before the last meal on the fortieth day. After the parting ceremony the daughter of the female departed collects the scarves and takes them to the grave. There she hangs them on the branches of a broad-leaved tree, usually a birch. As compensation she divides the scarves which belonged to the deceased among the women.

At noon relatives and near ones came to the house for the remembrance ceremony. At the forty-day ceremony a duck has to be cooked. When women prepared the duck, they collected all its feathers and down, which were to be used at the departure of the soul. At the meal all the participants have to taste the duck meat. All the bones have their special names. The breast bone, χŏn, "boat", is given to the most important guest. When the duck has been eaten, all that is left is collected on a plate. Bones and left-overs are put together with the feathers and down and hair of female relatives, which have been saved for forty days and kept in the *appa* together with the death doll.

At 16.30 the women organised in front of Pavel's home a ritual, which is called *upit šup uśʌa*, in which they built a small, 10–20 cm high ʌiʌ χot, "soul hut" (a tiny *chum* for the ʌiʌ-soul) for the deceased near the door of the house: four (for a man five) sticks were put up as supportive poles of the *chum* and birch bark was put on it. The duck bones, feathers and down and women's hair were put into this *chum*. A small fire was lit in order to burn everything properly. When the fire went out the women began to lament. Usually women lament at home only for funerals, when the departed is carried away from the house and when an outsider comes to a house where there is a dead person. When women lament near the remembrance fire, they cover their heads and faces with scarves. After lamenting, the faces are washed near the fire and a ritual meal is held outdoors at the same place. For the fire for a woman, there will be four (five for a man) pieces of food. Though dogs ate those pieces, it was said that they "were left for birds".

After the parting feast of the soul, the women went back to the house, untied their plaits and gave all four hair ribbons (*sevkel*, fake plaits, which contain three locks) to the daughter of the deceased, who took them with the scarves to the graveyard. If the deceased is a man, all the women give five *sevkel*. After this ceremony women retie their hair and put on the new scarf given to them. Only the daughter of the dead did not tie her plaits for four months. She has a scarf like in the parting feast. At 17.00 all the participants sat at the table again and continued the remembrance meal. The soul of the dead had already left the house.

44. Teal (*χenši),* wigeon (*vüjǝv*) and pintail (*kŭrek*) are grey ducks or "Khanty ducks" (*χănti vasịt*); black ducks are "Russian ducks" (*rŭś vasịt*).

Burning the soul hut at the parting feast of the soul on the fortieth day, Ust'-Voĭkar.
– Video picture by A.-L. Siikala 2000

In the parting feast, the shared meal of duck meat and the burning of duck bones and hair locks of relatives have symbolic meaning connected to the soul concepts. A little bird is painted in charcoal on *kaldanka* boats between the sun and moon marks. It represents the soul flying to the Otherworld. The fourth soul, ʌiʌ, the breath soul, is believed to live in a person's head and especially in the hair; it has a form of a little bird. The concepts of the breath soul seem to be behind burning pieces of hair and remnants of the duck seem to represent the boat for the trip to the Otherworld.

Remembrance rituals in graveyards

IN TWO GRAVEYARDS

On the Synya and Voĭkar rivers graveyards are situated 2–4 km from villages, often behind a river or brook. Orthodox graveyards are public places, which have their own landscape schemes, decorations and customs. So too do the Khanty graveyards, where people remember their late relatives, though they are not open to everybody. It is possible to visit them only with a specialist in ritual traditions. The following descriptions of two visits to Voĭkar graveyards reveal the ritual scheme and rules for behaviour in the remembrance rituals.

167

We went to the Vershina Voïkar graveyard with a group of Khanty and Komi people. The graveyard there is a very beautiful place: on both sides of the central path there are small houses for the dead, covered by turf and circled by sacrificial hides hanging from trees, sledges and kitchen utensils for the dead and the visitors. From the middle row of houses other paths lead to the right and left. The graveyard looks like a small village of the dead. The remembrance ritual was led by Anna Ivanovna Rebas', who wanted to recall memories of Anton, her sister's son, whom she had raised. Anna Ivanovna was accompanied by women from Vershina Voïkar. The women performed all the rites calmly and without any unnecessary discussions. They seemed to know the traditional customs, which today are not known to all Khanty. We were especially requested to follow the rules of behaviour in the graveyard and we did so by imitating Anna Ivanovna and other women. The remembrance ceremony was as follows:

A path to the graveyard from the river is not clearly visible. A person who wants to go to the place has to know the route. There were a couple of branches across the path; they prevent the souls of the dead from leaving the graveyard. Hence, the path should be opened by a person with the right knowledge.

When we came to the graveyard, all the participants in the remembrance rite went round the graves in the direction of the sun and after knocking at the hatches of the *još-vŭs* (*još*, "hand" + *vŭs*, "hole") windows on the graves, opened them and said: "I have come." After that the women and men began to do their tasks. At first, Anna Ivanovna treated the spirits of her relatives to cigarettes. This she had to do though she does not smoke and does not even like the smell of tobacco. She put an open box of cigarettes near the window of the grave of her nephew Anton, whom she especially wanted to remember. After she had lit the cigarettes she also gave them to other relatives, putting them on the shelf in front of the grave windows. Then she washed the dead: she poured a little water near all the graves of relatives. At the same time, a low table with food and vodka was laid in front of Anton's grave. Other women made tables for their dead, sat near them and began to talk with the dead. Anna Ivanovna talked mostly with Anton.

While the women washed and served the dead, the men made a fire. Every person had to put at least one log on. The one who lit the fire had to put some butter or fish oil (a better solution) in his mouth and squirt it five times on the fire. Volodya Konev, who lit the fire, squirted vegetable oil brought mistakenly by Martyn's son. "It should have been fish oil, I already said that. But, good, this also works."[45] Whoever had came for the first time to the graveyard had to mark a tree with an axe.

When the tea and fish were ready, the table was taken from Anton's grave to another place, where the shared table was laid. People talked with their dead relatives and friends and after that shared a meal with them. At first there was fish and fish soup and vodka to drink. Everybody poured vodka from his bottle for the others. But it was not allowed to offer thanks at the table, because the meal was shared with the dead. After the meal we had tea and discussed different topics. After the remembrance table was cleaned and kitchen utensils washed,

---

45. Anna Ivanovna Rebas', b. 1933, Vershina Voïkar, 2000.

Anna Ivanovna remembers her sister's son in the Vershina Voĭkar graveyard.
– Video picture by A.-L. Siikala 2000

the women sat near the main grave in this remembrance ritual, covered their heads and lamented for about ten minutes.

Before we left, everyone went round the graves, knocked on the roofs and closed the windows, saying: "I am leaving." The stand for the pots at the fire place has to be left in its place. Omitting this rule leads to people's starvation. The fire will feel offended if it is stamped on or extinguished with water. The embers can merely be spread a little. When we left the graveyard and came to the path leading to the graveyard, everybody had to shout three times "*Is χŏr jua! Jua! Jua!*" ("My shadow, come, come, come!"). The one who came first to the graveyard was the last to leave. She or he closes the graveyard, taking two branches or two young trees and placing them over the path. This time, Martyn's son closed the path.

When returning to the village we visited *Aj χăɭaś*, "little graveyard", of Vershina Voĭkar. *Aj χalaś* is situated behind a brook. The dead placed in the grove are small children who did not yet have teeth. It is not permitted to bury them near older people. There are also no remembrance ceremonies connected with them: "They do not drink vodka and do not eat fish." After the burial, parents seldom come to the children's graveyard. The graves were around a big "mother broadleaved tree", which does not have sap, only tears, said the women.

In Vosyakhovo we took part in a remembrance ritual with the families of

Nurislam Mutalabovich Magadeev and Anatoliĭ Lukich Tynzyanov, who is related to Magadeev's wife. Magadeev is a Tatar, but his wife Ol'ga a Khanty. Because Ol'ga said that she does not know all the rites, she asked her friend Nadezhda along because she knows "what to do". We walked but Anatoliĭ with his brother's sons came by boat, because we had to cross a brook. The graveyard is situated about 4 km from the village, but the water route was much longer.

We had to search out the path to the graveyard, because Ol'ga was not sure of its whereabouts. Her brother Anatoliĭ knew more, but thought it better to keep silent at first. Nadezhda led the ritual. She had not been in a graveyard for a while, but remembered what to do there. Still she omitted some of the acts, for example putting the table near the grave for the one remembered and lamenting. First the women changed their clothes.[46] Nadezhda had brought a Khanty dress for Ol'ga also, because "women have to wear *jernas* in the graveyard". After dressing, Nadezhda said: "OK, now we can make tea." The rite began:

> Oleg, who is a Komi and usually treated by the Khanty like one of their guys, was asked to make and light the fire. When he asked, should he squirt oil on the fire, Ol'ga said, "Well . . . only relatives do that when they light the fire". Nadezhda, in turn, was of the opinion that the one who lights the fire should squirt the oil. The problem was that nobody had remembered to bring any oil. She consented to taking grease from a tinned meat box. The women brought water for washing the dead and it was poured three times near all the graves of relatives. The cigarettes were given only to two or three of the dead.
>
> The table was made between the graves of relatives, not for every one, as happened in Vershina Voĭkar graveyard and in the Ust'-Voĭkar *ura*. Oleg was criticised, because he put an unopened vodka bottle on the table: it should be open for the dead. Oleg and Anna marked a tree, but because the axe was left in the boat we used a knife. Everybody had to put logs on the fire. Nadezhda said that the dead would discuss the visit: "When people leave the graveyard, the dead discuss and boast: 'To me, well, came my daughter, and brought logs', or 'To me there came such and such people, they brought logs and remembered.'" Magadeev commented: "Well, after you die we shall see what you are talking about." Ol'ga, who supported Nadezhda, retorted: "Well, everybody has to put at least a small branch on the fire. We do not know, but old people say that the dead gather after a remembrance ceremony and talk about the visitors."
>
> Vodka was poured by the one who laid the table: at first he poured one glass and then put the glass and bottle on the table. Then he poured another glass for himself and drank it. After that he poured some for everybody sitting around the table, serving them in the direction of sun. It is a terrible offence to offer thanks at the table, for example for a cup of tea or a piece of fish. "The dead are serving us, the living."
>
> Anatoliĭ pointed out some graves which, unlike the others, were dug a little into the earth. He said that drowned people were buried like that. Ol'ga did not agree; she said that was done only in Ovgort and Yamgort. Nadezhda thought that the different graves might not be for local people but those coming from Yamgort

---

46. *jernas* is a Khanty women's dress.

Konstantin Sergeevich and Varvara Pavlovna remember a relative who disappeared in the Afghan War in the Ovolyngort ura. – Photograph by A.-L. Siikala 2001

or somewhere else. This explanation did not seem right, because in Yamgort the graves are covered by pieces of turf. Actually, such graves were also found in the Vosyakhovo graveyard. Magadeev showed us, and said that the buried person collected the turf for his grave himself. But the grave was not made according to the local tradition. The grave had four levels of turf cover as in Yamgort, where women get four and men five turf covers. The boats on the low graves showed that Anatoliĭ was right. In one of the boat graves there was a man who had drowned and the boat on the grave was the one in which he was at the time of the accident. The bottom of the boat had been broken through with an axe.

Anatoliĭ closed the graveyard and Ol'ga said: "The one who is late in coming, is the last to leave", but Nadezhda corrected her: "No, the one who came first will shut the graveyard." When we left Nadezhda shouted: "*Is χŏr, jua, jua, jua!*" After that she mentioned the names of all the people who had left the graveyard "*Is χŏr Jura, jua, jua, jua! . . .*" After exchanging some words with Anatoliĭ she added, laughing, also the name of his dog running around: "*Is χŏr Mushka, jua, jua, jua!*" If somebody cannot call his or her shadow, for example a small child, a drunken person or an animal, other people have to do so.

Thus the graveyard is a magically closed area which can be opened by a ritual expert: he or she removes the branches blocking the path thither, and the visitors progress in order towards the graves. The dead are awoken by tapping on the graves and calling them by name. The grave windows are opened and gifts presented to those being remembered, in the form of food, tobacco and liquor. Food and drink are placed before the grave huts and both the dead and those commemorating them may partake of them. The visitor sits beside the departed, speaking to him and discussing matters with him. There are hearths in the graveyard for visitors to prepare shared meals. Fish is cooked and a table laid. All visitors partake, and the departed are the hosts. Much behaviour is proscribed; for example, it is not permitted to thank anyone, since the departed are the givers of the food. The dead may be remembered after the meal too, with laments forming part of the ritual. After the meal, the graves and graveyard are cleaned up, the departed are bidden farewell and the grave windows closed. The visitors depart in the same order as they came. Each person calls his or her own shadow soul. Last comes the person who opened the graveyard, who also closes the path to the graveyard, to prevent the departed from wandering from the area.

THE VILLAGE OF THE LOST

Graveyards are not only memorial places for dead relatives. Clothes and possessions of people who have been burned, drowned or lost have a memorial site with *ura* huts, for remembrance. In Ovolyngort we saw two *ura* groves in the forest. The one, belonging to one of the families, was about 700 metres from the village, the other, belonging to a neighbouring family, about 2 km distant. Paths leading to *ura*s were not well marked. A person had to know where the holy groves were in order to find them. *Ura* groves resemble graveyards in a miniature form. All dead relatives had their own miniature *ura*, a small house standing on a pole. Men had higher *ura*s (about 130 cm from the earth) than women. "You see, man is over woman. As a death doll of a man is put in the attic, so also in the *ura* the men are over the women."[47]

Making a memorial hut with clothes and possessions of the dead is based on soul conceptions. One of the souls is buried in the *ura*, and the dead cannot go around after that. Pëtr Nikitich said that an *ura* can be made at any time when it is permitted to make a sacrifice. A reindeer, ram or cock might be slaughtered, but not a cow or pig. When the *ura* is constructed, the sacrifice is carried out and the *još-vŭs*, the opening, is smeared with blood. A *porχa*, an image of the deceased wrapped in a shirt or dress they had owned, is put in the *ura*. For a man it is sewn of the hide of a young reindeer. A woman's *porχa* is like a woman's coat, sewn like a doll. Pëtr Nikitich emphasised that a *porχa* is not an *ittərma*, it is just a represention of the dead, the one who should be remembered in the grove: "If you go there, you should have vodka and something to eat with you, because the dead are remembered there. But, of course, you can remember them in the usual graveyard too. But if you do not make this kind of *χăʌa*, the soul will wander around and disturb relatives."[48]

Oleg visited Ust'-Voĭkar in 1997 with the Swedish researchers, Lars-Gunnar Larson and Söder Thornberg, but could not visit the local *ura* grove. Hence, he agreed to go with his Khanty friends to visit the "village of the lost people". The mother and stepfather of one of the visitors had drowned

---

47. Yuriĭ Semënovich Ozelov, Ust'-Voĭkar, 2000.
48. Pëtr Nikitich Longortov, Ovolyngort, 2001.

in 1997. According to local rumour the catastrophe happened because the stepfather had given a sabre from a holy storehouse to a museum, which may have been in Salekhard or in Muzhi. After a year the stepfather drowned and the mother died of something else. According to local belief the drowned often take their favourite child or grandchild. The family was afraid that in two years the mother would take away one of the relatives. Her children and grandchildren were not allowed to play near water. When Oleg was in Ust'-Voĭkar in 1997, the memorial day of the mother took place on 24 August at the grave of the stepfather. The stepfather was remembered at home on 25 August, though people were of the opinion that in this case the remembrance should have been done at the grave. The son made an *ura* for his mother on the main memorial day, the fortieth day from the death. Nowadays the family came to the *ura* in order to remember the parents.

The son of the drowned parents wanted to take with him a duck, but then he decided that it would take too long to cook a duck because we had to go to Vosyakhovo. Instead of a duck he took tinned meat and fish. The duck has a special ritual meaning, as shown for example in the ritual of the fiftieth- or fortieth-day memorial. The *ura* grove of Ust'-Voĭkar was different from some others we had seen. Instead of miniature huts it had normal graves, but of course without the bodies in them. The hut structures were larger than was described before: 1.5 metres or more. Only one *ura*, which belonged to the uncle of another visitor, was of a smaller size, at 70 cm x 70 cm, and it was placed on a metre-high stump. When Oleg asked why it is not like the others, men said that at the time of burial they did not have suitable material in the form of long boards. "We do not have such trees, all the boards have to be brought here." Especially women's grave structures were as in a graveyard: it is put in a usual type of deck, which is about 20 to 25 cm high. Only the grave structures of the men were put on holes; usually there were four of them, or on four supporting horizontal poles, which were nailed on four trees at a height of 60–100 cm. There were many new grave structures. The old ones were not taken care of. Men said that once it is made nobody is allowed to touch it afterwards.

The remembrance ritual went on as in graveyards. Men made tea and a meal of fish and meat. The graves were tapped and the *još-vŭs* windows opened in order to waken the dead. On leaving, the visitors tapped the huts and said good-bye. Food, an open vodka bottle and a full glass were put on a table in front of the small window of the hut, where also the offering was made. Men set the table in front of the mother's grave. Oleg lit the fire and had to put grease in his mouth and squirt it five times on the fire. The fire was served five times with vodka instead of grease. Because Oleg was for the first time in the *ura* grove, he made a mark on a tree with an axe. When the food was ready and had been put on the table near the grave, the men moved the table to another place, where the dead one was remembered. Because Oleg had the bottle, he had to pour for everybody in the ritual order: the one who is serving has to drink the first glass and then pour for everybody in the circle, selecting people according to the direction of the sun. He takes the last glass and after that the bottle has to be put on the table for a pause. A person who does not want to drink can just hold the glass. The difference between a remembrance feast and the usual drinking spree is that in the graveyard it is not possible to offer thanks or to express any hopes.

All kinds of matters were discussed at the table: the dead, their habits, events in life – all the matters of life and death. Men talked with Oleg about spirits and omens and discussed the objects around in the *ura*. Omens came up at the moment when a man who was tired fell down and began to sleep. His companion shook him a long time and tried to wake him up. When Oleg asked him to let the man sleep, he answered that in this kind of place you should not sleep. The Komi have similar beliefs: if a person falls asleep in a graveyard, they will not live even a year. Later, the men explained the cause of the prohibition: if someone falls asleep in a graveyard, the dead are calling him to themselves. When the meal was over, the men cleared the place, checked that everybody was with them and asked their shadows to come with them.

Rules and obligations in contact with the dead

It seems that visiting relatives in graveyards and in *ura* groves follows the same pattern. The only difference between memorial rites in the graveyard and in the *ura* relates to the possibility of visiting the place. It is possible to visit the graveyard every day, but the *ura* only once a week.[49] In visiting the dead it is not allowed to step over a grave or to blow at the fire when it is lit. The small windows of graves cannot be left open. A person has to go around the graves of his own relatives or possibly the whole graveyard or *ura* in the direction of the circling sun before "closing" them. The one who comes first closes the graveyard or *ura* with two branches of a tree, which are put across the path, and leaves last. When people leave they have to shout three times: "*Is χŏr, jua, jua, jua!*" in order to take their shadow with them in case it has liked being in the graveyard or is interested in conversing with the dead.

There are also rules which have to be attended to in serving the dead and in shared meals with them in the graveyard and *ura*. Conversing with the dead, telling of his or her life and habits, lamenting, and discussing serious life experiences create a close contact with the dead and lead to a situation in which the dead should feel himself or herself honoured. The rules and obligations guarantee that the dead and spirits in the graveyard, for example the spirit of fire, are not violated. They prevent the possible escape of the dead and ensure passage for the souls of visitors from a dangerous place back to their home.

The passages of souls and continuation of the family

The main scheme of ritual process is the same in different northern Shuryshkary villages: protective rituals, preparing the deceased for burial, collecting and producing equipment and objects for the grave, the building of the grave

49. N. A. Ozelova, b. 1974 in Ust'-Voïkar, Vosyakhovo, 2000.

or grave boat, burial, sacrificial rites, rites of mourning, the parting feast and remembrance rites. But the ritual acts and their supposed meanings vary. Similar variation can be found also in comparing detailed descriptions of Tegy, Kazeem and Azovy burials given by Marjorie Balzer.[50] The local variation in rites is typical for oral cultures. At the same time, the "right" way of doing things is continuously discussed and negotiated.

The complexity of burial process depends on the notions concerning the human being and the understanding of a peron's future after death. The souls of the deceased will have a different fate after death. The first soul *is, is-χŏr*, "shadow soul", stays in the graveyard with all the dead relatives and friends. The second soul, *urt*, will go down the river to the Otherworld, and the third soul stays in clothes and in possessions for some time. The deceased has to be equipped for staying in the graveyard, a village of the dead, and for the Otherworld. The fourth soul, *ʌiʌ*, the breath soul, will be reincarnated. In a fifty- or forty-day ceremony it flies by means of a complicated ceremony to heaven between the sun and moon. In the parting ritual, actions are based on an idea of the Otherworld journey of the breath soul. The measures to help the third and fourth soul to find their place also has to be taken into consideration. All the souls have their special characteristics and can be dangerous to relatives. Hence, Khanty burial rituals are not a simple scheme for a soul going to the Otherworld, as it has been described, but a complex ritual for the transitions of the several souls of the deceased. The protective acts are important in all the phases of the funeral process and the remembrance of the death. Hence it is not easy to explain meanings of single ritual acts in these processes. The ideas and the explanation of the rituals are discussed by people who have overseen the long process. Sometimes only a shaman or experts know the meanings of such symbolic acts. The actions in a complicated ritual process are connected to each other: they intermix and give power to each other. They are not thought about, they are simply done.

Marjorie Balzer has emphasised that funeral rituals maintain the cultural sense of "self". Because faith in reincarnation helps the Khanty to perceive themselves as an ongoing social group, rituals have value in keeping up social identity.[51] The main place for expressing the continuity of the kin is the graveyard and holy groves with *uras*. Remembrance rituals contain a great number of rules and obligations which shape the success of this continuation.

50. Balzer 1980; Saar 1998.
51. Balzer 1980: 78–9.

11 The reawakening of shamanic rituals

Did the Khanty have shamans?

The shaman is the problem-solver of ancient Khanty myths. He is also the best adviser in the crises caused by spirits and a functionary of common rituals even today. Researchers have nonetheless argued over the existence of Khanty shamanism. Lack of a proper shaman dress and equipment and especially of a common name for the shaman among the Khanty has been one of the main negative arguments.[1] Kulemzin noted that in Vakh, Vasyugan and the Middle Ob' the functions of healing, fortune-telling, dreaming and so forth were taken care of by different persons who were called by different names.[2] Sokolova, in her article "A Survey of Ob-Ugrian Shamanism", lists words referring to Khanty and Mansi shamanism in some of the publications:

> Indeed, the Khanty and Mansi have no uniform terminology to denote a person who scholars call shamans. Among the Khanty people *terden-khoi* or *tarten-khoi* means sorcerer, a foreteller, a wiseman (Karjalainen 1927: 249); *nait*, a magician; *sem-volyan-kho*, a contemplator; *chipänen-ku*, sorcerer (Karjalainen 1927: 252); *toteb, tocheb, tadyb*, a shaman (Georgi 1779: 74); *multe-ku*, a magician, or a man communicating with spirits (Kulemzin 1979: 61); *chirta-ku*, a shaman (Lukina *et al.* 1975: 170–1); *mant'e-ku*, a narrator; while among the Mansi *kojpyn nyalt* is a shaman; *valtakhten-pupi* is a summoner of spirits; *potrtan-pupi*, a foreteller; *penge-khum*, one telling fortunes with the axe.[3]

Most of these words are from the Eastern Khanty dialect, as for example the ending *khoi* or *ku* ("man") shows. *Toteb, tadyb* are loans from Nenets. Khanty *nait*, sometimes *näjt-ku* and Mansi *ńajt, ńajt-χum* are Finno-Ugric words found even in Baltic Finnic: Finnish *noita* means a witch but also a person with shamanic abilities.[4] To this list of names *jol*, and *jolta-ko*, "a witch, fortuneteller, a shaman", could be added.[5] Among the Shuryshkary Khanty, the shaman is called *šepən*.

1. Kulemzin 1976: 46, 64, 128.
2. Kulemzin 1976: 46, 64, 128.
3. Sokolova 1989: 155.
4. Siikala 2002a: 343.
5. Kulemzin *et al.* 2006: 93.

In the light of comparative study in Siberian shamanism, the variety of the tasks and names of shamans in one society is a commonplace. In shamanic cultures there are specialists for different functions and becoming a shaman is usually a long process during which a candidate has several titles. Hence, the many names of Khanty shamans represent a common practice in Siberia.

Karjalainen, who has been considered the main author in the research of Khanty religion, assumed that Khanty shamanism varied because the scattered population has been susceptible to influence from neighbouring cultures. He argues that the northern tribes, for example, have adopted the reindeer-breeding of the Nenets.[6] Kulemzin's view is that Khanty shamanism spread in ancient times from southern cultures and included the practices of local witches and fortune-tellers; Khanty shamanism is quite a new phenomenon and does not have a clearly expressed professional character.[7] These opinions, presented also by some other researchers into the early history of Ugric shamanism, are most debatable, because they are not based on religion but on the study of historical materials of an ethnic group. The fact that there is no complete shaman dress among the Khanty, or the idea of the shaman's journey or complex ritual activities, does not prove the case.[8] The picture changes when we look at Siberian shamanism from a comparative perspective.[9] Koryak and Chuckhi shamans do not have a dress, but rather undress like Inuits when shamanising. It is interesting to see that these palaeo-Asian peoples have similarities in their shamanic cult with the Khanty: for example, as a means to achieve ecstasy they use *Amanita muscaria*. The soul flight is not the only way during a séance to present the contact with the spirits – there are other possibilities: discussions with spirits (south-west Siberia: for example Minusa Tatars, Khanty), possession (mid and east Siberia: Yukagirs, Evenks, Yakuts, Manchus, Nanai, Orochi) and ventriloquism (palaeo-Asian peoples: Chuckhi). The séance structures, the position of the shaman and the shaman's tasks vary in different Siberian cultures.[10] The main problem in defining the different religious phenomena as shamanic or non-shamanic is a lack of common understanding of the main features of shamanism. For example, possession is not understood as a shamanic phenomenon even though it belongs to the complicated shamanic séances of Tungus-speaking groups, the Yakuts and Yukagirs.

The concept of shamanism

Shamanism is not a religion as Uno Harva and many early researchers assumed, but a complex of beliefs and rituals connected to different kinds

6. Karjalainen 1918: 563–71.
7. Kulemzin *et al.* 2006: 94.
8. Kulemzin *et al.* 2006: 94–5.
9. See Siikala 1987.
10. Siikala 1987: 303–41.

of religions. Åke Hultkrantz sees as crucial the *activities* of the shaman: "We may now define the shaman as a social functionary who, with the help of guardian spirits, attains ecstasy in order to create a rapport with the supernatural world on behalf of his group members."[11] Anna-Leena Siikala has stressed that ritual practices characteristic of shamanism, the process of ecstatic communication between shaman and representatives of the supranormal, are relatively uniform in Siberia with only a few variations of the basic structure, even though the details vary endlessly. The varying details reflect the position of the shaman in his society, which differed on the basis of social structure and the people's economy.[12] It should also be remembered that in all the cultures concerned there are different types of shamans, fortune-tellers, shamanic healers and so forth. The different themes in the discussion of shamanism depend not only on the disciplines but also on the perspectives: comparative work on shamanic phenomena finds similarities in various cultures when present-day field workers stress specific features of their "own" cultures.[13]

Discussion of the term "shamanism" arose with the new field-work boom. Because the Soviet authorities destroyed shamanism as a social and religious institution of oral Siberian cultures, the modern field workers of post-Soviet Siberia have met with only individual shamans and occasional performances instead of rituals connected to belief systems important in the life of communities encountered by ethnographers in the eighteenth and nineteenth centuries. The contact with post-Soviet shamans has affected the definitions of shamanism. Caroline Humphrey argues that the word "shamanism" gives a misleading impression of a single unified system. Hence she avoids it and talks about *shamanship*.[14] Rane Willerslev, who studies the Yukagirs, sees the shaman as a person with particular skills and powers. He states that the Yukagirs do not recognise any formal office of the shaman.[15] He uses the term shamanship and refers to the definition of Piers Vitebsky: "Like craftsmanship or musicianship, [shamanship] is a talent or inclination as much as an activity and is spread variously among persons who practise it to varying degrees."[16] Rane Willerslev is right when we talk about the Yukagirs and their neighbours the Koryaks and Chuckhi. Anna-Leena Siikala has emphasised the special type of shamanic vocation of these people; it does not have a solid connection to the shaman's own society as among the kin shamans of central, southern and eastern Siberia or the small-group shamans of north-west Siberia.[17] The term shamanship refers to the capability to act as a shaman, while *shamanhood*, used by some researchers, refers to a person's shamanic vocation.[18] In the studies of neo-shamanism, the stressing of the activities of

11. Hultkrantz 1973: 34.
12. Siikala 1987: 320.
13. Hoppál 2007: 3–16.
14. Humphrey 1996: 51.
15. Willerslev 2007: 124.
16. Vitebsky 1993: 22.
17. Siikala 1987: 301–9.
18. Pentikäinen 1998.

individual shamans seems to be convenient. But shamans are not performing for themselves. The shamanship, the ability to act as a shaman, has no value without the audience which calls for the performance. The new terms hide the basis of the shaman's activities: his connection to the society he serves. Hence, the old term "shamanism", even if it is vague and worn out, allows for shamans to be viewed as functionaries in their own societies and for an understanding of the social significance of their activities.

Shamans in Khanty society

After the Revolution the Soviet order tried to wipe indigenous religion out. In the 1930s shamans were sought out, their holy objects were taken and they were punished in jails and camps. In the Longortov family, Vasiliĭ, living in Ovolyngort, had three sons, Ivan, Kuz'ma, and Nikita. All the sons had to remain in jail, Kuz'ma for thirteen years, because they were assumed to practice shamanism.[19] Many other families have similar memories. They gave birth to local legends and memorates concerning people's fates, the destruction of holy objects and punishments of wrongdoers. At the same time shamanic tradition still lived on in secrecy. In particular the camps of reindeer herders, where Khanty and Nenets lived together, were the last refuges of shamanic activities and knowledge. Shamans were consulted when spirits were considered to be causing harm, in sicknesses and other crises.[20]

Oral narratives and early eyewitness accounts show that shamans had a central position in northern Khanty religion. They could communicate with spirits by using various methods. Zoya Sokolova notes that her fieldwork materials from 1957 to 1973 show that on the Lower Ob', Synya, Kunovat, Kazym, Vakh, Northern Sos'va and Lyapin rivers there were shamans who shamanised with a drum. Both men and women could shamanise.[21] In Synya, according to Sokolova, there were shamans who used not only drums, but shamanised also with axes or knives. Hence, a shaman in Yamgort was called Big Axe.[22] We found in our field trips that the best-known shaman in Shuryshkary, Vasiliĭ Petrovich Pugurchin, who lives in the Synya area, shamanises with a drum, axe or sword depending on the situation and purpose of the séance.

In Synya, shamans cured the sick, helped in child-delivery, tried to find the causes of diseases, found out the wishes of the deceased and communicated with spirits who might trouble people. They communicated with spirits in order to know where to hunt or fish and what kind of sacrificial rituals spirits wanted. They took part in funeral rituals and were important participants in common religious ceremonies.[23] Shamans were needed not

19. Rec. in Ovolyngort, 2001.
20. Rec. in Ovolyngort, 2001, 2003.
21. Sokolova 1989: 156.
22. Sokolova 1989: 156.
23. Sokolova 1989: 156–7; rec. in Ovolyngort, 2001.

only in rituals and for curing people but also in producing spirit idols and sacred objects. During our field work these functions of the shamans were mentioned several times. Quite often people complained about the lack of those who know and said that previously shamans knew how to deal with sicknesses and troubles caused by spirits and the dead.

Attitudes to shamans were mixed in the 1900s. Wolfgang Steinitz published a narrative written in Khanty of P. J. Pyrysev, a young Khanty from Yamgort, whom he met in Leningrad in 1937.[24] The first part of the narrative describes shamanising in a holy place, the second tells about the conflict of a shaman and a poor Khanty fisherman who could not pay enough money for the ceremony. The economic difference between Synya reindeer herders and fishermen is sharply defined. At the end of the narrative the shaman, Pilip-iki, and the fisherman, called Nameless, argue. The shaman threatens to help the fisherman no longer. The latter shouts that he never did any good. The shaman had tried to heal his wife and he had given his only reindeer for a sacrifice, but the wife died just after the shaman left.[25]

Local lore shows that some shamans were valued, some were thought to be frightening. In Kazym-Mys there was a shaman called Ivan Nakhrachëv before the Revolution and at the beginning of the Soviet regime. The shaman "went down the river" but later came back. Then the old and sickly shaman lived first in Kazym-Mys but settled afterwards in Lopkhari. A Komi man from Kazym-Mys who had seen the shaman said that he was feared and he played "dirty tricks" with people:

A Komi man passed by here, a fur collector. He gave a white [reindeer] bull to the shaman for fifteen squirrel pelts. Once he came for the pelts – he said he had none. A second time he came and Ivan had nothing and Ivan at night (it was dark, you know) said: "I'll go," he said, "I'll bring the fifteen squirrel pelts. He went off, at night. And they had a belt,[26] they put the game in their bosom into the belt. He untied the belt and dropped the game onto the floor. Well, the collector counted: "OK," he said, "it is exact." He went off. And 15 km up the river from our village there was a settlement. And 5 km further, there was another one. Kolya's ancestors on his mother's side lived there, the Sotruevs. In the nearer settlement he stopped: "I'll leave fifteen squirrels for you. I'll go now and you skin them meanwhile", he said to his assistant. He dropped the pelts from the sack – they were fir twigs! Well, where could the shaman get the squirrels at night? He had probably mastered hypnosis. And that one, the fur collector, one gave him a white reindeer.

And when he escaped from here, there was the place called Panaevsk, maybe you know it? Well, he must have lived there. I studied fur-farming there in the 1950s. Then a local guy told me. "He used to play hide-and-seek with us, the children," he said. "He went behind a storehouse , where actually there was no place to hide at all. And he was gone! But a dog was running here and there after us, playing with us. Well! So, we did not find him. And he comes out: "What,

---

24. Steinitz 1939: 53–79.
25. Steinitz 1939: 72–4.
26. Russian *tasma*, lit. "cloth band" [V. N.].

have you looked at all?" – "Well, you weren't anywhere." – "How is that? But what about the dog which ran around you?"

He drank terribly. He was old, but his health was probably very strong.[27]

The shaman was buried in Lopkhari separately from the main cemetery. There we heard another story of a shaman's grave. In the village, there lived a shaman whose name was Akshamov. He was called Liuli. Before he died he said: "When I die, three days later raise me up: I'll be alive again." In a big fire in Lopkhari, the forest burnt out everywhere. Only the headland, where the shaman's grave was, was untouched:

> They buried him separately, not in the cemetery. There, on that headland. Everybody was afraid to go there. Nobody did raise him from the grave, being afraid, otherwise, maybe, he would still be alive. As for me, I do not believe much in such things, but once they called me there: "Let's go and see!" they said. But I refused. To hell with him . . . Well, I do not believe especially, but, suppose, maybe, there is something in it. Especially since a big fire has taken place here. A really great fire. Everything around Lopkhari burnt out. All the forest. But his grave escaped it. Everything burnt out, but around his grave the forest stays as it was. Nobody visits this grave.
>
> One must not make a funeral repast there, they say. Everybody is afraid. The shamans are buried separately from the cemetery. And the cemetery is there, on the other headland. The old cemetery is also there. All the graves are already collapsed. And not so far from there are old pits [house sites]. It was probably an old village. However, old Lopkhari was in another place. A bit further away. This channel did not exist at all at that time."[28]

According to these stories, shamans were buried separately and remembrance ceremonies were not conducted for them. The reason was fear of shamans. But according to traditional customs shamans were buried like other people. On the other hand, their belongings, costumes, drums and ritual objects, were taken care of in a special way. Zoya Sokolova mentions that on the Synya river, the shaman's dress, drum and drumstick were put in a particular store house 1.5 km from the settlement. The remembrance feast was held both in the cemetery and before the store house.[29]

The shamanic séance

In Ovolyngort, we heard that in the house of Pëtr Nikitich's uncle, Kuz'ma, the *pătʌam χot*, "dark-house", ritual was being carried out. The dark-house ritual was organised in a room with no light at all. It is performed in especially hard times when there is no fish and famine threatens people. The ritual was carried out by Pëtr's uncle, Ivan, a strong shaman. His brother Kuz'ma

---

27. A Komi man, Kazym-Mys, 2003.
28. U. L., Lopkhari, 2003.
29. Sokolova 1989: 161.

helped him. The séance was first prepared as follows: the *šepən* (shaman) Ivan, an old man, was seated in the sacred corner, covered by a clean, new, never-used fur coat. Thereafter the windows were "closed" (thickly curtained). Before the *šepən* in the sacred corner a table with a bottle and a glass cup was put, and the light was switched off. Everyone gathered in the house and something unexpected happened:

> When all the people gathered in the house and sat around, one drunken man began to say something wrong. He was several times struck on the head with an arrow. Then the arrow was broken and bounced towards the door.
>
> The sacred corner opened and *ʌuχ-χŏr* [spirit-images] of the people present came in: a bear, an ermine, a loon and a reindeer. The bear tramped and grumbled, the ermine squeaked, the reindeer puffed.
>
> The last to enter was *Kŭl-ilpi-iki*, not from the sacred corner, but through the door.
>
> The sound of vodka being poured out was heard and then paper rustled. Then the *ʌuχ-χŏr* went away and the sounds they produced were heard, too.
>
> The cover of the *ʌarăś* [chest] opened.
>
> When the light was switched on, the people saw that the bottle of vodka was full, but remained on the *ʌuχ-ʌarăś*, and all the unnecessary things which had been situated in the sacred corner – pictures, cards, cigarettes etc. – were scattered about near the threshold.
>
> The old man was pierced with a sword from one side of his body to the other. The oldest man came, took the sword out and put it into the sacred corner, and it suddenly disappeared.[30]

The séance made a strong impression on people who were in the house. The rite closely resembles the Northern Selkup séance in a dark hut, as this description based on Prokof'eva (1981) and Gemuev and Pelikh (1999) shows:

> *qamịtịrqo* – "to perform a shamanic séance in a 'dark' hut":
> The séance was usually performed without a tambourine in "a dark hut" for various purposes, including healing, prophecy, searching for lost or vanished things. The participants came before the shaman, lit a fire and spread a bear's skin between the fire and the back wall of the hut. Near the skin they put a bucket of fine shavings, behind which they put a copper pot (used as a percussion instrument). Between the fire and the skin they put a stick. If the shaman was to use the tambourine during the séance they put this too on the ground. The shaman dressed himself in his usual clothes, undressed to the waist and sat on the skin, folding his legs underneath. Assistants of the shaman put the hat and the shamanic apron on him, while those present asked the questions to be answered after the ceremony: any number of different matters could be asked about, such as a forecast for the hunting season, the name of a person guilty of some misdeed, the location of lost items. Two of those present tied the whole body of the shaman with ropes. Following the signal of the shaman his assistants put the fire out, after which it was not allowed to light a match. After some time a bang was heard in the pot. The shaman started singing, calling his helping spirits

30. Pëtr Nikitich Longortov, Ovolyngort, 2002.

and asking them to untie him. A bear might appear, and those present could hear him stepping, grumbling and sniffing. Birds flew over the hut, their voices and flapping of wings audible. The rope used to tie the shaman might be thrown in the faces of those who tied him. The staff put on the ground turned out to be tied at chest level to the supports of the hut. Squealing helping spirits flew onto the staff. Finally the shaman was heard hoisting himself heavily onto the staff while continuing his singing. Slowly his voice became lower and seemed to sink away. The shaman flew off somewhere. Soon the voice became stronger – the shaman was coming back. In a few minutes an assistant of the shaman lit the fire. The people present saw the shaman sitting on the skin. Sweat was pouring off his face and his body; he removed the sweat with a wooden scraper. The shaman lit his pipe and had a rest for some time.

After his rest the second part of the ceremony started. The shaman cut himself with a knife, pricked his body with a ramrod, and stabbed a knife into his own abdomen. Everything looked very genuine, though not a drop of blood was spilled. Some Selkups testified that there had been shamans who were able to prick themselves with up to fifteen knives and continued to sing and dance as if nothing had happened.

At the end of the ceremony the shaman answered the questions asked at the very beginning by those present. One of the elements of the ceremony was guessing by the beater, which showed who had injured this or that person among those present.

Neither children nor women were allowed to be present at the séance.[31]

In his songs the shaman calls his spirit helpers, he flies off somewhere and comes back, which is heard in changes of his singing voice. At the end of the séance he cuts himself with a knife and then answers questions. Shamanising in a dark room with the tormenting of participants has also been mentioned by some earlier researchers of shamanism.[32] It may be associated with the experiences of flesh-cutting in the initiation period.[33] U. T. Sirelius's Vasyugan account mentions the lack of light at the place of shamanising: the windows are covered with a thick cloth and the fire is put out. If the fire were to be kindled during the séance the witch would fall ill.[34] It is further said of the preparations: "In the middle of the floor on which the witch conducted his sorcery a reindeer skin was spread. His hands and feet were firmly bound with the same belt. Some brass money was put on the skin and a Khanty took up the kantele [zither]".[35] A similar binding procedure was also familar to J. B. Müller and Novitskiï.[36] The latter, who knew the people of Irtysh and the northern Khanty, describes a séance as follows: When one of them wishes to know something about his daily needs in particular, the fish and forest animals to be caught, they take the witch into a dark room, bind him firmly and themselves sit down to play their

31. Tuchkova *et al.* 2004: 161–2; see also Tuchkova *et al.* 2010.
32. Karjalainen 1918: 567; cf. Siikala 1987: 221.
33. Siikala 1987: 221.
34. Karjalainen 1918: 587–8; cf. Siikala 1987: 221.
35. Karjalainen 1918: 587; cf. Siikala 1987: 221.
36. Karjalainen 1918: 579.

instruments. The bound man cries out a few magic words, calling his ally the devil. Usually they do this at night, and after a few hours of calling a wild spirit enters in fury. Those present rush out of the cottage, leaving the bound witch there. The spirit takes him and lifts him up, and torments him in every way; for this reason he was bound, so that, overcome by the torture, he would not in his flight be destroyed. A few hours later the unclean spirit makes false prophecies, just like the father of falsehood whispering in his ear, and goes away; the witch, barely alive, is freed from his torment, breaks free and announces the false predictions.[37]

The breaking free from chains or bonds is one of the trick-like measures indicating the skill and power of the shaman.[38] Novitskiĭ's explanation – the spirit tortures the shaman to such an extent that he must be bound, so that he may not flee – directs our thoughts, on the other hand, to the sufferings of the initiation period. In carrying out the cutting act the Samoyed shaman called the executors of his ecstatic initiation, "the flesh-cutting spirits", to his assistance and in his mind went over the events of his initiation period.[39] We may thus conjecture that in being tortured by the spirits during a séance the Khanty shaman is repeating scenes from his ecstatic initiation. Similar procedures are also reported by Gondatti among the Mansi: One dark night people, both men and women, gather at some wealthy house. The witch places on the floor a metal plate, on top of this iron-headed arrows, and begins to swear to god, hitting the plate with the arrows. In a short while the house quakes, the roof opens and *Mir-susne-χum* enters the house, manifesting his arrival by beating the plate with an arrow. Often he then tortures the witch, even to such an extent that he falls as if dead, piercing him, it is said, in all parts of his body with the arrow. Kindling the fire is then prohibited, for the unconscious witch, who has bouts of cramp, would die immediately. Once an arrow pierced one witch from the heart to the heel, but even so the witch only became more healthy than before.[40] In place of the indefinite "torturing" we here have the piercing of the shaman's body and the wounding with a sharp object, so that we are here approaching the meaning of the act of slashing the body in the séance.

Having quoted U. T. Sirelius's rather short description of a shamanising séance among the Vasyugan Khanty, Karjalainen continues with a more extensive account,[41] the source of which he does not mention. It is most probable that the account is based on his own observations, for he had become acquainted with the forms of Vasyugan shamanism on the spot, as is demonstrated for example by the subsequent account of the proceedings of a seer taking *Amanita muscaria*. The description of the séance is detailed and animated and the calling of the spirits including the snatches of invocatory songs is quoted.

37. Karjalainen 1918. 579.
38. Cf. for example Mikhaĭlovskiĭ 1892: 137.
39. See Lehtisalo 1924: 152–5.
40. Karjalainen 1918: 580.
41. Karjalainen 1918: 552–4; in English in Siikala 1987: 218–21.

Several spirits presented themselves in the dark-house séance in Ovolyn-gort: the *ʌuχ-χŏrs*, spirit-images of people in the hut, a bear, an ermine, a loon and a reindeer. Spirit animals came from the holy corner, where they were honoured. The shaman had invited them to help in this difficult situation. The same concerns also *Kŭl-ilpi-iki*, the Master of the Underworld, who came through the door. The Master of the Underworld is worshipped even today at secret places in the forest as a family helper (see pp. 144–5). The dark-hut séance of the Selkups is connected with the trip to the Lower World;[42] the same idea may lie behind the Khanty dark-house séance also. The comparison between Khanty and Samoyed rituals shows that in Synya the shamanic séance represented the classical form of north-west Siberian shamanism.

The dark-house séance is not the only ritual model for the Khanty shaman. P. J. Pyrysev from Yamgort described shamanising on Holy Cape where the Synya people worshipped *Jŏχan-iki*, Old River Man, the main deity of the Synya river.[43] The narrative shows that the authorities could not wipe out most of the important shamanic activities, particularly the performance in the ritual place. The ritual represents the traditional shamanism in which the shaman served a larger community, on this occasion the *Săńa joχ* (Synya people). In Synya, the extended families belonged to the *Moś*- or *Por*-phratries.[44] The sacrificial ceremonies have basically similar structures whether they were done by a shaman or somebody else. The sacrificial priest may, for example, be one of the elders of the family or village, the one who know the rules and modes of ritual. In private rituals, which we documented in Ovolyngort and in Ovgort, the rites were led by old persons who took care of the ritual place: in Ovolyngort a man belonging to a shaman family and in Ovgort a woman, who was the first wife of a known shaman. If a direct contact with spirits was needed, the shaman had to take part in the sacrifice.

Shamans are performing publicly again

We took part in the public midsummer celebrations on St Elijah's day (2 August) in Muzhi in 2000 and 2001 (see pp. 148–9). The first ritual was a part of the 160th anniversary of Muzhi and great numbers of politicians, journalists, researchers and others arrived at the festivities. The Khanty cultural festival formed one of the main events in the jubilee and there were many rumours about the coming ritual. The best-known shaman in Shuryshkary, Vasiliĭ Petrovich Pugurchin, from the Synya river had promised to lead the ritual. There was a rumour about the sacrificial animals, too. Two reindeer were selected for the sacrifice, but they ran away and the organisers had to buy a couple of sheep, or rams as the Khanty described them. Actually, Oleg helped Afanasiĭ Ivanovich to take the two rams by Zhivun motor boat to Muzhi. The rams, bought from the local Komi, were black and white. Oleg

42. Tuchkova *et al.* 2010: 206.
43. Steinitz 1939: 52–61.
44. See Perevalova 2004: 95–6.

had to carry the black ram on his shoulders because its feet were too feeble and it could not move.

The next day people gathered to celebrate the 160th anniversary of Muzhi. Muzhi museum planned to create an outdoor museum for Khanty-Muzhi and the sacrificial ritual was planned in order to dedicate the place. We awaited the sacrificial ceremony from the morning until two o'clock. Rumours went round that the sacrificial ceremony could not be performed as it should be. The shaman refused to take his drum away from his own village, but would work with an axe. The axe as a shamanising implement is typical of the Northern Khanty. Later we heard that Vasiliĭ Petrovich was somewhat reluctant to perform in the festival, but after discussions took on the job.

According to Oleg's field notes the ritual was as follows:

We filmed the dedication of the planned outdoor museum from beginning to end. Men prepared the sacrificial site and lit a fire. They put a bucket over the fire for tea and meat. Women, who came to the sacrificial place later than men, waited outside the holy area. Later they helped men to build a *chum* (a conical tent) on the field and laid the tables for men and women on the ground for a shared dinner. Men dragged the heavy black ram to the ritual site and tied it to a birch decorated with kerchiefs, ribbons, small bells etc. Everything was as it should be. Under a tree, there were a plate with bread, a vodka bottle and a full glass. The shaman stood with his back against the tree; he took the glass and said: "I do not drink to become drunk, but to divide the drink with those who give us happiness and health." He sprinkled the first glass with his right hand around the tree in the direction of the sun. The second glass he drank himself.

After that he sat opposite the axe, which was hanging on the red woollen lace of a right-foot shoe. He began to sing for about fifteen minutes. He sang seriously and went into a light state of trance. Then he rose, and turning to the audience said some words. His three helpers put the ram in the centre of the small opening so that its muzzle was towards the rising sun. Men rose and from the east side of the opening, crossed their hands and shouted three times: "O-o-o-o!" Then one of the helpers took the kerchief with orange, red and white decorations and moved it over the ram in the direction of the sun and put it on the animal's back. The other helper took the axe and moved it in circles over the head of the ram. He struck the animal with the axe. Helpers slaughtered the ram, dragged it in the direction of the sun and placed it so that the muzzle was towards the rising sun. One of the helpers dampened the kerchief with blood and hung it on a branch of the holy birch. The internal organs were hung on the next tree, and the flesh was cut up for cooking. The pelt and the head were put under the holy tree so that the ram was like an honoured guest looking towards the meadow where people were gathered.

When the meat was boiling, the *chum* was constructed. Then the meat was eaten and vodka and tea were served. After the feast Kolya Nakhrachëv put a gift, a blue check shirt, on the shaman. The shaman changed his clothes. Instead of his *kŭvś* he now had a normal coat, waistcoat and trousers.

Men took the pelt to the forest and hung it on a spruce. The helpers of the shaman bent the spruce, which was about 3 metres high, and put a branch of the spruce in the hole previously made in the neck side of the pelt. The tree with the pelt was let go and when everybody was around it, men again shouted three times "O-o-o-o!"

Women laid the "tables" on the ground. An assistant of the shaman took the innards of the ram (the heart, liver, kidneys and lungs) from the holy tree and gave them to local men. People dispersed and the dancing began on the meadow nearby.

Vasiliĭ Petrovich Pugurchin lives in Ovgort and has a house up the river in a Synya village. He has herded reindeer for thirty years and has become very learned. His father was a shaman, but because of persecutions he kept silent. Pugurchin learned most on the tundra where he herded reindeer with Nenets and Khanty shamans. He speaks Komi well and spoke about shamanism in Komi, because in Russian it is not possible to talk about shamanism.[45] In Muzhi, the feast continued. A Komi women's group performed songs and dances in the central space of the centre. Pugurchin had erected his *chum* in the front of the main government building and sang shamanic songs through the night. Oleg talked with him late into the night. The shaman, who left the centre in the morning, wanted small bells for the spirits, which he got a year later.

The midsummer feast in 2001 did not differ much from the great celebration of the 160th anniversary of Muzhi; the festival was again held on 2 August. Anna described the feast in her field notes:

2 August 2001. It is St Elijah's day in the Malaya Ob' region of Siberia. People arrive by boat from the administrative centre and neighbouring and distant villages. Next to a hut that has been erected in the village square towers a pole, on the top of which hangs a stylised shaman's drum. This is the staging area for the official part of the St Elijah's day festival, which the Khanty refer to as Midsummer's Day. A little further away from the square, in the holy place of the village, a fire is lit for performing the sacred ritual of the festival. The programme of this bilingual festival includes traditional plays, dances, and a wrestling tournament which the Khanty regard as their own sport although it is of Turko-Mongolian origin. However, the main event is the sacrificial ritual performed by the shaman Vasiliĭ Petrovich Pugurchin.

The seventy-year-old shaman arrives, having placed his rucksack under a holy birch tree that grows at the edge of the sacrifice area reserved for men. He leans both his sabre, which he uses for magic rituals, and his fox-fur trim shaman's hat against the holy tree. He exits momentarily to carve a stick one *eʌ* (cubit) in length which he will use to fumigate both his feet and equipment; he also fumigates pieces of red cloth used in sacrifice and hangs them on the branches of holy trees. In this location last year three birches were used for sacrificial rituals, but this year only two: the main tree used by the men, the other for women's equipment, and on which later are placed the internal organs of sacrificed animals. Pugurchin also places an essential ritual item under the tree after fumigating it: a red and yellow scarf "with a pattern of the sun". Standing with his back to the sacrificial tree, the shaman pours out a drink into a glass from a bottle wrapped in the scarf. After saying "I do not drink to get drunk, I drink to give the spirits a treat" he pours the vodka out

45. Vasiliĭ Petrovich Pugurchin, Khanty Myzhi 2.8.2000.

to the tree with a sweeping gesture of his right hand while simultaneously turning quickly towards the sun. After this four men lead out a sacrificial black ram.

In the Khanty view every ritual must have a specific purpose: this ritual is devoted to friendship. The shaman then calls on all the spirits beginning with *Torəm*. After asking the participants if a certain god should be invoked, and receiving a positive reply, the shaman summons the celestial god while drawing a circle with his sabre above his head. He summons the lower-range deities, by calling them while drawing a circle in front of himself; he summons the mythical heroes as he presses the sabre against his waist. After agreeing to the presence of the Master of the Underworld *Kŭl-ilpi-iki* or *Xịń-iki*, he touches his sabre to the ground, saying "Very well! If the sacrifice is dedicated to friendship, we will invite everyone and forget no one!"

At the start of the festival different foods were set on a long tablecloth spread over the ground: fish, biscuits, sweets, tea and vodka. The festival programme is informal: people listen to recorded popular music, and both watch and participate in plays and games. At a short distance from the festivities the sacrificial animal is slaughtered and its meat served according to a familiar prescribed ritual. The shaman himself does not participate in the slaughter, but dispenses advice when needed. The animal skin is placed under a birch in a sitting position; refreshments such as fish, bread and an open bottle of vodka and glass are placed in front of the skin. They throw the intestines into a hole behind the birch; the liver, heart, lungs and kidneys are placed onto the women's tree to give later to local people. They place the meat in a bucket and hang it over a fire to the left of the holy tree.

After the meat has been cooked, the shaman ties to the sabre's point and handle a red woollen garter taken from his right leg. While sitting under the birch he draws under him his left foot and extends his right and begins to sing. The men carry away the animal skin and hang it on a young spruce by piercing a hole in the animal skin's head; the tree is then bent to the ground and released with the animal skin still attached. This ritual is considered to be so holy that women are not allowed to attend. The meat of the sacrificial animal is then placed in dishes brought by the participants and eaten at the common table."

The scheme of both sacrificial rituals in Khanty-Muzhi and that described by P. Yu. Pyrysev in the 1930s presented above are similar in outline though the details vary. The basic ritual rules and performed acts are as follows:

1. *The time of the sacrifice* is a calendar day related to the means of livelihood. Because the equipment and sacrificial animals are taken to the ritual site the previous day, the ritual process might last two to three days.
2. *The sacrificial site* is a holy place. If it has not been used traditionally, it has to be specially consecrated. The shaman was said to have consecrated the place already before the feast in Khanty-Muzhi.
3. *The division of men and women.* Women can nowadays look at the sacrifice but cannot enter the sacrificial site. The men either act in the ritual in the role of the shaman and his helpers or help clear the site, making fire and slaughtering the animal. Some of the men represent families and only participate in eating. Women have a separate place to eat in the festival and eating is regulated.

4. *The holy tree* mediates between people and spirits. When women are allowed to come to the feast, they have their own holy tree near the sacrificial site but not in it.

5. *The actemes (sequences of ritual acts) of the ritual*: clearing the place, making fire, purifying acts, giving gifts to spirits by hanging them on the holy trees, invocation of the spirits by the shaman, treating the spirits to vodka, testing the sacrificial animal in order to see if the spirit/deity approves it, slaughtering of the animal, giving the blood to the spirits/god, cooking the meat, a shared meal, hanging the pelt on the holy tree in the forest for the deity.

These main actemes of the sacrifice are also found in the Eastern Khanty rituals, as can be seen from the article by Balalajeva and Wiget.[46] The writers witnessed a sacrificial festival on the Trom-Agan river, in the northernmost area of the Eastern Khanty. The ritual was performed in winter and lasted two days. The first day was a preparation for the rite: the shaman sang without outsiders. The sacrifice was performed on the second day and consisted of the gathering of people, the site's preparation, the sacrifice, the feast and thanksgiving, the distribution of gifts, the disposition of materials, the departure, and the evening's shamanising. The night-time shamanising of Vasiliĭ Petrovich in a newly constructed *chum* in Muzhi may correspond to the last act of the Trom-Agan river ritual.

Even though the basic model of sacrifice seems to be traditional and quite similar in different Khanty areas, the details vary. Notably the attire and shamanic equipment of Pugurchin differed from those of the Khanty-Muzhi rituals.

2000	2001
1. The shaman wore a grey broadcloth *kŭvś* (long coat).	1. He wore a civil costume.
2. He was in fur boots,	2. He was in rubber top-boots;
3. but without a cap.	3. every now and then he put on a cap with red and blue quarters on the top and a fox-fur edging.
4. He shamanised with an axe.	4. He shamanised with a sabre.
5. The bands hung on three birches: two grew in the sacrificial glade (the main one and the one to the right of it) and one in the women's glade.	5. There are only two birches: the one, which was the main one last year (now it is the men's one) and the other, the one growing to the right of the main one (now the women's one).

In general, we should note that the shaman's wardrobe is not of major ritual significance among the Khanty. Thus, in 2000 Vasiliĭ Petrovich performed the ceremony dressed in the Khanty costume: a long grey coat (*kuvś*), white fur boots and a traditional reindeer-breeder's belt. He also performed

46. Balalajeva and Wiget 1999: 114–24.

Shaman Vasilïĭ Petrovich and his assistant, Khanty Muzhi
– Video picture by Oleg Ulyashev 2001

shamanic rituals with an axe and honoured three sacred trees. In 2001 he wore a modern three-piece suit, but on his head he had on a pointed hat with fox-fur trim, the upper side of which was sewn from two blue and two red pieces of cloth. He also used a sword as his shamanic and ritual attribute. Only two of the sacred trees were decorated. What appears to define the choice of equipment is the nature of the ritual and the spirits who are summoned. In 2000, when the sacrifice was devoted to friendship, the shaman called upon the deities of the Upper and Lower Worlds. The assistants who cleared the ritual site and helped the shaman were also different each year. Of the assistants from 2000 only Prokopïĭ N. remained. In the absence of other helpers the shaman taught Nikolaĭ Nakhrachëv the secrets of the ritual.

The sacrificial ritual was accompanied and followed by an official festival organised by the government: boat races, lasso-throwing, pulling pegs out of the earth with one's teeth, waist-belt wrestling, song performances and so forth. The simultaneous performances on the festival site enabled the audience to choose the most interesting entertainment. The Khanty sacrifice, in fact, interested mostly the Khanty men who had a chance to take part and researchers who documented it. But at the end of the festival everyone took part in the ritual meal and merrymaking in the meadow.

Vasiliĭ Petrovich summons spirits under the holy tree, Khanty Muzhi
– Photograph by Valeriĭ Sharapov 2000

Different interpretations: belief and entertainment

Modern celebrations of the main festival days of the Khanty calendar (*Vŏrŋa χătʌ*, Crow's Day, and *lŭŋ-kŭtəp-χătʌ*, Midsummer's Day) have become a mixture of official celebration, festival programme and traditional ritual, which, however, fit into the common scene as generally self-contained units. In contrast to the old days when all participants took active ceremonial roles (leader, assistant, male/female participants' "choir"), and all knew their place in the ritual scheme (motives, structure, and the general outline of the action), now modern festivals have become events that require comment. Not all participants view traditional rituals equally since everyone interprets and explains ritual actions from their own point of view. For a shaman who specialises in holy rites, the most important goal is to perform the rituals as precisely as possible to achieve a high degree of positive spiritual interaction. Thus, when one woman approached the main tree of Khanty-Muzhi holy grove with a present during the ritual, the shaman Vasiliĭ Petrovich interrupted the rite, leaped to his feet, drew a circle around himself three times with a sword, and began to swear in the Komi language, in which he is fluent. Later Nikolaĭ, the shaman's disciple and our friend, in his anger at the woman's behaviour commented on the situation thus:

When a shaman calls spirits, the highest spirits, refreshments are made for them and they are at the host's table. But if someone breaks the rules concerning the ritual, if he does something in the wrong way, lower and evil spirits all come to the feast when they are not called. They will also sit at the table like the main guests. And this may turn out badly for the person who performs the ritual. This is especially a concern for the shaman, and after him the others who are present. It is the shaman who has called the spirits to the feast. That's why Vasiliĭ Petrovich became so angry with the woman. And, in fact, women used to be killed for this kind of action, and nobody said anything about it to the shaman. You know, everyone has said that it was the woman who wanted to call the evil spirits. The evil spirits are in fact waiting for this kind of action all the time.[47]

Not everyone involved has such a severe attitude towards all breaches of the rules: during the same ritual a little girl, after she had fumigated over the fire a ribbon with coins, hung it on the men's tree. She was scolded for this, but not severely because she was still a little girl and not yet a woman in either the biological or social sense.

Religious rites, in general, are never the same for all the executors, nor do all the participants have the same kind of relationship with the events of the rite. The woman who, out of ignorance, broke a prohibition such as approaching a holy tree was more interested in entertainment and representatives of this world than the next, whereas the belief in deities and hence the authentic way of sacrifice was important to the shaman and his helpers. The festival was in fact attended by people from all walks of life, including visitors from abroad, and for most participants, not raised according to Khanty tradition, both the sacred and profane elements were of equal interest. The religious element is lent authenticity through its performance by a practising shaman, despite its setting within a modern festival, and such a setting, despite being a modern creation, offers a channel for the continuance of Khanty religious tradition.

47. Nikolaĭ Nikitich Nakhrachëv, Ovolyngort, 2003.

12 Religion, kin and environment

The Northern Khanty were baptised so early that for a couple of centuries their religious world has consisted of two different spheres: public Orthodox Christianity and secret local cults. The long era of double religion has led to a syncretism of ideas and practices. The calendar festivals of the Church have been assimilated to traditional Khanty feasts and Orthodox icons decorate the holy corners of their homes. The saints of the Orthodox Church, especially Nicholas, have been assimilated to Khanty spirits. Sometimes divine beings of both religions have been understood as one being, which simply had both a Russian and Khanty name and image. The Soviet era made the religious situation and ideas even more complex. Both of the religions were condemned by the authorities. The result was a hidden religious domain of people who trusted each other, among close relatives and neighbours. In part the native religion was kept up secretly in the Soviet era, but the appeal of the Christian faith diminished.

Hallmarks of Khanty religion

Tradition, memory and keeping to ritual models are hallmarks of Khanty religion. As we know from studies concerning ethnic religions, these tendencies are common to most non-literate ethnic religions. The following features appear to describe Khanty religion today.

1. **Weak institutionalisation.** In oral ethnic religions institutionalisation is weak even when the cults are kept up publicly. In the situation created first by the Orthodox Church and after that by the Soviet Union, religion became even weaker as an institution. It was kept up by people who "knew" more than the average, such as shamans and heads of families, but always in secrecy. Religious practices were performed as people believed they had to be done, but people often repeated that nowadays there is no one who knows what to do, how to do it or where to do it. The collapse of the Soviet Union gave way to new specialists of religion and some young people have tried to learn the religious practices in attempts to revive the Khanty culture.

2. Rules of "traditional" ritualism. The imagined field of proper ritual is created by keeping to tradition. When a man spoke about a bear wake, he said: "When they got a bear and wanted simply to cook it, my uncle said: 'As it is customary, as our grandfathers ate, just so shall we eat.' And he did everything according to the rules."[1] Following the rules is especially important when people are dealing with spirits and the deceased. The obedience of norms marks everyday life. Visits to the graveyard, for example, cannot be undertaken without a guide to show the proper way to behave. For women the rules are much stricter than for men. For this reason, children are educated by adults and poor field workers by kind informants. The success of field work depends greatly upon the willingness to learn the rules. On the other hand, misbehaviour can elicit a lot of information about the accepted behaviour.

3. Strong variation in ritual practice. The basic models for rituals in the northern hunting cultures are widespread and observed in large areas of the Eurasian forest zone. But because of the non-existence of written guides or models for religious life, details of rituals vary even between settlements close to each other. The Khanty live in a very large area and are divided into three main dialectal groups and several smaller groups which have had contacts with several other nations. Among the Northern Khanty and even in Shuryshkary, the people have developed different ritual traditions. One reason for varying practices is the close connection with Nenets groups and reindeer-herding Komi, which can be seen also in the formation of dialects. The variation in ritual practice is discussed by people, especially at burials or other ritual practices connected with daily life, when everything has to be done according to the correct rules.

4. Holy places manifest social and gender hierarchy. The oral religion of the northern hunters, fishermen and reindeer herders is embedded in the environment. Landscape and its holy places, trees and cult objects frame the living world with places of varying degrees of importance. Although the ritual places are not constructed cathedrals or other impressive man-made objects, they are full of the power of the spirit world and honoured and feared in the same time. Holy places mark out sites distinguished for their dignity. Men and women, old and young can move between them, use them or are ordered to avoid them according to their position in society. Among the Khanty, holy places manifest the social and gender hierarchy.

5. Religious experts, memory and orality. Oral religion depends on social memory, which is usually transmitted by "those who know", specialists who have learned the knowledge from the older generations. But even the memory of shamans and seers is affected by the nature of communication. Oral knowledge has its own characteristics. It is based on transmitted models but recreated again and again in the course of continuous discussions.

1. Pëtr Nikitich Longortov, Ovolyngort, 2002.

Idiosyncratic and creative interpretations are often mixed with inherited ideas and beliefs. The truth and value of testimonies are commonly discussed and interpretations of religious ideas and narratives belong to everyday talk. Hence, oral religions represent a network of ideas and beliefs consisting of continually changing meanings and interpretations.

6. Emotion and bodily performance. Everyday rituals are practised according to the traditional rules. They are not emphasised, just carried out without much attention as normal daily activities. But rituals manifesting the connection with the Otherworld, practised usually in critical situations, are different. The contact with spirits and demons, for example in shamanistic practices, is marked by striking bodily movements. Emotions linked to such rituals might be strong and effective from the viewpoint of the onlookers. The relationship with the dead is also a delicate matter, full of concern and even fear. Following the rules obediently gives protection against over-close contacts.

7. Experiencing and doing instead of "believing". Spirits are very seldom "believed" in; they are seen and heard. Knowledge inherited from old people and ancestors gives a basis for the manifestation of the Otherworld, not for abstract belief in the supranormal. Experiencing things which are difficult to interpret from an everyday human perspective allows for varying interpretations. Omens seem to be right when they are interpreted in a suitable way. It can be said that in oral religion experiencing is more important than believing.

Unity of religion, kin and nature

The Northern Khanty have been hunters, fishermen and reindeer herders. The close relationship between people and environment is embedded in their religious ideas and its expressions. Myths offer an understanding of the universe, referring back to the time when the main heroes were animals or gigantic men and people lived between the worlds inhabited by spirits and spiritual animals. The Ob', the great mother, connects the world of the living to that of the dead. Tales tell how the first inhabitants came along the Ob' or from the Ural mountains. At the time of the great flood, the Ob' was filled with water. Shamans saved their people and directed them to proper settlement places. According to these myths, the flood divided people into smaller areal groups.

The relationship with nature is also expressed in the social sphere. The animal ancestors of kin groups link people closely to their environment. This link is symbolised by objects, furs and animal parts, found in homes and sacred storehouses. Despite the teachings of the Soviet state and the technology-driven urgings of the administration, they are still taken care of today. Ancestors are fed both in everyday and in festal rituals. For those who do not find Khanty religion important, the animal connected to the surname may still be significant. It tells something about the culture of the forefathers.

The landscape is full of holy places, usually situated in forests or along the Ob' and its tributaries. Holy groves emphasise the division between the sexes and social and geographical groups: there are sacred places for men and women, for the family, for the kin, for a village or for those living along the same river. The connectedness of religion and social hierarchy and the gender system is also close: there are spirits for the family, larger kin groups, villages, rivers and for both genders. Spirits are not seen only in the sacred areas. They act at home and in the village and the forests outside. They rule over fish and hunted animals, cause accidents and sicknesses and affect livelihoods. Forgetting the spirits may cause trouble. On the other hand, feeding ancestral spirits guarantees a prosperous life.

Religion and belonging

The reason for the persistence of Khanty religion lies in its connectedness to the kinship system. Rituals express the bond between the kin group and the protective spirits. The death dolls are kept at home for four or five years, and they may become guardian spirits of the family. Ancestral spirits create a sense of belonging to a certain kin or larger related group of people. For the Khanty, their own beliefs and sacred rituals are important identity-forming factors. While these factors make up their religion, they equally represent their culture. The interests of our informants reveal how and when religion is identified with culture. Modern young Khanty might appreciate Khanty religion only as a means to be noticed in the world, for example for economic reasons in building cultural tourism. For older people in distant settlements, for example the shaman Vasiliĭ P. Pugurchin, religion keeps its former value. The place and cultural context affect the assessment of religious tradition; people change their clothes and behaviour, and maybe their attitudes, according to the situation. In preserving and building up culture and therefore also Khanty religion the tradition-collectors and cultural workers are crucial. Nikolaĭ N. Nakhrachëv, who learnt myths when he was child, has begun to collect and publish them. He represents the teacher/cultural worker type of many Finno-Ugric peoples who aim to transform the oral tradition into written form. Nakhrachëv is a good expert on his culture today. As a worker in the Cultural Administration he helped to organise cultural festivals in Khanty-Muzhi.

Modern festivals do not reject religious feelings. They just broaden the arena of people and groups forming the community. In the St Elijah's day festival in Khanty-Muzhi two cultural tendencies, the official and the traditional, penetrate and infuse each other to form an event which reflects the modern state. In addition to the inhabitants of the village, the participants in the sacrificial festival in Khanty-Muzhi included researchers, local academics, government representatives and visitors from foreign countries. The goal of this kind of festival is to reconcile differing, even contradictory, interpretations of ritual by honouring the original Khanty culture as well as highlighting the importance of connections between ethnic history and ethnic values. This ritual, performed by a practising shaman and members of the ethnic group who are living representatives of tradition, remains authentic, even when it is included within the framework of a modern festival. The public performance of ritual is one means of preserving and transferring ethnic traditions in this era of modernisation and globalisation.

The Komi: Proliferating Singing Traditions III

13 The singing culture of the Upper Vychegda Komi

Studying Komi singing

Folklore collectives, which perform at festivals, on visits and at home during cultural events, have an important place in the creation of contemporary ethnic self-awareness. Understanding of local culture depends on the ideas given by ethnologists and folkloristists. Cultural portraits created by researchers have been transmitted to local people through museums, folklore publications and exhibitions. In Russia, the huge influence of the state in the creation of locally visible representations of ethnicity is evident in the folklore collectives in rural villages. During the 1930s, leading Russian folklorists recommended folklore as a basis for socialist folk art. Since the 1990s the celebration of festivals in individual villages and towns has been much favoured; the programmes include presentations by the republics' folklore groups both amateur and professional. The folklore collectives have been supported in most Komi villages. The Komi singing groups form a good target for studying the history and the present-day practices of the folklore collectives.

The Komi (earlier known as Zyryans) are aboriginals of the Komi Republic, which is a large area in northern Russia reaching as far as the eastern Ural mountains. The landscape is characterised by endless taiga forests, swamps and tundra, and slowly flowing serpentine rivers, the Vychegda, Mezen' and Pechora and their tributaries, which have been the most important routes for communication and on which the old villages are often situated. The Komi language belongs to the Permian group of the Finno-Ugric languages; its speakers moved to the area from the Kama and Vyatka rivers. In the tenth to fourteenth centuries, groups of Perms lived in the Lower and Middle Vychegda and in the basins of the rivers Vym', Vashka and Luza.[1] At the moment, there are several Komi groups living in different parts of northern Russia. Reindeer-breeding took the Izhma Komi as far as Shuryshkary in the Lower Ob' region. However, reindeer-breeding was a late phenomenon pursued only by the Northern Komi group from Izhma. The traditional economy was complex: hunting, fishing, cattle-breeding and slash-and-burn

1. Konakov *et al.* 2003: 15.

agriculture.[2] Though agriculture has improved in the southern parts of the area in recent centuries, hunting and the fur trade have provided important means for living in the northern areas.

The Komi were converted to Christianity by the Russian missionary St Stephen of Perm, who created the first alphabet for the Komi language in the late fourteenth century and became the first bishop of the Komi in 1379. The new Permian eparchy was situated in Ust'-Vym', at the cult centre of the old ethnic religion. Contact with Russians has been close over many centuries, and Russian immigrants have established their own settlements, for example Ust'-Tsil'ma near Izhma, which is a centre for Old Believers. After the Revolution the Komi became one of the minority nations of the area, because the Soviet government began to build up the mining industry and forest centres and large numbers of Russians and people of other nationalities moved to new settlements there. The Komi republic came to be known for its prison camps; prisoners built the railway to Vorkuta, and worked in the timber and mining industries. Many stayed in the Komi area after they got their freedom.

However, many old Komi villages continued their life on a traditional basis, though the farming system was replaced by kolkhozes and later by sovkhozes. In the basin of the Vychegda river, in the Ust'-Kulom and Kortkeros areas, the Komi language is spoken by 70 per cent of inhabitants. The villages look as they did before: grey log houses in rows near the river or on the tops of hills. Besides the traditional material culture, folklore too has had an important role in people's lives. Folklore genres survived until last century and were utilised in the time of the new Soviet cultural agenda in the creation of programmes for cultural festivals.

In the summers of 2000 to 2006 we undertook field trips to the Ust'-Kulom and Kortkeros villages, Vol'dino, Vyl'gort, Pomozdino, Pozheg, Bogorodsk, Troitsk and Nivshera,[3] and visited Izhma and Ust'-Tsil'ma. During the field work we interviewed members of numerous folklore collectives, took video films of performances and followed the preparations for the Komi eightieth anniversary, which was to be held in Syktyvkar. In the following chapters, we examine the history of the Upper Vychegda folklore collectives, their programmes and performances and the significance of singing as a building-block of ethnicity and the female community's sense of belonging. Because collectives form the main arena for performing folklore today, we are interested in their influence on people's understanding of folklore: how singers arrange and edit written poems for songs, which serve their aims, and how the folk-editing enlarges the domain of folklore.[4]

---

2. Konakov *et al.* 2003: 15–17.
3. Nivshera is called *Odyb* in Komi; the Russian name Nivshera derives from the Komi river name *Ńyvśer*.
4. In comparing Komi and Russian songs and in analysing macronic songs we use a scholarly transcription system, as is used in the transcription of Komi.

Did the Komi have a singing culture?

Ćiviľ, ćiviľ, ćiviľ, vorobej
Ispokhodilśa na nogy,
Ispokhodilśa na seńe.
Tudy-judy prošla.
Primolodeńka.
Ešśo žöńik – totara,
Totara ľi poltara,
Ešśo v śeni vćetverom,
Vćetverom ľi všestoju.
Zapretaj ľi zapretaj,
Zapevajśa truba,
Śeredi oteća,
Potom pisvaja devena.
Vśo lenok, vśo venok,
Vśo vo bortonty,
Vśo vo est vo sakarnyje,
vśo vo piťi medornyje.
Zaguľ devitsa,
I zaćistit on pole.
Ne ko śere, ne końa,
Ńe belykh i ńe lenta.
Poďi doćeri domoj,
Poďi śerevyj domoj.
A sama posvista,
Naterśe roža.[5]

This song was the start of our acquaintance with the folklore of Nivshera in the Kortkeros area. Singers to whom the song is dear cannot totally understand the Russian words, which, in fact, have been modified to resemble the Komi pronunciation, and therefore they cannot translate the song into Komi. The understanding of the words was difficult for us too, though Oleg is a Komi and speaks several dialects of his native language. The only way to have an idea of the meaning of the text was to compare it with Russian parallels. In Nivshera, people regard the song as ancient and local. The song belongs to the rituals of Christmas time:

> In Christmas we took hand in hand and sang the song *Ćiviľ-vorobej* (Chivily-sparrow). Smog houses were used at that time, and at that time there were no chimneys, but they said that the song *Ćiviľ* was already in existence.[6]

Three days we *ćivil* to Christmas, beginning from 7 January. The one who meets you will be blackened with soot. This Christmas, when all the leaders came from

---

5. Aleksandra Stepanovna Gabova, b. 1933, rec. A.-L. S. and O. U., Nivshera, 7.5.2000. The song is untranslatable.
6. Tat'yana Alekseevna Zhizheva, b. 1902, rec. V. M. Kudryashova and O. U., Nivshera, December 1989.

town, all were stained with soot, all leaders. Markov [a politician] was stained, he was stained with soot. Nobody was pitied.[7]

As I remember, for ages the *ćivil* was sung in Nivshera, and our grandmothers and our mothers sang it too. It is an *Odyb* [= Nivshera] song.[8]

In this connection we may recall the ideas on Komi songs presented by Russian academician Nadezhdin and N. E. Onchykov, a Russian researcher who studied Pechora *byliny*, Russian heroic songs. They claimed that Zyryans lacked songs: their whole lyrical programme was a borrowing, a collection of twisted Russian texts. According to Onchykov, who recorded Pechora *byliny* from Russians in 1901–2, the Izhma Komi had borrowed all their songs from Russian neighbours: "Zyryans do not have their own poetry at all; at least nowadays they are content just with Russian songs."[9]

It is true that the Komi song tradition includes many Russian and translated texts, but after several field trips in the Upper Vychegda, we cannot agree with the earlier researchers. Certainly the Russian influence on Komi culture has been strong. The connection with the Russians began already when the relations of the Komi with the Volga Bolgar were diminishing and close contact with the principality of Rostov-Suzdal' began to develop in the eighth and ninth centuries. The relationship with Novgorod was strong from the ninth to the fourteenth centuries and with the principality of Moscow from the thirteenth. Later Russian influence was increased by the alliance and vassal relations with the principality of Moscow, which needed allies in its conquest of the far side of the Ural mountain belt, and afterwards in the service of the Cossack army in Siberia and Alaska. This contributed to a process in which the Permians of Vychegda, called Perm' Velikaya in the Russian sources, became Christian in the fourteenth to fifteenth centuries. The pre-Christian hunting culture of the Komi was threatened,[10] but not annihilated. New contacts did not destroy the Komi song culture, and even less did they affect the whole culture.

The close contacts with Russians is reflected, in particular, in the wide distribution of Russian folk songs. They could be performed in Komi, translated into more or less close versions or sung in Russian or in bilingual (macaronic) Komi-Russian form. To the best known of these songs belong *Pedör Kiron*, *Tiga-tiga*, *Apitser molodoj*, *Izo-lesu* and *Końerej daj Vanykaej*. In most cases the songs were not simply translated from one language into another, but were adapted to the world view of Komi folklore. They obtained content, form, melodies and image systems characteristic of Komi culture. The special Komi epic songs and ballads, which had earlier been performed by men, retreated to the periphery of the folk culture. Today in parties when

7. Aleksandra Stepanovna Gabova, rec. A.-L. S. and O. U., Nivshera, 7.5.2000.
8. Aleksandra Stepanovna Gabova, rec. A.-L. S. and O. U., Nivshera, 7.5.2000
9. Onchykov 1904: 8.
10. P. L. Limerov and O. I. Ulyashev are working on the disintegration of the Komi culture in the change from a pre-Christian hunting culture to a Christian agricultural culture, but the results are not yet published.

people sit together, men sometimes sing war songs and heroic or lyrical-epic songs, or sometimes they join in the women's singing of lyric songs. Some men play musical instruments; there are famous harmonica players in several villages, for example in Kerchomya and Pozheg. Women sing lyric and wedding songs and *častuški* (short half-improvised songs) in their own gatherings. During the Soviet period women sang psalms and other religious songs in Komi in meetings they organised. Family rituals are still important contexts for singing. Laments have been performed at home after bringing the coffin out of the house and by the grave, before burial. This is especially characteristic of the Upper Vychegda culture.

However, the favourite folk songs changed over time. New song types and styles, new tropes, personages and heroes emerged in the song tradition; not all of them were straight loans from Russian folklore. The well-known Izhma-Kolva heroic epos has some Nenets roots, but it is difficult to evaluate all the Nenets features. A. K. Mikushev, a Komi folklorist, worked hard on solving this problem but at least both his Nenets and Komi sources are indisputable.

It is clear that the Komi of the nineteenth century could not sing in their native language to N. E. Onchukov, who collected Russian *byliny* and legends, or to other Russian researchers, because they did not talk in Komi. On the other hand, in the nineteenth to twentieth centuries and even today, the songs in mixed languages were dominant in the border areas of Russia and Komi: Udora, Vym', Izhma and Luza. Komi to this day perform Russian songs which have already been forgotten by native Russians long ago. N. E. Onchykov, for example, recorded some Russian *byliny* in Izhma. *Ilya Muromets* has been recorded as a folktale variant from the Vym' and Lower Vychegda Komi in their native language. Many plots and personages of the Komi wedding poetry texts have also been borrowed from Russian and it is possible to find regularities in the genre features of loans. We can, for example, show that in the twentieth century wedding songs and ritual poetry increased among the Komi at the expense of the wedding incantations. This has changed the dominant folklore elements: for example the role of recitative has diminished in ritual texts; the main reason for this change has been the adoption of lyrical and ritual songs from Russian folklore.

For example the song cycle in the play of taking captives *Ćužmar-nylej* ("Ermine-maiden") and *Krug šöryn mića nyv sulale* ("A beautiful girl in the circle"), which were recorded by A. K. Mikushev as heroic epic songs,[11] actually approach in their images and style the North Russian, Finnic, Veps and Karelian lyric-epic and wedding songs. The song *Dol'i-šel'i*, which is nowadays known as a lyrical song, comes from the Russian wall- or bridge-song *Vdol' le, vshir' le ulitsa*. The wall- and bridge-songs opened young men's traditional fights in calendar festivals. These songs were called by Russians *stenochnaya* (< *stenka*, "wall") or *mostovaya* (< *most*, "bridge") because the lads used to sing them on a bridge, at the edge of the village, before "going wall on wall", i. e. starting to fight with the lads from another village during

---

11. Mikushev 1969 and 1987.

the holiday outing. The old men from the villages of Vyl'gort and Vol'dino remembered with pleasure that in earlier times, during the Church holidays on St Stephen of Perm's day in Vyl'gort and on St Elijah's day in Vol'dino up to forty men on each side, not only the young lads but the married men too, used to step into the "walls". On St Stephen's day they came together on the bridge across the Machekha-shore brook near Vyl'gort, and on St Elijah's day on the bridge across the Rasyol' brook by the path to Vol'dino. Before the fight the youngest participants used to stir up the opposing side with bawdy *častuška*-songs and obscene flyting. The "walls" collided after staccato harmonica playing from both sides. Only the harmonica players, one or two on each side, were not touched in the fight. In the 1980s to 1990s during the Church holidays, which turned into secular communal outings, the "wall" fights were still preserved, but without any music and without any connection with the calendar rites. The strict order of the village fights was still followed too, but the cultural context was lost. From this perspective it is possible to study the transformation of songs. We are especially interested in the survival of local folklore and how connections with the other Komi groups, Russians and other peoples of the Uralic cultural area have changed the Upper Vychegda tradition.

The Upper Vychegda Komi

Boris Putilov wrote that ethnic communities form a culture defined locally in terms of history, society and geography.[12] The Upper Vychegda Komi form a separate ethno-local group, which developed relatively late, from the end of the sixteenth to the beginning of the eighteenth century. Because the Izhma and Pechora road of the northern Komi region, which passed through Cherdyn', Gaïny, Koïgorodok and Ust'-Sysol'sk (today Syktyvkar), went through the Upper Vychegda area, it connected geographically, but also historically, Western Vym', Northern Komi or Izhma, Udora and Pechora with Southern Sysola, Luza and the Komi-Permyaks. Hence the common annual Komi calendar festival, the Nikolaï market, connected to a local church festival, the Winter-Nikolaï feast, was held in Pomozdino. Komi from Pomozdino often married people from the Izhma and the most southerly Upper Vychegda, and the inhabitants of Dzol' village traditionally took Komi-Permyaks from Gaïn as wives. The Ekaterina II canal, nowadays blocked, connected the Vychegda and Kama rivers, and the northern Komi Permyaks and Upper Vychegda people kept in close touch with each other. The Upper Vychegda people, in turn, worked in the southern Urals and behind the Ural mountains, moved there, came back, hunted sables in hunting groups or brigades called *artels* behind the Urals, and hence had close connections with Siberian Russians, Samoyeds, Khanty, Mansi and Altaians. Even though the social, cultural and economic relations were close with Russians, the Upper Vychegda people never bordered geographically with densely populated Russian settlements,

12. Putilov 2003: 156.

The Upper Vychegda river at Vol'dino. – Photograph by A.-L. Siikala 2000

because both Upper Vychegda areas, Ust'-Kulom and Kortkeros, belong to that quarter of all the twenty Komi areas where the proportion of Komi population is 70 per cent. This might be the reason for the survival of folklore areas on the Upper Vychegda, such as have disappeared from the other areas or which have changed heavily because of influences from their neighbours or Soviet culture. A widely known saying refers to a kind of ethno-cultural autonomy of the Upper Vychegda: "I am tired of living in the Komi Republic, I shall move to Ust'-Kulom."

Upper Vychegda settlements have been traditionally divided into groups named *kusts* (*bush* in Komi), which indicate village groups situated near each other and which historically, religiously and administratively are connected to a larger village or *pogost*, a centre of a *volost* which has a church. *Pogost* centres developed further into wider settlements with local centres and village councils. Because of the politics of enlargement Pomozdino and the centre of Storozhevsk were joined administratively to a larger areal unity (the *rayon*; the first to Ust'-Kulom and the latter to Kortkeros) usually with a right to an ordinary village council. But they did not lose their democratic status. Today there may be some larger villages in a *kust* with a village council. On the other hand, when we follow the Vychegda river upstream there are Kortkeros, Storozhevsk, Bogorodsk (Viśer), Ust'-Kulom, Ust'-Nem, Pozheg and Pomozdino *kusts* as before. Although political and administrative alterations took place during the Soviet period and the relations of villages changed, the idea of the division of settlements into *kust* units and the understanding of relationships of these *kusts* is still vital. It is subject to changes brought about by other cultures, which are governmental and today even global. Long distances have shortened because of tarmac roads.

The house of a folk singer in Vol'dino. – Photograph by A.-L. Siikala 2000

On the other hand, many small distances seem to be long in the new perspective, which has changed the understanding of time and space. This change can be illustrated in legends told by many informants. One inhabitant of Badël'sk village related that his grandfather brought pilgrims going on foot from Badël'sk to the Stephan monastery of Holy Trinity through the forest. He left in the morning, went to the day service and after the whole ceremony returned home for the night. Today the distance from Badël'sk to Ul'yanovo through Pomozdino and Ust'-Kulom is 100 km along the tarmac road. A similar story is also told about an old woman from Badël'sk, who had lost all her relatives in the village and lived alone. Every Saturday she visited her relatives, who had a sauna in Malaya Kuzhba, and returned back home in Sunday. According to contemporary measurement the distance is about 120 km on the tarmac road.

Hunting artels as folklore arenas

Vishera healers, fullers and shoemakers earned their living in the *volost* of Pomozdino but they also visited the villages of Upper Izhma – Izvail', Lach (Komi: Lač), Roz'din – which belonged to the Pomozdino *pogost*. Hunters from different *kusts* formed common *artels* (brigades) and exploited neighbouring areas belonging to the *kusts*. Hunting *artels* were important arenas for intensive communication and oral lore, which were becoming strongly limited in the 1930s and 1940s.

Formerly our people fought a lot against the Ugra people – the Ostyaks, you know – about the hunting grounds on the Urals as well as behind the Urals. Even before the War (1941–5) it was so, they said. At that time, they used to go in hunting brigades. The brigades lit the fire to spend the night, and whoever lit the fire first, that one was slaughtered. If the Ostyaks lit the fire first, our men killed them. If they managed to catch our men, to sneak secretly up to the fire, they murdered our people. This was in the 1920s to 1930s, and even later. Well, maybe Siberia was not so rich with furs, and on our side there was everything, now only a few are left. However, they came with good prey from that side. Or they did not come back at all.

A man had his hunt on the border with Tyumen oblast', even further away from this Siberian route. And he came to the Ostyaks, a father and a son. They decided to kill him as he left. He was like a guest, so it seemed not to be good to kill him in the house. And he left his fur-cap in the house saying, I'll go out for a while. And he ran away. And it was night and a snowstorm, and the tracks were covered with snow. They lost him. "I'll never," he says, "go there alone." But somebody always went, anyway.[13]

Certainly, the stories about real war conflicts refer to more ancient times and belong to the sphere of folklore, but they nevertheless reflect the difficulties of relations between the brigades of different ethnic origin and the complexity of the hunting life. On the conflicts over hunting rights between the Upper Vychegda and Upper Pechora Komi in the 1930s to 1940s, which no longer resulted in fatalities, the children of the participants commented:

In olden days the autumn hunting began here in October. They went to Pechora. The Pechora people hated them and stole their furs. Once our people went to the forest. And what a household they had there: they made a hut, put down a sheepskin, *eshkyn* (a blanket with pocket for feet made from sheepskin), and that's all. One of them stayed to cook and to keep watch. The Pechorans came, beat him – he was alone – and took the furs they got yesterday (all the others our men managed to hide). The hunters came back: everything was plundered, scattered, their comrade beaten. And the people from Pozheg and Pomozdino [i. e. the countrymen from the Upper Vychegda] were hunting somewhere nearby. They called them and seven or eight men went to the Pechorans' camp. The Pechorans also had only one guard. They beat the guard, broke the guns, burnt the huts and took the furs. Then they came back.[14]

Judging by the domination of hunting themes and the image system in the folklore texts, hunting in Komi tradition occupied a place close to army service as a side of the men's culture deserving equal poetic and epic praise. The hunting-magic epic of the Komi predominates over the heroic epic in quantity and quality, which points to a special importance of the hunting culture for the Komis. The hunt may be poetically compared with the battle field as a comparable site for the application of the supreme forces of the hero. The image of a hunter in other folklore genres and in everyday speech

13. M. I. Ulyashov, rec. O. U., Priural'skiĭ, Troitsko-Pechorsk region, 2007.
14. E. E. Ulyashev, rec. O. U., Badʹěl'sk, Ust'-Kulom region, 2005.

is poetic enough and bears a positive emotional valuation, being a standard of a "real" man, called *vör kyrnysh*, "forest raven", *vador kaľa*, "shore gull", and the sphere of hunting is described as men's prerogative. The Komi epic hero is as a rule a hunter possessing majestic strength and magic abilities, and in the Komi fairy tales the peculiar transitional moment is the hero's penetration into the forest – as opposed to the coming into the open field of a Russian hero.

The Komi hunting season consisted of the pursuit of autumn game and the winter-spring great beast and fur chase. Whereas the autumn hunt, beginning from St Simeon's day up to the day of the Protection of the Virgin, took place on the grounds not far from the villages and included mainly the hunters going around along fixed routes (Russian *putiki*), the winter-spring one was represented by a brigade's campaign for hundreds of miles, often beyond the Urals, to the far-away wilderness. It lasted up to three or four months and was connected with a great physical tension. The main Komi means of transport was fur-soled skis and hand-pulled sledges, pulled with harnesses. The carrying capacity of a sledge was up to 10–12 *puds* (160–90 kg), but moving a load of more than 8–9 *puds*, even with help from dogs, was hard work. On the long climbs the hunters had to leave a part of the load and to harness the sledge in pairs, coming back for the abandoned load the next day. Therefore on the long and distant campaigns they took only the most necessary food, attempting to restrict the allowance.[15] The route's severities were reflected in the folk poetry. So, in a wedding song the hunter boy sings:

koköj menam ćukyľtćis	My legs are crooked
kuź tuj džendödömyś . . .	Because I made the long way shorter . . .
görböj menam bydmis	A hump has grown on me
kuź nort kyskalömyś . . .	From pulling the long hunting sledges . . .
nyröj menam ćukyľtćis	My nose is crooked
ur nyrisalömyś . . .	Because I nosed out the squirrels . . .
śinmöj menam tamyšmis	My eyes squint
koz jylyś ur kyjödömyś . . .	Because I spied out the squirrels on the fir-tree tops . . .[16]

Today it is difficult to find close personal relations between areas of the Vishera and the Upper Vychegda villages, because only a few hunters from Baděľsk have preserved their hunting rights in the Lymva tributary of the Vishera. The disputes about hunting grounds are resolved in a peaceful way and "inheritance" of the territory gives the right of priority:

When my father died, I abandoned the big hunting circuit, and for about four years did not go along that circuit. The near circuit was sufficient. And when after that I thought to repair my traps there, there was too little game. So I began to make the traps there but I saw somebody had already put his there. Three or

---

15. Konakov 1996: 126.
16. Mikushev 1969: 39–41.

four traps stood there. Once as I went around there, near a trap of mine a piece of birch-bark was nailed on a tree. It was scrawled there: "Who has so cheekily trodden on my routes? We have to talk about it." And a Vishera man from Lymva village had signed it. I went to him, took a bottle with me – he was about to start a fight: "Why have you got onto my hunting grounds, is there not enough room for you?" And I said: "What kind of threat is that? Already my father used to hunt there, I can show you his old cuttings on the trees." I led him there and showed him. There father's *pas* [kin sign cut on a tree] was preserved under the resin, and we picked it out. "Well," he said, "sorry. I looked: nobody was hunting here, and there was plenty of game, that's why I extended my range. I knew your father," he said, "but I had no idea he had come down here." So we agreed. He moved his traps away a bit and I moved my ones.[17]

The disappearance of hunting culture led to the domination of agriculture and cattle. The gender relations also changed with the change of occupation and especially with the new modes of life brought by the Revolution. Changes in gender relations affected folklore.

Gender relations and songs

Collectivisation in the years 1928–38 and after the Second World War broke the centuries-old way of life in the countryside and affected local cultures and folklore. The change was reflected in the gender relations of society: women began to dominate the traditional culture, first because of their numbers and then because of the quality of their interventions. This cannot be explained by the great conservativeness of women, as V. V. Nalimov and Zh. A. Drogalina thought when they referred to Alexander Borisov: "The Orthodox Church is archaic and for that reason non-active. It depends on old women."[18] In the Upper Vychegda, those Komi men who did not belong to the Old Believers or other religious groups were never very interested in the Church, because the male hunting culture was connected to the forest and its spirits. Women's culture in the countryside was linked with agriculture, which was dominated by the Orthodox Church. Hence it was natural that the priest through his position belonged to the world of women in tales, beliefs, omens, ideas of Komi men, fairytales and other folk narrative texts. Actually it could be said that the world view, beliefs and folklore of Komi men were more conservative than those of women. On the other hand, men, whose life was associated with long and continuous work shifts, in hunting, temporary jobs, factory work and so forth, adopted new cultural features, especially material ones, sooner than women.

Consequently the Upper Vychegda Old Believer centres, Kerchomya, Voch' and Vol'dino, and some Christian groups, for example "Singers of Good" (*Bur s'ylys'*) in Pozheg, Myёldino and Vyl'gort, were created by men who came from Pechora and the Urals and brought with them new ideas,

17. E. E. Ulyashev, rec. O. U., Bad'ёl'sk, Ust'-Kulom region, 2005.
18. Nalimov and Drogalina 1995.

books and prayers, which were not consistent with the doctrine thought by the Church. Teachers among the Old Believers and other sects were traditionally men, even though women took part in prayer meetings more than men. After the time of persecutions and the Second World War, when a great part of the men had been killed in the Finnish Winter War, the Great Patriotic War and Russo-Japanese war in the 1940s, women began to replace local men as teachers among the Old Believers and Evangelical sects. In the 1920s this would have been impossible, but after the war women had to take charge of many male domains.

The same process can also be seen in the area of male verbal culture. After the war it partly disappeared, and was partly taken over by women, who adapted tradition to suit their ideas. Therefore, the folklore collectives lacked the voice of men. Usually groups had two or three male singers and one or two accordion players. An exception to this was Kerchomya village in Ust'-Kulom with its original culture, in which the traditions of Old Believers were fused with acts of resistance against the authorities and anarchist attitudes towards the encircling world. The village was famous for its well-known accordion players and cruel habits. It was said that "In Kerchomya, forty accordions are played in a festival and forty guns are shot in a night." The saying is known even today, because the accordion player groups have operated there to this day.

Above all, the cultural processes which changed the gender relations affected folklore discourse. Both the amount and quality of folklore items, forms of performance and even detailed genre features reflected the female way of thinking and practices. In folk song, traditionally female lyrics began to dominate the epic singing, which had been a male genre. These changes can be illustrated by two examples. The one is a lyrical song well known in the Upper Vychegda, *Me gul'ajti lun daj voj* ("I partied [strolled] day and night").

Me gul'ajti lun daj voj,	I partied day and night,
Gorte lokti asjador,	I came home in the early morning.
Mamlen paćis vajmema,	Mother's stove was warm,
Pöś piregis petema,	Hot pies were baked,
Samevaris pużema,	The samovar was boiling,
Bat'e lokte udž vyliś,	Father came from work,
Voke lokte vorsaniś,	Brother came from the dances,
Ćoj lokte vojpukaniś,	Sister came from an evening party,
Me gul'ajti lun daj voj.[19]	I partied day and night.

The subject of the song is having fun the whole day and night and coming home in the early morning. The song refers to the doings of family members, mother, father, brother and sister, according to a common pattern in lyrical

19. Mariya Ivanovna Ivashova, Ėleonora Nikanorovna Ivashova, Dina Pavlovna Gabova, Lidiya Ivanovna Ivashova, Avgusta Semenovna Gabova, Tamara Efimovna Kalistratova, Natal'ya Ivanovna Ivashova, rec. A.-L. S. and O. U., Bogorodsk (Viśer), Kortkeros region, 20–21.5.2000.

songs of young women also known in the Baltic area. There are variants in which this song is a part of another song telling of a recruit who was taken to the army though he is small and insignificant:

Prijemas ke me lećći da,	When I went for review[20]
Meiś dźoľais abu,	Nobody was smaller than me,
Meiś końeris abu,	Nobody was more miserable than me.
Meiś omeľis abu.	Nobody was leaner than me.
Me ke ćajti, oz bośtni da,	I thought they would not take me,
Vidźeda da, bośtisni.	But I saw they would take me.
Jures ńaredź šyrisni da	They shaved my head bald and
Kolľedćini ystisni.	They sent me to say good-bye.
Me ke kabake pyri da	Then I went to an alehouse and
Parta vinase kori . . .	Asked a quarter[21] of vodka.

The song describes the subject as smaller, leaner and more miserable than the others in the way of some songs telling of a poor girl (see. pp. 158–9). But the army takes the wretched man on. The final lines resemble drinking songs (see p. 241); they change the mood of the song and cut through the sorrowful thoughts. This song ending with two or three additional lines was already in 1960s an independent part of a recruiting song. The other example is the song of *Pedör Kiron*, translated from a Russian religious poem, which told of Theodore of Tiran, the subduer of a dragon. The song is originally Greek. The Komi translation has lost all the references to Christian culture except the morning prayer of the hero. The Komi hero fights with a sword, not the word of God, and he does not fight for the Christian faith but for the Russian land and tsar. The image of the dragon opponent has been replaced by an image of enemy forces. The song is known only in the Vychegda river area, from the Upper Vychegda to the Vym' river. Two variants of the song texts were recorded on the Upper Vychegda in Skorodum and Voľdino and one in Pomozdino and Pozheg during the 1960s. Some of the texts were published in the collections which dealt with Komi folk songs and epic forms of Komi folklore.[22] During our field work we recorded parts of the *Pedör Kiron*, but could not find a complete version. When we asked Yuliya Pavlovna Sergatova from Voľdino to sing *Pedör Kiron*, she sang only the beginning of the ballad, which tells of the handsome Roman and beautiful Romanica (*Micha Röman*):

Mića Römanlen võli mića žö j götir.	Handsome Roman had a very beautiful wife,
Yle slavitće daj yle ńimale.	Famous far off, her name known far away,

20. Review refers to a reception of recruited men in order to examine their health and suitability for the army.
21. A quarter (*parta* in Komi) is an old measure, equivalent to 3 litres.
22. Mikushev 1987; Mikushev and Chistalëv 1966; Mikushev, Chistalëvand Pochev 1971.

Mića Römanliś mića götirse	The beautiful wife of handsome Roman,
Šöd totarajas pölöńiteni.	Lusted after by the black Tatars.
Mića Römanej mića götirse	The beautiful wife of handsome Roman
Karta vilas leććedis daj vorje puktis,	They set in the byre and put to a trough,
Daj vorje puktis, daj vorjen žej vejťťis,	Put to a trough and covered the trough,
Vorjen žej vejťťis, turun jur puktis,	Covered the trough and on it threw hay,
Turun jur puktis,	On it threw hay,
Ydžid öškes domalis . . .[23]	Next to the big ox they roped her . . .

Then she suddenly stopped singing and said: "That's all. I know only this far", though some years ago she performed a longer variant, which she had learned when she was a young girl from her mother's sister Anna in Pomozdino. Yuliya Sergatova knew, in principle, also two variants of the *Pedör Kiron* song: a Pomozdino variant from her aunt Anna and a Voľdino variant from her mother-in-law Natal'ya Il'inichna Ulyasheva. But she was too tired to remember them though she had performed them to students in the 1970s.

In Pozheg in 2002 we were luckier, because we found Natal'ya Andreevna Ulyasheva in the village of Kekur. She had known the whole song after learning it from her mother Aleksandra Mikhaĭlovna Shomysova (named in the traditional Komi way: Grish-Öprös'-Mikajlö-Sandrö) from Skorodum village. She sang only the beginning of the song to us:

Pedör Kiron, bur mortanöj,	Pedör Kiron, my good man,
Medydžyd saröj,	My greatest tsar,
Roć mu kutyśöj.	Upholder of the Russian country.
Pedör Kiron užis ij ćeććis,	Pedör Kiron slept and stood up,
Myśśis ij jurbitis, synaśis da	Washed, prayed and combed.
Vötse kutis ij viśtavni:	He began to tell about the dream:
Me pe talun vötaśi,	Today I saw in a dream
Kyz kymer i kypedćis,	A big cloud rise.
Kyz kymer i börśańis	After the big cloud
Kyk kyrniš i lebisni.	Two crows came flying.
Kerka jur vyle pukśillisni,	On the roof of a house they sat
Kurk-kurk!-vartisni,	"Croak, croak!" they screamed,
Da vörlańe ij lebisni . . .	and to the forest flew . . .

Though she tried many times to continue, she could not, but merely told the plot briefly and added:

Up to this [line] I know. I do not remember more. Mother, well, always sat spinning and sang. Mother sang. Men sang this song loudly. My uncle, according

---

23. Yuliya Pavlovna Sergatova, b. 1930 in Pomozdino, lived from 1951 in Voľdino, Ust'-Kulom region, rec. I. V. Il'ina, A.-L. S. and O. U., July 2001.

to mother, sang. I used to know it to the end, but nowadays age has made me shrivel.[24]

In the same village, we tried to ask other women about the same song. They remembered some fragments of the song, altogether twenty-six lines, but could not sing the whole song to the end:[25]

Oleg: And did you sing *Pedör Kiron*? Do you remember that kind of song?
Agniya Vasil'evna: Our men sang a lot of that song. My mother used to sing it. She began to rock the child to sleep and sang:

... *Śiźimdas śiźim rana.*	... Seventy-seven wounds.
Śiźimdas ranase šyen byčkemaeś,	He was pierced with seventy-seven wounds by a hoof,
Śiźim ranase pul'aen lyjemaeś ...	The bullets penetrated seventy-seven ...

Oleg: If you know the beginning, could you sing that too? Start from the beginning.
Evdokiya Arsent'evna: No, we know the beginning, but don't remember the melody.
Oleg: Just try.
Evdokiya Arsent'evna:

Pedör Kironej, roć mu kutiśej,	Pedör Kiron, my upholder of the Russian country,
Medydžid sarej, tene korisni ...	My eldest tsar asked of you ...

Agniya Vasil'evna: Oh dear, it's too long ... It had also these kind of lines:

Mamislen śinvais tuvsov lysva moz pete,	Mother's tears are running like a spring dew,
Bat'islen śinvais arśa lysvais moz	Father's like an autumn dew ...

Evdokiya Arsent'evna:

Mamislen ydžid šor moz vizulte,	Mother's like a great stream,
Bat'islen dźol'a šor moz vizulte	Father's like a small stream,
Babaislen vojtva moz t'opke ...	Wife's like drops dripped.
......	
Pedör Kironej, roć mu kutiśej,	Pedör Kiron, my upholder of the Russian country,
Medydžid sarej, vojujtni koremaeś	My oldest tsar, he invited you to a battle
...	...

He sat on the back of the horse and went, but more I do not remember. From mother the tears are shed like a big brook, but from the wife only the eaves are dripping ... the wife, seemingly, did not mind so much.

24. Natal'ya Andreevna Ulyasheva, b. 1917 in Pozheg, village of Kekur, rec. A.-L. S. and O. U., 3.7.2002.
25. Evdokiya Arsent'evna Shakhova, b. 1932, Agniya Vasil'evna Shakhova, b. 1933, Mariya Ivanovna Shakhova, b. 1933, rec. A.-L. S. and O. U., Pozheg, village of Kekur, 3.7.2002.

Poľe vylas pe ij šaťer zevtemaeś.	In the field, they construct a tent.
šaťer pytškas Peder Kiron kujle.	In the tent, Pedör Kiron lies.
Bur völis pe ij šuve:	And his good horse says:
- Bur köźajinej pe, bur köźajinej,	"My good master, well, my good master,
Lok pe me vyle söl da nuva.	Sit on my back and I will take you away."
- Og pe me vermi da kydźi söla?	"If I cannot, so how can I sit?"
Völis eśśa pidźeśćań vylas ij uśkedćas:	Then the horse knelt down on its knees:
- Bur köźajinej pe, bur köźajinej,	"My good master, well, my good master,
Lok pe me vyle söl da nuva	Sit on my back and I will take you away."
- Og pe me vermi da kydźi söla?	"If I cannot, how can I sit?"
Bok vylas śa uśkedćas da,	The horse threw itself on its side, and
oz že vermi sövni . . .	(Kiron) could not sit down . . .

Agniya Vasiľevna: When he jumps on the back of the horse, well

Vyľ kerkajas pe drögńitasni,	New houses, well, shake
Važ kerkajas pe pölińćasni,	Old houses lean of line,
Omeľ kerkajas kiśśalasni . . .	The age-old houses collapse . . .

Evdokiya Arsenťevna:

Völ kok uvśis muis pylśan gyrśa	Lumps like big saunas are flying from the
* lebe . . .*	feet of the horse . . .

Once I sent the recorders to Stepan-Ladim Serafim in Skorodum, he knew the whole song.[26]

It is clear that women remember the tears of the heroes, which fix their attention. The same is true of the suffering expressed by song: they remember the tragic death of a wounded hero. But the actual battle scenes do not seem to be interesting for women though the cause of the sorrowful events in ballads and lyric songs is a fiancé or husband who dies in a foreign country. All the women interviewed, born in 1910–30, said that they had heard the song from their mother or grandmother. At the same time they stressed that songs like *Pedör Kiron* belonged to men, who liked to sing them. Women might hum them when they worked at home or as a lullaby for children. Vasiliĭ Zakharovich from the same village, Pozheg, said that *Pedör Kiron* and other war songs were performed by men:

> My mother, Pelagaya Prokopʼevna Treťyakova, sometimes sang *Pedör Kiron* at home. I remember only the beginning "Pedör Kiron, you sustainer of the Russian country, good man, the oldest of tsars . . ." Mother was a sister of Sandrik Mikol.[27] I have never sung. Usually, women sing, but this *Pedör Kiron* I have heard many times from men.[28]

26. Evdokiya Arsenťevna Shakhova, b. 1932, Agniya Vasiľevna Shakhova, b. 1933, Mariya Ivanovna Shakhova, b. 1933, rec. A.-L. S. and O. U., Pozheg, village of Kekur, 3.7.2002.
27. Sandrik Mikol is Nikolaĭ Akeksandrovich Shakhov, an early-twentieth-century poet from Pozheg.
28. Vasiliĭ Zakharovich Treťyakov, b. 1918, rec. A.-L. S. and O. U., Pozheg, 4.7.2002.

This reference to male singing is the only one we heard in the Ust'-Kulom villages. But it seems that in the twentieth century women inherited a great part of the songs performed before by men. A part of the transition depended not only on the general change of gender roles but was also connected with the establishment of folklore collectives.

The fusion of singing traditions

Present-day folklore and common social features in the villages of the Komi Republic are the outcome of the unification and the fusion of national traditions and public and administrative sociocultural influences. It is difficult to determine where the influence of the "older" tradition ends and where a new one is emerging, because folklore elements are not just the repetition of old inheritances. They have been shaped on the basis of experiences of hundreds of years and reworked in new circumstances through cultural strategies and tactics.

Hence, we cannot talk about creation of Komi folklore traditions, though nowadays they have many new forms: ethno-pedagogical centres, folklore theatres, restored personal and local names or presentations of village folklore ensembles. Culture cannot entirely die and be born again from the mud. It might disappear or change or melt into the soil of new cultural traditions, but live again when fertilised. Hence the present-day women's folklore collectives of the Upper Vychegda are as traditional as women's festival gatherings or evening get-togethers in the nineteenth century. The only difference is the encircling modern culture and social interventions that have influenced the characters of performers, the programmes, the songs, the singing arenas and the times of performances.

14 Folklore, cultural institutions and festivals

Folklore as verbal peasant art

The origin of folklore collectives working together with modern rural clubs and cultural houses goes back to the inauguration of the work of reading rooms, clubs and libraries following Soviet tradition. These were established after the Revolution of 1917 under the aegis of cultural commissariats and later of corresponding ministries. Among the main objectives of these institutions was the initiation of the rural populace into the achievements of the "world proletarian culture" by raising reading and writing abilities. Before the 1940s a minor aspect of this was the so-called culture of the rural populace, represented by such folklore genres as dance, folk tales, music and song. Everything else, for example ritual folklore and beliefs, was regarded as magic superstition and hence as belonging to the leftovers from the past.

Such a categorisation of folklore is based on the notions of N. P. Andreev and Yu. M. Sokolov. They represented the "official Soviet science" in discussions touching upon the topic of folkloristics in Soviet Russia in the early 1930s. For them, folklore is a verbal art, comparable with literature and with aesthetic qualities like literature or art.[1] This was in opposition to the viewpoints of many other scientists, such as M. K. Azadovskiĭ (1928, 1939), A. M. Astakhova (1931), P. G. Bogatyrev (1971) and Vladimir Ya. Propp (1928), who understood folklore as part of culture, practically synonymous with tradition. Tradition, they argued, is not to be categorised by genre but functionally, as verbal, musical, dance and ritual folklore, as everyday folklore, as profession-related folklore and so forth. However, following the official Soviet scientific line, the "folkiness" of folklore began to be interpreted in the spirit of Marxist-Leninist ideology as class-based, where the main function is the expression of the ideology of the folk groups and the main task is the rural population's struggle against the bourgeois, the nobility and the priesthood.

Folk poetry, viewed according to class and artistic aesthetics, thus artificially lost its connection both with the cultures of other social levels and with the everyday life of the people, as well as with mythological concepts and viewpoints. It became a weapon of propaganda. On the other hand new songs

---

1. Andreev 1939; Sokolov 1926, 1931.

and rituals began to take root in traditional life. In 1925 V. I. Lytkin wrote in his article "What sort of literature is needed in the rural Komi village?":

Why do young people able to read and write not spread (popularise) revolutionary songs? Why are there no revolutionary songs in any of the villages? Why is there no one to write them and read them, no one to teach them to sing, no one to make them known?[2] From the 1930s folklore was supported officially, but only in an oral and aesthetic folk-art form. Maxim Gor'kiĭ's remarks to the First Congress of Soviet Writers in 1934 linked folklore with literature: as literature folklore could give heroic models for people, heroes who were both ordinary people but have extraordinary strengths. Gor'kiĭ's redefinition of folklore had wide consequences.[3] Folklore seemed to offer means for building socialism, but not all folklore. Feasts, folk and religious festivals, rituals, everyday linguistic use and traditional tasks were left outside the bounds of folklore. All that was left was participation in concerts and festivals, which nestled in special culture institutes, reading rooms, red corners, rural clubs, cultural houses and in time in new, official festivals and events.

Following the Soviet plans, the reading rooms and clubs had to replace both the village council in making economic decisions and also the church and local amusement places, theatres, concerts and so forth. The clubs were opened everywhere in closed church structures, but not for economic, but political, reasons. In Upper Vychegda, in eastern Komi, clubs were found in churches in nearly all the former parishes: Bol'shelug, Bogorodsk, Nivshera, Myëldino, Ust'-Nem and Pozheg.

> The locals built a timber, two-cupola church. Then they began making tiles. Masters came for the tile work, "ginnari, ginnari" – they just played the accordion in the evening. We just danced along, mother says. The bad times began [the Revolution] and the work was left off [of tiling the church]. The wooden church was turned into a club. I danced there as well. It's because of that that my feet ache: Go on now and dance in the church! By Alekseĭ Mikhaĭlovich's stream, on Mel'nich's quay we went to have fun. Now we gather at Vasiliĭ Ivanovich's.[4]

Gradually, ongoing dramatic collectives took shape in connection with the clubs. They consisted primarily of youngsters from the local Komsomol departments. To concerts of political agitation, where plenty of *ćastuška* songs and dramatisations of burning issues of the day were presented, as well as revolutionary and patriotic songs (originals and translations), were gradually added broader dramatic presentations, such as comedies, plays,

2. Illya Vaś 1994. Illja Vaś is a pseudonym for Vasiliĭ Lytkin, who was a well-known Komi linguist. He had contacts with Finnish, Hungarian and other foreign Finno-Ugric researchers and intellectuals. In 1925–1930 he was an ardent revolutionary romantic, but suffered a sad fate: because of his foreign contacts he was arrested in 1936 and accused of being a bourgeois nationalist and Finnish spy. He was imprisoned until 1938.
3. Olson 2004: 39.
4. Glafira Matveevna Larukova, b. 12.4.1922, rec. A.-L. S. and O. U., May 2000.

operettas and "oratorios" by V. Savin, N. Popov, V. Chistalёv and M. Lebedev. In other words, an amateur-based and everyday form of folk art began to change into something ever more semi-professional.

Drama circles and the growth of poetry

An indication of the increasing interest in theatrical art was the birth of drama circles everywhere in connection with the clubs. Thus in 1938, 313 drama circles were counted in the republic; in 1940, in addition to these, in Kortkeros, Ust'-Usa and Pechora amateur theatres were operating.[5]

The predominant materials were of course themes concerned with the Revolution, the civil war and the building of collective farms and industry. Some presentations were written from a folklore and ethnographic basis, although in the 1920s to 1930s they usually received an allegorical form and represented the class struggle. Thus M. N. Lebedev's operetta *Tun* (shaman, witch), performed in the folk house of Ust'-Sysol'skiĭ in 1920, presents a pagan shaman as preying upon peasants and as an enemy of enlightenment. N. A. Frolov's historical dramatic poem *Pemid parmayn* ("In the dark taiga") is a demythologised adaptation of a tale about the *pam*[6] Shypicha-Sukhanov, "oppressor of peasants". It was presented in the theatre of the Komi Republic in 1941, five years after it was written. Among comparable plays and arrangements is V. T. Chistalёv's play *Nyv śetöm* ("Wedding", literally "ceding of a girl"), which was performed in 1936 in the folk house of Pomozdino. It had preserved the traditions of the folk theatre. In fact *Nyv śetöm* was the wedding ritual in the guise of a play, which over the course of its several hours of performance preserved ethnographic and folkloristic details of the Pomozdino wedding festival. Yuliya P. Sergatova said that she was a child at that time but took part in the performance. Her aunt could perform laments and was one of the actors. Later the play was performed in the 1960s and 1970s by the forces of the drama collective in the cultural house of Pomozdino.

In the difficult social fragmentation at the beginning of the twentieth century many peoples of Russia took refuge in folklore. Peoples such as the Komi, whose literature was at that time torn loose from its nineteenth-century traditions, began to create literature based on folk tradition. Famous old poets such as I. Kuratov, G. Latkin, P. Rasputin and P. Klochkov were already forgotten. Precisely that folklore foundation which is alive in the poems of the generation following the older revolution, such as V. Chistalёv, V. Savin and M. Lebedev, brought the texts again into folk programmes, first of all as arranged songs. Later they received a second life as folklore with its many adaptations and folk recollections. The formation of folklore and

---

5. Kozlova 1966: 63.
6. *pam* (*pama*, *pan*) is a pagan priest and war chief. Pan-Šypića is a folklore figure, with whom a historical personage, a representative of the merchant Sukhanovy family of Ust'-Sysol'sk, has been confused.

the creation of oral variants were also much influenced by the sorrowful events of the 1940s, when all Komi poets were persecuted and their books condemned and destroyed.

From the beginning, when the "proletarian" regime began to form cultural institutes, it attempted to determine their work and exercise a firm hold over them. The peripatetic instructional Komi theatre worked from the early 1930s up to 1936; it formed the basis of the Komi theatre in 1936. In place of the theatre touring the countryside there arose theatres on the collective farms and sovkhozes, which obtained a professional status and which were subject to the office of the governmental art department of the folk-commissariats' soviets in the autonomous soviet socialist republic of Komi. The theatre of the collective farm and sovkhoz of Ust'-Kulom region was opened in 1941; the theatre director was M. K. Rastorguev. The theatre presented a Komi-language drama only in 1948, however.

The theatre's programme was fundamentally "corrected" after the central committee of the united Communist party promulgated its stance on theatre programmes and measures for their improvement on 26 August 1946. From the programme were ousted plays which were "of a low ideological value", i.e. which did not reflect the struggles of the "heroic" post-war recovery period, or the demands of socialist reconstruction, and which did not praise communist ideals. Naturally, among these were counted plays and concerts based on folklore themes, which were viewed as atavistic and as extolling the dark bourgeois or kulak past from before the Revolution. During this period the plays of dramatists persecuted in the 1920s and 1930s, V. Savin's *Nëbdinsa Vittor*, N. Popov's *Žugyl'* and V. Chistalëv's *T'ima Ven'*, were already forbidden.[7] Later the regime refused to financially support the rural theatres and collectives, as a result of which even Ust'-Kulom theatre was closed.[8]

Strengthening the village culture

N. S. Khrushchëv's time turned attention away from the previously focal ideology of industrialisation to the economy. At this period began the so-called cultural burgeoning in the village. Initially it manifested itself as mass-cultural propaganda and an enlivening of the work of clubs and theatres. Amateur theatres began to be established in many rural clubs in the 1960s. In 1969, seven folk theatres were already operating in the Komi Republic, three in rural areas, one being in the central Komi village of Kortkeros. In 1969, sixty amateur collectives took part in the regional festivals of the amateur theatres. In 1987, twenty-two folk theatres operated in the republic, eleven of them in rural districts.[9]

At the same time, amateur singing groups strengthened. Their programme consisted, apart from the obligatory, officially enlightening songs,

7. All these three poets are from the Ust'-Kulom villages.
8. Kozlova 1966: 147.
9. Kozlova 1966: 148.

also of many folksongs and songs favoured by the folk. They were presented after the supported entertainment pieces. Folklore festivals began to be arranged widely in the 1960s and 1970s: there were regional, republic-wide and national festivals. Many rural amateur groups sang not only in the Komi Republic but even travelled to Moscow.

In the 1980s to 1990s, the time of perestroika and the subsequent depression, the festivals were localised within the borders of the republic and they began to be celebrated in Syktyvkar and regional centres. For example, in Ust'-Kulom, the centre of Ust'-Kulom district, the Vasileĭ folklore and amateur group festival has taken place since 1991. It takes place on the winter St Basil's day and is arranged by three locals: the composer Vasiliĭ Gushchin, the self-taught composer Vasiliĭ Chuvёrov and the poet Vasiliĭ Lodygin, who are in close contact with Ust'-Kulom folk choir.

Since the 1990s the celebration of festivals in individual villages and towns has been much favoured; the programmes include presentations by the republic's folklore groups both amateur and professional. Folklore bands began at this time to work more actively, and in Syktyvkar a state folklore theatre was opened, which under its present name is the Komi Republic Music and Drama Theatre. A significant number of artists have gone to rural art schools. Mikhail Burdin from the small central Komi village of Nivshera created a new folklore band *Zarñi añ* ("The Golden Woman") after the band *Parma* ("The Taiga") which he founded joined the folklore theatre as an independent formation. Mikhail Lipin from Ust'-Kulom, producer of the drama *Gytsan* ("The Swing") (1994), also worked on the stage of the folklore theatre, as well as Anastasia Kazakova from Kortkeros, producer of the drama *Jöla gor* ("The Sound of Echo") and previously director of Kortkeros folk theatre. The rural theatres have gradually become amateur assemblages, where concert programmes have taken over from dramatic productions. In the post-perestroika era national consciousness has grown and folklore items have also broadened the popular programme.

The Upper Vychegda collectives

The folklore collectives operating nowadays in the Upper Vychegda region originated in the 1930s in connection with rural village clubs and culture houses: Vol'dino 1933, Vyĺgort 1936, Nёbdino 1927, Pozheg 1930 and Pomozdino 1926. Thereafter only the directors and composition changed. It is to be noted that the collectives in Pomozdino, Pozheg and Nёbdino, which were formed before the others, were organised by poets born in these villages: V. T. Chistalёv, N. A. Shakhov and V. A. Savin.[10] A great part of the programme in these years consisted of their poems, which later circulated in numberless oral variants. Usually the caretaker of the reading room, the club leader or the cultural worker gathered such a collective on a voluntary

10. All three of these were from the Upper Vychegda villages of Nёbdino, Pozheg and Pomozdino (author's observation).

basis. Connected with the club in the village was an adult amateur collective, whose membership was more or less unchanged. In connection with the school a children's collective operated, whose membership varied as the school children grew up. The school collective was directed by or worked in close collaboration with the corresponding village club.

Amateur collectives presented both dramatic and concert programmes on official festivals, such as the Soviet army day (23 February), women's day (8 March), Lenin's birthday (22 April), May day, Victory day (9 May) and Revolution day (7 November). Part of the Soviet celebration days are still current, as Evgeniya Ulyasheva from Vol'dino noted: "The next concert is the twenty-ninth anniversary of Sord'yv village . . . on 8 March we always meet, sometimes also on 23 February."[11] Centenaries and other village celebrations are nowadays important: we took part in the centenary of the Vol'dino school, where both the Vol'dino and Vyl'gort choirs performed. The celebrations of local cultural personages are remembered by singers. The centenary of the poet V. T. Chistalëv was celebrated in Pomozdino, noted Yuliya Pavlovna Sergatova. The photographs of performances help to commemorate the important celebrations. Polina Alekseevna Ulyasheva showed her album and explained the background of the pictures.

> This is the feast of T'ima Veń,[12] our poet, who is our local poet. The feast was held when it was 110 years since his birth. Then we went to his feast and sang and performed at his monument and performed at the Cultural House of Pomozdino. This picture was taken outside the Cultural House. This is near the Cultural House in Pomozdino, then it was the feast of T'ima Veń. And here we are performing at the seventieth anniversary of the region; we visited them and performed. And this is the anniversary of the artist Yuliya Pavlovna Sergatova, she is seventy-five . . .

Festival concerts were not usually confined within the walls of the local club: the collectives from time to time set off on a visitation of neighbouring villages. Dina Egorovna from Vol'dino said: "I have performed now for more than forty years. Oh God, how many times we walked to Kortkeros, to all the places we went where we performed, in town, in Kortkeros, Storozhevsk and in all the villages, Puzla and Jag Ködž. I was once in Jag Ködž, it was a long time ago."[13] Exchange visits were also arranged. Sometimes two groups from neighbouring villages arranged a concert together, performing in turn in each village. Such peripatetic activity attracted attention from the beginning. Visiting presentations by folklore and amateur groups mainly took place within a *kust*, the circle of neighbouring villages. Yuliya Pavlovna Sergatova described the visits:

> A.-L. S. Did you perform in different villages?

11. Evgeniya Ivanovna Ulyasheva, Vol'dino, rec. A.-L. S., 16.6.2001.
12. Polina Alekseevna Ulyasheva, rec. A.-L. S., Vol'dino, 18.6.2001.
13. Dina Egorovna Pystina, rec. A.-L. S., Vol'dino, 16.6.2001 .

Yu. S.: We performed in different villages. In Puzla, which is 30 or 40 km from Vol'dino, then Bad'ĕl'sk, Pomozdino, Vyl'gort, Skorodum . . . These are the nearest places. In all the places, in all the places. At first at home we were busy, performed and then travelled. Earlier it was a matter of how to travel. There were no cars, we had to use horses. A horse cannot carry much. So. We put things on it so that it could carry them and we walked. It was like that.

A.-L. S. Was it difficult?

Yu. S.: Of course it was difficult. We had to walk 10, 20 km. And then we had to perform.[14]

The concerts of visiting groups were popular: "The elderly and children, old and young, all kinds of people came, all wanted to listen", said Yuliya Pavlovna. Folklore collectives did not charge spectators in their own village, but in other villages they used to have tickets. It cost 20 kopeks, the same sum as a loaf at that time:

> So, in our village we did not arrange chargeable concerts. Therefore the hall was full of people. If we had to travel, then it was chargeable. It was two rubles. Two kopeks. The ticket cost the same as a loaf. But now they charge three. Then the ticket was 20 kopeks, like a loaf for 20 kopeks. But now if it was like a loaf, it would be 8–9 rubles, if we want to count.[15]

Yuliya Sergatova mentioned that in the home village there were no tickets, but in the other villages the ticket was two rubles. The payments were used for costumes and for other outfits: "It was like the budget of the club." At that time the collectives did not have much, only one cabinet and a table which was taken from one of the *kulaks* at the time of the confiscation: "We did not have any more; a lamp we had, but not electricity. We used an old-type lamp."[16] Nowadays clubs have their own rooms in the cultural centres of villages and folklore collectives' cabinets for their dresses.

Later performances by the groups developed into a regional phenomenon, and then into a national event in the republic's capital, Syktyvkar, and finally into a governmental festival in Moscow. In Syktyvkar, the festivals were planned and directed by professionals. Yuliya Sergatova remembered the name of Igor' Sklyar, an instructor, who came from Moscow. The festival tradition carries on even today:

> A.-L. S.: What kind of festivals do you have? Do many groups take part in them?
>
> P. A. U.: We have festivals. Even now, on 12 June, we have a festival: festivals for children, festivals for grown people. There is *Jurgan, Šondibanèj* in Syktyvkar. At first we walk as a group, then all the collectives come together, many, many collectives, and they perform in Syktyvkar. This year there will also be a festival because we have a feast, a big feast, the eightieth anniversary of the Komi Republic. And they are probably going there. I do not know if we are going. That's how it is.

14. Yuliya Pavlovna Sergatova, rec. A.-L. S. and O. U., Vol'dino, 16.6.2001.
15. Dina Egorovna Pystina, rec. A.-L. S., Vol'dino, 16.6.2001.
16. Yuliya Pavlovna Sergatova, rec. A.-L. S. and O. U., Vol'dino.

A.-L. S.: And where are people accommodated during festivals?

P. A. U. In hotels, schools, or whatever they provide, and in colleges they give places. Hotels are very expensive.

A.-L. S.: Does the club give some money for you? You said that you collected money and made everything at home.

P. A. U.: No. Free of charge. No. All is free of charge. No. We feel that this is nice; it is good that everybody can present something of her own.[17]

Groups were carefully divided at festivals into different levels according to their capabilities. The basis of the hierarchy was the quality of the choreography, the choice of costume and naturally the programme. Many Upper Vychegda groups have significant prizes and diplomas. All the singers got diplomas. Klavdiya Terent'evna remembered that Muza Alekseevna, Yuliya Pavlovna, Dina Egorovna and Mariya Anufrievna got diplomas in 1972, when the second festival of that time was organised in Syktyvkar.[18] International tours of course were beyond the dreams of most groups, even though the professional quality was often high enough. Real folklore presentations took place only in connection with the folklore festivals at different levels.

Today the state's attitude to folklore and amateur groups has changed, as have the groups' own views of the future and ways of carrying out their creative work. A reason for this is the Soviet and later Russian social and economic processes, which have resulted in the limitation of the field of activity of the groups. For economic reasons groups have not been able to travel to Moscow or Syktyvkar, or even to neighbouring villages very often.

The leader and director of the pensioners' choir of Bol'shelug in the Kortkeros region, Ol'ga Nikolaevna Pavlova, who founded the choir in 1986, told us of the choir's great problems in the 2000s. There are few singers: young pensioners, around fifty years old, do not join, and of sixteen singers only twelve are left. Secondly, the leader of the culture house will not give the choir any space, since he does not see the choir's work and existence as necessary or meaningful. Thirdly, it is difficult to do tours, as there are no funds to hire a bus or pay for fuel. Hence concerts are arranged only in nearby villages reachable by foot.

A.-L. S.: How expensive will it be, if you go to a festival? Does the government give money?

Yu. P. S.: No. They pay something, but we have to do everything ourselves. Last year, we went to perform in Ust'-Kulom, and paid ourselves for the petrol and the driver. They gave only a little, and that's all. For that reason it is difficult to travel to perform in concerts in other places, because, when we travel, all we get goes for petrol. So, we are not interested in travelling. You do not even earn anything whatever. Culture is always the lowest priority, and it has been and always will be.[19]

---

17. Polina Alekseevna Ulyasheva, rec. A.-L. S., Vol'dino, 18.6.2001.
18. Klavdiya Terent'evna Ulyasheva, rec. A.-L. S., Vol'dino, 16.6.2001.
19. Yuliya Pavlovna Sergatova, rec. A.-L. S. and O. U., Vol'dino, 16.6.2001.

The crisis in festival folklore is an axiom. The state does not give material support to small peripheral collectives, cultural institutes are poorly funded and cultural programmes are dwindling throughout Russia. On the other hand, the abandonment of festival structures, the weakening of the state's control and the decentralisation of folk culture may be seen in part as a return of folklore to its traditional form of existence. Presentations have achieved a relative independence in their local forms. Boris Putilov has put his finger on this by comparing local and regional folklore:

> It has become customary in the field of literature, theatre and professional music to oppose concepts of the centre and the periphery, the capital and the provinces, the national and the regional. This imperceptibly brings with it a value judgement: what is in first place, what second and so on. In the field of folklore there are no centres or capitals, nor any peripheries or provinces. Folklore follows its own path, and nothing rises higher above this living folklore – however deep an ethnic territory it may be found in – nor is anything more significant, "more collective".[20]

In the Upper Vychegda villages, we met both people who had sung previously in groups and those who nowadays work in folklore collectives. Folklore groups differ from each other for example in whether they have a director as leader, the age of the performers and the social position of the participants. In the villages of Myëldino and Pozheg we were told that there are no folklore collectives. However, the need to sing is manifest in the villages in two different ways. Firstly, in the singing of spiritual songs, favoured in these villages, and secondly in singing together with workmates. In Pozheg they are led by Lidiya Nikolaevna Vasil'chenkova, who tells of the singing thus:

> In Pozheg no one sings at funerals. The old women pray. When I came to work in the school in Pozheg in 1951, the teachers of the lower classes sang a lot. Now no one sings, not even at Kekur. They used to sing there more, and now there is no singing even in Pozheg. Peder Petyr's family sings at Vichkodor's house. The whole family of Kuchevs plays the harmonica, and sings very beautifully, but not the old songs from the 1920s and 1930s like Savin's, Lebedev's and Chistalëv's ... In the Pozheg area there were old singers only at Kekur. There are accountants', teachers' and school children's choirs, which perform revolutionary songs, favourites and classics. I "direct" them all. They sing polyphonically, but there are no folklore groups.[21]

The director of the culture house, or the so-called culture worker, who has attended Syktyvkar's cultural and folk-culture institute, directs the groups in many villages.

---

20. Putilov 2003: 158.
21. Lidiya Nikolaevna Vasil'chenkova, b. 1939 in Pozheg, rec. A.-L. S. and O. U.

*Yuliya Pavlovna Sergatova, Evgeniya Ivanovna Ulyasheva and Dina Egorovna Pystina
on the veranda of Vol'dino school. – Photograph by A.-L. Siikala 2002*

A life as a cultural director

In Vol'dino from 1954 to 1996 the director of the club was Yuliya Pavlovna
Sergatova, who told about her life, the activities of the club and the orders
given by the cultural ministry. Yuliya Sergatova was born on 7 July 1925 in
Pomozdino, the next village to Vol'dino. Her sister says that actually she was
born a month before, but Yuliya keeps to the day mentioned in her passport.
She began to sing already in childhood and took part in a theatre play on the
Pomozdino wedding when she was ten years old. After working in Syktyvkar
and Troitsko-Pechorsk, she came to Vol'dino in 1954 and dedicated her life
to the Vol'dino Cultural House and folklore collective.

> A.-L. S.: Polina Alekseevna said that you worked before that in a theatre.
> Yu. S.: I did not work in the theatre, only in a song and dance performance. It was
> always sold out. I was there for a year and a half. We sang something, whatever. By
> day we sang and in the evenings we went to the concert. There was no schooling.
> Later, when they cut back the staff, they kicked us out.
> A.-L. S.: Where was it?
> Yu. S.: In town, in Syktyvkar. We worked in the Philharmonia 1945. In 1947, they
> cut the staff.
> A.-L. S.: Did you live for long in Syktyvkar?
> Yu. S.: Maybe a year and a half. Then, because of staff cuts, I went to my sister in
> Troitsko-Pechorsk. I worked there for some time in the Cultural Palace. Then I

got ill and moved to Savin's library in Troitsko-Pechorsk. Then we went together with my husband, but nothing succeeded with us. I gave birth to twins and travelled back to Pomozdino. In Pomozdino I worked as an artist instructor from 1950 to 1954. Then I came here and worked here, and that's all.

A.-L. S.: How many years have you worked in this club?

Yu. S.: I have been here twenty-six years, thirty-six altogether.

A.-L. S.: A long time.

Yu. S.: A long time, altogether thirty-six years.

A.-L. S.: Now, what did you do in the club? It was a women's collective. That I know. But did you have other kinds of work?

Yu. S.: There were all kinds of work. Not like now. They demanded a lot. It was . . . how can I put it? . . . Like they led the party, they wanted it that way. Now I do not remember . . . now I cannot talk.

A.-L. S.: It does not matter.

Yu. S.: There, everyone asked for presentations and discussions and everything. They published posters, papers, war posters, all kinds of slogans. We had to organise many functions, not only concerts: evenings for cattle-breeders, autumn dances. There was all kind of evening entertainment. It was a collective . . . we had clubs, clubs for soloists, clubs for dance, and for theatre because we produced plays. Very big dramas with many acts.

A.-L. S. When you began the work, did you have a women's collective?

Yu. S.: No, not then. It broke down, what was going on. They used to have a theatre, I heard that it was Mariya Fëdorovna Trosheva who organised it. Women . . . we did not have even a house for the club, they did the music in a school. They had it before, but when I came, it did not function any more. I organised it for a second time.

A.-L. S. How did you know when you had to organise a festival? Who invited you to produce a festival?

Yu. S.: The Cultural Ministry, the executive committee of the district, the committee of the district, all of them together. They informed us, then we had a lot of documents. All the time there was something which we had to do, all kinds of things.

A.-L. S. Did they give any orders?

Yu. S.: They did, they did. And they demanded reports and programmes. We had to have a monthly programme, a quarterly programme and yearly programme. And we had to report on our activities: we had to make a monthly report, quarterly report and yearly report. And even in Ust'-Kulom they asked for seminars.

A.-L. S.: Did you have seminars?

Yu. S. Yes, there were seminars. They were in town.

A.-L. S.: What did you do in a seminar?

Yu. S.: In a seminar? There were seminars on dance. Then we danced. Because we could not dance. I do not know. They show us and we learn. Then we come and show the girls. And then we danced.

A.-L. S.: What kind of monthly programme did you have?

Yu. S.: What we did in a month I wrote on the programme: mini-concerts, or a lecture, or poster or evening party. I wrote all that.

A.-L. S.: Did the women's collective perform folklore song, or did they perform all kinds of songs? Did you have instructions on what kind of songs should be presented?

Yu. S.: We did not have instructions. We made up our minds ourselves. If we sang, they just did not allow the personal songs. Generally, we decided ourselves.

Polina Alekseevna
Ulyasheva, Vol'dino.
– Photograph by A.-L.
Siikala 2000

Then we rehearsed. Then they looked at these rehearsals and decided which kind of songs we could perform and which not.

A.-L. S.: How did you select the songs?

Yu. S.: We selected them together with the collective. They said what they knew and then they asked their parents – they told them and brought [the songs]. Then we went to our parents and wrote them down.[22]

The life story of Yuliya Sergatova reveals how tightly the Cultural Ministry and local authorities followed the work in the villages. Capable persons were elected to the positions of cultural director, they got orders for activities and they had to make monthly, quarterly and annual programmes. The reports had to be written similarly. Several seminars were organised for cultural workers and Yuliya Sergatova appreciated them. She was honoured in her own village because of her good voice, ability to dance and strict way of guiding the other performers. Singers said that she was a clever leader, ensuring that the choir had suitable dresses, for example trimming hems that were too long so that the traditional *köti*-shoes could be seen, and that she was the best singer and "could dance like a grasshopper". In 2004, she felt ill, and did not want to continue her interview, but came to the centenary of Vol'dino school and – after the choir had finished the performance – danced the whole night on the platform with the Finnish researcher.

22. Yuliya Pavlovna Sergatova, rec. A.-L. S., Vol'dino, 1.6.2001.

Women leaders

From 1996 the director of Vol'dino folklore collective has been the head of the culture house, Ol'ga Nikolaevna Belyaeva, who succeeded Yuliya Sergatova. It is to be noted that directors of culture houses are usually women. Ol'ga Nikolaevna Pavlova, choir director of the pensioners' choir in Bol'shelug, has worked in the Cultural Institute since 1986. The head of the culture house, Serafima Ionovna Kurochkina, directs the folklore group *Mića an'jas* ("Beautiful Women") in Vyl'gort. In Nivshera the leader of the culture house Mariya Aleksandrovna Popova and the choir director Nina Vasil'evna Eftene work together. In Troitsk the group *Oztuśjas* ("The Strawberries") is directed by the club leader Angelina Ivanovna Panyukova. Bogorodsk and Ust'-Nem villages do not have professional directors. Although cultural workers receive continuous directions from the ministry, in practice they direct folklore groups as they see fit. Thus local choir directors put in the programme regional songs and make use of the costume tradition of the villages. The directors also emphasise the importance of meeting together as moments of rest and enrichment in women's lives. "Here we can rest in the midst of the daily toil" was the usual director's comment.

In groups established in connection with cultural institutes and which have a director schooled in a professional subject, all sorts of people assemble. Only the very oldest, who are unable to travel and stand during the performance and whose voice has weakened, gradually stop coming to practices and concerts. Yet it is precisely from these people that we recorded the oldest traditions in unofficial circumstances, when they gathered in each other's houses to sing. The more elderly women gather independently everywhere, arrange concerts for various celebrations and sing together on feast days for their own pleasure. But the interest in folklore has enlivened the activities of folklore collectives. Yuliya Sergatova answered a question on the future of folklore collectives: "Life continues and folklore continues and the collective will always survive. We die and then the young ones come."[23]

23. Yuliya Pavlovna Sergatova, rec. A.-L. S. and O. U., Vol'dino, 16.6.2001.

15 "Singing for myself and for my soul"

At Anna Ivanovna's

We spent some days of the summer of 2000 in Bogorodsk in the Komi Republic. Anna Ivanovna Popova cooked pies in the kitchen on the lower floor,
where the heat did not stifle even at the height of summer. Anna was then
a tall and upright woman, firm-featured, in her mid-seventies. Her humour
was biting, but clear and well-intentioned. She said you can be as you like
here, there is space. Anna lived by herself in her large house, looked after her
plants and potato patch, and carried wood and water. Once or twice a week
she sat singing in the evening with her friends. Anna was a fount of countless
songs, learnt when young. She sang still, but her voice no longer reached the
height it did in her youth. Her daughter, Lidiya Loginova, a respected Komi
artiste, presents her lullabies and lyric-epic ballads as arrangements in which
old and new merge in a surprising harmony pleasing to the ear.

Guests arrived in the evening: one was a neighbour, a second came from
further afield. Around ten women ended up sitting in the tiny kitchen: all
old, from their sixties up to Anna's age. We understood why huge piles of pies
need baking on this scorcher of a day. But everyone had to put something on
the table: cakes, sweets, vodka, rowan-berry liqueur. Anna had also made *sur*,
a substance like honey, but treacherous, which needed to be enjoyed carefully. The women delved into their bags for clothes: all alike, green dresses
and *kokošnik* hats decorated with pearls. There was soon a tight circle around
the table. They drank tea, tasted the offerings, chatted. Then some word
roused a woman sitting at the head of the table into song. The others joined
in, and then moved on to the next and the next. Old Komi songs, lyric-epic
tales, then monitory songs of youth, Russian romances and finally *ćastuškas*.
Their short lines are sung in Russian and the light melodies bring to mind
the steps of a dance. Indeed, they end by dancing, before changing clothes
and leaving for home.

The next day we asked the story of the Bogorodsk singing group:

– How long have you been singing?
– We have always sung together, since we were young.
– Does the group have a name?
– We don't have a name, we are just called the grannies, but there isn't a name.

The Bogorodsk group sings at Anna Ivanovna's of a summer evening. The members have new kokošnik hats. – Photograph by A.-L. Siikala 2000

> – Do you sing publicly together?
> – Well, only here in the village.
> – But you have performance costumes.
> – Yes, we made them a couple of years ago when we thought we would go to the nearby villages to perform.

The women have known each other since their childhood, have spent the heavy years, both good and bad, together. There is no formal leader to the group, and the songs are performed from memory. The forming of company, the presentation of songs, their themes and the general enjoyment are reminiscent of many other Komi and Udmurt women's circles, which we had got to know in homes and festivals. Folklore collectives are such a central part of Russian village life that they are found not only in everyday life but also whenever people want to hold a celebration, or want to recount who they belong to, who they are.

Polyphonic singing

The harmonic connection of singers can be heard in their polyphonic singing. Singing in parts is characteristic of the traditional performance of Komi songs. The leaders of singing groups can determine the type of part singing in some of the villages, whereas in other places women themselves decide what

The Bogorodsk singers have changed clothes before going home. The departure is accompanied by ćastuškas and dances. – Photograph by A.-L. Siikala 2000

kind of songs will be performed and in what registers, who is the leader, who a soloist and at which moment others will follow. Therefore, the performers themselves put the final touches to every song and there will not be any discussions or arguments about these questions.

Not all groups can sing in four or five parts as in the Vol'dino group. The old leader of the group, Yuliya Sergatova, explained the practice, which follows old local ways of singing:

A.-L. S.: You sing in many parts.

Yu. S.: We seem to have different . . . too, but I do not know. Some think that we don't. We sing some songs in four parts, some in two.

A.-L. S: Do you sing different songs with different parts?

Yu. S.: Oh, as it is best. We give expletive voices in some songs, when we can. But when it is not possible, we sing in two parts; if we can, we sing with four parts.

A.-L. S.: But how you do it?

Yu. S.: We do it ourselves. In olden times we sang as anybody could. But nowadays we cannot sing like that, and all sing one part. But we sing sometimes with a second voice, but as they say . . . girls cannot sing the second voice any more. I do not know why. Only some sing like that a bit. Because of that they always want us [old women] to sing the second part.

A.-L. S.: Do all begin together usually?

Yu. S.: As it chances. It has been like that always. We begin sometimes without anything, without the accordion, without accompaniment, and for that reason we have to begin with one voice so that we can start.

A.-L. S.: Do the women usually begin?

Yu. S.: No, usually I was the one who began. Now, I am already ill and cannot. They use whoever begins.[1]

The free gatherings of old singers differ from the planned performances especially in the use of polyphony. The women who master the local tradition and have sung together for decades enjoy singing with many parts. Their polyphonic songs, sometimes even five-part improvisations, form a harmonious whole which is not easy to compare to the modern ways of performance.

Transmitting traditions

All the best singers of the older generation had learned singing from their parents – not as pupils, but through spontaneous singing. Most women said that they had learned singing from their mothers, grandmothers or aunts. A. A. Popova said that her aunt taught her to sing:

My mother's sister, Marfa Ivanovna Popova, taught songs to me. She was born in 1892 and died in 1968. She was a wife of my father's cousin; she was also born here in Pozheg. She was the one who sang and also told folk tales well. I remember many songs from her, especially childrens' songs . . . like "The goat goes for berries", *Tuk-tuk, ćurbaćok*, and many more. Then I learnt from the old teachers of elementary classes who sang here, too.[2]

Yuliya Pavlovna Sergatova also knows wedding songs and epic songs, which she heard from her mother's sister, who taught her many songs. Two of her mother's sisters, Anna and Elena, "served", as she said, in the choir of Pomozdino from 1936 until their deaths. Now she cannot sing solely from memory and has written down her aunts' laments and songs. She also recalled *vojpuk* ("night sitting", evening party), in which some of the most popular songs and plays were performed, but had lost the notes:

Some student girls came, they might have been from the university of Syktyvkar, from the Teachers' College or from Leningrad. They took my notes in order to copy them, but did not return them. I asked and looked for them . . . But how you can find someone, if you do not remember even the family names. Now, I do not have them myself, I would like to show the songs, but how can I?[3]

1. Yuliya Pavlovna Sergatova, rec. A.-L. S. and O. U., Vol'dino, 2001.
2. A. A. Popova, b. 1938, in Pozheg, rec. A.-L. S. and O. U., Pozheg, 2002.
3. Yuliya Pavlovna Sergatova, rec. A.-L. S. and O. U., Vol'dino, 2001.

Evdokiya Arsent'evna Shakhova, born in 1932 in Pozheg, Kekur village, learned songs from her playmates smaller than herself:

> You [Oleg Ulyashev] must know Gelya from Yarash'yu village? He was the husband of Rimma Ionovna. Really an ugly man, but with a beautiful wife. He was five or six years old and I was eight. He knew everything, all kinds of songs and different *ćastuška*s. I learned from him. We sang together very loudly.[4]

During the interview, we found that she had learned a lot of songs and melodies from famous singers later:

> I did not learn from books. I learned everything when I followed those who sing well. They were of course older, and knew more. I did not like to go to parties, I did not take part, that's why I do not know so many songs.

We also met whole generations of singers. In the choir of Vol'dino, Klavdiya Terent'evna Ulyasheva (1923–2005) performed until her later years. When we met her, she had finished with singing but her daughter Valentina Konstantinovna Ulyasheva (born in 1952) and two granddaughters, Tanya and Lena, were active members of the choir.

Other hobbies and pursuits might outdo the choir interest among the young people nowadays and they may come for a short time and then leave the group. But the love of singing has not vanished altogether. Quite often, when age cuts back other forms of social activities, a need for intercourse with like-minded people may grow and people wish to have fun by singing together in choir groups.

Performing traditions

Performance habits and songs of folklore collectives did not emergence from nothing: they made use of known ways of performing and singing. Local festivals included gatherings of people interested in singing and dancing. Collectives performed at calendar feasts introduced first by the Church and afterwards the Soviet Union but also at events organised by the youth. Traditional *vojpuk* get-togethers or "night-sittings",[5] *rytpuk* evening parties[6] and the inspections of girls before the wedding or *kol'pavny* evening parties,[7] which were popular among unmarried twelve- to twenty-one-year-olds, were before the beginning of the twentieth century one of the most common ways to spend leisure time in the Komi countryside as in the whole of Russia. Youngsters paid for the evening entertainment with a small sum of

4. Rec. A.-L. S. and O. Ulyashev, Pozheg, 2002.
5. *voj* "night" + *pukavny* "sit".
6. *ryt* "evening" + *pukavny* "sit".
7. *kol'pavny* – figurative sense: to have fun, to drink together, to have an unregular sexual life.

money or as a treat paid for by lonely people or small families.[8] The evening parties, where young people communicated with each other or with older people, were events of cultural exchange where the older taught the younger and those who knew more instructed those who knew less.

Evening party songs were primarily lyrical or play songs mostly performed by girls. Young ladies organised plays, sketches and competitions and played string or wind instruments, sometimes singing with the girls. Both men and women sang ritual songs and popular tunes. Primarily men sang epic songs, which were performed at feasts and family festivals and in the evening among working or hunting groups. Singers of these types of songs were well known over large areas outside the borders of their own villages.

In the 1920s and 1930s the traditions of evening parties were preserved, though now the arena for singing and playing was very often the so-called red corners and reading houses. The programme (see pp. 147–50) was widened to include songs created by known composers and *ćastuška*-songs which handled contemporary themes. Because *ćastuška*-songs belong to minor song genres, are easily created and similar to some forms of folk songs (for example teasing and chain songs), they were important in the propaganda of new ideology.

Dressing up for performance

Up to the 1960s men and women belonging to amateur groups dressed as they did in the ordinary evening parties. Women performed in *sarafan*s, which represented the fashion of their villages. Everybody had her own *sarafan* either made by herself or inherited from her mother or grandmother. Even today some women dig old *sarafan*s out from their chests and say that they used to perform in them. Some of them are sewn of linen and silk; they might be from the nineteenth century or later, even from the 1930s and 1940s, but made according to traditional models. Performers of the Upper Vychegda collectives usually had leather *köti*-shoes and socks with multicoloured decoration. On their shoulders girls or women put a cotton scarf, a flowery cashmir shawl, which had tassels, over their lower shawl. Men, who gave up using folk clothes earlier than women, if we discount working, hunting and fishing garments, and preferred factory-made suits, dressed in those years more "democratically": they had trousers, riding-breeches, jackets and boots. Before the 1970s they were ordered from local makers. A sign of popular tradition was and still is decorated cossack shirts and woven belts.

Polina Alekseevna Ulyasheva, who was born in 1944 in Udora but had lived for more than forty years in Vol'dino, showed her dress and spoke about the traditional dress used in folklore performances:

A.-L. S.: You have a very beautiful dress.
P. U.: Yes, this is the national dress.

8. Startsev 1929.

A.- L. S.: Did everybody make the dress or were there people who sewed them?
P. U.: Most people probably sewed them themselves. The most important is the blouse, an embroidered blouse. If it had three-quarter sleeves, they were decorated here over the elbows, but if it had long sleeves, the lower part was embroidered. The decorated blouse was embroidered on the bosom near the neck. It was the festive blouse. But armpit patches, definitely armpit patches were sewn – they are . . . like shoulders, like suspenders. There were also armpit patches. They are called *kunlös*. A blouse had *kunlös*. They are in the armpits. Then there is a *sarafan* [dress]. There are different *sarafans*. The festive *sarafan* was sewn here [shows the place] horizontally on the bosom, and very many, many, many quiltings were done. Very many horizontal quiltings. The skirt in the *sarafan* was broad and tightened at the waist. There were no pleats. In Udora and in the north they had large pleats, very large pleats, but here they did not have them, only folds. But now it is already simple, we just sew like this without any horizontal quiltings. The sewing takes a lot of time, a great deal of time. Here we have such *sarafans*, we can look for them. For a concert, all were made by dressmakers, but they also tried to sew themselves. There were also women who sewed for themselves and others.
A.-L. S.: But this dress is . . . red?
P. U.: The colour is red, red.
A.-L. S.: When did you make this kind of costume?
P. U. Red colour. Red was for festivals . . . mainly red colour. But for work, blue. So, for work. It is *šušun*, *sarafan* is called *šušun*, it has been made of thick fabric for work. And the apron is necessary, but not the bossom patch . . . The apron and bossom patch are also embroidered. They were sewn like that with a ribbon – to that place they sew a ribbon. And broad ribbons were sewn together on the hem of the apron. And the lace definitely, lace like this. These are my aprons, I have sewn them myself . . .[9]

Polina Alekseevna continued by telling that the oldest representatives of the Vol'dino group had made their aprons themselves. Some of the garments were given to relatives when they began to sing. Polina had given her *köti*-shoes to a field worker who visited her home, but had her scarf and the belt, which she had sewn herself, left. Nowadays the belts are replaced by factory-made bands. She is proud of her dress and mentioned that it is "beautiful and festive".

In the 1970s the use of folk clothes was not as trendy as before. New types of dresses were made or ordered from professionals. Performance attire became more uniform and suitable for the stage, but still in the 1980s retained typical details and the local colours. Then the conflict between new, fashionable stage dress and age-old local clothing began. For example, women from Vol'dino and Skorodum complained to their director about the performance dresses: in the competitions between towns and in the performances of the amateur groups of the republic, they looked poorer than Kortkeros women, because they had measly clothes, actually traditional, even decorated with inherited patterns, which differed from others also because the material was more simple, cotton instead of silk.

9. Polina Alekseevna Ulyasheva, rec. A.-L. S., Vol'dino, 2001

In the 1990s costumes were ordered and made according to common models with the financial support and suggestions from the area administration. The reason for this was the increasing self-esteem among Komi and generally all people of Russia and performing outside of one's own village began to develop into forms of modern festivals.

Amateur and folklore groups began to have clothes which were not typical for Upper Vychegda people. For example, the Bogorodsk group discussed above wanted to have *kokošnik* headdresses, though they said that their mothers and grandmothers never used such attire. Many men changed boots to *köti*-shoes and began to wear decorated multicolour knee socks. Men had previously used with *köti*-shoes only woollen socks in one or two colours (*latšč*) or grey, white or black linen or cloth knee socks (*čörös*). Many folklore groups began to use non-folkloric colours in their attires. They dressed for example in green gold-decorated *sarafans* instead of Upper Vychegda festival *sarafans*, in which the main colours were red, blue and white: for example red or blue *šušin-sarafan*, white *sos*-shirt with red ornaments and on the hem and the upper side of the *sarafan* black decorated stripes. If at the time of the performance it was important to change clothes quickly, some collectives began to order *sarafans* which could be fastened with a small catch in the side seam.

Being together

Feasts and all kinds of competitions have been and still are the main official places in which talents are expressed. In the meetings organised by the authorities, collectives communicate with each other and exchange news, not only about the stage and theatre, but about personal and local matters, because the Upper Vychegda villages are joined by kin relationships and cultural ties. But the feast is a feast, events proceed fast and inconsistently; sometimes groups can present just some of the songs of their programme. The intercourse in a group or between groups usually happens at other kinds of events and places.

Travelling together seems to create a space or border between everyday life and the festive, which offers opportunities for self-expression. Women who walk together or sit in a transport vehicle have free time for discussion and remembering. They evaluate former performances, think about their programme and rehearse their songs or sing songs which better suit the travel atmosphere. The past performances and events are recreated and the emotions strengthen. This also happens when women go to or come from collective work, to hay gathering, collective cleaning of homes, chopping wood, sowing or ploughing. At this kind of time women usually sing traditional work songs or lyrical tunes. The best travel songs are not those which include an image of the road, but the songs which are presented slowly and strongly so that there is no need to strain the midriff or voice. These are for example *Pukśini kutis bur šondi* ("The good sun began to sink"), *Komi nyvjas, komi zonjas gažedćeni jona zev* ("Komi girls and Komi boys rejoice greatly"),

Jagyn bydmis zev mića požöm ("A beautiful pine has grown in a pine forest").

Besides festivals and competitions of folklore collectives the performers and people interested in choir activities come to rehearsals, which do not follow "official" models. Tea parties are common to the meetings of collectives, which are organised by members, often in the local traditional feasts reflecting the visiting habits of the Komi. The food and suitable drinks offered spontaneously by members are an important part of such meetings. Polina Alekseevna spoke about the habits of sitting together:

A.-L. S.: When you sit together, who brings the food?

P. A. U.: We bring it ourselves. Everybody brings something from home, whaevert they happen to have. Everybody bakes something. It is our tradition. We do not collect money. They do not give money to us, only for big festivals they give a bit. But if we want for example to meet, if for example somebody has a birthday party, or if we celebrate some feast, for example 8 March [Women's day]; we had now all . . . only one man came. All the others were women. Everybody brings from home whatever delicacy she has. And then we meet and have a very full table.

A.-L. S.: What is there on the table?

P. A. U.: *Šan̄gi* [round pies], different *šan̄gi* . There are sweet *šan̄gi*, flour *šan̄gi*, potato *šan̄gi*, but also sour-cream *šan̄gi*; *maljok, maljok* [little fish], they are called *jos, joska šan̄gi*. Round pies like this. Also different pies, very different ones, from flour or from hulled grain. They are not very big, flour or hulled grain pies. So, and then fish pies, fish pies are baked. Anything people can manage. And food: cabbage salad, and ones with mushrooms in. Different, very different. Nowadays, everybody grows cucumbers and tomatoes. If it is autumn, they are taken from our own plant frames, if it is spring, then we have to buy them. We also make our national dishes and bring them. Someone brings home-made beer, someone else stewed milk, sour cream, home-made beer.

A.-L. S.: And tea too?

P. A. U. Of course tea. Tea, we are used to drinking tea. We put a samovar there, the director of the Cultural House has fine sugar. She also buys chocolate and cakes.

A.-L. S.: And vodka?

P. A. U.: Yes . . . We drink only a bit, we shall never be drunk. We do not like drinking, only a bit in a decent way. We shall take only a bit, because there can be fun without drinking. Nobody from our collective drinks much . . . Just to be happy, to have fun.[10]

We took part in some of the gatherings and found that women sang a short song at the beginning when they sat at the table; the song was termed a drinking song.

Ovlö šöd kymör da, jur veśtyn gymalö.	It happens that black clouds rumble overhead.
Ovlö i šondia, šondia löń.	There is also sunny, sunny weather, too.
Med eśkö šudlunys šedödćas kutlyny.	May the happiness be contagious.
Med eśkö Jen da, Jen da bur jöz.	May God be there, God and good people.

10. Polina Alekseevna Ulyasheva, rec. A.-L. S., Vol'dino, 2001.

Ńimkoďys-dolydys zev dyr oz voly da,	Gladness and joy did not come for a long time,
Em na i šogydly, šogydly saj.	But against misfortune, against disaster there is a protection, too.
Juyštam vajö da, jurö med kajö da.	Let's drink, may it go to the head.
Šo majbyr! Löśalö, löśalö taj.	Hundred-fold bliss! Well, it's right, it suits [us].

Polina Alekseevna mentioned that at the table women sing *ćastuška*s: "They are in principle the table-songs or evening songs. When we sit at table we sing them and also when we dance."[11] During the common feast at the club or in some other place where the choir meets their visitors, nowadays usually in a beautiful natural setting near the village, a feeling of understanding and friendship is created, which does not disadvantage the song competitions.

Especially popular in common gatherings are songs which praise a local place or people of a river area or a village. They became popular in the early 2000s and were composed according to a model which tells of the great rivers Izhma, Pechora, Vychegda and Mezen'. One of these local praise songs tells about the Nivshera river, the Vishera river and the centres of population in Vishera:

1. *Ńyvśer viľiš nyvka moz*	Nivshera like a joking girl
Viśer julań koterte.	Runs to Vishera.
Nöris jylin mića koz	On the hill, a beautiful fir-tree
Poneľjasen vorsedće.	Plays with small trees.
Vorse gudek «Šondiban»,	The accordion plays Šondiban,
Śylem-jöktem sen i tan:	Singing, dancing here and there:
Ydžidvidźin, Viśerin,	In Bol'shelug, in Bogorodsk,
T'ipe śiktin, Odibin ...	in Troitsk, in Nivshera ...

In Troitsk, the song *T'ipe śikt*[12] from the time of collectivising the countryside was thought to be composed by the famous Komi poet V. Savin.

1. *Parma šörin, Ńyvśer ju bokin*	In the middle of the forest, by the Nivshera-river
Zumida sulale važ komi śikt.	A Komi village stands powerfully.
Paśkida yledź ńimale, kyle	Famous far and wide
Kypid bur udžen T'ipe śikt.	For enthusiastic work, this village of Troitsk.
2. *Ńyvśer ju šlyvge, vizuv va kyvte,*	Nivshera pours, the quick water flows,
Eziśen vorsedće śordjiś va vyv.	The surface of water plays with silver.
Gudek šy ule T'ipe śikt śyle,	When the accordion echoes, Troitsk sings,
Gažaa jurge zboj śylankyv ...	the cheer song reverberates gladly ...

11. Polina Alekseevna Ulyasheva, rec. A.-L. S., Voľdino, 2001.
12. The Komi name for Troitsk.

This kind of song also appeared later, in the 1970s and 1990s. V. Lodygin, a poet from Ust'-Kulom, wrote a song about Vol'dino; it split into different variants, probably because local performers found in the text "factually" inaccurate notions, which were, of course, fixed by the folk censorship:

1. *Va doryn, Ežvalön jylas,*	At the water, in the upriver of Vychegda,
Važön ńin vužjaśim dźiködź mi.	we have rooted ourselves deeply long ago.
Öťi lun kö šogalam, kuim lunsö śylam.	If we grieve one day, then we shall sing three days.
Kerka pomyn emös nyv i pi.	At home both sons and daughters,
Völ'dinöj, Völ'dinöj, mijan śölömśöröj,	Vol'dino, you Vol'dino, the centre of our heart.
Artmis öd te jylyś gaža śylankyv.	We dedicate to you a cheerful song.

The drinking or table songs were not imitated in "local-patriotic" songs or praise of visitors. Competitions at table are a special form to vary and enrich the programme, because in these situations some unusual or forgotten songs, which are not performed in stages, pop up. Unwritten canons are performed as table songs, but they could not be presented in stage performances. The festival table is "opened" with a special song when people have taken their seats. After the short songs singers turn to popular Komi songs, which do not need much attention and are easy to perform. After the popular tunes singers continue with complicated folk songs, which are presented alternately with Russian songs. When the best-known songs have been sung, the popular melodies come up and after that *ćaštuska*s accompanied with dance. After dancing the evening meeting might end. Today *ćaštuska*s seem to belong to the secondary elements of folklore programmes though they are socially flexible and informative and were in the 1940s and 1950s liked by young people. They offer a useful means for expressing different relations in the society, for example love confessions, accusations of treachery, forecasting of traditional feast fights and reflections of changes in social and political life.[13]

We noticed several times that evening meetings when table songs were presented were more rewarding than the stage performances. The official frame of cultural institutes is not a very good milieu for collecting folklore. On the other hand, meetings in formal situations can be a first impetus for later communications. The best songs are usually recorded at homes or other familiar places, when first meetings have woken the memories of dear old songs. Then the singers can remember occasions of everyday life or ritually important moments, jokes of singers and other events and feelings connected to songs. Visitors awake memories connected to Church feasts, when relatives met each other and sang jointly together or memories of evening parties or work trips. Of course performers also meet in private parties, in feasts, weddings, in the farewell parties for those who join the army and so on, and

13. See Adon'eva 2004: 134–97.

also remember songs which do not belong to their programme.

Spontaneous gatherings held in the countryside are an important form of meeting: spontaneous evening parties at a fire in summer time are traditional but also favoured by the young people of today. Especially those who belong to a folklore group sing besides the popular modern songs also old folk songs, as with us in Nivshera, Ust'-Nem and Vol'dino.

From politics to women's culture

As resources dwindled for politically organised activity a unifying change took place for the village women in their shared life, particularly important for those elderly women whom the spectrum of song had affected in the various stages of life. The Vol'dino collective, led for decades by culture secretary Yuliya Pavlovna, began its work in 1936. The collective has no special name though it was at one time called "The Strawberries"; nowadays it is just a village choir of Vol'dino. At the time we met them, at the beginning of the third millennium, the activists were great-grandmothers, grandmothers, mothers and daughters; the collective's membership stretched over five generations in certain cases. Yuliya Pavlovna said that in her time, in the 1950s, Vera Yosifovna, Mariya Pavlovna and Ekaterina Vasil'evna were the oldest: "they were old, some more than seventy years, just as we now sing with Klavdiya Ulyasheva".[14] Polina Alekseevna spoke about the oldest members of the Vol'dino collective in the following way:

> Klavdiya Terent'evna Ulyasheva was born here. Her mother was from Vyl'gort, her father from Vol'dino. She worked all the time in a kolkhoz. During the war, she got a medal for "devoted work during the time of the Great Patriotic War". She had many children, her husband died and she became a widow. She has a very good and low second voice, very good . . .
>
> Then there is Dina Egorovna Pystina. Her mother sang well and also her grandmother Dar'ya Stepanovna sang very well. They have been singing already a very long time. Dina Egorovna was also a kolkhoz worker, and she was a milker in the sovkhoz. Her husband also died, and four children were left. She brought them up without a father. She has a very beautiful first part high voice, very beautiful. I have to say that this collective is somehow specific, as many people as there are, so many are the voices. As many voices as women. All have different voice-parts and they blend in very well.
>
> Then there is Svetlana Petrovna Ulyasheva. She said that out of her sixty years she has been on stage fifty years. She has a second voice too. We have all been working in the kolkhoz and sovkhoz. She was also a milker. Also Klavdiya Terent'evna was a milker. All three were milkers. She brought up a son and daughter.
>
> But for forty years they were guided by Yuliya Pavlovna Sergatova. She is from Pomozdino. Her aunt sang very well, they [aunt and mother of Yu. P.) also lamented in weddings. Yuliya Pavlovna also has an exceptionally outstanding, distinctive voice. She is also a widow. Now she is on a pension.

14. Yuliya Pavlovna Sergatova, rec. A.-L. S. and O. U., Vol'dino, 2001.

But I have been in the collective for forty years. I came in December 1962. They put me straightaway on stage and we have been together all the time. This [shows a picture] is Valentina Konstantinovna, she is the daughter of Klavdiya Terent'evna. All the daughters sing beautifully, now all the daughters' daughters sing well, they have beautiful voices. The daughter's son of Dina Egorovna, Maksim, also sings beautifully, and her daughter's daughter Inna has been with us in festivals and taken part in concerts. She sings well and very beautifully. This is the core group, but usually in the collective we have eighteen to twenty persons. These are the oldest.[15]

Polina Alekseevna did not mention that her daughter Evgeniya also sings in the collective and takes her four-year-old daughter, called Polina after the grandmother, with her so that she can listen and learn the songs. In its early stages, male singers attended the collective, and the accordion was traditionally played by a man. One Vol'dino woman told how her jealous husband had prevented her singing, because the practices held at the club concluded with dancing and general merry-making.

The Vol'dino collective now consists of a tight-knit group of women, and the practices are finished off by sitting and nattering about village and world affairs. The older members meet others more often, usually at the home of one of the singers. Singing together is central to their life, uniting them with close relatives and friends and lending form to their existence. In the evening sittings of Vol'dino's old women, singing in many parts, the old songs of the Soviet period come to the surface. Somewhat embarrassed, someone eventually says: "These are the war-time songs. It was tough: the men were at war and we had lots of work, but we were happy in the fields when we sang together."

Collectives performing traditional material are very varied; groups range from those which live the tradition to those which present it on stage and professional school directors. The Vol'dino collective is firmly attached to the village tradition and is led by a cultural worker resident in the village. Its oldest women are capable of five-part improvisation, which younger members can no longer cope with even when taught. In the neighbouring village of Vyl'gort, whose collective began a few years later, the group has its own choreographer, its costumes are strongly stylised and the songs widely known. The modern style of the songs has in fact been made well known by folklore singer Lidiya Loginova from Bogorodsk, daughter of Anna Ivanovna introduced before, and has since permeated the general consciousness.

Vyl'gort's young female singers enjoy performing, their songs are controlled and their movements coordinated. In summer 2003 we promised to video their performance. Everyone in the village club was business-like: wearing handsome and coordinated folklore costumes the singers performed on the stage and an ample table stood on display in the hall. In the middle of the performance, however, three old women arrived, in work-worn clothes, boots on their feet. They sat on the other side of the hall and called Anna, the

15. Polina Alekseevna Ulyasheva, rec. A.-L. S., Vol'dino, 2001.

The Troitsk folklore collective rehearses a performance
– Photograph by A.-L. Siikala 2000

Finnish researcher, to join them to hear the songs. We sat, we got to know each other and we moved to a table where the grannies at last got seats. As the evening progressed, one of the grannies got up and began a song, which her two companions joined in with, and then some of the singing group. Not all could manage these songs. Anna asked the woman next to her, in her forties, why the singing group didn't join in. The woman said that she had learnt when young, but the others could no longer manage the songs. The grannies were singing "in the old way", traditionally. Their powerful and self-conscious performance completely possessed the audience. Once they had sung enough, one of the grannies got up to dance, "in the old way", lifting her feet rapidly in the necessary fashion. The singers on stage then followed her and afterwards the visitors also.

The situation where the grannies take control of the whole show, even concretely, was not new to the Finnish researcher. Those performers who stayed in charge of the show longest after the festivals, both in southern Udmurt villages and in Vol'dino, were precisely the grannies. Before the centenary celebrations of Vol'dino school, held in 2003, Yuliya Pavlovna, a small and slender woman, was so aged and infirm that she could not even manage to be interviewed. After the singing performance, however, she was sufficiently refreshed to dance with Anna on the stage before the school later into the evening. In the village of Karamas Pel'ga in Udmurtia the folklore singing festival was joined in the early hours by a ninety-year-old woman,

The tea table of the Troitsk singers. – Photograph by A.-L. Siikala 2000

who enthusiastically taught some Finns, Pekka Hakamies and the writer, the steps of the old dance. Age indeed is, in traditional Komi and Udmurt cultures, of value in itself, and the old women are a deliberate and core part of the collectives with their singing and dancing, even if performed in a ramshackle manner. Old women are the emotional and social leaders of their villages, who can express *joie de vivre* in such a colourful manner, unknown in the various cultures with their hierarchies of age and gender formed under the influence of Protestant tradition.

The activities of the groups are still directed by the Ministry of Culture. The group leaders gather for several weeks of instruction, and they receive written advice about the composition of programmes, dances, etc., but financial assistance is not forthcoming. Costumes and snacks or food on singing evenings are prepared with no outside help. So singing demands resources and this can be tough before major presentations. Why do the women gather together? The standard answer to the question, "Why do you sing?", was "For myself and for my soul". The groups are displays of creative female togetherness. Culturally and politically, however, they have a broader significance. Folklore and its dissemination are important tools for belonging together.[16] It is precisely here that the festivals' vital force lies.

The central tool in the sense of belonging is the songs, "our songs". The repertoire of some groups was established originally by listening to well-known traditional songs of the village; the modern repertoire, determined in the main by the choir director, consists of interesting-sounding songs. In the Soviet period the performance began with songs praising the Communist

16. Cantwell 1993.

party and its leadership. In the war period various songs spread quickly throughout Russia expressing the collective worry and sorrow. In addition to the traditional Komi-language songs, the groups' repertoire contains nationally adopted Komi lyrics, Russian folk songs and literary translations, as well as emotional Russian-language romances. Even though the programmes of folklore collectives were purged fundamentally in the 1930s and 1950s, performances include old epic and ritual songs. Epic performed by men has in fact shifted to being performed by women. A similar shift also appears in the organising of religious festivals.[17] As was already said, some of the Komi songs are associated with known places. Thus the lyric-epic song "Along the Vychegda", concerning the river which unites the villages and is visible everywhere, is an Upper Vychegda visiting card.

"Belonging" is also exhibited by means of costume.[18] The Komi folklore collectives' costumes have in part followed local tradition, and in part details revived or derived from elsewhere, for example the Bogorodsk grannies' *kokošnik* hats do not belong to the local tradition. In recent years groups have had uniform performance costumes made by urban seamstresses. Thus the costumes of Vyl'gort's singing group were sewn from bright material and to a uniform design familiar from festival performances.

However, there are not the resources or the will for uniformity everywhere. The women's group of the small central Komi village of Troitsk wished to perform for us in the summer of 2000. The women came to the club house and took up positions for filming in rows along the wall of the hall. They tried out the singing and dance steps for some time. In the tense situation, however, it did not work. In the end the director said that it would be best to go and sit in the club room in a circle, as they usually did. So we moved to the table, which the women quickly turned into the festival venue. Drinking tea, they checked the costumes. Each had prepared her costume herself with all its ornate stitchwork; in the varied group there merged the work of the skilled and the not so skilled. In the middle of the evening a young drunken man joined the group. His wife and mother-in-law, members of the group, shoved him into the yard. Soon the man came back, sat crossly among the old women and said: "Look how beautiful the girls of our village are. But there aren't any men." To the question: "Why aren't there any men?" he answered: "They got drunk and died." After the shattering of the old structures of society, there was no work. Migration and alcoholism consequently took a great part of the village's men. The power of women to carry on life, however, still dominated the village: the weekly gatherings are part of the process of survival. Beauty is created in the singing groups, beauty "for the soul and for the self" as the singers say, the possibility of harmony even in gloomy circumstances.

17. Heikkinen 1992, 1998; see also Heikkinen 2006.
18. Lehtinen 1996.

16   Folk-editing and variation in songs

Programmes of folklore groups

From the period after the Revolution to the perestroika of Gorbachëv, the programme of folklore and amateur groups consisted of mainly folk songs, translations from Russian popular melodies and songs based on the Komi poets. During the Soviet times, patriotic and internationally known political songs representing Soviet ideology belonged to all performances. Komi folklore texts formed about a half of the programme though there were local variation in favourite songs. Some folklore collectives have saved their old programmes and it is possible to see how the selection of the favourite songs changed over the years.

Yuliya Pavlovna Sergatova from Voľdino, who planned the programmes for the local folklore group, gave a manuscript of favourite songs for the decade from 1960 to 1970:

1. *Nyvjas va dorö vorsny leććisny*, "Girls came down to the river to play" (Pëtr Klochkov, nineteenth century)
2. *Kodi vežö Ľenin ďadöc?*, "Who replaces/compensates uncle Lenin" (folk song, 1930s–1940s)
3. *Zev dözmöma omľyalö lećyd voj töv*, "Very angrily howls the sharp northern wind" (Pavel Shebolkin, poet)
4. *Görd armija ľok jedžydjasös zyrö*, "The Red Army presses the evil Whites" (Viktor Savin, 1924)
5. *Talun petis gaža šondi*, "Today the merry sun rose" (Illja Vaś)
6. *Jenežyś iskovtis kodźuv*, "A star slid from the sky" (composed song)
7. *Völi šonyd gaža tulys*, "It was a warm merry spring" (composed song)
8. *Tundrayn*, "On the tundra"
9. *Uśis kodźuv, uśis möd*, "A star fell, another fell" (folk song)
10. *Mamö menö pińalö*, "Mother scolds me" (folk song)
11. *Šondiöj-mamöj*, "My mother, my sun" (folk song)
12. *Gögrös ćužömjas*, "Round faces" (Sandrik Mikol)
13. *Buzgö tölys*, "The wind whistles" (folk song, translated from Russian)
14. *Kyk geroj*, "Two heroes" (folk song, translated from Russian.)
15. *Myjla talun, musa kajöj . . .*, "Why today, my dear bird . . ." (T'ima Ven')
16. *Rytja vojö, matuška . . .*, "In the evening night, mother" (folk song)
17. *Mamöj, mamöj, mamuľöj . . .*, "My mother, mother, mother . . ." (folk song)

18. *Jagyn bydmis zev mića požöm*, "A beautiful pine has grown up in a pine forest" (Ivan Vavilin)
19. *Dumajti öťikös*, "I thought about one" (folk song, translated from Russian)
20. *Paśkyd gaža uľicha . . .*, "Wide merry street",(folk song)
21. *Lèććis-munis nyv vala*, "A girl went for water" (folk song)
22. *Pukala köť vetlödla*, "I sit although I walk" (Mikhail Lebedev)
23. *Asja kya*, "Morning dawn" (Pëtr Klochkov)
24. *Mića nyvjas Ežva dorö leććisny*, "Beautiful girls came to Vychegda" (Viktor Savin)
25. *Jugyd kodźuv*, "Bright star" (Viktor Savin)
26. *Zarńi ćikyš*, "Golden swallow" (Mikhail Lebedev)
27. *Bereg doryn, ju doryn . . .*, "On a shore, by the river" (folk song, translated from Russian)
28. *Pastukjaslön šmońa ćastuškajas*, "Funny ćastuška*s of herdsmen" (folk song)
29. *Oj-oj, tuvsov voj . . .*, "Oh, oh, spring night" (Viktor Savin)
30. *Köni svaďba, sen ij gaž*, "Where the wedding is, there is fun" (Mikhail Lebedev)
31. *Śylim, jöktim, gažödćim*, "We sang, we danced, we had fun" (folk song)
32. *Šondibanöj, olömöj*, "Sun-faced, my life" (folk song)
33. *Das kvajt arösödź oli da, vek na ved me götirtem*, "I've lived to sixteen and I'm still without a wife" (folk song)
34. *Pöputćik*, "Fellow traveller" (S. Popov, composed and translated from Russian)
36. *Majbyr nyvjas*, "Happy girls" (folk song)
37. *Svaďba mijan pansöma*, "We began the wedding" (folk song)
38. *Olis-vylis vöryn*, "Once they lived in a forest" (Mikhail Lebedev)
39. *Oj, jona žö nin vojys kuź*, "Oh, the night is too long" (folk song)
40. *Vež vidź vyvti muna*, "I go along a green meadow" (Viktor Savin)
41. *Ylyn-ylyn roć Kavkazyn*, "Far, far away in the Russian Caucasus" (Egor Kolegov, translated from Russian)
42. *Džudžyd kerösyn*, "On a high hill" (Pavel Shebolkin)
43. *Konda lösyd tušaöj*, "My body beautiful as a resin tree" (folk song)
44. *Šölöm veśt kiń uśködyśöj*, "In the hearth sparked" (folk song)
45. *Öšińjasyn śarvidźis*, "In the windows many are seen" (folk song)
46. *Bur baťköd-mamköd olöm*, "Good life with father and mother" (Mikhail Lebedev)
47. *Mirtuj doryn*, "By a wide road" (folk song)
48. *Myj mem gažtöm*, "Why I'm sad" (folk song)
49. *Kön olam mi, sen sulavlis . . .*, "Where we live, there once stood . . ." (Mikhail Lebedev)
50. *Saldatjasöj, mića vojtyrjasöj*, "My soldiers, my beautiful people" (folk song, translated)
51. *Tulys vois, gaža lunjas . . .*, "The spring has come, merry days" (folk song)
52. *Mića Römanöj*, "Beautiful Roman" (folk song)
53. *Kačaśinjas*, "Camomiles" (Serafim Popov)
54. *Jukmös doryn*, "By a draw-well" (folk song)

55. *Tölöću-völöću* (folk song)
56. *Kak pošol molodec*, "As a young boy went out" (Russian folk song)
57. *Una nyvjas ćukörtćisny*, "Many girls gathered together" (folk song)
58. *Myjla nö, šondiöj, vör sajö leććömyd*, "Why do you, sun, set behind the forest?" (Mikhail Lebedev)
59. *Śiźim vo nin vojna kyśśö*, "Seven years already the war has lasted" (Viktor Savin)
60 *Suskin sadjyn*, "In a cedar grove" (folk song)
61. *Alöj l'entoćka*, "Rose hair ribbon" (folk song)
62. *Gögör-gögör me vidźödla*, "Around, around I look" (folk song)
63. *Sad jöryn kö nyv gul'ajtö*, "A girl is strolling in a garden" (translated, folk song)
64. *Me gul'ajti lun da voj*, "I partied [strolled] day and night" (folk song)
65. *Ökśińja pökrasa*, "Oksinya the beautiful" (folk song)
66. *Votyśej daj votyśej . . .*, "Berry picker, berry picker" (folk song)
67. *Ćuži-bydmi*, "I was born and grew up" (Viktor Savin)
68. *Kučöm šonyd da lön*, "How warm and calm" (Mikhail Lebedev)
69. *Mem öťi arśa rytö*, "For me once on an autumn evening . . . " (Mikhail Lebedev)

The Dances: 1. *Kapusta*, "Cabbage"; 2. *Krug gögör*, "In a circle"; 3. *Kačaśinjas*, "Camomiles"; 4. *Komi kadril'*, "Komi quadrille"; 5. *Völ'dinsa kadril'*, "Vol'dino quadrille"; 6. *Šen*.

Round dance songs: 1. *Nyvjas va dorö vorsny leććisny*, "Girls came down to the river to play"; 2. *Talun petis gaža šondi*, "Today the merry sun rose"; 3. *Mića nyvjas Ežva dorö leććisny*, "Beautiful girls came to Vychegda" 4. *Oj-oj, tuvsov voj*, "Oh, oh, spring night"; 5. *Köni svad'ba, sen ij gaž*, "Where the wedding is, there is fun".[1]

The manuscipt of Yuliya Pavlovna consists of sixty-nine songs of which thirty-six are folk songs and five dances. "Official songs" do not belong to her list though they belonged to the normal performance. "Official" political and patriotic songs of the Soviet time were known by most people and they usually began the performance according to the situation and the type of the feast. Usually the group sang two or three of them at the beginning of the festival. During the performance the tunes became lighter, ending in *ćastuška* songs and dance. The list of Yuliya Pavlovna lacked *ćastuška* songs, because they varied according to the theme of the performance. Songs for performances were selected from the manuscript, but if needed, other popular songs, usually Russian, were added to concerts.

Folklore groups collected folk songs from the best singers of their own villages. In the collective they were passed to new generations like other folklore items. The composed songs were transmitted like folk songs: they were remembered but also reinterpreted and changed. Hence, the programmes of folklore collectives vary according to local traditions and we were able to record several variants of some well known songs. In what follows, we look more closely at the texts of the most popular songs of the Ust'-Kulom groups.

1. Yuliya Pavlovna Sergatova, rec. O. U. and A.-L. S., Vol'dino, 14–15.6.2001.

We shall pay attention to the relationship of literal and folk texts, modes of translation, new and old variation of local songs and to the deliberate folk-editing of them brought about by cultural and political motivations. The main questions are: Which types of songs were selected for the programmes and how and why were they edited by the women?

Textualisation and variation of songs

Because the Komi became Christian at the end of the fourteenth century, they became familiar with literary culture at an early date, though it was at first in Slavonic. In addition to the work of the Orthodox Church and monasteries, the Christian faith also spread informally, through peasant leaders of the Old Believers who moved to the northern areas of Komi. Ust'-Tsil'ma, not far from the Komi centre of Izhma, known for its commerse and wealth, was a base for Old Believers, who have preserved a great number of medieval literary works to this day. Some peasants of the Ust'-Kulom villages could read already in the eighteenth century and more than a hundred books and translations in the Komi language were published in the nineteenth century in Cyrillic alphabets. Local schools have a long history; the Vol'dino school had its centennial festival in 2003. The national school system for Komi was established in 1918 and the dialect of Ust'-Sysol'ski (later the capital Syktyvkar) was chosen to be the Komi literary language. The Komi alphabet invented by V. A. Moldotsov was officially confirmed. In 1932–5 the Komi language was published in Latin alphabets, but soon Cyrillic was back again.[2] The directors of clubs and song collectives had access to publications of folklore and national poetry and they copied songs in their notebooks, as did the singers. Because of the early literacy and bilingualism the ideas of the literary form of poetry followed the popular Russian model.

Song publications gave the model for textualising songs in the notebooks of performers. Copying songs from books is still going on, but media spread music later. A young woman in Vol'dino choir said that she has a habit of listening to the radio and copying the words in her notebook.[3] The songs of this chapter were recorded at the informal meetings of singers or in their public performances. We also saw notebooks of singers and choir leaders. In this chapter the textualisation of songs follows the folk habit of Ust'-Kulom, which in turn has been adapted from the Komi literary culture. The lines and verses, if there are any, are shown by spacing the text and the beginning of lines are marked by capitals. The pauses are marked as in literary forms of the texts known to singers. The transliteration of the Komi words written originally in Cyrillic is presented according to a modified scholarly system, which suits the Komi language better than Cyrillic. The word order could not always be followed in translating the lines, but the accurate meanings of words are given, which may lessen the poetic quality of the lines in English.

2. Konakov *et al.* 2003: 16.
3. Valya Ulasheva, rec. A.-L. S., Vol'dino, 2001.

The method of textualisation of performed songs is connected to the method of studying variation of the songs. The words of importance in the analysis are underlined.

The study of variation in song texts has a long history in folkloristics. Already Kaarle Krohn, who wanted to renconstruct the original form of the *Kalevala*-metre epic poems in 1918, tried to fathom the reasons for variation of texts of poems. He believed that every folk poem was created by a singer, and later singers only performed it, so that the poem could degenerate from its orginal textual form. The variation was connected to the processes of *remembering* and *forgetting*. According to him, so called laws of "thought" and "metre" are reasons for variation in oral poems. The "law of forgetting" means not only that a part of the poem or a line can be forgotten, but that lines can be added, when the orginal phrases were not remembered. Besides the larger parts of the text and lines, also phrases and words can be added or altered. General words can be replaced by special expressions and vice versa. Krohn also refers to the use of analogic expressions in varying the text.[4]

Krohn's idea of the key position of memory did not fit song genres in which improvisation or continuous recreation was a typical feature and his ideas were contested by researchers studying for example long epics. Researchers who wondered how performers could remember long epic poetry tried to find the rules of reproduction of the poems. Albert Lord and Milman Parry, who studied the performance of Balkan epic poetry, developed a research approach called *oral formulaic theory*, the main proponent of which today is John Miles Foley.[5] Lauri Harvilahti has combined the ideas of oral formulaic theory with cognitive approaches in studying the memorisation and reproduction of songs and narratives and text linguistics in his study of Ingrian epics recorded in the nineteenth century.[6] In the study of songs which are recreated in long performance sessions, the oral formulaic theory has shown its value. though the commonly accepted definition of "formula" always seems to have been a problem.[7]

Though not all songs of Komi folklore groups are folklore, they share many features with it. In their variation and liberal editing, the singer's knowledge of *registers* of oral genres affects the adoption of new expressions. Foley defined the concept of register following Dell Hymes: "major speech styles associated with recurrent types of situations".[8] When trying to find registers we should according to Foley look for "any linguistic, rhetorical, or other performance-constituting phenomenon that marks an otherwise inexplicable departure or change in emphasis from the standard language and presentational mode employed for ordinary, unmarked discourse".[9] In

---

4. Krohn 1918: 51–77.
5. For example Foley 1985.
6. Harvilahti 1992. Anna-Leena Siikala has approached the problems of variation in incantations (1986) and legends on the basis of schema theory (1992).
7. Harvilahti 1992: 114.
8. Foley 1995: 50.
9. Foley 1995: 51-2.

studying strategies and registers of performers Lauri Harvilahti has noted that different levels of regularity and variation cannot be described by a single, blueprint-like model or set of models, since such strict delimination would reflect only a part of a system of reproduction.

> The production of oral poetry utilises a system of linguistic and poetic strategies determined by multidimensional, oral-traditional means. One prerequisite for the fluency of the production process is the use of "pre-existing" overall structures, core subject matter, episodes and substitution, groups of words, and formulae, which rely on primary poetic features and are "located" in the singer's memory.
>
> Each performance is, however, one manifestation of a process of countless reproductions. Singers neither compose nor create. When interpreting a song they reproduce it as they experience it, influenced as they are by their own prior familiarity, competence, interest and aims, as well as the demand of the collective tradition and performance situation. From the standpoint of oral poetry tradition the extremes – word for word repetition and free improvisation within the performance situation – are spurious assumptions.[10]

Naming the use of *"pre-existing" overall structures, core subject matter, episodes and substitution, groups of words, and formulae* as the marks of fluency of the production process Harvilahti gives a helpful list of tools for the textual analysis of songs. The Komi collectives mastered an extensive number of songs and in their performances they also used parts of songs when this was needed. *Intertextuality*, which, argues Lotte Tarkka, in the folk poetry is based on repetition, indicates a text or text fragment in a new context.[11] Tarkka has studied intertextuality in the *Kalevala*-metre poems and her observations could illuminate Komi epic lyric also.

Anna-Leena Siikala has claimed that variation in oral poetry should not be studied only as a mechanism within oral texts but as a product of changes in the field of discourse. Basing her arguments on the ideas of linguistic anthropology, especially William F. Hanks, she has claimed that genre constitutes the strategy for reproduction and is the key to possibilities and forms of variation. Changes of the value of the discourse field affect all the practices connected to it.[12] Accordingly sources of variation are many and could not be studied by analysing only the text. If we compare genres representing different cultural traditions or analyse variation within a culture, we can see genres as orienting frameworks, sets of expectations and interpretive procedures for the production and reception of discourse.[13] Strategies for reproduction – the practice of genre – can be analysed on different levels closely connected to each other. These crucial domains for variation can be found at least in the following areas: 1. cultural significance / value of the discourse field and accordingly the genre, 2. the degree of institutionalisa-

---

10. Harvilahti 2000: 67–8.
11. Tarkka 2005: 65.
12. Hanks 1987, 1996: 240–6.
13. Siikala 2000d; Siikala and Siikala 2005: 90–1; Hanks 1987: 670; see also Briggs and Bauman 1992: 142–3.

tion of performance practices, 3. habitus of the narrator/singer, 4. discourse strategies and generic models of narrating/singing, 5. performance settings (place, event, audience), 6. memorising and performing (including stylistic and linguistic strategies), 7. political, moral, religious etc. evaluation of narratives, and 8. shared and individual ways of giving meaning to narratives/songs.[14] These domains of examination do not reveal all the possible levels of discourse strategies. In order to understand the sources of variation in songs of Komi folklore collectives we should grasp the factors guiding the practices of patterned discourse processes in question. The value of the discourse field, institutionalisation of the practice, habitus of singers, performance settings, political background have been discussed in previous chapters. In this chapter we analyse the memorisation and performance of songs, their evaluation and ways of giving them meaning.

Old Komi folk texts

Though the programmes of folklore collectives and amateur groups were "cleaned" thoroughly for political reasons from the 1930s to the 1950s, some of the old songs were preserved. To these belong mainly epic and ritual songs; for example the ballad *Mića Römanöj* ("My beautiful Roman") was performed on stage still in the 1970s. Of the wedding song *Krug šöryn mića nyv* ("In the circle a beautiful maiden") we recorded four variants, from Vol'dino, Nivshera, Troitsk and Vyl'gort. The song *Svad'ba mijan panśöma* ("We began the wedding") we recorded twice. One of the most popular songs is the lyric-epic *Ežva ju kyźa* ("Along the Vychegda"), the UpperVychegda calling card, of which we recorded eight variants. The difference between the various singing modes noted by performers themselves is recurrent: in Badël'sk, Vyl'gort, Troitsk and Ust'-Nem only the second part of the second verse is repeated; in Bogorodsk, Vol'dino, Nivshera and Bol'shelug the whole second verse. The lexical differences and repetitions are not so important as to change the plot. On the other hand, they mark every text and are firm signs of local traditions, which can be recognised by analysing different examples. Five variants are compared here. The variant recorded in Troitsk, Kortkeros area, is the longest, containing twenty-four lines:

I

1. *Ežva ju kuźa, **teryb** gy vyvti*	Along the Vychegda river, on a **quick** wave,
2. *Lebźe ydžid pyž jedžid parusa.*	A big boat **flies** with white sails.
3. *Pyžas pukale das vit udal zon.*	In the **boat** fifteen brave lads sit.
4. *Öťi zon kyndźi stavis gažaeś.*	All but one lad, all are cheerful.
5. *Naje vorseni kujim gudeken,*	They play with three accordions,
6. *Naje śyleni das ńoľ gölesen.*	They sing with fourteen voices.
7. *Öťi burlak-zon mića ćužemnas*	One lad with handsome face

14. Siikala 2000d: 216.

8. *Arśa kymer moz vaas vidźede.*	Looks at the water like an autumn cloud.
9. *Jurse ledźema, oz i leptivli,*	He presses down his head and doesn't lift it up,
10. *Vomse **tupkema**, oz i goredli.*	His mouth **shut**, he does not sing
11. *«Myjla **burlak-mort**, tadźi žugiłtćin?*	"Why young **man**, have you become downhearted?
12. *Myjla **jortjasked** te on gažedći?»*	Why do you not rejoice with your **friends?"**
13. ***Kinas** šeništis **šogśiś burlak-mort,**	The **grieving** young man **waved** with his **hand,**
14. ***Šuis-goredis** nora gölesen:*	He said with a **sad voice:**
15. *«**Jona**, jortjasej, udal zonjasej,*	"**Harsh**, my friends, reckless lads,
16. *Ene divitej, ene lögaśej.*	Do not judge, do not be offended.
17. *Menam śölemej šogen tyrema,*	My heart is full of sorrow,
18. *Menam dolidej yle kolema.*	My joy was left far away.
19. *Musa Mašukej mene enovtis.*	Dear Mashenka has deserted me.
20. *Jugid šondiej menam kusema.*	My bright sun has faded.
21. *Me ke mustemmi **mića** Mašukli,*	If I was rude to beautiful Mashenka,
22. ***Ovni mu vylin** menim ńinemla.*	It is pointless for me **to live on the earth.**
23. *Bośtej šybitej mene końeres*	Take me, throw the wretched one
24. ***Džudžid va pyčke**, gudir kyrkeče."*	In the **deep water**, in the **muddy** bend of a river."[15]

II

The second variant was recorded in Bogorodsk (Viśer) in the Kortkeros district in 2000. The lines are numbered as in the Troitsk text (above). The words and phrases which differ from the first variant are in bold.

1. *Eźva ju kuźa, **gylyd** gy vyvti,*	Along the Vychegda river, on a **vast** wave
2. ***Kyvte** ydžid pyž jedžid parusa.*	A big boat **floats** with white sails.
3. *Pyžas pukale das vit udal zon,*	In the boat, fifteen brave lads sit,
4. *Öti zon kyndźi stavnis gažaeś.*	All but one lad are cheerful.
5 (6). *Naje śyleni das ńoľ gölesen,*	They sing with fourteen voices,
6 (5). *Naje vorseni kujim gudeken.*	They play with three accordions,
7. *Öti **burlak-zon** mića ćužema*	One young lad with handsome face
8. *Arśa kymer moz vaas vidźede.*	Looks at the water like an autumn cloud.
9. *Jurse ledźema, oz ij leptištli,*	He presses down his head and doesn't lift it up,
10. *Vomse **tupjema**, oz ij goredli.*	Mouth **shut**, he does not sing.
11. *«Myjla burlak-**zon**, tadźi žugiłtćin?*	"Why, young **lad**, have you become downhearted?
12. *Myjla jortjasked te on gažedći?»*	Why you do not rejoice with your friends?"

15. *Oztuśjas* (Strawberries) choir: Anna Stepanova Shuchalina, Elena Ivanovna Gabova (with her daughter Veronika), Nina Petrovna Gabova, Anna Dimitrievna Gabova, Nina Stepanovna Gabova, Nina Mihaïlovna Gabova, Angelina Ivanovna Panyukova (instructor, director of the club), Nina Aleksandrovna Gabova, Valentina Aleksandrovna Podorova, Anna Aleksandrovna Gabova, Margarita Anatoľevna Gabova, rec. A.-L. S. and O. U., Troitsk, Kortkeros district, 2000.

13 (21). «*Me ke mustemmi **musa** Mašukli,*

"If I was rude to beloved Mashenka

14 (22). ***Ovnim, ok, öni** menim ńinemla.*

Oh, it is pointless for me to **live now.**

15 (23). *Boštej šybitej mene końeres,*

Take me, throw the wretched one

16 (24). *Džudžid va pyčke, **pemid** kyrkeče.*"[16]

In the deep water, in the **dark** bend of the river."

III

The third variant was recorded in Kekur village, Pozheg area, in 2002. The lines are again marked as in the first variant and the differences in the text marked in bold.

1. *Ežva ju kuźa, **teryb gy vyvti***

Along the Vychegda river, on a **quick** wave,

2. ***Kyvte ydžid pyž jedžid parusa.***

A big boat **floats** with white sails.

3. ***Seni pukale dasvit burlak-zon.***

Fifteen **young lads** sit **in it**.

4. *Öťi zon kyndźi stavnis gažaeś.*

All but one are cheerful.

5 (6). *Naje śyleni das ńoľ gölesen.*

They sing with fourteen voices.

6 (5). *Naje vorseni kujim gudeken.*

They play with three accordions.

7. *Öťi burlak-zon mića ćužema*

One young lad with handsome face

8. *Arśa kymer moz vaas vidźede.*

Looks like an autumn cloud at the water.

9. *Jurse ledźema, oz ij leptivli,*

He presses down his head and doesn't lift it up,

10. *Vomse **šiptema,** oz ij **voštivli.***

His mouth **closed, he does not open it.**

11. «*Myjla **burlak-zon,** sidźi žugiľťćin?*

"Why **young lad,** have you become downhearted?

12. *Myjla **mijanked** čöč on gažedći?*»

Why you do not rejoice with us?"

13 (13+14). *Šogiś šuištis nora gölesen:*

He **said sadly** with sorrowful voice:

14 (15). «***Burlak-zonjasej, musa vokjasej,***

Young lads, my brothers,

15 (16). *Ene **d**ivitej, ene lögaśej,*

Do not judge, do not be offended,

16 (23). *Boštej šybitej mene końeres*

Take me, throw the wretched one

17 (24). *Džudžid va **pije,** džudžid kyrkeče.*

In the deep water and in **the deep** bend.

18 (21). *Me ke mustemmi **musa** Mašukli,*

If I was repulsive to dear Mashenka,

20 (22). ***Ovni mu vylin** menim ńinemla.*»[17]

It is pointless for me to **live on the earth.**"

IV

The next variant was recorded in Voľdino village, in the Usť-Kulom area, in 2001:

16. M. I. Ivashova, Ė. N. Ivashova, D. P. Gabova, L. I. Ivashova, A. S. Gabova, T. E. Kalistratova. N. I. Ivashova, Bogorodsk, rec. A.-L. S. and O. U., Bogordsk, 20–21.5.2000.
17. Yuriĭ Vasiľevich Timushev, b. 1941, Dina Vasiľevna Treťyakova, b. 1944, Evdokiya Arsenťevna Shakhova, b. 1932, Agniya Vasiľevna Shakhova, b. 1933, Mariya Ivanovna Shakhova, b. 1933, rec. A.-L. S. and O. U., Kekur, Pozheg, 3.7.2002.

1. *Ežva ju kuźa, **džudžyd** gy vyvti*	Along the Vychegda river, on a **high wave,**
2. ***Lebźe** ydžid pyž da jedžid parusa.*	A big boat **flies** with white sails.
3. ***Pyžas** pukaleni das vit udal zon.*	**In the boat**, fifteen young brave lads **are sitting.**
4 (6). *Naje śyleni das ńoľ gölesen.*	They sing with fourteen voices.(2)
5 (5). *Naje vorseni kujim gudeken.*	They play with three accordions.
6 (7). *Ôťi burlak-zon mića ćužema*	One young lad with beautiful face
7 (8). *Arśa kymer moz vaas vidźede.*	Looks at the water like an autumn cloud.
8 (9). *Jurse ledźema, oz i leptivli,*	He has pressed down his head and doesn't lift it up,
9 (10). *Vomse **tupkema**, oz i goredli.*	Mouth shut, he does not sing.
10 (11). *«Myjla **burlak-zon**, sidźi žugľaśan?*	"Why, young lad, are you so downhearted?
11(12). *Myjla **jortjasked** te on gažedći?»*	Why do you not rejoice with your friends?"
12. *+**Śinjasse vośtis šogśiś burlak-zon,***	**The sorrowful lad opened his eyes.**
13 (14). ***Sidźi** goredis nora gölesen:*	He started to sing like this with a sad voice:
14 (15) *«Dona jortjasej, musa zonjasej,*	«**My dear** friends, my dear lads,
15 (16). *Ene divitej, ene lögaśej,*	Do not judge, do not be offended,
16(23). *Bośtej šybitej mene końeres*	Take me and throw the wretched one
17 (24). ***Gudir** va pyčkas da **pemid** kyrkečas.*	In the **muddy** water and the **dark** bend of a river.
18 (21). *Me ke mustemmi musa Mašukli,*	If I was repulsive to dear Mashenka
19 (22). *Ovni mu vylin menim ńinemla.»*[18]	It is pointless for me to live on the earth."

V

The fifth variant was recorded in Vyľgort, a neighbouring village of Voľdino, in 2001:

1. *Ežva ju kuźa, **džudžyd** gy vyvti*	Along the Vychegda river, on a **high wave.**
2. ***Lebźe** ydžid pyž da jedžid parusa.*	A big boat **flies** with white sails.
3. ***Pyžas** pukaleni das vit udal zon.*	**In the boat**, fifteen young brave lads **are sitting.**
4 (6). *Naje śyleni das ńoľ gölesen.*	They sing with fourteen voices.(2)
5 (5). *Naje vorseni kujim gudeken.*	They play with three accordions.
6 (7). *Ôťi burlak-zon mića ćužema*	One young lad with beautiful face
7 (8). *Arśa kymer moz vaas vidźede.*	Looks at the water like an autumn cloud.
8 (11). *«Myjla **burlak-zon**, sidźi žugľaśan?*	"Why, **young lad**, are you so downhearted?
9 (12). *Myjla **jortjasked** te on gažedći?»*	Why do you not rejoice with your friends?

18. Dina Egorovna Pystina, Yuliya Pavlovna Sergatova, Valentina Konstantinovna Ulyasheva, Klavdiya Terenťevna Ulyasheva, Polina Alekseevna Ulyasheva, Svetlana Petrovna Ulyasheva, rec. I. V. Iľina, A.-L. S. and O. U., Voľdino, 16.7.2001.

10 (16). *Ene d̄ivitej, ene lögaśej,*	Do not judge, do not be offended
11(23). *Bośtej šybitej mene koṅeres*	Take me and throw the wretched one
12 (24). **Gudir** *va pyčkas da džudžid* **kyrkečas.**	In the **muddy** water and the **deep** bend of a river.
13 (21). *Me ke mustemmi mića Mašukli,*	If I was repulsive to beautiful Mashenka,
14 (22). *Ovni mu vylin minim ṅinemla.»*[19]	It is pointless for me to live on the earth."

The lyric epic song tells how fifteen young lads are sailing on the Vychegda river and all are glad, singing and playing the accordion, except one. When asked he says that his loved one has left him, because he was rude to her, and wants to be punished by his friends. They should throw him in the river. The scene is simple: a description of the trip and persons, questions and answers which tell the sad story. The Bogorodsk variant is shorter than the others and in all the variants the first lines are more stable than the last ones. The enduring components are descriptions of events which carry the story ahead, lacking explanations or descriptions of emotions. The differences between variants are not extensive, but some lines are discarded or added, uniting two lines or words expressing the quality of persons or action. Changes in wording like "high/vast/quick wave" or "deep/muddy water/bend of the river" show Vol'dino-Vyl'gort-Pozheg in the Ust'-Kulom region and Bogorodsk-Nivshera-Troitsk in the Kortkeros region have their own singing traditions. Also, the women of Pozheg and Troitsk, which lie a little further away from other villages, have developed their own ways of singing. The melodies of the song vary like the texts.

The opinion of one performer from Vol'dino who said that "Komi don't have joyful songs, all are so sad" was probably caused by a large number of sorrowful lyric epic and lyric songs like *Mamö menö piṅalö* ("Mother scolds me"), *Šondiöj-mamöj* ("My sunny mother"), *Oj, jona žö nin vojys kuź* ("Oh, too long is the night"), *Konda lośyd tušaöj* ("How parched my body has become"), *Myj mem gažtöm?* ("Why am I longing?"), *Šölöm veśt kiṅ uśködyśöj* ("In the hearth sparked"), *Una nyvjas ćukörtćisny* ("Many girls gathered together"), *Suskin sadjyn* ("In a cembra forest [garden]"), *Alöj lentoćka* ("Rose hair ribbon"), *Das kvajt arösödź oli da, vek na ved me götirtëm* ("I've lived to sixteen and I'm still without a wife"), *Šondibanöj olömöj* ("My sunny life"), *Gögör-gögör me vidźödla* ("Around, around I look"), *Vež lud vyvti, kladbišče vyvti* ("In a green meadow, in a graveyard"), *Ruć ku da köć ku* ("A furcoat of fox and a furcoat of hare") and others.

The conflict themes, which usually form the nucleus of sad songs, often tell about a sorrowful situation in everyday life, for example the separation of a loving couple, going to the army, imprisonment, deception or forced

19. Vera Semënovna Ignatova, b. 1927, Nina Stepanovna Kurochkina, b. 1925 in Veliko Pole village, Anna Timofeevna Ulyasheva, b. 1925 in Bad̄ël'sk village, Serafima Ionovna Kurochkina, rec. A.-L. S. and O. U. in the club house of Vyl'gort, 13.6.2001, and at the home of Aleksandr Davydovich Ignatov, b. 1927, 28.6.2002.

giving of the daughter to an unwanted man. The next song places the people and events in a far-away village, and gives a background for the maiden, a daughter of a widow, who is poor but very beautiful. She is not allowed to marry her beloved, but has to take an old man, who beats her severely:

Ylyn-ylyn pe da ju sajin,	Far away, far away, behind the river,
Ju sajin da va sajin	Behind the river, behind the water,
Vyľ slöbeda tydale.	A new village is seen.
Vyľ slöbedajas tomińik döva j ole.	In the new village, a young widow lives.
Tomińik dövajislen	The young widow
Tom že pe daj nyv vijim.	Has a young daughter.
Sečem mića nylis ńinekyteni abu.	Nowhere is there such a beautiful girl.
Da ćužem vilas vir vorse.	In her face the blood surges.
Eta slavais kuźa	Because of her fame
Pöriś starik saje love munni.	An old man she had to marry.
Starik saje munas da,	To an old man she went,
Bördas da, bördas da,	And she cried, she cried.
Ćölöj ćyšjan kötaśas.	The whole scarf was wet.
Kiľći vylas petas	She came to the porch
Da drugisked panid love.	And met a friend.
Drugisli žeptas śujas da:	She put [a note] in the pocket of the friend:
«Kydź pe etije ćyšjanis siśmas da,	"When this scarf decays,
Sidź že menam śölem kośmas».	Then my heart will dry up."
Starikis pe kaźoolas,	The old man found it
I kujim voža da pľeť pyrtas.	And took a three-lined lash.
Nöjtas da, nöjtas da,	He hit and hit.
A uľić vylas da tojištas.	And into the yard he pushed her.

There are also joyful songs like *Śylim, jöktim, gažödćim* ("We sang, we danced, we had fun"), *Ökśińja-pökrasa* ("Oksinya the beautiful"), or *Votyśej daj votyśej* ("Berry picker, berry picker") or humorous ones, from playful songs to joking ones: *Mamöj, mamöj, mamuľöj* ("My mother, mother, mother"), *Lèććis-munis nyv vala* ("A girl went for water"), *Parpoń* ("Parfen"), and *Sarjov kabak* ("The tavern of the tsar").

The same text can be interpreted both in tragic and humorous ways in the context of different local traditions. For example, Yuliya Sergatova showed this in the song called *Majbyr nyvjas* ("Happy girls"). In Pomozdino it is performed as a sad song on the fate of a poor girl who is given to an old man,[20] but in Voľdino the song is performed playfully:

Majbir nyvjas, gyriś nyvjas,	Happy girls, good-sized girls
Votes votni kajisni.	Went to pick berries.
Me końerej, dźoľa nylej,	I, poor girl, small girl,
Votes votny kaji že.	Went to pick berries too.
Mića nyvjas, majbir nyvjas,	Beautiful girls, happy girls,

---

20. The song resembles folklore texts of the Soviet time, which tell of oppressed women in class society.

Dozjen-džynjen votisni,	One and a half bushels everybody got.
Me końerej, dźoľa nylej,	I, poor and small girl,
Sodźdźen-džynjen voti že.	One and a half fistfuls picked too.
Majbir nyvjas, gyriś nuvjas,	Happy girls, good-sized girls,
Veressaje petisni.	Were wedded.
Me końerej, dźoľa nylej,	I, unlucky, small girl
Pöriś saje peti že.	Went to an old man, too.
Majbirjaslen tom mužikjas	The young men of the happy ones
Vöre kyjni kajisni.	To the forest went to hunt.
Menam pöriś, aslam pöriś,	My aged man, my old man,
Vöre kyjni kajis že.	To the forest went too.
Majbirjaslen tom mužikjas	The young men of the happy ones,
Śoen-pölen vajisni.	One and half hundred hauls brought.
Menam pöriś, aslam pöriś,	My aged man, my old man,
šyren-džynjen vajis že.	One and a half mice brought too.
Majbirjaslen tom mužikjas	The young men of the happy ones
Krövatjas ńebalisni.	Bought beds.
Menam pöriś, aslam pöriś,	My aged man, my old man,
Požjas čöč vöćalis že.	A lattice also made.
Majbirjasej, tom gozjajas,	The happy young couples,
Krövaťe vodalisni.	Into beds tumbled.
Mi końerej-pöriśejked	We unlucky with my old man
Pož göger kyčiľććim že.[21]	On the lattice wrapped us too.

This is not the only case in which the verbally identical text has a different meaning in a new context, because the contextual change affects the way of performance and the melody adopted. For example in a meeting of the Voľdino singing group other women objected to the aim of Yuliya Sergatova to perform the song *Myjla bördan, mića nylej?* ("Why do you cry, beautiful girl?") as a lament:

> Kl. T. Ulyasheva said: They do not sing like that in Voľdino.
> Yu. S.: In Pomozdino and Vyľgort they sing like that. It is a wedding song and they also lamented in weddings.
> P. A. Ulyasheva: They can sing what they like, and those [the researchers] have to compare them, how and where people sing . . .
> D. E. Pystina: In them of course, the girl is lamenting, but with us, I do not know how they sing with us.[22]

After discussion Yuliya Sergatova covered herself with a scarf and showed how the bride lamented: "It begins in the same way as people sing in Pomozdino, Vyľgort and Sorď'yv villages. The people sing together the same song as in Voľdino, a lyric song with a Russian motif, *Lućinuška* ("The little torch"). The text in the *kust* of Pomozdino is scarcely different:[23]

21. Yuliya Pavlovna Sergatova and Voľdino choir, rec. A.-L. S. and O. U., Voľdino, 2001.
22. Klavdiya Terenťevna Ulyasheva, Yuliya Pavlovna Sergatova, Polina Alekseevna Ulyasheva, Dina Egorovna Pystina, rec. A.-L. S. and O. U., Voľdino, 2001.
23. Variants are marked "var" in the text.

1. *Myjla bördan, mića nylej,*	Why do you cry, beautiful girl,
2. **Nora gorzan** (var. **goralyštan**) *ńöžjöńik?*	Miserably sing (*var.* sing /another verb) quietly?
(2) (var. **Nora gorzan guśeńik**)	(*var.* Miserably sing in the low voice)
3. *Myjla kištan **sosjas*** (var. *ćyšjan*) *vylö*	Why do you shed on your shirt (*var.* scarf)
4. *Jugid śinva ńöžjöńik.*	Bright tears quietly.
5. *Eg i* (var. ***me***) *tödli musa mames,*	I don't (*var.* I) even know my dear mother,
6. *Eg i* (var. ***me***) *tödli musa bałes,*	I don't (*var.* I) even know my dear father,
7. *Eg i* (var. ***me***) *tödli aśśim gort.*	I don't (*var.* I) even know my own home.
8. *öliś börin, vežalune*	After a month, on Sunday,
9. *Veressaje śeteni.*	They get me married.
10. *Bałe ńimen ydždedleni,*	You call me by my father's name,
11. *Eziś-zarńi doľeni.*	You talk about gold, silver.
12. *Myj men eziś, myj men zarńi?*	What is gold to me, what silver?
13. *Eziś-zarńi šud oz vaj.*	Gold and silver don't give happiness.
14. *Šudej ponda šogśa-börda,*	I cry, I mourn for my happiness,
15. *Koľi menam tom pöra-aj.*[24]	My time of youth has passed.

The texts of *repetition and praise songs* were performed at the time of traditional evening gatherings (*voĭpuk*) by participants; songs preserved as they were in oral culture, though their meanings changed after the 1940s. Previously they were connected with real persons who took part in the gathering, but later they had a general object. In the evening parties, songs were presented to boys and girls who were interested in each other or to couples or bridegrooms and brides, who were praised. Nowadays these short songs are used in singing groups in the training of voices or as accompaniments to humorous plays performed on stage, but seldom in everyday life. Sometimes they are performed in modern weddings, and then their context is not a "pseudo-wedding" but a real wedding, and they lose their ironic tendencies and overt emotionality. Here are five typical examples of the songs we recorded in villages.

I

Ylyn-ylyn čyn čynale,	Faraway-faraway smoke is hanging,
Matin-matin pu sulale	Nearby-nearby a tree is standing.
Pu vužys dinas da,	Next to the root of the tree, so,
Ńoľ ker kujle da,	Four logs are lying, so.
Ńoľ ker dinas da,	Near the four logs, so,
Ńoľ karťina da.	Four images are so.
Öťi tuś uśe da	One berry is dropping so,
Ardalľon vyle da,	On top of Aral'ľon, so.
Möded tuś uśe da	The second berry is dropping, so,
Ivanović vyle da,	On top of the son of Ivan, so.

24. Dina Egorovna Pystina, Yuliya Pavlovna Sergatova, Valentina Konstantinova Ulyasheva, Klav'dya Terenť evna Ulyasheva, Polina Alekseevna Ulyasheva, S. P. Ulyasheva, rec. I. V. Iľina, A.-L. S. and O. U., Voľdino, 16.7.2001.

Kojmed tuś uśe da
Nastaśśa vyle da,
Ńoľed tuś uśe da Ľeovna vyle[25]

The third berry is dropping, so,
On top of Nastas'ya, so.
The fourth berry is dropping, so, on top
of Leo's daughter.

II

Ylyn-ylyn čyn čynale,
Matin-matin dub dubale,
Dub ulas ńoľ ker,
Ńoľ ker ulas ńoľ kor,
Ńoľ kor ulas ńoľ tuś.
Öťi tuś – Kaťa,
Möd tuś – Matvejovna,

Kojmed tuś – Mikulaj,
ńoľed tuś – Vaśiľjović.
Kaťase da Mikulajse
Gide śujam-ignalam,

Idźas voľes voľsalam
Da asiledźis sen vidźam.[26]

Faraway-faraway smoke is hanging
Nearby-nearby an oak is growing,
Under the oak four logs,
Under the logs four leaves,
Under the four leaves four berries.
One berry is for Kaťya,
The second berry is for the daughter of
Matveï,
The third berry is for Nikolaï,
The fourth berry is for the son of Vasiľiï.
Kaťya and Nikolaï
Are pushed by us to a cowhouse, closed
up,
We spread a straw mattress under them
And keep them until the morning.

III

1. *Pyžen more kuźa,*
Poden dores kuźa,
Svet Jelena da Mikajlovna,
Svet Ivan daj Öndrejović,
Bergedći-bergedći,
Garušnej ćuki vaja,
Oj, og bergedći,
Og bergedći.
Me sijes eg dumajt,
Me sijes eg bažit.

1. By boat across the ocean,
On foot along the beach,
Dear Elena Mikhaïlovna
Dear Ivan Andreevich
Turn around, turn around,
I bring decorated woollen socks.
Oh, I do not turn around
I do not turn around.
I did not think about this,
I did not wait for this.

2. *Pyžen more kuźa,*
Poden dores kuźa,
Svet Jelena da Mikajlovna,
Svet Ivan daj Öndrejović,
Bergedći-bergedći,
kašimer dörem vaja,
Oj, og bergedći,
Og bergedći.
Me sijes eg dumajt,
Me sijes eg bažit.

2. By boat across the ocean,
On foot along the beach,
Dear Elena Mikhaïlovna
Dear Ivan Andreevich
Turn around, turn around,
I shall give you a cashmir shirt.
Oh, I do not turn around,
I do not turn around.
I did not think about this,
I did not wait for this.

---

25. *Oztuśjas* choir, rec. A.-L. S. and O. U., Troitsk, 25.5.2000.
26. Mariya Aleksandrovna Popova, b. 1958, Bogorodsk village, director of Nivshera cultural house; Nina Vasiľevna Eftene, b. 1964. , rec. A.-L. and O. U.,Nivshera village, Kortkeros.

3. *Pyžen more kuźa,*	3. By boat across the ocean,
Poden dores kuźa,	On foot along the beach,
Svet Jelena da Mikajlovna,	Dear Elena Mikhaĭlovna
Svet Ivan daj Öndrejović,	Dear Ivan Andreevich
Kujimiś okaśam.	Three times we kissed.
Oj, bergedća, bergedća.	Oh, I turned around. I turned around
Me sies dumajta, Me sijes bažita.[27]	I think of this, wait for this.

IV

Teś gežemej daj Matrenej,	Beautiful-faced Matrĭona,
Sur vóćemej daj Mikajlovnaej.	Ale made by the daughter of Mikhaĭl
Oj dum, razum, razum, razumnöjej.	Oh dum, razum, razum, razumnaja.
Köšeľ vöća daj zev ydžid tugjen.	I made a tobacco-pouch with big tassels,
Zev ydžid tugjen daj vetymyn molľen.	Big tassels and fifty glass beads.
Kodli śeta? Da musukli śeta.	To whom shall we give it? To the dear one we give it.
Kodli musukli? Da Mitrejli śeta.	To which dear one? To Dimitriĭ we give it.
Kodli Mitrejli? Da Öndrejovićli.[28]	To which Dimitriĭ? The son of Andreĭ.

V

Oľ kuźa lećće,	To a dell (she) descends,
Keres kuźa kaje.	To a cliff (she) climbs.
Kod keres že kaje?	Who is climbing the cliff?
Ögaš keres.	Agaf'ya is [climbing] the cliff.
Kujim jagod.	Tree berries I saw.
Menim jagod oz kov,	I do not need the berries.
Menim Karlom kole.	I need Kharlam.
dĭve kole, dĭve kole,	I need a wonder, I need a wonder.
śölem pote kole,	My heart splits, I have such need,
Śölem ćećće kole.	My heart jumps, I have such need.
Siteg oz poź lun ooni,	It is impossible to live a day without him,
Siteg oz poź voj užni.[29]	It is impossible to sleep a night without him.

A lyric epic song *Krug pyčkyn mića nyv* ("A beautiful girl in the circle"), belongs to the thematic domain of wedding and evening party songs on the basis of its plot and the comments of performers. Performers interpreted it seriously. In Troitsk, this song was sung already in the middle of the evening party, when performers had "warmed up", attained an emotional state and practised a bit. Then we heard somebody say: "OK, now we can sing *Krug pyčkyn*."

27. Mariya Aleksandrovna Popova, b. 1958, Bogorodsk village, director of Nivshera cultural house; Nina Vasiľevna Eftene, b. 1964, rec. A.-L. S. and O. U., Nivshera village, Kortkeros.
28. Mariya Aleksandrovna Popova, b. 1958, Bogorodsk village, director of Nivshera cultural house; Nina Vasiľevna Eftene, rec. A.-L. and O. U., Nivshera village, Kortkeros.
29. Mariya Aleksandrovna Popova, b. 1958, Bogorodsk, director of Nivshera cultural house; Nina Vasiľevna Eftene, b. 1964, rec. A.-L. and O. U., Nivshera village, Kortkeros.

I

1. *Krug pyčkyn mića nyv,*
   Mića nyv göger ľok vojtyr.
   Mića nyvlen mam lokte.
   «Mamej pe da, musa mam,
   Mene etatiś vešti.»
   «Nylej pe da, musa nyv,
   Myjen že me veštišta?
   Šök plaťťe don on suloo.»

1. A beautiful girl in the circle,
   Evil people around the girl.
   The mother of the beautiful girl comes.
   "My mother, well, my dear mother,
   Redeem me from this."
   "My daughter, well, dear girl,
   With what can I redeem you?
   You are not worth a silk scarf."

2. *Krug pyčkyn mića nyv,*
   Mića nyv göger ľok vojtyr.
   Mića nyvlen aj lokte.
   «Ajej pe da, musa aj,
   Mene etatiś vešti.»
   «Nylej pe da, musa nyv,
   Myjen že me veštišta?
   Noj šľapa don on suloo.»

2. A beautiful girl in the circle.
   Evil people around the girl.
   The father of the beautiful girl comes.
   "My father, well, dear father,
   Redeem me from this."
   "My daughter, well, dear girl
   With what can I redeem you?
   You are not worth a cloth hat."

3. *Krug pyčkyn mića nyv,*
   Mića nyv göger ľok vojtyr.
   Mića nyvlen ćoj lokte.
   Ćojej pe da, musa ćoj,
   Mene etatiś vešti.»
   «Maše pe da, musa Maš,
   Myjen že me veštišta?
   Šök parća don on suloo.»

3. A beautiful girl in the circle,
   Evil people around the girl.
   The sister of the beautiful girl comes.
   "My sister, well, dear sister,
   Redeem me from this."
   "Masha, well, dear Masha,
   With what can I redeem you?
   You are not worth a silk brocade cloth."

4. *Krug pyčkyn mića nyv.*
   Mića nyv göger ľok vojtyr.
   Mića nyvlen vok lokte.
   «Vokej pe da, musa vok,
   Mene etatiś vešti.»
   «Ćojej pe da, musa ćoj,
   myjen že me veštišta?
   Roć kepiś don on suloo.»

4. A beautiful girl in the circle.
   Evil people around the girl.
   The brother of the beautiful girl comes.
   "My brother, well, dear brother,
   Redeem me from this."
   "My sister, well, dear sister,
   With what can I redeem you?
   You are not worth a Russian mitten."

5. *Krug pyčkyn mića nyv.*
   Mića nyv göger ľok vojtyr.
   Mića nyvlen Vaś lokte.
   «Vaśej pe da, musa Vaś,
   Mene etatiś vešti.»
   «Mašej pe da, musa Maš,
   Tulup pölanam vešta.»

   Tulup pölanas veštis,

   Čygirććisni-munisni.[30]

5. A beautiful girl in the circle.
   Evil people around the girl.
   The beautiful girl's Vasiliĭ comes.
   "My Vasiliĭ, well, dear Vasiliĭ,
   Redeem me from this."
   "My Masha, well, dear Masha,
   With the hem of a fur coat I redeem
      you."
   With the hem of a fur coat he redeemed
      [her].
   They embraced and left.

30. *Oztuśjas* choir of Troitsk, rec. A.-L. S. and O. U., 26.5.2000.

II

The sceme of the second variant is practically the same as the first variant. The difference is found in the girl's ransom list, the order of relatives to whom she turns in her unbearable situation and the direct mention of a *wedding*. In the example, the first two lines are not included, because they are the same as in the first variant.

1. (...) «*Ajej pe da, musa aj,*
Mene etatiś vešti.»
«*Nylej pe da, musa nyv,*
Myjen ne te veštiśan?
Ruć šapka don on suloo.»

1. (...) "My father, well, dear father,
Redeem me from this."
"My daughter, well, dear girl,
With what can you be redeemed?
You are not worth a fox-fur hat."

2. (...) «*Mamej pe da, musa mam,*
Mene etatiś vešti.»
«*Nylej pe da, musa nyv,*
Myjen ne te veštiśan?
šök plaťťe don on suloo.»

2. (...) " My mother, well, dear mother,
Redeem me from this."
"My daughter, well, dear girl,
With what can you be redeemed?
You are not worth a silk scarf."

3. (...) «*Vokej pe da, musa vok,*
Mene etatiś vešti.»
«*Ćojej pe da, musa ćoj,*
Myjen že me veštišta?
Roć kepiś don on suloo.»

3. (...)"My brother, well, dear brother,
Redeem me from this."
"My sister, well, dear sister,
With what can you be redeemed?
You are not worth Russian mittens."

4. (...) «*Ćojej pe da, musa ćoj,*
Mene etatiś vešti.»
«*Ćojej pe da, musa ćojej,*
Myjen že me veštišta?
Roć ćyšjan don on suloo.»

4. (...) "My sister, well, dear sister,
Redeem me from this."
"My sister, well, dear sister,
With what can I redeem you?
You are not worth a Russian scarf."

5. (...) "*Zonmöj pö, musa zon,*
Menö etatyś vešty."
"*Nylöj pö, musa nyv,*
Öni me tenö bošta."
Krug pyčkyś petisny,
Kuććyśisny, munisny.
Kuććyśisny, munisny,
Gaža svadba vorsisny.[31]

5. (...) "My lad, dear lad,
Redeem me from this."
"My girl, dear girl,
Now I shall take you to be mine."
They came out from the circle,
Embraced and left.
Embraced and left
And had a merry wedding.

III

1. *Krug šörin mića nyv sulale,*

A beautiful girl stands in the middle of the circle,

Krug gögeris ľok totara bergale.
Vidžedlas ke baťis lokte.
«*Baťej, pe baťej da, vešti že vešti.*»

Evil Tatars roll around the circle.
She looked, her father comes.
"My father, father, redeem me, redeem me."

«*Nylej, pe nylej da,*

"My daughter, daughter,

31. Voľdino's choir, rec. A.-L. S. and O. U., 13.6.2001.

Myjen me tene vešta?» With what can I redeem you?"
«Baťej, pe baťej da, kaftannad.» "My father, father, with your kaftan."

2. *Krug šörin mića nyv sulale,* 2. A beautiful girl stands in the middle of the circle,

Krug gögeris ľok totara bergale. Evil Tatars roll around the circle.
Vidźedlas ke, mamis lokte. She saw her mother come.
«Mamej, pe mamej da, vešti že vešti.» "My mother, mother, redeem me, redeem me."
«Nylej, pe nylej da, "My daughter, my daughter,
Myjen me tene vešta?» With what can I redeem you?"
«Mamej, pe mamej, mića jurkyčnad.» "My mother, mother, with a beautiful jurkyč."[32]

3. *Krug šörin mića nyv sulale,* 3. A beatiful girl stands in the middle of the circle.

Krug gögeris ľok totara bergale. Evil Tatars roll around the circle.
Vidźedlas ke, drugis lokte. She saw her friend come.
«Drugej, pe drugej, da, vešti že vešti.» "My friend, my friend, redeem me, redeem me."
«Nylej, pe nylej da, Myjen me tene vešta?» "My girl, my girl, with what shall I redeem you?"
«Drugej, pe drugej, medbur sapegnad.»[33] "My friend, my friend, with the best boots."

When we compare variants, it is clear that though the compositions of the texts are structurally similar, the variants from different villages are unlike. At first, the antagonist model varies: in the songs performed in wedding rituals the side of the bridegroom is depicted as "evil people" or "evil Tatars". In the Baďël'sk variant the antagonist model is built in the home space of the girl: *«Kerka šörin mića nyv sulale, porog ulin **Guriluki** bergale»* ("In the middle of the house a girl is standing, Guriluki on the threshold rolls").[34]

For the second, the variants differ on the basis of the list of items (wedding gifts) by which the girl could be bought and for which the girl is not valuable enough. In Upper Vychegda weddings, the gifts and return gifts were usually towels and accessories like scarves, trousers, shirts, sarafans, decorated socks and mittens, but not domestic animals, which were given to the young only when they left the family. Hence the songs do not list horses, cows etc. as in the variants of other parts of Komi.

For the third, the differences of rhythm lead to different local melodies and tunes.

"The song of the redeemed girl" is known over large areas of North Europe, for example in Ingria, Karelia and Finland (Savo). In the Baltic Finnic area the song belongs to the repertoire of young girls and represents

32. *Jurkyč: jur* "head"+ *kyč* "frame".
33. Aleksandra Stepanovna Gabova, rec. A.-L. S. and O. U. 2000, Troitsk, Kortkeros.
34. Anna Timof'evna Ulyasheva, b. 1925, Baďël'sk village, rec. Z. Novotny, A. Smorchkov and O. U., Vyľgort, 10.7.2003.

a singing tradition in which the girl compares her loved one to her relatives. When father, mother, sister and brother betray her, the loved one saves her and pays the necessary items for her. The basic scheme of the song is similar over the whole area and the variations seem to be in the same compounds of texts as in the Komi songs though the singing contexts vary. In Savo (central Finland), the gifts for redeeming the girl are domestic animals, as in many parts of Komi. The wide distribution and several different functions of this song testify that it belongs to the old North European lyric epic tradition. Matti Kuusi has shown that this and other repetition songs comparing relatives, typical in Russian and Baltic Finnic cultures, are connected to ballads and belong to the medieval tradition. He argued that "The redeemed maiden" brought the comparison of relatives scheme with the "climax of relations" to the Baltic from the west and the context may have been originally a new form of circle dance. The Komi tradition shows the song has been popular also in Eastern Europe.[35]

Macaronic and Russian songs

Macaronic verses or songs are those in which words of different languages are mixed. Such verses with Latin inclusions were very popular among university students and wandering singers in the late Middle Ages and in the Renaissance. Russian–Komi examples in Komi folklore are most often used for humour. Sometimes the texts are decorated with standard Russian poetic images like *selena vina* (< Russian "zeleno vino", lit. "green wine"), *krasnoj devitsoj* (< Russian "krasny devitsy", "beautiful girls"), *mölödèj mölödeč* (< Russian "molodoĭ molodets", "young man"), *apitsèr mölödèj* (< Russian "ofitser molodoĭ", "young officer"). Some of these texts appear as the results of Komi linguistic adaptation of the old Russian songs borrowed in the sixteenth to seventeenth centuries and became incomprehensible not only for the Komi performers but also for native speakers of modern Russian. In this case we have songs such as *Ćivil'-vorobej, Jedet milenkoj da-jna troećkoj, Tiga-tiga*, in which the Russian source can hardly be guessed or not even guessed at all, and the Komi words added in phonetic accordance with the Russian words provide no new sense either. In these cases, the melody and the situational connection of the song with a peculiar rite or a group of performers become the main point for the Komi.

In Upper Vychegda are found macaronic and Russian-language songs. In the song *Tiga-tiga*, the second and third line have clearly changed. Because there is no gender in the Komi language, the performers make mistakes in their references. Some of the words have been changed, for example in place of the expression "the maiden's beauty" in the Russian song there is "the maiden's agony" in the Komi variant. On the other hand, the plot, personages and experiences of the lyrical heroine are quite understandable in the *Tiga-tiga* song though there are mistranslations in repetitions. The song

---

35. Kuusi 1963: 344–6; Kuusi 1958.

Iz-zo lesu in turn is totally incomprehensible except for a couple of lines. The words are so hard to understand that the textualisation of the song is difficult, though it is known that the song has possibly been performed in bride evenings of wedding rituals. The song was presented at the entertainment parties of young people. In Troitsk, this song was danced like a known, originally Russian dance song, *Rućejok*. One woman begins the dance, then, gradually, others are invited one after another. At the end of the song everyone was included in the dance. As it ends, they form a half-circle, bow and offer their hands to each other.

Some of the songs begin with Russian words or lines and continue after that in Komi:

Kak po piterskoj da po doroženkoj	Kak po Piterskoĭ da po doroge,
jeďet milenkoj da-ju-na-trojećkoj ke.	Edet milen'ki na troĭke.
Nyv vala lećće da,	A girl goes to get water,
Čaj vala lećće.	Goes to get water for tea,
Da zon vöv juktale, daj vylas pukale.	And a lad gives water to a horse, and sits on its back.
Daj löśida pukale, mićaa j śorńite.	And he sits fine and talks beautifully.
laskov ved sije.	He is tender.
*Da **primetliv** sije.*	And he is observant.
Yli kare möde . . .[36]	He leaves for a town far away . . .

Or:

Apitser molodoj da,	Young officer, so,
Mića mundǐra.	In a beautiful uniform.
Zarńi pogona da,	Golden braces and
Lasko kyvja.	Tender speech.
Yle munis.	He went far away.
Kise vajlis,	He gave his hand [to me],
Ötnames kolĭs,	He left me alone,
Ćuńkyča kijen,	A ring for the hand,
Kaga mozdoren.	A child on my lap.
Mića novli,	I dressed beautifully,
Gažaa śyyli.[37]	Sang gladly.

In the first song, instead of the loan-word *primetliv* (< Russian, "observant") after the word *laskov* (< Russian, "tender, caressing") in the previous line, logically there should clearly be *privetliv* (< Russian "privetlivyĭ", "affable, friendly") – the more so, since in Russian everyday speech and in folklore *laskov da privetliv* ("caressing and affable") is a stable expression. Probably it was more important for the Komi performers to stress that the boy was

36. Mariya Aleksandrovna Popova, b. 1958, Bogorodsk, director of Nivshera cultural house; Nina Vasil'evna Eftene, b. 1964, rec. A.-L. and O. U., Nivshera, Kortkeros.
37. Mariya Aleksandrovna Popova, b. 1958, Bogorodsk, director of Nivshera cultural house; Nina Vasil'evna Eftene, b. 1964, rec. A.-L. and O. U., Nivshera, Kortkeros

handsome and sporty, hence the use of the Russian loan-word with a slight shift of meaning: *primechateľnyĭ* ("remarkable") to *primetlivyĭ* ("observant").

Songs translated into Komi

The basic corpus of folk songs of the Upper Vychegda is completed by a great number of translated folklore genres, ballads, historical and lyric songs, melodies belonging to urban milieux and spectacular romances and later patriotic and lyric songs. The *Saldatjasöj, mića vojtyrjasöj* ("My soldiers, my beautiful people") is a translation of the Russian song *Soldatuški, bravy rebʹatuški* ("Solders, brave fellows"), *Buzgö tölys*, ("The wind whistles"), *Bereg doryn, ju doryn* (On the beach, by the river), *Dumajti öťikös* (I thought one [person]), *Sad jöryn kö nyv guľajtö* (In garden a girl is walking) – *Vo sadu li v ogorode* (In forest or in garden), *Kor rytys völi gažtem* (When evening is sorrowful; an urban romance), *Maruśa otravitćis* (Marusya went, an urban romance), *Leźavlej vaj, zonjas, vövte* (Lads, take the harness of the horse; a Ukranian song), *Ötćid ij mića nyla-zonma*. The last song begins sometimes "Once a beautiful lad and a girl", sometimes it is called "Rush rustled". Translations do not repeat word by word the content of the original Russian song. This is evident if we look at the last song:

Russian orginal	Translation from Russian
Šumel kamyš, derevʹa gnuľiś,	Rush rustled, trees bent
A noćka ťomnaja byla.	And the night was dark.
Odna vozľubľennaja para	One loving couple
Vśu noć śidela do utra.	Sat the whole night until morning.
A poutru oňi prosnuľiś,	But in the morning they woke up,
Krugom pomʹataja trava,	Around them trampled grass,
To ne trava byla pomʹata,	But trampled was not only the grass,
Pomʹata devićja krasa . . .	Trampled was the beauty of the girl . . .

The beginning of the Komi variant	Translation of the Komi text
Ötćid ij mića nyla-zonma	Once a beautiful lad and a girl
Kust ulin kujlis asileź.	Under the bush rested until morning.
Nylid ćeććis da ij vidźedlis:	The girl woke up and saw:
Göger dźugśema turunis.	Trampled grass around.
Ćyšjanjasnas śinse tupkis	With her scarf she covered her eyes.
Da śinvanas bördni kutis . . .	And began with tears to cry . . .

In the Komi translation the introduction of nature images is missing and the focus is not on the night of love but on the repentance of the girl the next morning. The adequacy of translations, their independent character and the use of traditional metaphors in the Komi texts can be illuminated by the following example. It is the first verse of the Russian Katyusha song, which was very popular in the 1940s:

Russian
Rastsvetaľi jabloni i grushi,
Poplyľi tumany nad rekoĭ.
Vykhodila na bereg Kaťusha,
Vykhodila na bereg krutoĭ.

Translation from Russian
Blossomed apple and pear trees,
Mist clouds hung on the river.
Came to the beach Katyusha,
Came to the steep beach.

Komi text
Zöridź ludjas, mića badjas pölen

Šonid tölen gyale nyrvyv.
Gožśa ryte džudžid bereg vyle
Petavlivle mićańik tom nyy.

Translation form Komi
Meadows blossom, through beautiful
   willows
Warm wind makes waves in the swamp.
On a summer evening to a high beach
A young beautiful girl comes.

In the Komi variants the details of southern nature, for example apples and pears, have disappeared. Instead the songs use Komi images, such as meadow flowers (*zöridź*) and willows, the symbols of the beauty of a young woman, and emotional signs of gentle sorrow. The girl is faceless and without a name, she represents a generic young woman. If we look at the unusual rhymes and clear metre of the poem, the translation seems to have been made by a professional poet. But through its longevity – it is about a century and a half old – the poem has adjusted to the demands of folk poetry.

The translation of the favourite Soviet poem "Blue scarf" belongs to the time of the Second World War. It has been adapted to the Komi language very freely.

1. *Löń Ežva ju kyrköč doryn,*
Pelyśjas bydmeni kön,
Pelyś pu ulin
Te korke šulin:
«Radejtni kuta me pyr».

On the quiet bank of Vychegda,
Where rowans grow,
Under a rowan
You said once:
"I shall love you always".

2. *Vetlö,vetlö sad jörö*
Tom jözys, ton,
Gažödćö-śylö.
Šölömšör nylöj,
Ńekor te menam on vun.

2. Go, go to the garden
Young ones,
Sing, have fun.
In my heart, girl,
I shall never forget you.

3. *Tene pöśa*
Syvtyrjen kutli me sek.
Özjeni śinjas,
Dźoridźainjas,
Özjej ti kodźulen vek.

3. Warmly you
I then embraced.
Shining eyes,
Blooming regions,
Shine always like stars.

4. *Te mene puľaiś vidźan,*
Tyš vyle teteg og pet.
Morejas-jujas, görajas-mujas
Vörögly ńekor og śet.

4. You protected me from bullets,
To battle I do not go without you.
Seas, rivers, hills, earth
To enemies we shall never give.

The translation from Russian into Komi is free: the basic image of the Russian text, "a small modestly blue scarf" (*sinen'kiĭ*, modestly blue, the old meaning of the word is also "worth five rubles"), has gone. Instead, in the translation there are images of the Vychegda and the rowan, a sacred tree for the Komi.

FOLK TRANSLATIONS

In the long interaction with Russians, unknown singers have translated a great number of Komi songs from Russian. The time of translation cannot be precisely ascertained. Hence, the origin of the above mentioned (see pp. 213–17) epic song *Peder Kiron* should be sought in Russian religious poems. The translations of Russian literary poems written from the eighteenth to twentieth centuries or Russian folksongs from that time into Komi do not much resemble the original texts. Sometimes the plot and some lines survive, sometimes only key words and images are left. The translated songs may also have a great number of variants. On the other hand, there are old songs which have spread to all districts with only small variations. Thus, in Upper Vychegda, a song called *Paśkid-gaža ulića* ("Broad, gay street") has little variation: the song is known in the other Komi areas by the name *Doľi-šeľi* or *Dor ľi, šör ľi*:

Paśkid-gaža ulića-ulića,	Broad, gay street
Doľi-šeľi, noľi šeľi. Govorinskej ulića.	**Doľi-šeľi, noľi šeľi. Govorinskej** street.
Ulićaas nyv ole, nyv ole.	On the street, a girl lives.
Doľi-šeľi, noľi šeľi. Govorinskej nyv ole.	**Doľi-šeľi, noľi šeľi. Govorinskej** a girl lives.
Nyv doras pe zon vole, zon vole.	To the girl a boy is going, a boy is going.
Doľi-šeľi, noľi šeľi. Govorinskej zon vole.	**Doľi-šeľi, noľi šeľi. Govorinskej** a boy comes.
Zonmej, zonmej, myj volan, myj volan?	My son, my son, why do you go, why do you go?
Doľi-šeľi, noľi šeľi. Govorinskej myj volan.	**Doľi-šeľi, noľi šeľi. Govorinskej** why do you come?
Mene mame pińale, pińale.	Mother blames me, blames me,
Doľi-šeľi, noľi šeľi. Govorinskej pińale.	**Doľi-šeľi, noľi šeľi. Govorinskej** blames me.
Mene baťe kyjede, kyjede.	Father tracks me, tracks me.
Doľi-šeľi, noľi šeľi. Govorinskej kyjede.	**Doľi-šeľi, noľi šeľi. Govorinskej** tracks me.
Vaj že, zonmej, mun gortad, bör gortad.	Oh, son, go back home, back home.
Doľi-šeľi, noľi šeľi. Govorinskej bör gortad.	**Doľi-šeľi, noľi šeľi. Govorinskej** back home.
Gaške, korke addźiślam, addźiślam.	Maybe some time we shall meet,
Doľi-šeľi, noľi šeľi. Govorinskej addźiślam.	**Doľi-šeľi, noľi šeľi. Govorinskej** meet.
Grad kostas mi okaśam, okaśam.	Between the [flower]beds we shall kiss.
Doľi-šeľi, noľi šeľi. Govorinskej okaśam.	**Doľi-šeľi, noľi šeľi. Govorinskej** we shall kiss.

This is a free translation from the north Russian "bridge" or "walking" song "Along the wide street" (*Vdol'le, všir' le ulica*). It was performed by groups of boys who were going to fist-fight in a closed row against another closed row of boys. The song has been interpreted from a new perspective and became a lyrical song in the programmes of Komi women. The end lines added by the women of Vol'dino and Vyl'gort are not easy to understand:

Pośńi lukse šyblalam, šyblalam.	A small onion we throw away, throw away.
Gyriś lukse vesalam, vesalam	A large onion we clean, we clean.

Only one variant, which we recorded in Pozheg, refers indirectly to the original Russian text and the motif of the fist-fight:

Pośńi löpse[38] *šyblalam, šyblalam.*	Small devastator we throw away, throw away.
Gyriś löpse lösalam, lösalam[39]	Large devastator we hit with the fist, hit with the fist.

Anonymous translations can be dated accurately only rarely, though through various cultural indications they may hint at when Komi singers got to know and perform them. For example, the song *Kyk geroj* ("Two heroes"), which was performed to us in every village, was popular during the Second World War period but may have been translated earlier: Aleksandra Arkhipova and Sergeĭ Neklyudov have shown that the Russian song was created around the First World War.[40] Only in one exceptional case was the song performed in Russian and even then the singers said that it was performed earlier in Komi. We recorded the most complete variant (I) in the village of Vyl'gort.

1. *Lokteni kyk geroj*	1. Two heroes return
2. *Pinskej pront vyvśań gortas.*	2. Home from the Finnish front.
3. *A pinjasked tyšin*	3. And in the fight with the Finns
4. *Moresej rańiććis kujimiś.*	4. My breast was hurt three times.
5. *Tövaryš, tövaryš,*	5. Comrade, comrade,
6. *Viśe menam rana ćorida.*	6. My wound aches hard.
7. *Öťi rana burde, möd rana vośśe,*	7. One wound is healing, the other is opening,
8. *A kojmednas kuvni men love.*	8. But with the third I shall die.
9. *Tövaryš, tövaryš, vajli men gumaga,*	9. Comrade, comrade, give me paper,
10. *Me tenid gižišta piśmetor.*	10. I will write to you a letter.
11. *Gortin menam ćeľaď, tom götirej menam.*	11. At home I have children, a young wife of mine.
12. *Naja viććiśeni mene.*	12. They wait for me.

38. In Komi: *löp* = 1. rubbish; 2. a bad thing; 3. a devastator, bad person.
39. In Komi: *lösavny* = 1. level off or cut with an axe; 2. hit with a fist, hit both sides of face.
40. Arkhipova and Neklyudov 2008.

13. *No med viććišeni, abu važnej ďele,*	13. But though they wait, that has no meaning.
14. *Šorovno me gortedź og vo.*	14. I do not come home anyway.
15. *Kor bydmasni ćeľaď, juvalasni mamliš:*	15. When children grow, they ask mother:
16. *«Köni mijan röďimej baťnim?»*	16. "Where is our own father?"
17. *Sek mamis žugiľććas daj šinvanas, börddźas*	17. Then mother becomes sorrowful and bursts into tears,
18. *Daj ćeľaďli öťvet vidźas:*	18. And holds back from answering:
19. *«Tijan rödnej baťnid*	19. "Your own father
20. *Ij pinjasked tyšin ušis».*	20. Was killed in the fight with the Finns."
21. *Menam götir tom na, addźas aslis mužik,*	21. My wife is still young, she finds a new man,
22. *A ćeľaďli bať ńekor oz lo.*	22. But the children will never have a father.
23. *Tövaryš, tövaryš,*	23. Comrade, comrade,
24. *Guav menšim lyjas pydedžik.*	24. Bury my bones deeper.
25. *Pröššaj, menam drugej, pröššaj, menam ćeľaď,*	25. Good-bye, my friend, good-bye my children,
26. *Pröššaj, tom götirej menam.*[41]	26. God bye my young wife.

The variant from Kekur differs from the above text so that lines 5, 6, 9, 10, 25 and 26 are missing, in line 18 the words *ötvet vidźas* ("holds back from answering") are the words *ötvet šetas* ("gives an answer"). In the line 21 the words *menam götir tom na* ("my wife is still young") are the words *menam tom götirej* ("my young wife").[42]

From the Voľdino variant lines 4, 5, 17, 18, and 21–6 are missing. In line 10 *me **tenid** gižišta pišmetor* ("**To you** I shall write a letter") are words *me **gorte** gižišta pišmetor* ("**To home** I write the letter") .[43] The Pozheg variant lacks lines 5, 6, 9, 10 and 21–6. Lines 19 and 20 are *Tijan rödnej baťnid ij pinjasked tyšin, pinckej grańica vylin ušis* or "Your own [your kin] father in a fight with the Finns, on the Finnish border, was killed".[44] This variant refers to the original Russian folk song, which was heard by writers as a performance by the Cossack chorus from Ekaterinburg a little later: "Two heroes served on the German front, on the Finnish border in a war . . .".

This song was presented to us for two reasons. First, we asked singing groups to sing something old, which to singers means "not modern or popular, but something which was performed by the former generation". For the second, it was especially presented to the Finnish researcher. Interestingly

41. A. T. Ulyasheva, N. S. Kurochkina and, V. S. Ignatova, rec. A.-L. S. and O. U., 18.6.2001

42. E. A. Shakhova, A. V. Shakhova and M. I. Shakhova, rec. A.-L. S. and O. U., 3.7.2002.

43. D. A. Pystina, Yu. P. Sergatova, V. K. Ulyasheva, K. T. Ulyasheva, P. A. Ulyasheva and S. P. Ulyasheva, rec. I. V. Il'ina, A.-L. S. and O. U.

44. Nina Vyacheslavovna Treťyakova, b. 1924, Nina Sergeevna Treťyakova, b. 1932, rec. A.-L. S. and O. U., Pozheg, 4.7.2002.

enough, the women never thought that a Finnish woman would not understand the song as they do. In one village, it was said that they know a Finnish song – maybe, because Finland and the Finnish front were mentioned in the song. Only in Bogorodsk did friends of the researchers stop a woman who wanted to sing this song: "What, are you mad? How can we sing to a Finnish woman about the war with Finns?" But the next day, we were able to persuade the women to sing the song. Anna said that her father, too, had died on the Finnish front at the same time, though the Finns looked at the front from the opposite direction.

It is not amazing that this song is so widely known and popular among women born in the 1920s to 1940s. First, the song describes in a lyrically sorrowful way the fall of the war hero who speaks his last farewell and sends regards to his closesest relatives. The theme is handled in *Pedör Kiron*, "Far, far away in the Russian Caucasus", "My mother blames me", *Kazań-göra*, "Once I had, I had one whom I loved". A motif of a message given by a bird or a bird which flies to the place of the killing of mother, wife or bride of the hero, in order to "bury the bones of the hero deeper" is quite often joined in this kind of songs. For the second, a great number of Komi men who were experienced hunters, skiers and shooters were mobilised for the Winter War between the Soviet Union and Finland and later, in the time of the Great Patriotic War of the Soviet Union, for the Karelian front. From all the villages where we recorded this song at least three or four men were on the Finnish front and many of them did not come back; some of them became prisoners of war in Finland.[45] Naturally losses from the peaceful period of fifteen years after the Revolution and the Soviet propaganda about the unbeatable Red Army were reflected in the oral epic tradition of that time: the songs did not praise the heroic deeds of the war, but people's tragic fates.

TRANSLATIONS OF KNOWN POETS

Women's groups also perform songs which were translated by poets in the 1930s to 1950s. In those years the translation efforts came to a head, in a way which had not been achieved in the whole history of Komi literature. Not only poems of Mayakovskii and the Internationale but also works of Pushkin, Lermontov and Zhukov were translated into Komi. The quality of translations was not always excellent, but their great number was surprising; the reason seems to be the rise of a new generation of poets. People arranged many poems for music. Then the texts were recreated again according to popular ideas and traditional fashions.

Menim mame dolis pyr ("Mother always talked to me") is a reasonably good translation by Zhan Morös (I. T. Chistalëv), a poet not much known today, into Komi from the song "How my mother" of Dem'yan Bednii. The names Nikolai and Mariya in the original text have changed. In the last passage, an addition of four lines, the song gives a picture of the enemy in typical Komi fashion:

---

45. See folklore texts recorded by Uotila (1986) from the Upper Vychegda war prisoners.

. . . Doliḏlunnim oz na kus. Virej pue.	Our rejoicing will never fade away. My blood boils.
Gaž korśni ved me og mun, śölem nue.	I do not go to seek for joy, my heart takes me.
Ozirjasked panśis tyš, panśis ćorid.	With the rich the fight began, the hard [fight] began.
Kyrnyšliś čöčkörtny gyž vlaśtnim kore.	The regime asks us to cut the nails of the raven.

Ylyn-ylyn roć Kavkazyn ("Far, far away in the Russian Caucasus") is a translation by E. Kolegov of a Russian historical song "Along the Caucasian line". Unlike the original text, the Komi variant is connected to the Civil War. The lyrical heroes are a Red commander and a Komi lad, who succeeds in a battle. These songs are used as folk songs like the modified songs written originally by Komi poets.

Songs to the words of Komi poets

Many songs which were composed to the words of Komi poets of the nineteenth and twentieth centuries, the 1960s–1970s and 1990s–2000s have been preserved among the people. Songs with words by I. A. Kuratov *Rytja vojö, matuška* ("Late in the evening, dear mother") and P. F. Klochkov *Asja kya* ("The red of dawn"), *Tölyś vyvsa nyv* ("The girl in the moon"), *Myjla bördan, mića nylöj* ("Why do you cry, beautiful girl?") have been handed down from the nineteenth century. From the 1920s and 1930s there are many songs by V. Savin, of which the best known are *Ćuži-bydmi* ("I was born and grew up"), *Śölöm śylöm* ("Song of the heart"), *Jugyd kodźuv* ("Bright star"), *Mića nyvjas Ežva dorö leććisny* ("Beautiful girls came to Vychegda"), *Vež vidź vyvti muna* ("Along the green meadow I go"), M. Lebedev's *Köni svaḏba, sen ij gaž* ("Where the wedding is, there is fun"), *Ovlis-vyvlis vöryn* ("Once they lived in a forest"), *Bur baťköd-mamköd olöm* ("Good life with mother and father"), *Kön olam mi* ("Where we live"), *Myjla nö, šondiöj, vör sajö leććömyd* ("Why do you, sun, set behind the forest?"), *Kučöm šonyd da lön* ("How warm and calm"), *Mem öťi arśa rytö* ("To me one autumn night"). These poets were persecuted in 1937–41 and their publications were removed from public use. Hence singers who knew the oral poetry but could not read the poems any more significantly modified the texts, which were communicated orally. Songs which were composed for the poems by later writers from the 1940s to the 1960s[46] have not changed as much as the poems of earlier generations. Hence, the song *Jagyn bydmis zev mića požöm* ("In a pine forest there grew a beautiful pine tree") written by I. Vavilin has been performed without changes.

The only characteristic feature of the Upper Vychegda variants is the end lines. After the last line *viśö völöm śölömys* ("[her] heart got ill") there is a repetition line *viśe völem möd vesna* ("[she] got ill because she [loved]

---

46. For example I. Vavilin, P. Shebolkin and S. Popov.

another"). The Pozheg variant differs from the literal text and other folklore variants because in the second stanza the line *medbur jagśis kerala* ("from the best pine forest I fell [a tree]") is replaced by the line *śemja pyčśis ńečišta* ("from family I separate [her]"); the line *asiv kaji pues pöredni* ("next morning I went to chop a tree") in the the third stanza is replaced by the line *rytnas muni nyles koravni* ("in the evening I went to woo a girl"). In other words, in this song variant the second and third stanzas have been combined. The fourth stanza differs from the literal text but is close to folklore variants. The last line ends the song as in the Voľdino variant: *šogśe völem möd vesna* ("longed for another").

The song *Džudžyd kerösyn* ("On a high hill"), written by P. Shebolkinin, has a folklore version, which is mostly similar to the literal text, only some words and the order of lines having been changed. The penultimate line and an added last line give a new interpretation to the hero of the song: 6. *Korke-nekorke, rytjalan kade, Tom jözlen virid pyr vorse-pue* ("sometimes in the evenings, in youth the blood plays and boils"); 7. *Öni vovema, tölka lovema, Ńiga vajema dźik mešek tyr* ("now he came, had became wise, of books he brought a whole sack"). The image of a man coming from the fight has been replaced by the image of a man coming back from the town with books.

The texts of M. Lebedev have not changed much. For that reason it is difficult to see them as folk poems, though they could have been greatly transformed because they are written mostly on the basis of motifs of folk works. In Upper Vychegda, singers have edited only the last lines. Thus, the roots of the poem *Bur batked-mamked olem* ("Good life with mother and father") are in wedding poetry, rituals and laments, and the life with parents and with the family of the husband has been opposed in a traditional way. The penultimate line is normally omitted from the song:

Bur olöm menam völi,	Good life I had,
Ľok olöm loi zev.	Very bad began.
Tom gažöj, dolydlunöj,	The joy and happines of youth
kydź byťťö ez i vöv.	As if it never existed.

The last farewell of the heroine has changed slightly. The mother and father of the original lines, "Father, mother, dear lad, farewell, farewell, farewell", are replaced by sister and brother and the main attention is paid to the description of the beloved young man. The saying **kört sadök piyn kaj** ("in an iron cage a small bird") has been substituted by a more poetic and less expressive saying **görd sadek piin kaj** ("in a red cage a small bird"), which identifies marriage with a cage.

To another song of the same poet, *Pukala köť vetledla* ("Though I sit, though I walk"), the Vyľgort and Bogorodsk women added a last, sixth, line:

Važen völi milojej jona raďejte,	Before my beloved loved me a lot,
Sija raďejtemjasse dźikedź vunedis.	That love he just forgot.
Myjla ne te, milojej, dźikedź lögaśin?	Why were you, darling, just so hurt?
Taje lögaśemjaste dźikedź vuned bör.	Forget these resentments for ever.

Some marks of folk-editing are also found in the songs which have become popular recently. An example of this was composed to the words of G. Butyreva, an Udoran poet. In its first phrase *džudžyd jenežys pyž moz potľašö* ("deep heaven, how the boat floats"), the Upper Vychegda performers replace a dialect word *potʹʟʹaśö*, "float, glide", with a word they understand better: *potlaśö*, "tear up, burst". Hence, the phrase gets a grimmer meaning, as if referring to thunder: "deep heaven, how the boat bursts".

Folk variants of the poems of known writers

The older songs written by known writers may have changed so much and are so far from the original text that we can call them folk poems. An example is the song composed to a poem of P. Klochkov, *Tölyś vyvsa nyv* ("A girl from the moon"). It is based on fairy-tale and mythic motifs of an orphan girl, whom the moon will take to himself and who is married to the moon. The motif is also handled in the wedding poetry, in the poem "The wooing of the son of Sun and the son of Moon" and from the folk tales which tell about stepmother and stepdaughter: Moon donates silver to the girl and lays her down on earth. The greedy stepmother follows the girl and tries to get the riches, but loses the chance to go down to earth and has to stay on the back of the moon. Because of the intertextual relationship of the song and folklore – the plot and personages are from fairy tales and myths – the song suits a folklore context, and it spread from the beginning of the nineteenth century widely to many Komi areas and the knowledge of its writer was lost.[47] The text of the song has changed deeply. Singers from different villages noticed the local differences in performance and texts in their discussions and in humorous arguments. They drew parallels between features of performance, and melodic and textual forms in different villages. In Vyľgort there was a playful dialogue between singers representing neighbouring villages. Though they had married and moved to another village in their youth they had perceived a form of "local patriotism", which in the Upper Vychegda becomes apparent in joking and banter.

> Kurochkina (born in Velikopole): In Baďëľsk people sing quickly, but with us in Poľľes (Veliko Pole) and here in Vyľgort people sing slowly.
>
> Anna Timofeevna Ulyasheva (born in Baďëľsk): Well, Baďëľsk is on a hill, on one high place, hence, people sing hard and quick and not like in Vyľgort, where they sing from a small knoll. And people in Baďëľsk are quick. They have to reach all the places. In the time you take to sing one song, we do two.[48]

47. Some old singers from Vyľgort assumed that this song was written by T'ima Ven' (V. T. Chistalëv) from their neighbour village, while people from Pozheg in turn thought it was was written by Sandrik Mikol from their village. Similarly the folk poem composed of the words of V. Savin, *Ćuži-bydmi* ("I was born and I grow up") is performed by Komi-Permyaks in the Perm'yak language, and they believe that it was created by a Perm'yak poet, Piťu Öňö.

48. V. S. Ignatova, N. S. Kurochkina, A. T. Ulyasheva and S. I. Kurochkina, rec. A.-L. S.

In performances of the song "Girl in the moon" there are few textual differences in the culturally coherent Pomozdino *kust* (Baďëľsk, Voľdino, Vyľgort). But if we compare the variants from Pozheg, which is further away though it belongs to the same *kust* as Pomozdino, we already find some distinctions. Among these belong the replacement of passages of text by gaps or omissions and additions of lines. Greater differencies become apparent when we compare variants representing different *kust*-areas as the next variants from Pozheg and Vyľgort. In the Pozheg variant the lines are numbered and in the Vyľgort one the corresponding lines are marked by numbers in brackets. The lexical differences and additional lines are in bold.

I

1.	*Öšiń ulin ködźid švačke, zel ed sije ľok.*
2.	*Töliś juger śinme vaćke, menam un oz lok.*
3.	*Pukala me öšiń dorin, kylza mamliś mojd,*
4.	*Kydźi olis šöd vör šörin ďetina me kojd.*
5.	*«Mame, mame, töliś vilas, ďert že, kodke em?*
6.	*Ješše karnan peľpom vilas. **Kod ne, kod ne sen?**»*
7.	*«Korke, taje zel nin važen, **olis mića nyl.***
8.	***Olem silen ez völ löšid, ez kylli bur kyl . . .***
9.	***Tomen końer koľis mamteg, völi-j ićińvodź.***
10.	*Ićiń nyles vidźis ľoka, **vidźis ponjes moz,***
11.	*Udžedis dyr rytin śoredź, asiv ćeććis vodź.*
12.	***Korke völi-j öťi pöra, sečem ködźid voj.***
13.	*Ićiń nyles ystis vala: – ‹Lećći pe va vaj.›*
14.	*Nylid leććis jukmes dore, nyles bośtis šog:*
15.	*‹Tačem olemśis pe bara, korke mynla-j og?*
16.	***Töliś, töliś, ted me kevma, töliś, kylan-on?›***
17.	*Töliś kylis, kyvzis nyles, bośtis as sajas.*
18.	*Nylid öni töliś vilad zel nin una vo,*
19.	*Ješše karnan peľpom vilas, byťťe katle va.»*

II

1 (3).	*Pukala me öšiń dorin, **kyvza** mamliś mojd,*
2.	*Töliś juger śinme vaćke, menam un oz lok.*
3 (5).	*«Mame, mame, töliś vilas, ďert že, kodke em?*
4 (6).	***Kute** karnan peľpom vilas, byťťe katle va.»*
5 (7).	*«Korke **öťćid**, zev nin važen, **(kyvzi menśim mojd)***
6 (10+8).	*Ićiń nyles ľoka vidźis, **ez šuli bur kyv . . .***
7 (13).	*Nyles ićiń **vala ystis:** – ‹Lećći pe va vaj.›*
8 (14).	*Nylid leććis jukmes dore, nyles bośtis šog:*
9 (15).	*‹Tačem olemśis pe bara korke mynla-og?*
10 (16).	***Jugid töliś, verman ke te, bo¦uu¦t as vilad vaj.›***
11 (17+18).	***Töliś nyles bo¦uu¦tis. Sije öni na vek sen.***
12 (10).	***Kute** karnan peľpom vilas, byťťe katle va.»*[49]

and O. U., in the club house of Vyľgort, 13.6.2001, and at the home of Aleksandra D. Ignatova, b. 1927, 28.6. 2002.

49. V. S. Ignatova, N. S. Kurochkina, A. T. Ulyasheva, S. I. Kurochkina, rec. A.-L. S.

1.	Out of the window . . . the frost cracks, it is very fierce.
2.	The moonlight strikes into my eyes, sleep does not come to me.
3.	I am sitting near the window and hear a tale from mother,
4.	How there lived in a black forest a young lad like me.
5.	"Mother, mother, in the moon, who might be there?
6.	Still with yoke on her shoulders. Who is there, who might be there?"
7.	"Once, long ago, there lived a beautiful girl.
8.	She lived but she she had it hard, did not hear a good word . . .
9.	The young one was left without mother, she became a stepdaughter.
10.	Stepmother dealt with the girl badly, treated her like a dog,
11.	Forced her to work late in the evening, to wake early in the morning.
12.	Once upon a time, such a cold night,
13.	Stepmother wanted the girl to bring water: 'Go, fetch water.'
14.	The girl went to the hole in the ice, the girl was overwhelmed by sorrow:
15.	'Can I never give up this kind of life?
16.	Moon, moon, I pray you, do you hear or not?'
17.	Moon heard, heard the girl, took her to himself.
18.	Already now the girl has been many years in the moon.
19.	Still with yoke on her shoulders, as if going to fetch water."

1 (3).	I am sitting under the window, heard a tale from mother.
2.	The moonlight strikes into my eyes, sleep does not come.
3 (5).	"Mother, mother, in the moon, who might be there?
4 (6).	She carries a yoke on her shoulders, as if going to fetch water."
5 (7).	"Once, long ago (listen to my tale),
6 (10+8).	Stepmother treated a girl badly, said not a good word . . .
7 (13).	Stepmother told the girl to bring water: 'Go to fetch water.'
8 (14).	The girl went to the ice hole, she was overwhelmed by sorrow:
9 (15).	'Can I never give up this kind of life?
10 (16).	Bright moon, if you want, take me to you.'
11 (17+18).	The moon took the girl. She is still there.
12 (10).	She carries a yoke on her shoulders, as if going to fetch water."

Line 20 of the folklore variant I and line 12 of the folklore variant II are in the place of four verses (sixteen lines) of P. Klochkov's poem. However, the mythic plot of the poem is still unchanged. The personages and key phrases remain in spite of their volatile expansion and tightening. In the folk variant of the poem of the same writer presented above *Myjla bördan, mića nylöj* ("Why do you cry, beautiful girl?") there are left only the two first lines. The narrative structure with its key words and thus the whole song belongs already to folk tradition in its typical form.

An interesting example of the folk-editing is the texts based on the song of V. Savin's *Tuvsovja* ("Spring-like"). Among the people the song is known according to its first line *Oj-oj, tuvsov voj* ("Oh, oh, spring night"). V. Savin wrote the poem as a testimony of an old man, who feels the loss of youth

and O. U., in the club house of Vyl'gort, 13.6.2001, and at the home of Aleksandra D. Ignatova, b. 1927, 28.6. 2002.

and his coming death as a great tragedy, and who is irritated by the joy of the world around him:

4. *En kök, kökińöj,*	Don't cuckoo, my cuckoo
Gaža sadja nörysyn!	On a merry garden hill!
Kusi bi kińöj	The fire sparkle has died out
Menam pöryś morösyn.	in my old breast.
5. *Okma! kynmöma*	*Okma!* Has frozen
Śyli gögör garććyś soj.	The hand bending round the neck.
Śölöm izmöma,	The heart has turned to stone,
Sömyn vek žaľ tuvsov voj.	Only it still resents a spring night.

Folklore poems lack the the fifth stanza, which is very tragic, and the the last line of the third verse has changed slightly:

3. *Majbyr, śo majbyr,*	Happy, hundred [times] happy is
Nyvgaž dyrśa tuvsov voj,	the spring night of the time of a girl's
	merriment,
Dolid olandyr,	Happy lifetime
Myjla mödiś te on vo?	Why won't you come again?

The slightly revised form of the third verse of Savin ends the folk poem:

5. *Majbyr, śo majbyr,*	Happy, hundred [times] happy is
Nyvkad dyrśa tuvsov voj,	the spring night of the time of girlhood,
Dolid olandyr,	Happy lifetime
Mödiś on vo myjla te?	Why won't you come again?

In Troitsk, Kortkeros area, and in Voľdino, Ust'-Kulom area, the folk-edited text is about the same, but it differs from the original poem of Savin in the order of lines, the lack of the fifth verse, and the alteration of some words: *žugyľ śölömön*, "with sorrowful heart" > *kypid śölemen*, "with exalted heart", *nora śylömön*, "mournfully singing" > *meli śylömön*, "tenderly singing".

Savin hopes that the cuckoo will be silent (st. 4); the folk variants also turn to the cuckoo, but ask it to cheer up the heart (st. 4). The result of this remodelling is a new song, like this kind of basic variant:

1. *Oj-oj, tuvsov voj*	1. Oh, oh, the spring night
*Važ **tomdyrös** kypede,*	The former **youth** arouses,
Gaža jugid voj	Merry light night
Unmes menśim paľede.	Drives my sleep away.
2. ***Kypid** śölemen*	2. **With elated** heart
Dźirja öśiń vośtišta,	I'll open the window leaf,
***Meli** śylemen*	With **tender** singing
Tom olemes kaźtišta.	I'll remember young life.

279

3. **Addźas**-*gažedćas*	**Will see**, will have fun
Mijan pyddi dźoľa ćoj,	instead of us the young sister.
Med že j kažiććas	May then please (her)
Jugid-dolid tuvsov voj.	The light and happy spring night.

4. **Atte-j**, *kökińej,*	**So**, my cuckoo,
Gaža sadja nörisin!	On a merry garden hill!
Kökej-kökińej,	**My cuckoo, my little cuckoo,**
Gažed menśim śölemes.	**Have fun, my heart.**

5. *Majbyr, śo majbyr,*	Happy, so happy,
Nyvkad dyrśa tuvsov voj,	the spring night of the **time of girlhood**,
Dolid olandyr,	Happy lifetime,
Mödiś on vo myjla te?[50]	Why won't you come again?

Tragic overtones are transformed into lyrics expressing milder, sad feelings. The subject of the song is not an old man, but a woman who is not yet old. She says good-bye to carefree youth and the joys of girlhood for ever.

L. N. Vasiľchenkova from Pozheg sang *Oj-oj, tuvsov voj* using a melody which differed from the one used in many other villages. She explained the background of their way of singing. Viktor Savin was from their village and they knew his poems very well. After he was persecuted his songs should not have been performed. Singers had to change the text:

In Pozheg, the teachers of the first school classes sang. It wrung the heart when they began to sing . . . From them I heard this song *Oj-oj, tuvsov voj* for the first time. This song is performed in the Vychegda river villages only in Pozheg. I have never heard this melody in the other places. Once the late Yakov Sergeevich Perepelitsa[51] told me off severely for singing like this: "The music of the composer is totally different, so why do you, who are a talented person, sing in a different way?" After that I thought a lot. I asked those teachers [they were alive at the time of the discussion]: "Why do you sing like that?" And Viktor Savin came here. And so, when he was persecuted, it was forbidden to sing his songs. And then they began to sing "nu-dan-da-na-dan", because everybody knew what kind of song it is . . . The words are from Viktor Savin, but who has composed it, nobody knows. Maybe, when he was persecuted, some of us in Pozheg thought if only we could sing his songs. I went to Yakov Sergeevich and said that this is a folklore variant. We sing like that in Pozheg, but about other kinds of songs I do not know . . .[52]

In the village of Vyľgort, the choir *Mića ańjas* ("Beautiful women") sing the song in their own way. The director of the choir, Serafima Ivanovna Kurochkina, began a song based in folk motifs in the presence of women

50. The Voľdino group: Yu. P. Sergatova, D. E. Pystina, S. P. Ulyasheva, V. K. Popova, P. A. Ulyasheva, V. K. Ulyasheva, A. V. Pystina, E. I. Ignatova, V. M. Ulyasheva, T. Maľceva, N. Ignatova, rec. A.-L. S. and O. U., Voľdino, 14.6.2001.

51. A Komi composer, who arranged a great number of melodies to popular songs, for example a variant of the song *Oj-oj, tuvsov voj*.

52. L. N. Vasiľchenkova, Pozheg, 2001.

belonging to the older generation. But she could not remember the song. Hence, she asked for help from the old *babushki*. They refused, saying that they did not remember the words, and in the Vyľgort group, in which the age range is from twenty to twenty-five, the song is performed in a different way: "We performed this *Gundari* song. Somebody has messed up its theme. Not like they sing in the *Mića ańjas* group, but in a different way, in the old way, better."

1. *Oj-oj, tuvsov voj **gažse** kypede,*
Gaža jugid voj unmes paľede.
Refren: Gundar'-gundar'-gundar'-gundar'-gundar'-gundar'-gundar'ga!

2. ***Jugid** śölemen dźirja vośtišta,*
***Gora** śylemen tomlun kaźtišta.*
Refren: Gundar'-gundar'-gundar'-gundar'-gundar'-gundar'-gundar'ga!

3. ***Eziś** kökińej, gaža nörisin!*
Kusis bi kińej menam moresin.
Refren: Gundar'-gundar'-gundar'-gundar'-gundar'-gundar'-gundar'ga![53]

1. Oh, oh, the spring night arouses **merriment**,
the merry light night drives away our sleep.
Refrain: Gundar'-gundar'-gundar'-gundar'-gundar'-gundar'-
gundar'ga!

2. With **light** heart I'll open the wicket,
with loud singing I'll remember young days.
Refrain: Gundar'-gundar'-gundar'-gundar'-gundar'-gundar'-
gundar'ga!

3. Silver cuckoo on a merry hill!
Died has the fire sparkle in my breast.
Refrain: Gundar'-gundar'-gundar'-gundar'-gundar'-gundar'-
gundar'ga!

In the stage variant of an amateur group the song is a dance arrangement of V. Savin's poem. It has been greatly shortened; from six stanzas there are only three left. The verses are not in the same order as in the original text of the writer. There are reminiscences of lyric folklore; some words have changed, for example *žugyľ śölömön*, "with sorrowful heart", *jugid śolemen*, "with light heart", *dźirja öšiń*, "window with hinge" has changed the word *dźirja*, "gate of the yard". An addition is an epithet *eziś kökińej*, "silver cuckoo". These changes have made possible a new rhythm and melody suited to dancing. The lyrical sorrowfulness has been transformed into joyfulness by changing the emotional tones of the song.

---

53. *Gundari* performed by *Mića ańjas*, rec. A.-L. S. and O. U., 13.6.2001.

Creating the programme

The programmes of Komi folklore collectives include mixed song genres heard, read from poetry books and song collections, and presented again and again in different private and public performances. As can be seen in the programme of Yuliya Sergatova (see pp. 247–50) half of the songs are folk songs and half translations or written by known poets. Some of the published poems were composed by famous musicians, but unknown songwriters arranged music too. The variation in melodies is identical to that of the texts.

The cultural significance of folklore groups and the degree of institutionalisation of folklore performances determined the songs suitable for collectives. According to the idea of a "folklore group" the old ethnic folk songs were preferred in the first years of the new cultural institution and they were collected by singers themselves for performances. But the Soviet state soon "cleansed" the programmes, especially from the 1930s to the 1950s. However, some of the old epic songs remained in the programmes. One of them is "Along the Vychegda", which resembled the popular poetry of the Soviet times praising the local landscape and hence maintained its favour in public performances.

Most of the folk songs are epic-lyrical or lyrical songs performed traditionally by women. They suited well the singing groups because they gave opportunities to express women's moods and desires, their hopes and worries. The epic-lyric songs seem to form a *ruling genre*, which determined the way in which songs representing other genres were interpreted and performed. Traditional epic lyric offered a register in editing poems of known writers for popular songs. Even traditional male songs were performed in the collectives by women and interpreted from the women's point of view. Many of the songs have a connection with wedding rituals, which has preserved their traditional position up to today. Two contexts of the Komi peasant culture, weddings and evening parties in which young people met each other, gave for the organisers of performances an idea of the traditional context of folklore and were played on the stages of cultural houses.

The long cultural contact with Russians has greatly affected the folk tradition. Some of the songs were translated already in the sixteenth and seventeenth centuries and are a part of traditional Komi folklore. The translations from Russian consisted of several genres, ballads, historical and lyric songs, romances and later also patriotic songs. Besides old folk translations from Russian folk songs into Komi, there were macaronic songs using a mixture of Russian and Komi. The words of these songs are difficult to understand and they survived because they are usually connected to religious festivals or rites. In the Soviet period, translations of known Russian poets, for example Mayakovskiĭ, Pushkin, Lermontov, were popular.

Poetry written in Komi presented an opportunity to express emotions inspired by "our" people, culture and local landscape. The first Komi poems were written in the nineteenth century and the trend has continued to this day. Unfortunately in Stalin's time many of the poets were executed or imprisoned and their songs were forbidden. Instead, songs praising the great Soviet leaders and celebrating the great motherland belonged to all performances. During the Second World War, the Great Patriotic War, songs supported the endurance of the home front. Many old singers of today were young in those years and they remembered the stress and common efforts of the time. Singing comforted women on the home front and they still enjoy the songs of the war time, be they Russian or Komi. "Two heroes", telling about the fate of a soldier on the Finnish front, was performed to the Finnish researcher in every village.

The political aims and individual ways of lending meaning, but also the performance setting, have an effect on variation and deliberate editing of songs.

As has already been mentioned, poetry and written folk tradition published in folklore collections provided models for the textualisation of songs. Therefore, the programmes of the folklore collectives form a special type of tradition, a discursive domain expressed both in texts and songs which influence each other. This discursive domain is not coherent but it comprises both orally learned and sometimes textualised songs and those which have spread first in text form but have changed over time into orally transmitted tradition.

In orally transmitted tradition of old epic-lyric songs, the variation of songs follows cultural areas so that different *kusts*, village groups, have their own ways of singing. Though the basic structures of songs are quite stable, there are lexical differences and changes in repetition. In different areas especially the metaphors, images and adjectives describing the heroes or landscape varied and like them the emotional depth of songs. The difference of cultural milieux is also seen in variants, for example the list of ransoms in the song of a girl who should be redeemed. This originally medieval song is widely known in northern Europe and is also old in Komi tradition. The list of ransoms refers to the wedding gifts, which followed local traditions. The context of singing, in this case a presentation on stage, affected the type and overtone of performance; that could be humorous, tragic or just a reconsruction of a ritual, which changed the wording of some songs. The folk songs of evening parties, which in the early twentieth century pointed to people, young boys and girls, taking part in the singing event, endured, but had a more general tone in presentations of the folk groups.

Macaronic songs and songs translated from the eighteenth to twentieth centuries, for example "Broad, gay street", resemble only partly the original Russian texts. The lines, words and sometimes even plot are recreated in these folk-translated songs. Sometimes only key words and images are left. These kind of old translations have so many variants that they are seemingly a part of Komi folklore and not understood to be Russian songs. In many translated songs, the variation is more than that between the original and the new language. Culturally unknown or unsuitable expressions are changed to those which suit the familiar area.

Songs to the words of Komi poets from the nineteenth and twentieth centuries and also from 1960–1970 and 1990–2000 are near the form in which they were written, though some features of "natural" variation can be seen, for example in the order of lines, in words and in ending lines of verses. The variation of final lines is typical in orally transmitted folk songs and is connected to the memory processes and the way of reproduction. Songs of the Komi folklore groups illuminate the relationship of literate and oral tradition. Researchers studying the relationship of oral and literal texts usually focus on the process from oral presentation into literal text.[54] In Komi songs the way of adaptation has two directions: literal poems have been transformed and arranged into oral songs and – in some cases – oral poetry has given a starting point to the literal poem. A good example of the intertextual relationship of folklore and literary works of Komi writers is P. Klochkov's "The girl in the moon", which uses fairy tales and mythic motifs as its thematic elements. The literal text was transformed again in the process of composing it into a song: the structure of text became simpler and wording changed. Only the the mythic plot and key phrases were left from the original poem.

There are also changes caused by deliberate folk-editing. At first, the condemned poets were well known and honoured in villages and their songs were popular. In the changed political contexts they were performed in new ways, for example humming parts of the song. Singers kept up the memory of their native writers in a way which was not too apparent. This led to local variation in singing.

Women singers changed the songs also for emotional reasons. Even new, recently published songs may have new adjectives and phrases which change the tone. Songs were recreated, or we might say edited into performances which expressed the life experience of singers. For example Viktor Savin's "Spring-like" poem changed from a tragic testimony of an old man into a song telling the sad feelings of women of mature age.

Folk-editing expresses the understanding of life and emotional world of women singers. The ruling genre, a register in folk-editing in collectives which consists of middle-aged and old women, is epic-lyric and lyric, though humour and nostalgia have their place in the programme too. The structure of performance, in which the patriotic and locally important songs turn into epic-lyric songs and romances and which ends in short humorous songs and dance, provides space for many-sided emotional innovation and for the joyful viewpoint of the mature women who want to create for themselves the beauty and happiness of life.

54. See for example Finnegan 1988; Goody 1991.

17 A state project leads to multiple forms of tradition

The Komi folklore collectives were a result of the country-wide state project which aimed to develop the peasant culture of farmers and other inhabitants of countryside villages. New programmes in the 1930s were based on an idea of folklore as the verbal art of the folk, which was set forth by prominent folklorists in Russia. The red corners and cultural houses established after the Revolution gave good frameworks for singing though the material infrastructure was poor. The public performances of singing groups were not created from nothing. The local knowledge, dress and songs were systematically gathered from family members for presentation. Therefore the Komi singing groups continue local village traditions and this can be seen even in the present-day performances. In the twentieth century, the gender relations and also the folklore tied to gender changed. The old male culture, which was connected to hunting brigades, vanished and this had an effect on the programmes of the singing groups.

The long connection with Russians has influenced the Komi culture, not only in the conversion to Christianity but also in new forms of folklore and the early knowledge of literary culture. Russian folksongs were translated into Komi and adapted to local traditions. The Komi literature and the way of textualisation of poetry had Russian models. After the Revolution, poetry in Komi, which had its initiators in the nineteenth century, began to increase. In Stalin's time, the ethnic poetry and folklore performances were "cleansed" in accordance with the favoured policy. Still, the work of folklore collectives continued under the auspices of the Ministry of Education. New political and patriotic substance was given to local cultural performances. The cultural secretaries of villages had the main role in educating the singers and leading their performances; they in turn had their instructions from higher levels of the cultural administration.

In the 1960s, the Soviet rule increased the activities in theatre and local cultural centres: the work of cultural clubs and amateur theatres was revitalised. Songs representing the production of Komi poets were an important part of the performances. In the 1980s and 1990s, the interest in folklore and local culture increased again, but the poor economic situation weakened the opportunities to perform in far-away areas. Many of the old women of

A group from Izhma at the eightieth anniversary celebrations of the Komi Republic, Syktyvkar. – Photograph by A.-L. Siikala 2001.

the 2000s told us about the difficult trips to neighbouring villages without transport and finance for performance outfits. The solution was self-help: women made their dresses, cooked food for feasts and walked if needed to other villages to perform.

Men were involved in the first of years of the collectives, but over time their interest diminished. Collectives became mostly female groups, in which men took charge of the playing of the accordion or flutes. This increased women's dominance in the groups. Songs were selected and written poems arranged according to the tastes of singers. The cultural project, which initially was political, became an activity representing female village culture; the group meetings were important spaces for rest and stimulus, in which women regained strength to live on in economically hard times. Today, many women say that they sing for "the soul and the self"; folklore groups are a place for emotional recreation and a feeling of belonging.

Many generations of women have sung in the collectives. The knowledge of the long history of folklore collectives has increased the emotionally loaded meanings of the institution. Actually, singing groups are a form of tradition themselves and at the same time they continue to preserve the established local singing customs. Old women have learned their ability to sing in many voices from their mothers and grandmothers. The models for performance dresses are sought from local ways of making clothes. Singers build feasts as their mothers did before. Folklore collectives strengthen the local singing tradition and make visible the customs of villages representing different *kusts*, village areas. It is because of singing groups that many old

Folklore groups perform on the streets of Syktyvkar at the eightieth anniversary celebrations of the Komi Republic. – Photograph by A.-L. Siikala 2001

Komi songs are still known, for example in the Ust'-Kulom area.

But the groups are not refrigerators of tradition. Over the last decades the contests and competitions on stage have led the collectives, sometimes led by professional choreographers, to renew their attire, often according to models used in town theatres and the media, and find fresh forms of dance and music. New songs have been sought over the whole life of groups and they have been adapted to the performances. The distinction between the generations of singers in the 1930s to 1940s and the 1950s to 1970s is, of course, very significant. The reasons are partly cultural, partly political and directed by the authorities, changing of programmes, new attitudes to concert activities and performance practices. This came up in several discussions in Vyl'gort and Bol'shelug; O. N. Pavlova stressed that at first choirs performed the Komi folk songs. When the choirs were reformed in the war time and afterwards, the collectives began to favour popular songs. Today young singers write and compose songs and can even sing karaoke in Komi and in Russian.

Comparison of programmes and the favourite songs of folklore collectives reveal important aspects of folklore processes. First, a socially established institution like folklore collectives organised or supported by state authorities widens, strengthens and reformulates the ideas and practices of folklore. Second, the comparison illuminates the practice of variation: part of it is due to "natural" variation discussed by folklorists but part is based on *folk-editing*, a conscious effort to produce relevant items for performance. Third, folk-editing easily changes the genre boundaries of folklore items and their modes of performance. Both genres and strategies of performance increase and the idea of folklore widens.

Folk collectives have transformed the image of folklore at the local level and especially at the regional and republic levels. A great deal of Komi poetry written by known poets has become folklore in its various forms and interpretations. Because of their work the idea of folklore is more colourful, impressive and many-sided than before. In the villages, the folklore collectives present an image of beauty and at the same time something which is our "own" and tells of belonging to a home village, culture and landscape.

Comparisons and Observations

IV

18 An Udmurt case: from sacrificial rituals to national festivals

In the 1980s it was believed that the Udmurt religion already belonged to the past. Only a few groups had been able to preserve their own traditional religion into the twentieth century despite the pressure of world religions. Since the atheist revolution had wiped out even the stronger religions, it was highly unlikely that the ritual life in small villages could have survived the pressures of modernisation. However, the director of the Estonian National Museum, Aleksei Peterson, told me[1] in 1990 that the rituals of the holy groves were still alive. During the summer of 1991, with his help, I was able to take part in an ethnographic field trip of the Udmurt Ethnographic Museum led by Serafima Lebedeva in southern Udmurtia and Udmurt villages in Tataria with Tiina Tael and photographer Arp Karm from the Estonian National Museum. In Kuzebaevo village we were able to take part in the sacrificial ritual which I recorded on video with the help of Arp Karm. The first field trip was followed by annual contacts with Udmurts in the 1990s. Pekka Haka-mies from Joensuu University also collaborated on the project. One of the aims of the field trips was to document the sacrificial places.

JULY 1991

> I wake up in a remote village of the Udmurt Republic, situated between the Kama and Vyatka rivers. The trip has been difficult: the Soviet Union is collapsing, there is no food in the shops, nothing to drink on the trains and the weather is hot. But the beauty of the village with its old log houses, green fields and galloping horses fascinates the eyes of a folklorist, raises nostalgic feelings and memories of something belonging to the lost past.
>
> Serafima Lebedeva, an Udmurt ethnologist respected and loved by village people, comes to find us. Half of the village would gather for the annual sacrificial feast honouring Inmar, the sky god of the Udmurts, and we cannot be late. "Do you have your scarf?" she asks when we hurry along a path which seems to lead nowhere, only to the thick forest.
>
> People come from different directions, walking and driving through fields, bushes and forest. There are no roads leading to the secret place of the sacrificial

---

1. "I" in this chapter refers to Anna-Leena Siikala.

grove. Some years ago, in the 1980s, the Soviet authorities found the *kuala*, the tiny sacrificial house without any windows, and demanded that it should be destroyed. Instead of destroying it, people repaired it.

Without warning we come to a small clearing in the woods where a row of fires is already burning. The principal sacrificial priest, who has a red woollen belt round his waist, looks at me suspiciously. "Anna-Leena belongs to our kinfolk", says Serafima, and I can stay, as can my young companions Tiina Tael and Arp Karm from the Estonian National Museum. People do not pay attention to us, they are busy building their fires and slaughtering sacrificial geese.

I record the ritual – trying to avoid disturbance – from the sides of the clearing; my feet are burning from stinging nettles, but I pay no heed. The ritual repeats in voices, colours, smells and tastes what I have learned from the works of Uno Harva and the other older ethnographers who witnessed similar rituals.

The *kuala* is small, a fire burns in the middle of it and benches are decorated with fir branches. At first, I have to stay on the crowded women's side because the sacrificial priest is killing the geese there. White birds for Inmar! Then the main priest asks me over to the side of the men and hands me an age-old wooden cup with blessed *kumyshka*. I drink the toast to Inmar as the priests do and make an offering like them by sprinkling the *kumyshka* on the fire so that the smoke will take it, through a hole in the ceiling, up to Inmar. The priests begin their prayers.

People seem to notice something unusual: new voices in the clearing, and a big television-camera! A car with intellectuals and journalists has arrived from the capital city, Izhevsk, to produce a television-programme for the local television. When asked, I give a speech on the special character and value of the Udmurt culture, in the spirit of the UNESCO principles.

Villagers do not pay attention to the television group. They continue their ritual: women pour home-made *kumyshka* for everybody and invite each other, and specially the Baltic relatives, to taste their sacrificial porridge.

When one of the priests collects money for the next ritual, I give some rubles on behalf of myself and some on behalf of Finland.

During the night, another cult group has its ritual, offering to Keremet, a frightening being who needs a blood sacrifice and revenges all violations of his *lud*, the holy grove. Intellectuals return to the capital city, but we are accepted with the help of Serafima to the *lud*, though outsiders are not allowed to be present at the ritual. The *lud* is a fenced area between fir trees on the top of a high hill; the remains of a huge tree show that, once, a holy tree had marked the grove.

The four priests come early, at seven o'clock, to slaughter the sacrificial animals and light the fires. After the sun has set, men begin to gather at the holy grove. One by one they come out of the darkness, from different directions, silently, without a word.

The Keremet-cult is a male ceremony and I film it standing behind a tree. Arp Karm takes the close-up pictures of the slaughtering of the lambs. The night is long and dark, but fires warming those who sleep on the ground of the holy grove give some light. The only voices heard in the darkness are *tikha*, *tikha*, silent, silent in Russian. Men sneak to the fields near the grove to smoke their cigarettes and to drink warming *kumyshka*. Keremet does not tolerate impurity or bad manners in his grove.

Just on the boundary between night and day, when the first rays of morning light can be seen, men kneel in rows and pray for good life and peace. The porridge is divided and we get our portion. The priests, at least, are not offended.

In the early morning, before the village awakes, people go home, one by one in the same silent way they came.[2]

These memories from my first field trip to the Udmurt Republic reflect a period of time which began a rapid transformation of society and culture. The Udmurts (earlier known as Votyaks), 700,000 strong, are a minority population of their republic among other even smaller ethnic groups: Mari, Tatars, Bessermens and others. Udmurts have also moved to the east because of the threat of Christianisation and Russian pressure, and are living in a diaspora outside the republic bearing their name. Through their history, Udmurts have become accustomed to living in multicultural areas where every village has its own language and customs. In 1991, a kolkhoz worker referred to the multicultural situation and said that a man has to learn languages, his father for example speaking four languages. When I was wondering what kind of languages they might be, he said: Udmurt, Tatar, Mari and Russian. These were the languages of four villages united into one collective agricultural unity.

Holy groves and social order

The Udmurt villages have retained their ethnic religion with its rituals and cult grounds between two world religions, Islam and Christianity, up to the twenty-first century. The Udmurt traditions and ways of life have been formed by many kinds of cultural influences over the centuries. Despite all the pressures the villages worshipping Inmar have kept features of ancient Finno-Ugric traditions, which have been observed not only by Russian researchers before the Revolution, but also by the Finnish scholars Torsten Aminoff, Uno Harva (Holmberg) and Yrjö Wichman. Later the Udmurt religion was analysed by Udmurt scholars, above all by Vladimir Vladykin (1991, 1994) and the Estonian Aado Lintrop (1993).

Historically the holy groves of the Udmurts and Mari continue an old tradition. They can be traced back to the oldest pre-Christian traditions of cult grounds in Europe. Some information about this tradition can be found also in Finland. In 1229 Pope Gregory IX gave the Church the right to confiscate the holy groves or *hiisi* of the Finns. In the Finnish interior, Savo, the Church destroyed the sacred sites of the ethnic religion in the eighteenth century; in Karelia and in Ingria, however, sites of ancient communal cults survived in Christian disguise into the last century. The groves of the Baltic Finns correspond to the sacred sites of some other European peoples. In the Greek *temenos athanaton*, the grove of the immortals, grew trees dedicated to nymphs. Some Germanic peoples organised communal meals in forests and the Lithuanians would make sacrifices in family groups in holy groves after midsummer and the autumn sowing time. In pre-Christian Europe the holy groves were the sites of seasonal sacrificial rituals. They were temples in the natural world described accurately by the historian Pliny: "We do not

2. On the description and interpretation of rituals in Finnish see Siikala 1998.

worship with greater reverence the idols made of gold and ivory than the groves and their uplifting silence."[3]

The so-called "nature religion" of the Udmurts is practised by kin-based cult groups and depends on oral tradition. During seasonal rituals the god of the heavens, the ancestors, the guardian spirits of the fields, earth and forest are approached in the ritual places dedicated to each of these. The sacrifices and prayers for the well-being of the family are conducted in the homes. Belief tradition and sacred prayers have been passed down from one ritual expert to another as esoteric knowledge. When interviewing in 1998 an Udmurt *vesas*, a guardian of the *kuala*, a kind of a priest, he said that he did not want to, and besides could not, tell about rituals in Russian. The information was given in the Udmurt language and without the chance to use modern recording equipment.

It is appropriate to use the term "nature religion". The holy groves are located on the hills and in forests surrounding the villages. Describing the Udmurt religion, Uno Harva paid special attention to the majestic holy groves used by large kin groups: "The greatest among many Votyak sacrificial feasts are those which are organised jointly by several villages. The sacrificial site, which has remained the same from generation to generation, a fenced holy grove, is usually located on a beautiful, noticeable place, if possible, near some spring or stream."[4] These holy groves used by large kin groups and described by Uno Harva can be found in several villages on the borders of Udmurtia and Tataria. They gathered people from several villages to take part in calendar celebrations.

The most important groves are, however, not the only ritual grounds of the Udmurt villages. The public life of Udmurt villages and the rows of grey log houses are surrounded by a circle of sacred sites. In Varklet Bodya, an Udmurt village in the Tatar republic, we documented in 1991 ritual grounds on the borders of the village area in the forests and fields and the main *kuala*, a windowless sacrificial house with an open fire in the middle of it, in which a great number of people gather and that is located in the middle of the village in a small grove. People performed sacrifices for the guardian of the fields under a tree growing in the field surrounding the village. The guardian of the earth is worshipped on his own ritual ground and the initiation ritual for the girls is celebrated and the appropriate feast porridge is eaten in a grove on the edge of the village. The most impressive sacrificial site is the skull forest near the tree of the ancestors. On the branches of the spruces in a dark forest dangle the bones and skulls of the sacrificial animals sacrificed during the "wedding of the dead" ritual. These bone trees are located in Karamas Pel'ga village outside the inhabited area in a grove, though in the village centre I also saw one similar, old sacred tree. The Udmurt village landscape seems to consist of places dedicated to the re-creation of everyday life and surrounding chain of holy places dedicated to the actions which ensure that this re-creation is successful.

3. Haavio 1961: 3.
4. Holmberg 1914: 124.

Because the cult groups are based on kin relationships, the social organisation is represented in the organisation of holy places. This can be seen clearly in Kuzebaevo village, which today is perhaps the best-known Udmurt village practising the ethnic religion. The village is divided into two endogamous groups[5] of which one worships in the *kuala* and the connected grove the old Udmurt deity of heaven, Inmar. The name is a cognate of the Komi *Jen* and Finnish-Karelian *Ilmarinen*, and the ritual follows the common models of the Finno-Ugric sacrificial ceremonies. The other group worships in *lud*-groves a being called Keremet according to the Russian habit, and the cult as well as the name bear marks of Tatar influence.[6] Both groups organise their principal rituals around Petro's day in July in order to secure the harvest; and there are spring and autumn rituals as well. Besides the *kuala* and *lud* there also exists a third ritual place of larger groups, the *bulda*. In the *bulda* the sacrificial rituals are organised every three years.

The Inmar sacrificial place, *kuala*, of Kuzebaevo is one of the last sacrificial buildings of a cult group of any ethnic religion in Europe. The sacred *kuala* and its grove is situated in a forest 1 or 2 km from the village and it is not connected to the village by any road. People arrive at the grove, which is cleaned on the morning of the rituals, through forest and fields. The Kuzebaevo *kuala* in its old form was described by P. Härmäs in 1980.[7] The building represents an ancient model of a north European house with an open fireplace and no windows. The most important place is the right corner of the back wall, the holy corner in all the Finno-Ugric areas, where the holy shelf containing sacred objects and offering cups is situated. Priests control the inside of the *kuala*, which is divided into the left side for men and the right side for women. The open grove area in the front of the *kuala* is filled during the ceremony with fires and porridge kettles, one for each family. The rows of these porridge kettles has became an identity symbol for the Udmurts of today. Besides the common *kuala* of a kin group, there are still *kuala* buildings attached to the home yard. These buildings have been used as prayer places for family celebrations and as summer kitchens. They are so holy that they cannot be destroyed. For this reason it is possible to see the decaying *kuala* buildings between new houses.

Besides great offering groves (*budzim kuriskon-inti*) joining several kin groups, which can be found only in the old mother villages, there were holy groves of kin groups in all the Udmurt villages. These *lud* groves, called *keremet* by early Russian writers, are areas with a fireplace and a construction for sacrifice; they are often situated in the forest near the village. Previously all the *lud*s were fenced, but nowadays only some are. The fenced *lud* of Kuzebaevo village can be found in the middle of the fields on a high hill covered by a few old spruces. Next to the hill there is a spring where the water for ceremonies is taken. The Kuzebaevo *lud* is newly renovated; people still remember the sacred oak that once grew there. Only the *lud-ul'is*, the

5. Vladykin 1991: 29.
6. Lintrop 1993: 48–57.
7. Lintrop 1993: 43–5.

Lud hill in Kuzebaevo, Udmurtia. – Photograph by A.-L. Siikala 1991

guardian of the *lud*, and his helpers can enter the fenced area, in which there are three fireplaces, a sacrificial construction and a huge stump of an oak tree felled by thunder. The holy fenced area, the holy tree and the holy well are signs common to all the north European sacrificial groves; the fireplaces and offering constructions complete the assemblage.

The Udmurt word *lud* means a field or forest outside the village, but also a specific sacrificial site.[8] The guardian spirit of this *lud*, its master, is called Keremet. The sources describing Udmurt religion describe Keremet – probably a result of Christian influences – as an "evil spirit". According to my observations the guardian spirit of the *lud* is, compared to Inmar and other spirits, more frightening and must be approached with great care.

In the Kuzebaevo *lud* old night rituals have survived, which, according to Uno Harva's description, were rare already in the early twentieth century. In the night following Petro's day, 12 July, a blood sacrifice is made to Keremet, the guardian of the *lud*, who nowadays is regarded as the provider of general well-being. The Keremet cult with its Tatar influences is a male sacrificial ritual. Thus women have to keep a safe distance about 60–100 metres from the fenced area. The assistants of the *lud* guardian make a fire for women and outsiders on the border of the grove and fields. The holy groves are highly gendered, where the power relationships between genders, age groups and families are continually established. Daphne Spain has paid attention to the institutionalised spatial barriers in different ethnic sacred places. She writes:

8. Holmberg 1914: 85.

Spatial barriers become established and then institutionalised for reasons that have little to do (manifestly) with power, but which tend to maintain prevailing advantages. This is because space is a "morphic language", one of the means by which society is interpreted by its members. The reciprocity between space and status arises from the constant negotiation and re-creation of the existing stratification system.[9]

As a matter of fact, only a few elderly women took part in the night ritual I observed. When the guardians of the *lud* were cutting trees for fires one of the women said to me: "Lets go to the fence and look at the *lud*." The woman broke the rule and did it on purpose. The sacrifice in the *lud* is clearly a male ritual – not only because of the use of space, but also because of the mode of performance. The behaviours of the *lud*-guardian and his assistant and the members of the cult group are organised both in military-like body movements and the hierarchical formation of the praying group: elders are seated nearest the fenced area, middle-aged men behind them, and youngsters in the back row. Boys gather in smaller groups separated from the praying men. The Keremet cult differs greatly from the cult of Inmar, where the segregation of women concerns only the holy *kuala* building. In the grove women move about freely and also have an important role in the ritual by producing the sacrificed animals, bread and *kumyshka* drink.

The grove is so holy that even loud talk is forbidden. "Quiet, quiet" – with these whispers the adults admonished the few children moving around the forested area; the children were not allowed even to come near the *lud* itself. The *lud* has a specially terrifying quality; the intruder who breaches its sacredness must pay with his health or even life. Even a member of the cult group will be punished severely. The awe of the *lud* derives from the fact that the spirit is believed to reside there and can only be approached in its abode. Keremet always requires a blood sacrifice and at the end of the last century some Udmurts were accused of human sacrifice. These kind of tales can even be heard today. A Mari woman warned me jokingly about the rituals and told stories of people who had recently disappeared and were assumed to be sacrificed by Udmurts. These narratives belong to a vast oral tradition concerning the *lud* containing different themes, for example the building of the *lud* or transferring it to different place.

Visible and hidden: the battle of ideologies and religions

The holy groves of the Udmurts were earlier hidden in forests and often on a hill. Uno Harva noticed that because of cultivation of the forest many groves have been made visible in the landscape.[10] Because of its location on a high hill, the Kuzebaevo *lud* dominates the village landscape. At the same time it fuses with the surrounding nature in a way that hides it from the

9. Spain 1992: 17; Spain refers to Hillier and Hanson 1984: 198.
10. Holmberg 1914: 96

people who do not know about the *lud*. Archaeological findings show that the cult place has been in use for centuries, and that the hill was already an important place during the Bronze Age. In its visibility the Kuzebaevo *lud* is not only a village grove with specific meaning but a monument representing the present-day values of Udmurt culture.[11] The same can be said of the *kuala* building, which has been pictured both for ethnographic and artistic purposes. The groves are at the same time visible and hidden and they represent central ethnic values cherished by the people but kept secret from outsiders for several hundred years. Udmurts tried to avoid Christianisation and the pressure of the Orthodox Church by moving eastwards to new areas and hiding their holy groves. The religious dispute continues to this day. When I asked in Kuzebaevo why the annual sacrificial rituals are so important, one villager, a young female teacher, told me: "Once we disregarded the prayers in the *kuala* and went to the Orthodox Church. The harvest was poor that year. So we have to pray in our own way." The sacrificial rituals are part of "our own way", or tradition, preserving which is regarded as important for maintaining the moral order of life. After the Soviet Union's collapse missionaries have been active in Russia. The head of the Udmurt cultural society Kenesh phoned me and said that Finnish missionaries have found the "pagan" villages, and he said that the economic problems were due to "bad gods" propagating the Christian faith.

During the Soviet era the sacrificial sites survived in the vicinity of the villages in forests or fields beyond the roads, and the rituals were disguised as ordinary village celebrations. The Kuzebaevo *kuala* was in danger as late as 1986 when a local administration chief ordered it to be destroyed. The cult group did not destroy the building, but repaired it and after that it has been used regularly. The destruction of holy places was part of the strategy of the Soviet authorities. Since the churches were demolished after the Revolution, the holy places of ethnic groups have been in danger until recent times. One typical feature is the destruction of graveyards, something I have witnessed in several republics. The authorities responsible are usually kolkhoz or sovkhoz directors and the reasons for destruction are economically and culturally legitimised. In a village in northern Udmurtia the graveyard was destroyed and a big and beautiful house for cultural activities was built on the site. The more usual reason is the need for land for cultivation. In Bogorodsk, a Komi village, the graveyard was moved to the other end of the village and in the place of the old one there is a new field. Only one cross was left, and villagers tell the story when seeing the cross. These kinds of renovations are usual, of course, also in Western countries. They arouse, however, always a lot of feelings and discussion. Burial grounds tell openly about the common past of the group, and establish a bond between those who belong together.

The burial ground of the Khanty in Vershina Voïkar village is a concrete example of collective memory connected to a burial ground and the on-going construction of ethnic groups practised in these grounds. The Khanty were

11. Tuan 1989: 164.

buried together with Nenets in the same burial ground, but earlier they were always separated from Russians and the Komi, who had their own graveyards (see pp. 58–9). The recently built houses of the dead along the path in the middle of the ground and the fresh sacrificial gifts for the loved ones are surrounded by decaying and decayed graves. They reveal that the same group has used this burial ground for decades, in fact centuries.

Beside their religious significance the sacred places, graveyards and holy groves are essential parts of the village landscape and symbolic vehicles of its collective memory. The holy groves are known by all the members of the community but kept secret from outsiders if needed. They are part of the landscape and invisible to outsiders. Known only by insiders, the groves create a boundary between those who move in the landscape and establish the divide between us and them, and are thus major markers of the communal identity. Rituals are not the only manifestation of social bonds. As Catherine Bell puts it:

> ritual systems do not function to regulate or control the systems of social relations, they are the system, and an expedient rather than perfectly ordered one at that. In other words, the more or less practical organisation of ritual activities neither acts upon nor reflects the social system; rather, these loosely co-ordinated activities are constantly differentiating and integrating, establishing and subverting the field of social relations.[12]

Used by different kin groups, the holy groves create social distinctions inside the village.[13] As sites of gatherings for the kin groups and both genders they constantly recreate the social order of the community. This re-creation is an interesting feature of the present-day use of groves when people who have left the villages come back in order to take part in ceremonies. They redefine the locus of every member of the group and provide them with history functioning as traces of past events. Representing tradition of importance for the previous generations they create a sense of continuity in which the moral order and the notions of "living right" are anchored.

The holy groves are not in use everywhere any more; respect and fear of consequences has, however, prevented the places from being destroyed. Discarded groves are overgrown in peace and transform into parts of the landscape occupied by extraordinary beings. Despite the overgrowth the places act as symbolic vehicles of the collective memory. They represent the past of the group, a tradition which in the present does not necessarily have the same meaning as before, but which despite this provides materials for experiencing the continuity of the group culture.

12. Bell 1992: 130.
13. Cf. Basso 1996: 179.

These breast decorations may be very old. Lisa and Lena Artamova in Karamas Pel'ga, Udmurtia. – Photograph by A.-L. Siikala 1993

From secret ritual into national festival

JUNE 1993

After inviting a village folklore group from Karamas Pel'ga to Finland, I am asked with Pekka Hakamies to take part in the Gerber, the national festival orgainised by the Udmurt Cultural Society. Kirsikka Moring, a journalist from Helsinki, and Kaija Heikkinen from Joensuu University, who came to know Udmurt women in Joensuu, come with us.

The yearly festival established in the early 1990s gathers representatives of the whole Udmurt population, members of the government interested in the Udmurt culture, intellectuals and ordinary people from villages and towns. A day-long feast has many forms: folklore groups from different villages sing and dance on the festival field and young men perform their skills in horse races.

At first sight this celebration, which is supposed to revive the traditional spring festival held after the ploughing season, resembles any other folk festival. The traditional costumes of sacrificial priests and the row of sacrificial pots on the corner of the festival field could be decoration organised for the pleasure of the public. Or is it? I meet the priests, they are familiar from the secret sacrifical village groves. For them the Gerber festival is an event of prayer which differs from the village prayers only in its magnitude and publicity.

The Gerber festival is a show of folk dresses. Women singing and dancing in the field wear dresses typical of their village, old women favouring their own

Members of the Karamas Pel'ga singing group at Ol'ga Mazitova's (standing)
– Photograph by A.-L. Siikala 1993

folk garments used on Sundays and family festivities, the younger ones wearing standardised performance dresses. During the previous night, the women of Kuzebaevo had sown dresses for Kaija, Kirsikka and me so that we could, in proper fashion, take part in the festival.

In the middle of a dance, Lidiya, the head of the Udmurt Cultural Society, takes me to meet an older dignified man and says: "Talk now about the school." Kuzebaevo village wants a new school building and a programme in which the Udmurt language could be taught. I recommend the idea of an Udmurt school and learn later that the man, unknown to me, is the president of the Republic, himself also an Udmurt.

The festival ends in the administration building of the village, where the head of the parliament, ministers and distinguished guests gather for the dinner. The president expresses thanks for the idea of a school focusing on the Udmurt culture; he knows the dream of the teacher of Kuzebaevo, a young woman keeping up the Udmurt heritage. The only problem is that other villages would also like to have such a school. How to finance this kind of programme?

I sit in the table wearing my new Udmurt dress, now wet because of rain, give a speech on the importance of cultural traditions and get a pair of bast-bark shoes to complement my attire. The car which takes us back to the capital city is full of intellectuals talking about their dreams of the cultural awakening of the Udmurts.

The festival, initiated by the Udmurt Cultural Society Kenesh, was organised in a small village. A look at the festival field revealed groups dancing and singing together in flexible groups, each wearing a folk dress, either a traditional village dress or a garment made for performances. The folklore groups had come from all parts of Udmurtia. The rain did not seem to spoil people's enjoyment, which partly arose from reunions with friends. The visible homogeneity and homely feeling of the feast hid, from an outsider, the underlying social order: ministers and the president of the republic made their speeches but took part in the festival like other participants. On the side of the field, a long row of pots was cooking. The highlight of the celebration was the sacrificial ritual behind its name, performed by village priests of the ethnic religion.

The intimate sacrificial offerings and prayers of villages unite the members of families and small social groups. The Gerber festival, in turn, creates an arena in which not only ordinary people but all the constitutive social institutions of the Udmurt population are represented. No wonder that the main speaker in 1993 was the president of the parliament, who at that time happened to be an Udmurt himself. In 1993, old sacrificial rituals were an important part of the Gerber festival, which also included revived folklore performances, speeches and competitions. When gathering Udmurts, it symbolised their ethnic identity. At the same time, the feast underlined the peaceful co-operation of different ethnic groups: the Russians of the villages nearby had their own festivities on the same vast green field.

In the former Soviet republics, the yearly celebrations organised by different ethnic groups were a characteristic feature of cultural life during the 1990s.[14] In 1996, I witnessed with Pekka Hakamies a festival of a small minority, the Bessermens, in the northern part of Udmurtia. The arrangement of the events and layout of the festival field followed the model of the Gerber celebration. The state was represented by the authorities of the district, and the songs and dances were composed by local masters of tradition. The characteristic feature of the Bessermen celebration was a display of old folk dresses with coin decorations, preserved by grandmothers and grandfathers, but not used as everyday garments like the folk dresses of the southern Udmurt villages. The strong advocator of the Bessermen culture has in recent years been a local teacher, and Udmurt herself, who had built with the help of her students a museum of Bessermen culture. She has also gathered and trained a folk singing group performing Bessermen music.

The appearance of the Bessermen, a tiny population with Turkic and Udmurt roots, into the arena of cultural display, is not a coincidence. One of the most marked phenomena of new forms of globalisation is the emergence of representation of the margins. Stuart Hall has called the processes where marginalities become powerful spaces a most profound cultural revolution of the twentieth century[15] (see pp. 23–4). This process includes the emergence of new subjects, new genders, new ethnicities, new regions, communities which before were excluded from cultural representation.

In their studies of nationalism and tradition processes, Eric Hobsbawm

14. See for example Heikkinen 1998: 148–57; Toidybekova 1998.
15. Hall 1991: 34.

(1984) and Benedict Anderson (1991, originally 1983) have paid particular attention to the legitimisation of state power. This kind of state-centred approach omits the problems presented by ethno-nationalism which as a counter-reaction of globalisation – or Sovietisation – seeks the cultural empowerment of the marginal and the local. When recreating their culture, northern Russian minorities react to the current situation in a way which at the same time is traditional and modern, in transforming their private rituals and objects into public performances. They are both executing and representing their access in agency, their opportunity to be different from others, yet in a similar way to the others: performing cultural features, both past and present, defined as heritage. Though the cultural elements of festivals and their interpretations represent and revive different ethnic cultures, the background ideology and structuring of events are common, following the Soviet models of folk festivals. The festivals manifest the differences, the cultural distinctions, according to common transcultural patterns.

The secret sacrificial village rituals may lose their former meaning or even vanish altogether. But they have already been transformed into new cultural forms with an aura of dignity, and been defined as a part of a nationally important heritage. Ethno-mimesis, the imitation of former forms of culture, is an instrument for striving for visibility and in the case of small minority peoples much more than just an entertaining carnival. The tradition processes of minority groups, in the present world, represent the pursuit of identity-formation, and survival in a world where economy, technology and information flows change the interconnections of the local and the global.

Female agency and marked diversities

JUNE 1996

This year the Gerber festival is going to be held in a Christian village, near the capital city. There has been a hot negotiation on the character of Udmurt culture and the right ways of representing it. "Pagan" nature-religion belongs only to small portion of the Udmurts, while others are Christians or non-religious. To keep up earlier forms of tradition might spoil the image of modern Udmurt culture! The coming presidential election in Russia also influences the body of organisers: instead of the Udmurt Cultural Society the government is responsible for the preparations. Pekka Hakamies and I have got a new invitation, signed by the Ministry of Foreign affairs instead of the Cultural Society.

Soviet and Western models for the festival mark the layout of the feast. A large market place welcomes the guests with global commodities from Coca Cola to numerous sweets with familiar labels. On a high stage, a female rock singer performs popular music in a short mini-skirt. Priests have not arrived at the festival – or they have not been asked – but Lidiya finds a pot of porridge which is situated in between two market huts. We taste the porridge. which seems to be the genuine Udmurt delicacy.

Finnish and Hungarian guests are advised to dine in a separate house for important guests. Interested in events of the festival, I run away with Lidiya to dance and sing with folklore groups already gathering in a green field. In a dress made by Kuzebaevo women, I disappear into the dancing crowds away from the hosts, who are looking for me.

The field is divided in two. In a smaller section there is a table with food for established guests who do not take part in the folklore events. When Lidiya, who herself has a coat over her Udmurt dress, takes me there, a guard refuses me entrance to the section on the basis of my dress. When he hears that I do not belong to the village people, but to the guests, he lets us pass. The Russian folklore group entertains guests in this exclusive section of the festival area during the dinner. The dresses of the professional group are richly decorated, and the Russian folk songs skilfully performed and enjoyable.

In the afternoon, when the rock singer leaves the stage, the old *babushki* from a village nearby take over. When we are dancing on the stage they examine my dress, asking from which village it is, and praise the handicrafts of their own village.

Pekka comes and we drive to Karamas Pel'ga to see our friends. After embracing and crying for the joy of reunion, Ol'ga, my friend, a former kolkhoz baker, dresses me again, now in her own Karamas Pel'ga dress, for a village festival.

Ol'ga and her four aunts are famous for their traditional handicrafts. There is a plan to transform her home into a living museum of Udmurt culture.

The national symbols for European state-building projects have been largely determined by men. European nationalism can then be seen as a male enterprise. National awareness was created mainly by the spread of literacy – as Benedict Anderson has stated. The post-modern world is characterised by new ways of taking action and wielding influence. Not only are women's efforts to define their own identity undermining conventional gender systems; they are also producing alternative expressions of ethnicity. It is necessary to study the relationships among various cultural processes such as detraditionalisation, the preservation and revival of traditions, as well as the points of contact between different populations, gender and age groups. A closer examination of female agency could enliven the nationalism debate and reveal how identity is produced in many contradictory yet related ways. In Udmurt villages, work and the use of space are still governed by traditional ways. Nevertheless, the women – partly owing to old models of agency, partly because of the high male mortality rate in the Soviet era – hold key positions as organisers of village events. According to Marjorie Balzer, the maintenance of traditions of belief and organisation of village festivals were the domain of women even before the Revolution.[16] If this view is true, the explanation may lie in the overall social structures of the Russian feudalist state. It seems, in particular, that in the feudal cultures of Eastern Europe, in which men were deprived of public agency, the women had a far more important role in managing the joint village activities than in Western Europe.

Since women are, besides acting as organisers of village feasts, taking part in the national folk festivals more actively than men, the ethnic symbols are

16. Balzer 1992.

Going to the Gerber feast in 1996. The third person from the left is Lidiya Orekhova, the chair of Kenesh, the cultural society of the Udmurts; the fourth is a visitor from Finland, whose dress is a gift of the Kuzebaevo women; and the fifth is the wife of V. K. Putylov, the president of the republic.

defined more and more from the point of view of the women's world. Singing, which forms a common form of entertainment among village women, was already during the Soviet time channelled into an activity underlining the unity of a work society, the kolkhoz and so forth. In every village, there is a club house and a folk-music group consisting of singing women and an accompanist who is usually a man. Because seniority is highly valued, old women are the ones who select and lead the singing, whereas the accompanists of folk groups, in turn, might be younger men. In many respects it seems that *babushki*, old women, are the social and emotional village leaders. In 1996, the occupation of the festival stage after the rock star by a group of *babushki* reminded us in its exuberance of "women's porridge", women's festivals which had carnevalistic features among the Finno-Ugric groups. The chance to show *joie de vivre* in such colourful ways has not been permitted for old women among the Baltic Finns, suppressed by gender and age hierarchies formulated and sanctioned by Lutheranism. The importance of food, specially baked delicacies, in rituals of hospitability, emphasises the warm female element in the display of Udmurt ethnicity.

The message of the Gerber festival is belonging,[17] belonging to a group of relatives and a village, but also to a nation. Singing together, singing "our" songs loaded with emotion and memories, and dancing in a great field in a group from "our" village with the groups of our neighbourhood villages, heightens the sense of belonging through participating in a strong emotion. Belonging is expressed also by dresses, which represent village fashions. I have several dresses representing different Finno-Ugric groups; these gifts are symbols of belonging, being one of us. In 1996, the lecturer of Finnish language in the Udmurt university was wearing her own Finnish national dress, modelled on the basis of a Karelian folk dress. She said that she always wears the national dress in Udmurt celebrations. It is her way of saying that I am different but belong to a greater unity like you, and just that belonging to a greater unity unites us even though we are different. The similar logic enforces the importance and multiple variations of Udmurt dresses. Even though the Udmurt dress, whatever form it may have, is a symbol of Udmurt culture, it has not achieved national character. On the contrary, the dresses are instruments of competition between villages and individuals. Dresses and heavy decorations of old coins which might be large shields over the breast or headgear, are admired and compared. Coin decorations, used formerly in weddings, are family treasures and only part of them survived the Second World War, when women had to sell them to get money for food. Dresses make distinctions, but distinctions are formulated in a competition to express a sense of belonging to a greater unity, which, embracing all, weaves a strong emotional bond between participants.

The growing symbolic value of dress, especially women's dress, has been noted among other Finno-Ugric groups, too. Ildikó Lehtinen stated in her article on the Mari living outside the Mari Republic that while the Mari dress has disappeared from towns and areas where the Mari population is sparse, it is used in most of the Mari-speaking villages. She also pays attention to the activity of women as promotors of the Mari culture. In several villages teachers or female committees organise clubs where girls are taught to produce their ethnic dresses. Old decoration patterns are remodelled to suit contemporary taste and the dresses are displayed in so-called tradition feasts organised by female committees.[18]

The active role of local teachers has, of course, been crucial in tradition-formation processes of various European countries. Similarly, the establishment of female committees consisting of semi-professionals, mothers and grandmothers, in order to revive the interest in handicraft, song and dance, is at the moment a global phenomenon supported by different international and developmental cultural and religious organisations. The women's federation of the Cook Islands supported by the Church, for example, encourages groups of local women to produce traditional handicrafts. Products of this kind of tradition-building are marketed from developing countries in Western countries.

17. On "belonging", see also Cantwell 1993: 102.
18. Lehtinen 1996: 760.

While private, female elements in the form of women singing in their ethnic dresses seem to characterise the visible and public image of the Udmurt national festivals, the aura of importance is created by other means. In 1996, the coming election of the Russian president seemed to affect the festival. The organiser was no longer the Cultural Society of Udmurts but a branch of government, which also gave weight to the festival. The opening speeches with political references, the division of the field into two halves for a cultural show and for a commercial market, and also by fences literally separating performers and ordinary visitors from important national and international guests, reflected the growth of the importance of the festival and the diplomatic aims of organisers. It told of the transformation of the Gerber from an ethnic festival into a national celebration.

In national festivals the international audience with guests specially invited by authorities connects the participants to the other nations of the world. Speeches of dignified guests and hosts grow into a dialogue between participants cherishing not only local traditions but common cultural values. At this level, the Gerber celebration performed – and enjoyed – by village men and women transformed into a pursuit of visibility in the sea of nations, into participation of an on-going international dialogue strengthening possibilities for co-operation with economic, educational, cultural and social implications.

The role of intellectuals and the media

August 1997

Again in Udmurtia with Pekka Hakamies. We are invited to a *vil*-feast held in a family *kuala*. We do not know much about the event, but I have taken my Udmurt dress and scarf with me in order to be dressed properly. In a village near the holy grove we meet a woman called Tamara and her old mother. When discussing rituals Tamara seems to be a really good informant. On the other hand, her mother's memories are fresh and detailed. Later I hear that Tamara is from the university. No wonder she knows so much, she might have read the work of Professor Vladimir Vladykin on the Udmurt ethnic religion.

The holy grove, which is not far from the village, is calm and green, with just the tinkling of a brook originating from the holy well breaking the silence. The *kuala* is new, built in 1993, but behind it we can see the remains of the old one. Another university teacher, originally from the village, has been active in the rebuilding of the *kuala*.

The sacrificial ram is reluctant, but the man acting as priest manages to take it to the *kuala* for slaughter. Soon the pot of sacrificial porridge is boiling and Ivan, our driver, who belongs to the same family, is taking care of it. The structure of the *vil*-celebration follows the scheme of sacrificial rituals, but the atmosphere is intimate: family members meet each other, talking about the revival of old rites. Youngsters are sitting on benches; girls have their town clothes, but their heads are covered with scarves.

There are no common prayers: everybody enters the *kuala* alone, praying and making offerings in private. I follow the example and leave some coins to Inmar. To my astonishment there is an icon, the Vladimir Mother of God, in the holy corner of the *kuala*. Afterwards, I ask what the icon represents and get an answer: "It is an image of Inmar." Why not? Gods can certainly change their gender and religion.

People ask why I do not have my video. They seem to be disappointed. I should have fulfilled my role as a mediator between this family – the Udmurts – and the world.

Memories of the *vil*-ceremony tell of the double consciousness of intellectuals. Intellectuals partake in negotiation of their traditions on an academic and public level, but may also establish private frameworks for displaying their ethnic values. The *vil*-ceremony resembled the sacrificial rite of Kuzebaevo village described earlier in its intimacy and in the desire to repeat the ritual as such, with only a few inventions due to contemporary circumstances. For the acting ritual priest, a deaf old man, and old grandmothers, the feast seemed to be a continuation of a familiar custom broken only for some years. For the revivers, academicians from town, it had personal meanings connecting memories of childhood to the present-day efforts at ethnic self-expression and better living. At the same time, it was a performance, a performance for revivers themselves and for us, outsiders, performing our own part.

The double consciousness of intellectuals with ethnic backgrounds is not necessarily displayed openly. On the contrary, in many cases, intellectuals who have roots in villages tend to stay in their personal life among the Russianised or – today – globalised elite as did the builders of the European national cultures in the nineteenth century. The reality of life forces people working in academic circles to prefer Russian, an international language, even in private. For that reason, children of ethnic activists do not always speak their mother language. Urbanisation increases the loss of interest in ethnic languages. In Udmurtia, 79 per cent of children living in the countryside can speak their native language, in town the proportion is 30 per cent.[19] Similar developments can be noticed among other Finno-Ugric groups in Russia. The decline of ethnic languages is not solely created by the language policy of the state or by the tendency of people to select such means of communication as guarantees their success in life. It is also an economic question, of how to finance equal opportunities for multiple languages in small multicultural societies.

There are considerable efforts to improve the status of minority languages in Russia, but these efforts need strong economic investments to be succesful. The Udmurt cultural foundation Shundy, for example, organises with the help of the government children's summer schools where artistic skills are taught, in addition to the Udmurt language. Festivals and material culture offer a shorter and cheaper way to the building of ethnic awareness. Performing features of culture in a visual form also suits well the media-centred character of a globalising world.

During my field trips, people often asked: "Did you bring your video camera with you?" Some of them know that I filmed the sacrificial ritual of

19. Belorukowa 1996: 97–100; Rasin 1993.

308

Kuzebaevo and that a television film was produced from the material. Some just refer to the role of video in recording private life or in the expression of ethnic culture. Art, theatre and literature have had a decisive role in establishing and displaying national values in the nation-building processes. Today, their role has largely been replaced by mass media, which reaches people in different geographical and social locations.

Traditions which individuals and groups employ to construct their self-definitions in a dispersed world are mediated in various, often far-reaching ways. Individuals and groups create their selfhoods on many planes of interaction, not only within their own immediate social and societal context but also in the worlds to which the media transports them and – at the insistence of the media – influence the local construction of the self. Through the media people are present in other worlds. They also have images and premonitions of what this presence means, of how they appear in others' eyes. The elements and ways employed in the search for self and the interaction between them are a challenging subject for the folklorist: when, where and how is the individual and collective self constructed by means of mediated folklore; in what sorts of social and societal relations do these manifestations acquire meaning; whose rhetoric does folklore belong to; in whose voice does it speak in the different worlds propagated by the media?

Media not only establishes arenas for performing valued forms of ethnicity, it also creates dialogues between people with different insights and opinions. In selecting what has to be seen it acts as a partner in an on-going negotiation of tradition. During many field trips to Udmurtia, I have been involved in different broadcast events, the range of which extends from television-debate to interviews at folklore festivals. The character of these discussions and speeches have been predetermined by the journalists and editors in question. The promoting of tradition needs legitimisation and revival of traditions has to be authorised. A researcher representing the outside world suits these purposes well.

Participation in the processes studied is, of course, nothing new in the study of culture. As a matter of fact, that was just what folklorists were doing in the era of European nation-state-building. But acting in another state and dealing with matters which have religious and political implications poses even more severe responsibilities than usual. The ethics of field work and the problems of the multiple consciousness of a researcher who acts as one of the negotiators in complex cultural and political situations is a topic which should be considered more deeply. Here, I can only refer to my commitment to the UNESCO principles, which are accepted in Russia, and which have formed a solid basis for defending cultural diversity and equal cultural rights of people living in multicultural circumstances.

Construction of tradition and cultural identity

During the post-socialist era the republic of Udmurtia has changed from a society which was firmly closed to outsiders because of its military industry, into an open country with a lot of contacts with the outer world. When in 1998 I visited a village where I had in 1991 recorded the sacrificial rituals, the relationship with other regions, marked concretely by a new road, had been established on different levels. The village – and Udmurtia – was in the 1990s opening up to the outer world, and at the same time towards its own history and cultural traditions. The sacrificial rituals of villages which were kept alive secretly during the Soviet time have been transformed into elements of national festivals. They have become ethnically important traditions, though there are competing interpretations of what is characteristic of the Udmurts, what the Udmurt heritage is. The ideas and ways of performing and reviving of traditions are fertilised with new possibilities opened by globalisation. Intellectuals, journalists, researchers, museum-builders, artists and international audiences taking part in ethnic celebrations have a decisive role in these processes. Thanks to the intellectuals and artists tradition is not only negotiated in local villages and towns, but in international conferences and festivals, and even in distant homes where people gather to follow the pictures of the world mediated by television.

For that reason, construction of tradition and cultural identity for today must be viewed against the tendency towards globalisation, within the framework of the interaction between nations, and not on a local level or only as a national, local, ethnic, gender or social-class signifier. The minorities of Russia and Siberia belong to a multicultural state in which identity is formed in relationship to other nationalities. The ethnic religious traditions found in these regions and the reawakening of traditions cannot be studied as isolated cases separate from the whole, but must be examined in relationship to the corresponding traditions of other groups.

19 Traditions symbolising cultural distinction

In recreating their culture, the northern Russian minorities are reacting to the current situation in a way that is both traditional and post-modern, in transforming their private rituals and objects into public performances. They both realise their chance to enter the public arenas of society and represent their difference from others, yet in a way similar to that of the others: performing cultural features, both past and present, defined as heritage. It should be added that reference to "tradition" occurs not only in public festivals but also in everyday practice. Not all cultural features are good enough to be symbols of the cultural "own" of an ethnic group. The selected cultural features have to represent continuity, lasting values and commonly approved aesthetics and be emotionally effective. They also have to attract public attention and in some cases be entertaining. A religious world view and rituals, folklore, dress and food make for something distinctive. They belong to the cultural domains symbolising self-awareness presented in public performances.

Myths and rituals as political practice

The recontextualisation of mythic heritage in the present day is a typical feature of ethnic movements. We may also ask whether Finno-Ugric myths and rituals still have any meaning today. How are they accommodated within an innovative society and in political situations? By creating a connection with the unchanging and foundational events of the past, myths, like sacred rites, possess a power to unite communities and to act as a tool for national self-determination and for political interests. Myths have also had a significant role within movements seeking to create nationhood or ethnic self-awareness. On account of their nature, they have presented themselves as the symbolic capital sum of identity processes which promote nationhood.[1] An examination of the pursuit of mythology linked to the construction of European national powers gives a good point of comparison with research

1. For example Branch and Hawkesworth 1994.

into present-day ethnic movements. In mythological research it is also worth paying attention to those processes of tradition in which myths are employed for the construction of ethnic and national self-consciousness. For in a multicultural society mythic and ritual traditions present themselves as means for distinction, for the construction and presentation of the self.

Ethnic religion and traditions of belief, as shapers of world view, are nestled in the deep structures of culture and have an effect upon them. The period of state-sponsored atheism did not uproot the ways of religious thought or rituals of Russia's ethnic minorities. In 1991–2006 during our field work in Udmurtia, Komi and the northern Ob' region we noticed that many religious traditions thought long dead were alive and were even being revived in connection with local identity processes. For example in the Volga and Kama areas and among the Khanty there are still villages in which the sacrificial groves are in use and function as stages for sacrifices performed for the promotion of means of sustenance. The significance of an ethnic religion as a builder of national identity has given rise to a discussion among intellectuals of the areas concerned. A corresponding development may be noticed in Siberia, where for example the traditional forms of shamanism have been revived as material for artistic expression.

The mythic traditions of the Komi have been transformed into literature and drama. The Komi Folklore Theatre has specialised in plays based on ethnic tradition and myths.[2] But myths do not live only in texts produced by poets and writers. One of the most visible forms of the recontextualisation of mythic traditions is to be found in art. Ethno-futurism has revived mythic images in its search for Finno-Ugric roots. The exhibition "Ugriculture. Contemporary Art of the Fenno-Ugrian Peoples" held at the Gallen-Kallela Museum in Espoo, Finland, in 2000, and several other Finno-Ugric exhibitions in Russia and Estonia reveal the central position of mythic symbols in present-day art. Mari artists Alexander Ivanov, Sergeǐ Evdokimov, Ismail Efimov and Yuriǐ Tanygin favour themes and subjects from Mari mythology and ethnic religion. The "Tree of Life" (1990) by Ivanov and the animal symbolism in the paintings "Under the Sign of the Wolf" (1990), "Irke Bird, the Mother of the Earth" (1996) and "Under the Sign of the Bear" (1996) represent an ethno-futuristic orientation.[3] In the 1990s Ismail Efimov became more interested in abstract-symbolic art combining Mari mythical figures and philosophical thinking. The paintings by Efimov have been interpreted as an example of the revival of national identity and knowledge of ethnic psychology.[4] "The Lord of the Forest" (1997) by Sergeǐ Evdokimov with a huge bear in a deep forest in itself symbolises the basic ethos of the ethnofuturists. Of Komi artists Pavel Mikushev, Yuriǐ Lisovskiǐ, Irina Fedosova and Valeria Ostasheva are well known in many countries. Mikushev's work "Going Hunting" has been influenced by rock art and his work "In Search of the Lost Souls" by ideas of shamanism. The painting "Jirkap" presents

2. Konakov *et al.* 1999: 70–4.
3. *Ugriculture* 2000: 77–9.
4. *Ugriculture* 2000: 80 and 87.

a mythic act: the Komi hero Jirkap is hunting a very swift elk. Lisovskiĭ's "Universal Tree", "Cutting the Sky" and "The Gold Girl" have mythic bases. Lisovskiĭ has impressive shaman pictures too. Some of his paintings show the relationship of the Christian and ethnic Komi religion.[5]

Ancient mythic tradition is connected to the need to live in harmony with nature. A close relationship with nature and especially the symbolically important animals, such as the elk and bear, has indeed assumed the important role of mythology in the changing cultural atmosphere experienced by most Uralic peoples. Finno-Ugric peoples have, for example, been defined as the offspring of the bear, as indicated in the name of Pekka Hakamies's work of 1998, or in that of a broad selection of Finno-Ugric folk poetry.[6] Bear rites function today as identity symbols of the Eastern Khanty and Mansi. They appear to have a recognised symbolic value also in modern Finland, where bear rituals have been revived in recent decades, thanks both to students and theatrical groups. Representatives of every ethnos seek materials for the construction of an identity from the circles of their own tradition. A common feature of artists representing Finno-Ugric peoples is their search for roots in the region of common northern culture, even though they might in many cases be sought equally in Indo-European cultures or the various divisions of Christianity.

The use of myths in the reinforcing of the ethnic identities of Finno-Ugric peoples and in the construction of cultural self-portraits is a blatant feature of modernity, which follows contemporary trends of the globalised world. Its foundation, however, lies in the nature of myths. The power of religion, myths and rituals to form a society is not a discovery of our post-modern world, nor is it based simply on models which have proved effective in the construction of nation-states. Concepts touching upon a group's past and the nature of the world are the fundamental forms of human knowledge, traditions whose preservation for succeeding generations has been guarded by means either of specialists in memorisation or of writing.

Myths, the history and explanation of the world, unite ancestors and people of the present in the circle of one and the same experience. As Émile Durkheim has shown, repeated common rites and the myths connected with them can create a unity of the community in a greater authority time and time again; at the same time they lay bare the ways in which the sacred which gathers the community together is manifested. Although a shared myth or rite does not signify the same thing to all those taking part, it gives to the different experiences a common background reference. Myth and ritual both unite and create a unity of defined difference. Against this background the meaning to many ethnic minorities of the manifestations of their own ethnic belief-systems may be understood. They offer one possibility, and a powerful one, when ethnically relevant tradition is sought, even though they may no longer function within a religious framework.

The exciting side of mythic research is that myth never has only one sole

5. Lisovskiy and Mikushev 2007.
6. Honko, Timonen and Branch 1994.

meaning nor do its meanings remain fixed. How mythic narratives, images and metaphors are conceived in different cultural contexts varies. The character of mythic discourse, however, defines the possibilities for the renewal of tradition and of accommodating it within new relationships.[7] Thus the mythic tradition forms a heritage with a long history, which moreover is in a perpetual state of modification.

In the renewal of mythic traditions the visibly continuing negotiation process leaves room for creative imagination. Myths are used for new purposes, as cultural materials are created, but their use is not a straight copying of the old but an absorbing of mythic materials as new and unique performances and new forms of modern art are produced. The examination of the recontextualisation of myths, a sort of meta-tradition, as an essential part of identity processes will in the future be an ever more important area of mythic research.

The revival of nature religion

Once, in 1991, my friend Ol'ga, a baker on a kolkhoz in a southern Udmurt village, raised an important question: "Communists said that there is no God, but the Russian Orthodox have their god, *musulman*s in the Tatar village have theirs and we Udmurts have Inmar. Tell me, Anna, which of these gods is the best?" The long period of atheism sustained by the Soviet regime failed to uproot the ways of thinking or the rites cherished by religious minorities. Even the heightened forms of Marxist education and the new Soviet ritualism of the 1950s and 1960s under Khrushchëv and Brezhnev[8] did not wipe out the local annual celebrations. Cults of ethnic religion were practised secretly at home and in hidden groves. When Mikhail Gorbachëv opened the way to the freedom of religion, a renaissance of religions was the result.[9] Atheism could not answer the needs of people and soon after the collapse of the state, the empty place left by it began to be filled with different religious alternatives. Although the Russian Orthodox Church has been and is a powerful and deep-rooted home of spiritual life for Russians, other churches began their missionary work in both towns and rural areas. In Ingria, where Arno Survo has done field work, the competition of religions has long historical roots connected to the geopolitical situation of the area and the interests of the Russian and Swedish states in it. The role of the Lutheran Church became more prominent during the 1990s and the interrelationships of different religious "dialects", the Russian Orthodox and Lutheran, are an interesting research topic today.[10]

In the field of competing religions, ethnic religions occupy a special position as bearers of world view important for the self-awareness of the

---

7. Cf. Hanks 1996: 274–7.
8. Luehrmann 2009: 37–8.
9. Powell 1994.
10. Survo 2001: 232–3.

minorities. The Khanty and Mansi, and the Finnic peoples near the Volga and Kama rivers, especially the Udmurts and Mari, preserved their ethnic cults to a far greater extent than had been imagined.[11] Sonja Christine Luehrmann, who studied religious life in the Mari Republic, notes that in the 1920s an important annual celebration of kolkhoz farmers was organised in a new form, in which religious elements were deliberately played down. In the 1930s and 1940s, the official discussion of ethnic celebrations highlighted the importance of such gatherings for the proletarian performance and sought to transform them into Soviet-type festivals.[12]

Among the Mari, the ethnic religion is nowadays called a "nature religion". The term refers to the central position of nature gods and spirits in religious life, which acquires its most visible expression in the sacrificial ceremonies led by specially elected priests. The concept was actually developed by Uno Holmberg (Harva) in 1926 in *Die Religion der Tscheremissen* (published in Finnish in 1914). The main sections of the book are headed "Die Belegung der Natur" and "Der Opferkult der Naturgottheiten". When Holmberg (Harva) described the Udmurt religion, he based his interpretation on the social organisation of cultic life and especially the role of kin groups maintaining the sacrificial rituals.[13] The theoretical modes of the history of religion had, it seems, affected his interpretations. On the other hand, describing the nature deities and spirits as the main objects of cults seems to make the point. Lidiya Toĭdybekova also emphasises the central role of nature in the religious mythical worldview of the Mari.[14] Even though the Mari have adopted numerous mythic features and religious practices from neighbouring peoples, especially Turkic-Tatar groups, the basic elements of their nature religion are Finno-Ugric.

The focus on supranormal beings and elements representing nature is as such a typical feature of most ethnically based Finno-Ugric religious systems. The structural hallmarks of the mythology of Uralic and Finno-Ugric cultures are linked to the demands of a nature-oriented way of life and observation of both nature and the positions of cosmic elements in the sky. For many cosmological myths and images documented among Uralic peoples, analogous forms have been discovered from such a broad area that these traditions have been considered age-old. Categories of the supranormal have undergone continuous alteration under the influence of neighbouring religions, so that it is difficult to identify the oldest divine beings. Beliefs held in common, however, include the concept of the sky-god, female deities having power over life and death, and above all the nature spirits and animal spirits essential to a hunting and fishing culture.[15]

The best experts on the Mari mythic traditions and sacrificial ceremonies

---

11. See, for example, Toĭdybekova 1997; Gemuev and Baulo 1999; Siikala 2000a; Minniyakhmetova 2000: 114; Moldanova 2001; Shutova 2001; Siikala and Ulyashev 2003.
12. Luehrmann 2009: 79–84.
13. Holmberg 1914.
14. Toĭdybekova 1997: 112.
15. Ajkhenvald, Helimski and Petrukhin 1989; Napol'skikh 1992; Siikala 2002b.

are the sacrificial priests known in the eastern areas as *molla* (Tatar *mulla*) but in other areas as *kart*, the Old One. The *kart*-to-be usually, according to Holmberg, acts as a helper to a sacrificial priest and learns the necessary tradition.[16] Many observations testify that there are still *kart*s in action in Mari villages. But, and this is more interesting from the point of the identity-formation of the Mari, the *kart*s also operate in towns and can even be taught among Mari intellectuals. The Oš Tsimari movement led by Mari intellectuals aims to win a kind of "official" status for the Mari nature religion.[17] Leena Laulajainen reports that at a meeting of the movement in 1991 there were fifty men who were studying to be sacrificial priests.[18] The transfer of the nature religion from villages to towns follows the common pattern of the religious practices of ethnic movements.

To intellectuals, the "nature religion" of these minorities represents an ethnically based philosophical idea of living harmoniously with nature. For participants representing the grass-root level of society, tradition and the values of ancestors are manifested in rituals. Holy groves are no longer in widespread use; respect and fear for the consequences has, however, prevented them from being destroyed. According to Laulajainen, there are thirty-two sacrificial groves in Meadow-Mari that are nowadays protected.[19] On the other hand, interest in taking part in sacrificial rituals has grown significantly in recent years. Vladimir Kudryavtsev refers to a sociological study in which Mari people were asked about their attitudes towards the revival of holy groves. In the Mari Republic 54.6 per cent of the respondents were in favour, and in Bashkorstan the percentage was even higher: 73.4.[20]

It is interesting to note that women, particularly, take part in these rituals and that many people participate in both Orthodox and Mari rituals.[21] Kaija Heikkinen, who witnessed a Syrem sacrificial feast of the Mari in 1992, reports that, "The participants were mostly middle-aged and older women, but there were also a few men, and the sacrificial priests were men. The men sat in the shade of trees at one end of the grove, and were joined by the outsiders – the researchers and reporters. In the centre were the places where the animals were sacrificed, and fires with pots heating over them. At this point the scene bore a masculine stamp. A man sacrificed the animal and said the accompanying prayers."[22] Heikkinen also noted that the gender division of the feasts had changed in the course of the twentieth century. According to ancient sources, only men attended most of the Mari sacrifices.[23] A parallel phenomenon is the active role of women in keeping up the Orthodox Christian traditions during the Soviet era.[24]

16. Holmberg 1926: 113.
17. Toidybekova 1998: 261.
18. Laulajainen 1995: 53.
19. Laulajainen 1995: 48.
20. Kudryavtsev 2001: 384.
21. Toĭdybekova 1997: 344.
22. Heikkinen 1992: 13.
23. Heikkinen 1992: 14; Holmberg 1926.
24. Heikkinen 1998: 151–5.

Reconstructing sacred histories

One feature of the time is that people with a higher education who have distanced themselves from village life take part in the reconstruction of groves and their rituals.[25] Shared historical experience is with language and other cultural forms an important basis of identity. Thus the domestic landscape telling of shared historical experience functions as an important basis for the experience of identity. Belief tradition, on the other hand, is important in expressing one's own ethnic identity and the difference from others. The importance of sacred sites is based in their ability to connect a group not only to the supranormal world but above all to a world gone by; ancestors and their life, and this opens up a view to the collective past. Rituals not only link social groups, but recreate and establish them in practised ceremonies. It is no wonder that the interest in the sacred sites and their reconstruction is an essential part of the ethnic revival in Russia and elsewhere.

The sense of continuity and with it one's own history motivates the tending and rebuilding of holy groves in several villages in southern Udmurtia, even among those with an academic education who have already left the village. Udmurts have also revitalised and created many new ritual forms better adapted to the modern life-style. One of the most important of these new rituals is the Gerber feast, which annually attracts people from different villages together from the whole Udmurt area.

The proper ways of organising the Gerber feast are subject to disputes. Some of the Udmurts are of the opinion that the heathen rituals of ethnic religion are unsuitable for expressing Udmurt identity. Revitalising tradition and highlighting the importance of the holy groves is thus not an uncontested process. One has to remember that ethnic processes are not without their internal contradictions but entail different interpretations and conflicting practices. The meaning and significance of the holy groves is always determined by these conflicting interests, intentions and ideologies in the community. We have to be able to differentiate between the social memory of the Khanty hunter's oral tradition and reconstructing history through reviving the ritual life in Udmurt holy groves.[26] Emphasising sacred sites, reconstructing and maintaining them is revitalising the past in a way which corresponds to the demands of the present political situation. It is a way to reconstruct a history which is a significant part of the identity of ethnic minorities.

Performing ethnicity in festivals

If the authority of the past is sought by intellectuals, researchers and artists in using ancient mythic traditions in their creative work, ordinary people establish symbols for "self" and "us" in their practical everyday

25. Kudryavtsev 2001: 384; Toĭdybekova 1997: 336, 344.
26. Cf. Connerton 1989: 13–14.

lives. "Identity" is a rigid concept which does not illuminate the ways of placing oneself in the multiple frameworks of practical relationships in the grass-root social world. People belong to their families, to their network of relatives and neighbours, to their village or co-operative farm, to an ethnic group or nation, to an area, republic and state. All the relationships of belonging have different emotional and cognitive values depending on the situation. In everyday life, the belonging is experienced through reciprocity and mutual help. Special acts, performances and arenas heighten the feeling of belonging. So does taking part in discourse over the common past and experiences. Folklore and its public performance are powerful instruments in creating the emotional experience of belonging, as Robert Cantwell (1993) has pointed out.

The folklore collectives serving the Soviet and post-Soviet cultural policy depended only partly on these policies. The reasons for the activity of folklore groups have to be sought elsewhere. First, these groups differ greatly as regards their participants and performances. Besides groups aiming at standardised stage performances there are groups of enthusiasts relying on local traditions and performing only in intimate events in their home villages. During the Soviet era, men took part in these activities, but nowadays the collectives are mostly in the hands of women. The negotiations of performances and interpretations of songs reflect the understanding of ethnic values and people's own history.

The annual festivals organised by ethnic groups have recently been a characteristic feature of cultural life in rural areas. The festival creates an arena in which both ordinary local people and the constitutive institutions of society are represented. Festivals underline the peaceful co-existence of different ethnic groups. The message of the folk festivals is belonging: to a group of relatives and village, but also to a nation. Performing "our" rituals and games, singing together "our" songs loaded with emotion and memories heightens the sense of belonging to a strong emotion.[27] Belonging is also expressed in dress and handicrafts representing local fashions.

Although the cultural elements of festivals and their interpretations represent and revive different ethnic cultures, the background ideology and structuring of events are shared by all, following the Soviet models of folk festivals. The festivals present the differences, the distinguishing cultural traits, according to the common trans-cultural patterns. The state is represented by the district authorities, and the songs and dances are composed by local masters of tradition. The appearance of the tiny Finno-Ugric populations in the arena of cultural display is not a coincidence. New forms of globalisation have enabled the margins to present their cultural difference.[28] Since women organise village feasts and take part in the national folk festivals more actively than men, the ethnic symbols are defined more and more from the point of view of the women's world. Now the role of women is visible even in such male-dominated societies as that of the Khanty. Not only are women's efforts

27. Cf. Durkheim 1971: 382–3.
28. Hall 1991: 34.

to define their own identity undermining the conventional gender systems,[29] they are also producing alternative expressions of ethnicity.

Political and economic implications of neo-traditionalism

The neo-traditionalism of the northern Russian minorities follows general trends in the globalising world of today. However, it is rooted in local cultural practice and reflects the changing Russian society. The ways of performing the heritage are more and more various. The active role of women in these processes reflects not only the special development of Russian society but also international trends. The intellectuals, journalists,[30] researchers, artists and international audiences at which the performance of heritage is directed are important mediators in these processes. Thanks to them, the heritage is not negotiated only in local communities but also in the media.

In giving visibility to minority groups, neo-traditionalism answers the challenges of political – and economic – aspirations. Arctic minorities have presented the best-known forms of ethno-nationalistic demands in northern Russia and Siberia.[31] In order to maintain the traditional lifestyle and gain their share of the new prosperity produced by the oil and gas industry, they have developed relations with the international circumpolar community.[32] Tradition movements have always had political functions. The political and economic implications have to be taken into account in examining the neo-traditionalism of Russian minorities. The meanings of administrative and political action in these processes should be traced at local, areal and national level. The cultural ministries of the republics already occupied an important role in the Soviet era in formulating the concept and representations of heritage. Today, discussions among representatives of the international community, such as in UNESCO, aim at supporting and preserving local tradition. The aims and forms of tradition revival cannot be reduced to a single level of the administrative hierarchy or cultural life. On the contrary, the goals and means of heritage politics are negotiated and reformulated at all levels of socio-cultural integration: from the practices of everyday life to the conscious politics of administrative institutions.

29. Kotovskaia and Shalygina 1999: 129–30; see also Warshofsky Lapidus 1979.
30. Cf. Sugney 2002.
31. Vakhtin 1993.
32. Fondahl 1997a: 202–4 and Fondahl 1997b; Prokhorov 1999: 172–5; Slezkine 1994: 384–5; Stoner-Weiss 1997: 180–1.

20 Dynamics of tradition among the Khanty, Komi and Udmurts

Discussion of the invention of tradition in the 1990s by sociologists and historians aimed to show how the cultural capital dependent on local culture in building European nation-states was a creation of politically oriented intellectuals. The notion is true, but we have to remark that the discussion itself had a political background: an effort to help to constitute the European and global unity. The discussion led further to the claim that invented traditions are not authentic, and hence not true and valuable.[1] This kind of argument rests on a poor understanding of cultural elements used in culture-building projects, which themselves are today international and even global. The selected cultural elements often have a local or ethnic base and they are called "traditions". From the viewpoint of folklore studies the endless variation and continuing change of tradition is a rule though the change concerns inherited cultural models. In this work, our aim has been to see how traditions performed among the Finno-Ugric people are selected. In studying the Khanty and Komi traditions we have tried to see which of the selected traditions are inherited, which recreated or invented and how they continue the local culture and its models for expression of culturally crucial ideas. What is the people's point of view in the tradition processes and what has the negotiation with authorities meant for their actions?

Field work done during the 1990s and 2000s in three different places, the Shuryshkary region on the Northern Ob', the Alnash district in the Udmurt Republic and the Ust'-Kulom district of the Komi Republic, shows that answers to these questions are not simple and similar in all the places. All areas are multicultural and local cultures have different histories. In Shuryshkary, the Khanty live with Russians, Komi, Nenets and representatives of some other peoples, for example Tatars. In Ust'-Kulom the Komi live with Russians. In Alnash, the main ethnic groups are Udmurts, Russians, Mari and Tatars. When performing their own culture groups have to take into consideration the aims of the others. Festivals are, actually according to the old Soviet practice, a place for cultural co-operation and also for contests.

We noticed that the distinctive cultural elements in presenting one's own

---

1. See the discussion in Siikala and Siikala 2005: 39–46.

culture are quite limited and they belong to the same schemes of cultural items. Myths and rituals represent the most valuable and safeguarded ethnic traditions; songs and folklore items have an ability to express emotionally loaded ideas and dress, food and handicrafts offer visual and visible ways to be distinct. These domains of cultural representation in public performances are not unique or typical only to the Finno-Ugric cultures. They are found in many other places of the world and have been created by the long work of intellectuals, museum creators, writers, researchers and journalists, who described the distinct cultural features and sometimes also odd features of the other peoples. Studies on negotiations between people and those who have produced representations of them, who created a picture of their heritage, illuminate these questions.[2]

The closer look at the post-Soviet Khanty, Komi and Udmurts shows that opportunities to perform ethnic culture vary among Russian minorities with different histories and administrative organisation. In this variation the dialogue of local and administrative needs is decisive. The modes of performing local culture in our field-work areas are:

1. The Shuryshkary Khanty: Persistence of ethnic culture in everyday life and public local festivals in performing it. Cult performances and shamanic acts were more important than the folklore in the first years of the third millennium.
2. The Ust'-Kulom Komi: The cultural project of the Soviet state provided the organised model for the performance of ethnic culture, especially songs and folklore suitable for presentations on stage. In peripheral areas, for example in Ust'-Kulom, it redesigned and multiplied folklore items.
3. Udmurts: The cultural awakening of Udmurts provided the basis for organising national festivals (the Gerber festival). Organising of festivals in the 1990s was characterised by a contest of religions (Christianity/ethnic rituals) and the re-establishment of the Soviet festival models.
4. Intellectuals have had their own arenas: journals, books, television and internet. In Komi and Udmurtia these are stronger than among the Khanty.

The interest and control of authorities vary from local administration to areal and even national. Hence, the festivals we saw were local among the Khanty, local and areal among the Komi and local, areal and even national among the Udmurts. The Gerber festival of the Udmurts was used as an arena for political propaganda in the election of the president in 1996. In the 2000s the financial support of the state diminished and local help is more important than before. A great deal of work is paid for by singers and other performers themselves.

The Soviet programme gave models for cultural representation in performances of folklore collectives and festivals in the European side of Russia already before the Second World War. In post-Soviet Siberia, however, people have turned to their old ethnic religion in performing their distinctive

2. See Olsen 2004; Conrad 2004; Durrah Scheffy 2004; Kuutma 2006.

culture. Though the northern Khanty became Christians a couple of hundred years ago, they secretly preserved many features of the old ethnic religion. During the Soviet time religions lost their meaning as a socially unifying phenomenon, but lived on in homes and smaller circles of people. The Khanty have established folklore groups too, but they are a new phenomenon in settlements and do not have as important a role in the public presentation of culture as sacred rituals.

The domain of culture presented in festivals determines the gender roles in them. Men are the main actors in the Khanty revived rituals; according to traditional models women cannot come to the holy area. However, women are not totally excluded from the festivals, as they help in making and serving food and take part in the merrymaking of festivals. The Komi, who were Christianised several hundred years ago, prefer in their festivals folk songs and family rituals, for example weddings, and they create plays and art representing their myths. Udmurts, who in the southern area have preserved their ethnic cults and have a living singing culture, favour both sacred rites and folklore and united in their 1990s festivals sacrificial rituals and singing and dancing of folklore groups. Male priests take care of sacrificial rites, but otherwise the situation is totally different among Udmurts and Komis from among the Khanty: women are important organisers of feasts and the main performers. Both rituals and singing, dress and food are gendered symbols of ethnicity presented by them. They are important means of raising emotions and a feeling of belonging to the home village, culture and nation.

Though the idea of "tradition" follows the common, global scheme, the understanding and practice in the tradition processes is local. "We have to do as our ancestors did", said one of the Khanty elders. The Khanty, who have maintained their culture, have more chances of continuing their old customs than for example the Komi, who have already long lived in a close and economically and culturally complex relationship with Russians. The Khanty religious rituals, too, should be performed following the inherited rules so that "the spirits will not be insulted". Hence, the concept of neo-tradition is not suitable for describing Khanty rituals, not even those which have been performed publicly in the festivals organised by the authorities.

The entertainment folklore, on the other hand, is a free domain for change. The performance of songs is open to alterations even though the mode of singing follows the learnt practice. When Komi women multiply their song store by adopting and composing poems of known writers, they are not inventing tradition but recreating it according to old models. They transform poetry, Komi and Russian, into their own tradition. So, the dynamics of tradition operate on several levels: it includes all kinds of elements, old and new, inherited, recreated and adapted, and is guided by inherited performing models which are followed when people are creating their presentations today. The media's role is to pass on the "tradition" to larger audiences. In this work they select again the items of performances according to their ideas and reshape them to suit the common ideas of what the tradition should be.

Bibliography

Abrahams, Roger D. 1993. Phantoms of Romantic Nationalism in Folkloristics. *Journal of American Folklore* 106 (419): 3–37.

Adam, Barbara 1996. Detraditionalization and the Certainty of Uncertain Futures. In Paul Heelas, Scott Lash and Paul Morris (eds.), *Detraditionalization*: 134–48. Cambridge and Oxford: Blackwell.

Adon'eva, S. 2004. Pragmatika chastushek. *Pragmatika fol'klora*: 134–97. St Petersburg: St Petersburg University.

Ahlqvist, August 1880. *Über die Sprache der Nord-Ostjaken: Sprachtexte, Wörtersammlung und Grammatik. 1. Abtheilung, Sprachtexte und Wörtersammlug von August Ahlqvist*. Helsinki: Edlund.

Ahlqvist, August 1883. *Unter Vogulen und Ostjaken. Reisebriefe und ethnographische Mitteilungen*. Helsinki: Suomalainen tiedeseura.

Ajkhenvald, Aleksandra, Eugene Helimski and Vladimir Petrukhin 1989. On the Earliest Finno-Ugrian Mythologic Beliefs: Comparative and Historical Considerations for Reconstruction. In Mihály Hoppál and Juha Pentikäinen (eds.), *Uralic Mythology and Folklore*. Ethnologica Uralica 1: 155–9. Budapest: Akaémiai Kiadó and Finnish Literature Society.

Anderson, Benedict 1991 [1983]. *Imagined Communities. Reflections on the Origin and Spread of Nationalism*. London and New York: Verso.

Anderson, David G. 2002. *Identity and Ecology in Arctic Siberia. The Number One Reindeer Brigade*. Oxford Studies in Social and Cultural Anthropology. Oxford: Oxford University Press.

Andreev, N. P. 1939. *Velikaya Oktyabr'skaya sotsialisticheskaya revolyutsiya i narodnoe tvorchestvo*. Sovetskiĭ fol'klor: Sb. stateĭ i materialov 6. Otv. red. M. K. Azadovskiĭ. Moscow and Leningrad.

Anttonen, Pertti J. 1993. Folklore, Modernity, and Postmodernism: A Theoretical Overview. In Pertti J. Anttonen and Reimund Kvideland (eds.), *Nordic Frontiers. Recent Issues in the Study of Modern Traditional Culture in the Nordic Countries*. Nordic Institute of Folklore Publications 27: 17–34. Turku: Nordic Institute of Folklore.

Anttonen, Pertti J. (ed.) 1996. *Making Europe in Nordic Context*. NIF Publications 35. Turku: Nordic Institute of Folklore.

Anttonen, Pertti J. 2005. *Tradition through Modernity. Postmodernism and the Nation-State in Folklore Scholarship*. Studia Fennica Folkloristica 15. Helsinki: Finnish Literature Society.

Anttonen, Veikko 1987: *Uno Harva ja suomalainen uskontotiede*. Helsinki: Suomalaisen Kirjallisuuden Seura.

Anttonen, Veikko 1996. *Ihmisen ja maaŋ rajat. "Pyhä" kulttuurisena kategoriana*. Helsinki: Finnish Literature Society.

Appadurai, Arjun 1996. *Modernity at Large. Cultural Dimensions of Globalization*. Public Worlds 1. Minneapolis and London: University of Minnesota Press.

Arkhipova, A. S., and S. Yu. Neklyudov 2008. Dva geroya/dva urkana: prival na puti. Natales grate numeras? Sbornik stateĭ k 60-letiyu Georgiya Akhillovicha Levintona. SPB. *Studia Ethnologica*, Vyp. 61: 27–75. St Petersburg.

Astakhova, A. M. 1931. Diskussiya o sushchnosti i zadachakh fol'klora v Leningradskom institute rechevoĭ kul'tury (IRK) 11 yulya 1931 g. *Sovetskaya étnografiya* 3–4.

Azadovskiĭ, M. K. 1928. *Mesto i rol' fol'klora v organizatsii kraevedcheskikh izucheniĭ.* Tr. Pervogo (sibirskogo) kraevogo nauchno-issledovatel'skogo s"ezda. T. V. Novosibirsk.

Azadovskiĭ, M. K. 1939. *Sovetskaya fol'kloristika za 20 let.* Sovetskiĭ fol'klor: Sb. stateĭ i materialov 6. Otv. red. M. K. Azadovskiĭ. Moscow and Leningrad.

Bagramov, É. A., A. I. Doronchenkov, M. M. Morozova and P. I. Nadolishnyĭ 1993. *Razdelit li Rossiya uchast' soyuza SSR? (Krizis mezhnatsional'nykh otnosheniĭ i federal'naya natsional'naya politika).* Mezhdunarodnyĭ fond Rossiĭsko-éllinskogo dukhovnogo edinstva. Moscow: Tsentr issledovaniya natsional'nykh otnosheniĭ RNIS i NP.

Badone, Ellen (ed.) 1990. *Religous Orthodoxy and Popular Faith in European Society*. Princeton: Princeton University Press.

Balalaeva, Ol'ga 1999. *Svyashchennie mesta khantov v sredneĭ i nizhneĭ Obi. Ocherki istorii traditsionnogo zemlepol'zovaniya khantov (materialy k atlasu).* Tezis: 139–56. Ekaterinburg.

Balalajeva, O., and A. Wiget 1999. Sacrifice, Shamanism and Cultural Specialists among the Khanty. In *Proceedings of the International Congress "Shamanism and Other Indigenous Spiritual Beliefs and Practices"*: 114–24. Moscow.

Balzer, Marjorie M. 1980. The Route to Eternity: Cultural Persistence and Change in Siberian Khanty Burial Ritual. *Arctic Anthropology* 17.1: 77–89.

Balzer, Marjorie 1981. Rituals of Gender and Identity: Markers of Siberian Khanty Ethnicity, Status, and Belief. *American Anthropologist* 83.4: 850–67.

Balzer, Marjorie Mandelstam 1987. *Strategies of Ethnic Survival: Interaction of Russians and Khanty (Ostiak) in Twentieth Century Siberia*. UMI Dissertation Information Service. A Bell and Howell Information Company (1979). Michigan: University of Michigan.

Balzer, Marjorie (ed.) 1992. *Russian Traditional Culture. Religion, Gender and Customary Law*. Armonk, New York and London: Sharpe.

Balzer, Marjorie Mandelstam (ed.) 1995. *Culture Incarnate. Native Anthropology from Russia*. Armonk, New York and London: Sharpe.

Balzer, Marjorie Mandelstam 1999. *The Tenacity of Ethnicity. A Siberian Saga in a Global Perspective*. Princeton: Princeton University Press.

Barkalaja, Anzori 2001: Some Personal Notes about the Fieldwork (on the Examples of the Eastern Khantys). In Pille Runnel (ed.), *Rethinking Ethnology and Folkloristics*. Vanavaravedaja 6. Tartu Nefa rühm. Tartu.

Barkalaya, Anzori 2002a. "Chameleons" of Siberia: Identity and Survival Strategies of an Eastern Khanty Family. In Anzori Barkalaya, *Sketches towards a Theory of Shamanism: Associating the Belief System of the Pim River Khanties with the Western World View*. Dissertationes Folkloristicae Universitatis Tartuensis 1. Tartu.

Barkalaya, Anzori 2002b. On the Aspects of Space in the Khanty World Outlook. In Anzori Barkalaya, *Sketches towards a Theory of Shamanism: Associating the Belief System of the Pim River Khanties with the Western World View*. Dissertationes Folkloristicae Universitatis Tartuensis 1. Tartu.

Barkalaya, Anzori 2002c. A Continuing Tradition: The Changing of Spirit Dolls by the Pym River Khantys. In Anzori Barkalaya, *Sketches towards a Theory of Shamanism: Associating the Belief System of the Pim River Khanties with the Western World View.* Dissertationes Folkloristicae Universitatis Tartuensis 1. Tartu.

Bartens, Raija 1986. *Siivekkäille jumalille, jalallisille jumalille. Hantien ja mansien runoutta.* Helsinki: Finnish Literature Society.

Basso, Keith H. 1996. Wisdom Sits in Places. Notes on a Western Apache Landscape. In Steven Feld and Keith H. Basso (eds.), *Senses of Place.* School of American Research Advanced Seminar Series: 53–90. Santa Fe: Scholl.

Bell, Catherine 1992. *Ritual Theory, Ritual Practice.* New York and Oxford: Oxford University Press.

Bellah, Robert 1970. *Beyond Belief: Essays on Religion in a Post-Traditional World.* New York: Harper and Row.

Belorukowa, Galina 1996. Nationale Entwicklungsprozesse im heutigen Udmurtien. In *Congressus Primus Historiae Fenno-Ugricae. Historia Fenno-Ugrica I:1.* Oulu: Oulu University Press.

Berezkin, Yuri 2005. The Cosmic Hunt: Variants of a Siberian – North-American Myth. *Folklore, Electric Journal of Folklore* 31: 79–100. Tartu.

Bhaba, Homi K. 1994. *The Location of Culture.* London and New York: Routledge.

Bogatyrev, P. G. 1971. *Voprosy teorii narodnogo iskusstva.* Moscow: Iskusstvo.

Branch, Michael 1973. *A. J. Sjögren, Studies of the North.* Helsinki: Suomalais-Ugrilainen Seura.

Branch, Michael (ed.) 1999. *National History and Identity. Approaches to the Writing of National History in the North-East Baltic Region, Nineteenth and Twentieth Centuries.* Studia Fennica Ethnologica 6. Helsinki: Finnish Literature Society.

Branch, Michael, and Celia Hawkesworth (eds.) 1994. *The Uses of Tradition. A Comparative Enquiry into the Nature, Uses and Functions of Oral Poetry in the Balkans, the Baltic and Africa.* London: School of Slavonic and East European Studies, University of London and Finnish Literature Society.

Briggs, Charles L., and Richard Bauman 1992. Genre, Intertextuality, and Social Power. *Journal of Linguistic Anthropology* 282: 131–72.

Bunzl, Matti 1996. Franz Boas and the Humboldtian Tradition: From Volksgeist and Nationalcharakter to an Anthropological Concept of Culture. In George W. Stocking, Jr (ed.), *Volksgeist as Method and Ethic. Essays on Boasian Ethnography and the German Anthropological Tradition.* History of Anthropology 8: 17–78. Madison, Wisconsin: The University of Wisconsin Press.

Cantwell, Robert 1993. *Ethnomimesis. Folklife and the Representation of Culture.* Chapel Hill and London: The University of North Carolina Press.

Cassirer, Ernst 1953 [1946]. *Language and Myth,* trans. Susanne K. Langer. New York: Dover.

Castrén, M. A. 1853. *Nordische Reisen und Forschungen, Teil I. Reiseerinnerungen aus den Jahren 1838–1844.* St Petersburg: Akademie der Wissenschaften.

Castrén, M. A. 1856. *Nordische Reisen und Forschungen. Teil II. Reiseberichte und Briefe aus den Jahren 1845–1849.* St Petersburg: Akademie der Wissenschaften.

Castrén, M. A. 1853. *Nordiska resor och forskningar af M. A. Castrén. Tredje bandet: M. A. Castréns föreläsningar i finsk mytologi.* Helsinki: Finnish Literature Society.

Castrén, Matias Aleksanteri 1967. *Tutkimusmatkoilla Pohjolassa. Matias Aleksanteri Castrénin matkakertomuksista suomentanut ja johdannon kirjoittanut Alis J. Joki.* Porvoo: Werner Söderström.

Castrén, M. A., and T. Lehtisalo 1940. *Samojedische Volksdichtung.* Mémoires de la Société Finno-ougrienne 83. Helsinki.

Castrén, M. A., and T. Lehtisalo 1960. *Samojedische Sprachmaterialen gesammelt von M. A. Castrén und T. Lehtisalo .* Mémoires de la Société Finno-ougrienne 122. Helsinki.

Chernetsov, V. N. 1947. K istorii rodnovo stroya obskih ugrov. *Sovetskaya Ėtnografiya.* T. T-VI–VII.

Chernetsov, V. N. 1959. Predstavleniya o dushe u obskikh ugrov. Issledovaniya i materialy po voprosam pervobytnykh religioznykh verovaniĭ. *Trudy instituta ėtnografii im. N. N. Miklukho-Maklaya,* new series 51: 114–56. Moscow: Izdatel'stvo Akademii Nauk SSSR.

Chernetsov, V. N. 1963. Ob Ugrian Concepts of the Soul. In Henry N. Michael (ed.), *Studies in Siberian Shamanism:* 3–45. Arctic Institute of North America, Anthropology of the North, Translations from Russian Sources 4. Canada: University of Toronto Press.

Clifford, James 1986. On Ethnographic Allegory. In James Clifford and George E. Marcus (eds.), *Writing Culture. The Poetics and Politics of Ethnography:* 98–121. Berkeley, Los Angeles and London: University of California Press.

Clifford, James 1988. *The Predicament of Culture.* Twentieth-Century Ethnography, Literature, and Art. Cambridge and London: Harvard University Press.

Clifford, James, and George E. Marcus (eds.) 1986. *Writing Culture. The Poetics and Politics of Ethnography.* Berkeley, Los Angeles and London: University of California Press.

Cohen, Percy 1969. Theories of Myth. *Man* 4.3: 337–53. London: Royal Anthropological Institute of Great Britain and Ireland.

Comaroff, John L. 1996. Ethnicity, Nationalism, and the Politics of Difference in an Age of Revolution. In Edwin N. Wilmsen and Patrick McAllister (eds.), *The Politics of Difference. Ethnic Premises in a World of Power:* 162–84. Chicago and London: The University of Chicago Press.

Connerton, Paul 1989. *How Societies Remember.* Cambridge: Cambridge University Press.

Conrad, JoAnn 2004. Mapping Space, Claiming Place. In Anna-Leena Siikala, Barbro Klein and Stein R. Mathisen (eds.), *Creating Diversities. Folklore, Religion and the Politics of Heritage.* Studia Fennica Folkloristica 14: 165–89. Helsinki: Finnish Literature Society.

Crapanzano, Vincent 1977. The Writing of Ethnography. *Dialectical Anthropology* 2: 69–73.

Crapanzano, Vincent 1992. *Hermes' Dilemma and Hamlet's Desire. On the Epistemology of Interpretation.* Cambridge, Mass., and London: Harvard University Press.

DEWOS: Wolfgang Steinitz, 1966–93. *Dialektologisches und etymologisches Wörterbuch der ostjakischen Sprache.* Berlin: Akademie-Verlag.

Donner, Kai 1919. *Sibiriska noveller.* Helsinki: Söderström & Co.

Donner, Kai 1923 [1915 in Swedish]. *Siperian samojedien keskuudessa 1911–1913 ja 1915.* Helsinki: Otava.

Donner, Kai 1933a [1933 in Swedish]. *Siperia. Elämä ja entisyys.* Helsinki: Otava.

Donner, Kai 1933b. *Ethnological Notes about the Yenisey-Ostyak in the Turukhansk Region.* Mémoires de la Société Finno-ougrienne 66. Helsinki.

Doty, William G. 2000. *Mythography. The Study of Myths and Rituals.* Tuscaloosa and London: The University of Alabama Press.

Drobizheva, Leokadia 1996. Russian Ethnonationalism. In Leokadia Drobizheva, Rose Gottemoeller, Catherine McArdle Kelleher and Lee Walker (eds.), *Ethnic Conflict in the Post-Soviet World. Case Studies and Analysis:* 129–48. Armonk, New York and London: Sharpe.

Dumézil, Georges 1970. *The Destiny of the Warrior,* trans. from French by Alf Hiltebeitel. Chicago: University of the Chicago Press.

Dumont, Louis 1994. *German Ideology from France to Germany and Back.* Chicago and London: University of Chicago Press.

Dundes, Alan 1984. Introduction. In Alan Dundes (ed.), *Sacred Narrative. Readings in the Theory of Myth*: 1–3. Berkeley, Los Angeles and London: University of California Press.

Durkheim, Émile 1971. *The Elementary Forms of the Religious Life*, trans. from French by Joseph Ward Swain. London: George Allen & Unwin.

Durrah Scheffy, Zoë-hateehc 2004. Sámi Religion in Museums and Artistry. In Anna-Leena Siikala, Barbro Klein and Stein M. Mathisen (eds.), *Creating Diversities. Folklore, Religion and the Politics of Heritage*. Studia Fennica Folkloristica 14: 225–59. Helsinki: Finnish Literature Society.

Dwyer, Kevin 1977. On the Dialogic of Field Work. *Dialectical Anthropology* 2: 143–51.

Dwyer, Kevin 1979. The Dialogic of Ethnology. *Dialectical Anthropology* 4.3: 205–24.

Dwyer, Kevin 1982. *Moroccan Dialogues: Anthropology in Question*. Baltimore: Johns Hopkins University Press.

Ehn, Billy, Jonas Frykman and Orvar Löfgren 1993. *Försvenskningen av Sverige. Det nationellas förvandlingar*. Stockholm: Natur och kultur.

Ekholm-Friedman, Kajsa, and Jonathan Friedman 1995. Global Complexity and the Simplicity of Everyday Life. In Daniel Miller (ed.), *Worlds Apart. Modernity through the Prism of the Local*. London and New York: Routledge.

Eliade, Mircea 1984. Cosmogonic Myth and Sacred History. In Alan Dundes (ed.), *Sacred Narrative. Readings in the Theory of Myth*: 137–51. Berkeley, Los Angeles and New York: University of California Press.

Erdélyi, István 1972: *Ostjakische Heldenlieder aus József Pápay's Nachlass*. Budapest: Akadémiai Kiádo.

Fabian, Johannes 1991. *Time and the Work of Anthropology. Critical Essays 1971–1991*. Harwood: CHUR.

Finnegan, Ruth 1988. *Literacy and Orality. Studies in the Technology of Communication*. Oxford: Basil Blackwell.

Flinckenberg-Gluschkoff, Marianna, and Nikolai Garin 1992. *Ugrien mailla. Suomalaisten tutkimusmatkailijoiden jalanjäljillä Obvirralta Uralille*. Helsinki: Otava.

Foley, John Miles 1985. *Oral-Formulaic Theory and Research. An Introduction and Annotated Bibliography*. New York and London: Garland.

Foley, John Miles 1995. *Singer of Tales in Performance*. Bloomington: Indiana University Press.

Fondahl, Gail A. 1997a. Siberia: Assimilation and its Discontents. In Ian Bremmer and Ray Taras (eds.), *New States, New Politics. Building the Post-Soviet Nations*: 190–234. Cambridge: Cambridge University Press.

Fondahl, Gail A. 1997b. Environmental Degradation and Indigenous Land Claims in Russia's North. In Eric Alden Smith and Joan McCarter (eds.), *Contested Arctic. Indigenous Peoples, Industrial States, and the Circumpolar Environment*: 68–87. Seattle and London: University of Washington Press.

Friedman, Jonathan 1992a. Myth, History and Political Identity. *Cultural Anthropology* 7: 194–210.

Friedman, Jonathan 1992b. Past in the Future. History and the Politics of Identity. *American Anthropologist* 94.4: 837–57.

Friedman, Jonathan 1994. *Cultural Identity and Global Process*. London and Thousand Oaks, New Delhi: SAGE Publications.

Gaster, Theodor H. 1984. Myth and Story. In Alan Dundes (ed.), *Sacred Narrative. Readings in the Theory of Myth*: 110–36. Berkeley, Los Angeles and London: University of California Press.

Gellner, Ernst 1983. *Nations and Nationalism*. Oxford: Basil Blackwell.

Gemuev, I. N. 1990. *Mirovozzrenie mansi: dom i kosmos*. Novosibirsk: Nauka.

Gemuev, I. N., and Baulo, A. B. 1999. *Svyatilishcha mansi verkhov'ev severnoĭ sos'vy*. Rossiĭskaya Akademiya Nauk. Sibirskoe otdelenie, Institut arkheologii i ėtnografii. Novosibirsk.

Gemuev I. N., and G. I. Pelikh 1999. Categories of Selkup Shamans. *Shaman* 7.2: 123–40.

Gemuev, I. N., *et al.* 2008: I. N. Gemuev, A. V. Baulo, A. A. Lyutsidarskaya, A. M. Sagalaev, Z. P. Sokolova, G. E. Soldatova, *Mansi Mythology.* The Encyclopaedia of Uralic Mythologies 3, ed. Anna-Leena Siikala, Vladimir Napol'skikh and Mihály Hoppál. Budapest and Helsinki: Akadémiai Kiadó and Finnish Literature Society.

Georgi, I. G. 1779: *Opisanie vsekh obitayushchikh v Rossiĭskom gosudarstve narodov – O narodakh finskogo plemeni.* St Petersburg.

Giddens, Anthony 1991. *The Consequences of Modernity.* Cambridge: Polity.

Giddens, Anthony 1994. Living in a Post-Traditional Society. In Ulrich Beck, Anthony Giddens and Scott Lash, *Reflexive Modernization. Politics, Tradition and Aesthetics in the Modern Social Order*: 56–109. Standford, California: Standford University Press.

Golovnëv, A. V. 1995. *Govoryashchie kultury. Traditsii samodiĭtsev i ugrov.* Panorama kul'tur Yamala. Ekaterinburg: Akademiya Nauk.

Gondatti, N. L. 1888. *Sledy jazychestva u inorodtsev Severo-Zapadnoĭ Sibiri.* Trudy Obshchestva Estestvenii Nauk Antropologii i Etnografii. Moscow.

Goody, Jack 1991 [1987]. *The Interface between the Written and the Oral.* New York, Port Chester, Melbourne and Sydney: Cambridge University Press.

Grant, Bruce 1995. *In the Soviet House of Culture. A Century of Perestroikas.* Princeton: Princeton University Press.

Guthrie, S. E. 1996. Religion: What is it? *Journal for the Scientific Study of Religion* 35:4.

Haavio, Martti 1961. *Kuolematonten lehdot.* Porvoo and Helsinki: Werner Söderström.

Haekel, Josef 1946. Idolkult und Dualsystem bei den Ugriern (zum Problem des eurasiatischen Totemismus). *Archiv für Völkerkunde*: 95–163. Vienna.

Hakamies, Pekka 1998. *Ison karhun jälkeläiset. Perinne ja etninen identiteetti yhteiskunnallisessa murroksessa.* Helsinki: Finnish Literature Society.

Häkkinen, Kaisa 1990. *Mistä sanat tulevat.* Suomalaista etymologiaa. Helsinki: Finnish Literature Society.

Halbwachs, Maurice 1992. *On Collective Memory*, ed., trans. and introduced by Lewis A. Coser. The Heritage of Sociology. Chicago and London: University of Chicago Press.

Hall, Stuart 1991. The Local and the Global: Globalization and Ethnicity. In Anthony D. King (ed.), *Culture, Globalization and the World-System. Contemporary Conditions for the Representation of Identity*: 19–39. Houndsmills, Basingstoke and London: MacMillan.

Handler, Richard 1988. *Nationalism and the Politics of Culture in Quebec.* Wisconsin, Madison: University of Wisconsin Press.

Hanks, William F. 1987. Discourse Genres in a Theory of Practice. *American Ethnologist* 14.4: 668–98.

Hanks, William F. 1996. *Language and Communicative Practices.* Boulder, Colorado, and Oxford: Westview Press.

Hannerz, Ulf 1996. *Transnational Connections. Culture, People, Places.* London and New York: Routledge.

Harva, Uno 1927. *Finno-Ugric, Siberian.* The Mythology of All Races 4. BostonArchaeological Institute of America.

Harva, Uno 1933: *Altain suvun uskonto.* Porvoo: Werner Söderström.

Harva, Uno 1993 [1938]. *Die religiösen Vorstellungen der altaischen Völker.* Folklore Fellows' Communications 125. Helsinki: Academia Scientiarum Fennica.

Harvilahti, Lauri 1992. *Kertovan runon keinot. Inkeriläisen runoepiikan tuottamisesta.* Helsinki: Finnish Literature Society.

Harvilahti, Lauri 2000. Variation and memory. In Lauri Honko (ed.), *Thick Corpus, Organic Variation and Textuality in Oral Tradition.* Studia Fennica Folkloristica 7: 57–75. Helsinki: Finnish Literature Society.

Harvilahti, Lauri, with Zoja S. Kazagačeva 2003. *The Holy Mountain. Studies on Upper Altay Oral Poetry*. Folklore Fellows' Communications 282. Helsinki: Academia Scientiarum Fennica.

Hastrup, Kirsten 1987. Presenting the Past. Reflections on Myth and History. *Folk, Journal of the Danish Ethnographic Society* 29: 257–67.

Heelas, Paul 1996. Introduction. In Paul Heelas, Scott Lash and Paul Morris (eds.), *Detraditionalization*: 1–20. Oxford: Blackwell.

Heikkinen, Kaija 1992. Women, Marginality and the Manifestation of Everyday Life. A Study of the Present-day Feasts of the Veps and the Mari (in Russia). *Ethnologia Fennica* 20: 5–17.

Heikkinen, Kaija 1998. Vepsäläisten etninen identiteeti ja ongelmallinen julkisuus. In Pekka Hakamies (ed.), *Ison karhun jälkeläiset. Perinne ja etninen identiteetti yhteiskunnallisessa murroksessa*: 141–59. Helsinki: Finnish Literature Society.

Heikkinen, Kaija 2006: *Metsänpelko ja tietäjänaiset. Vepsäläisnaisten uskonto Venäjällä.* Jyväskylä: Gummerus.

Hillier, Bill, and Julienne Hanson 1984. *The Social Logic of Space*. New York: Cambridge University Press.

Hobsbawm, Eric, and Terence Ranger 1984 [1983]. *The Invention of Tradition.* Cambridge: Cambridge University Press.

Holmberg [Harva], Uno 1914. *Permalaisten uskonto*. Suomen suvun uskonnot 4. Helsinki and Porvoo: Werner Söderström.

Holmberg [Harva], Uno 1926. *Die Religion der Tscheremissen*. Folklore Fellows' Communications 61. Porvoo: Suomalainen Tiedeakatemia.

Honko, Lauri 1979. Theories concerning the Ritual Process: An Orientation. In Lauri Honko (ed.), *Science of Religion: Studies on Methodology. Proceedings of the Study Conference of the International Association for the History of Religions, held in Turku, Finland, in August 1973.* Religion and Reason 13: Method and Theory in the Study and Interpretation of Religion: 369–90. The Hague, Pris and New York: Mouton.

Honko, Lauri 1984. The Problem of Defining Myth. In Alan Dundes (ed.), *Sacred Narrative. Readings in the Theory of Myth*: 41–52. Berkeley, Los Angeles and London: University of California Press.

Honko, Lauri (ed.) 1988. *Tradition and Cultural Identity*. Turku: Nordic Institute of Folklore.

Honko, Lauri, Senni Timonen and Michael Branch 1994. *The Great Bear. A Thematic Anthology of Oral Poetry in the Finno-Ugrian Languages*, with the poems translated by Keith Bosley. Oxford and Helsinki: Oxford University Press and Finnish Literature Society.

Honti, László 1982. *Nordostjakisches Wörterverzeichnis*. Studia Uralo-Altaica 16. Szeged: Attila József University.

Hoppál, Mihály 2007. *Shamans and Traditions*. Budapest: Akadémiai Kiadó.

Hufford, David J. 1995. The Scholarly Voice and the Personal Voice: Reflexivity in Belief Studies. *Western Folklore* 54.1: 57–76.

Hultkrantz, Åke 1973. A Definition of Shamanism, *Temenos* 9: 25–37.

Humphrey, Caroline, with Urgunge Onon 1996. *Shamans and Elders. Experience, Knowledge, and Power among the Daur Mongols*. Oxford: Clarendon Press.

Humphrey, Caroline 2002. *The Unmaking of Soviet Life. Everyday Economies after Socialism*. Ithaca and London: Cornell University Press.

Huttenbach, Henry R. (ed.) 1991. *Soviet Nationality Politics. Ruling Ethnic Groups in the USSR*. London and New York: Mansell.

Huttenbach, Henry R. 1996. The Impact of Soviet Rule on the Suppression or Encouragement of Finno-Ugric Ethno-national Self-consciousness: The Policy of Contradictions. In *Congressus Primus Historiae Fenno-Ugricae*. Historia Fenno-Ugrica I:1. Oulu.

Illja Vaś 1994. *Myj medsja lona da musa*. Syktyvkar: Komi kn.izd-vo. 84 lb.

Jääsalmi-Krüger, Paula 1996. Hanti- ja mansinaisten kokemuksia kuukautisista. In *Congressus Octavus Internationalis Fenno-Ugristarum*, Jyväskylä 10.–15.8.1995. Pars VI. Ethnologia and Folkloristica: 118–20. Jyväskylä: Jyväskylä University.

Jääsalmi-Krüger, Paula 2001. Hecht, Stör und Quappe – ein lebendiges Relikt frauenspezifischer Vorschriften bei den nördlichen Obugrien. In *Congressus Internationalis Fenno-Ugristarum* 7.-13.2000. Pars VII: 351–9. Tartu: Tartu University.

Jacknis, Ira 1996. The Ethnographic Object and the Object of Ethnology in the Early Career of Franz Boas. In George W. Stocking, Jr (ed.), *Volksgeist as Method and Ethic. Essays on Boasian Ethnography and the German Anthropological Tradition.* History of Anthropology 8: 185–214. Madison: University of Wisconsin Press.

Jensen, Jeppe Sinding 2001. Universals, General Terms and the Comparative Study of Religion. *Numen* 48: 238–66.

Jordan, Peter 2003. *Material Culture and Sacred Landscape. An Anthropology of the Siberian Khanty.* Archaeology of Religion 3. Walnut Creek, Lanham, New York and Oxford: Altamira Press.

Kálmán, B. 1968. Two Purification Rites in the Bear Cult of the Ob-Ugrians. In V. Diószegi (ed.), *Popular Beliefs and Folklore Tradition in Siberia*: 85–92. Bloomington and The Hague: Indiana University Press and Mouton.

Kannisto, Artturi, and Martti Liimola 1951–1963. *Vogulische Volksdichtung. Gesammelt und übersetzt von Artturi Kannisto. Bearbeitet und herausgegeben von Martti Liimola I-VI.* Mémoires de la Société Finno-ougrienne 101, 109, 111, 116 and 134. Helsinki.

Kannisto, Artturi, Martti Liimola and E. A. Virtanen 1958. *Materialen zur Mythologie der Wogulen. Gesammelt von Artturi Kannisto. Bearbeitet und herausgegeben von E. A. Virtanen und Martti Liimola.* Mémoires de la Société Finno-ougrienne 113. Helsinki.

Kappeler, Andreas (ed.) 1996. *Regionalismus und Nationalismus in Russland. Nationen und Nationalitäten in Osteuropa.* Band 4. Baden-Baden: Nomos.

Karjalainen, K. F. 1900–2. Ostjakkeja oppimassa I–V. *Journal de la Société Finno-ougrienne* 17, 18, 20. Helsinki.

Karjalainen, K. F. 1901–3. Matkakertomus ostjakkien maalta. *Journal de la Société Finno-ougrienne* 19, 20, 21. Helsinki.

Karjalainen, K. F. 1918. *Jugralaisten uskonto*. Suomen suvun uskonnot III. Porvoo: Werner Söderström.

Karjalainen, K. F. 1921–7. *Die religion der Jugra-Völker*. Folklore Fellows' Communications 41, 44, 63. Helsinki: Academia Scientiarum Fennica.

Karjalainen, K. F. 1948: *K. F. Karjalainens Ostjakisches Wörterbuch. Bearbeitet und herausgegeben von Y. H. Toivonen.* Lexica Societatis Fenno-Ugricae 10. Helsinki: Suomalais-Ugrilainen Seura.

Karjalainen, K. F. 1983. *Ostjakit. Matkakirjeitä Siperiasta 1898–1902.* Suomalaisen Kirjallisuuden Seuran Toimituksia 394. Helsinki: Finnish Literature Society.

Kar'yalaïnen, K. F. 1994–6. *Religiya yugorskikh narodov / per. s nem.* N. V. Lukinoï. I–III. Tomsk: Izdatel'stvo Tomskogo Universiteta.

Kemiläinen, Aira 1999. Nationalismi ja "universaalinen nationalismi" eli lähetystehtäväajatus muutostekijänä historiassa. *Tieteessä tapahtuu* 2. Helsinki: Tieteellisten seurojen valtuuskunta.

Klein, Barbro 2000. Folklore, Heritage Politics and Ethnic Diversity: Thinking about the Past and the Future. In Pertti J. Anttonen in collaboraton with Anna-Leena Siikala, Stein R. Mathisen and Leif Magnusson (eds.), *Folklore, Heritage Politics and Ethnic Diversity. A Festschrift for Barbro Klein.* Botkyrka, Sweden: Multicultural Centre.

Koepping, Klaus-Peter 1983. *Adolf Bastian and the Psychic Unity of Mankind.* The Foundations of Anthropology in Nineteenth Century Germany: 23–36. St Lucia, London and New York: University of Queensland Press.

Konakov, N. D. 1996. *Traditsionnoe mirovozzrenie narodov komi: formirovanie i sovre-mennoe ėtnokul'turnoe sostoyanie*. Moscow: Nauka.

Konakov, N. D., *et al.* 1999: D. N. Konakov and authors' collective (A. N. Vlasov, I. V. Il'ina, N. D. Konakov, P. F. Limerov, O. I. Ulyashev, Yu. P. Shabaev, V. Ė. Sharapov), *Mifologiya Komi*, ed. Anna-Leena Siikala, Vladimir Napol'skikh, Mihály Hoppál. Ėntsiklopediya ural'skikh mifologiĭ 1. Moscow and Syktyvkar: Akademiái Kiádo and Finnish Literature Society.

Konakov, N. D., *et al.* 2003: Nikolaĭ Konakov in collaboration with I. V. Il'ina, P. F. Limerov, O. I. Ulyashev, Yu. P. Shabaev, V. Ė. Sharapov and A. N. Vlasov. Scientific editor Vladimir Napol'skikh. *Komi Mythology*. The Encyclopaedia of Uralic Mythologies 1, ed. Anna-Leena Siikala, Vladimir Napol'skikh and Mihály Hoppál. Budapest and Helsinki: Akadémiai Kiadó and Finnish Literature Society.

Korhonen, Mikko, Seppo Suhonen and Pertti Virtaranta 1983. *Sata vuotta Suomen sukua tutkimassa*. Espoo: Weilin & Göös.

Kotovskaia, Mariia, and Natal'ia Shalygina 1999. Love, Sex and Marriage: The Female Mirror. Value Orientation of Young Women in Russia. In Hilary Pilkington (ed.), *Gender, Generation and Identity in Contemporary Russia*: 121–31. London and New York: Routledge.

Kozlova, D. T. 1966. Deyatel'nost' kolkhoznyh teatrov v Komi ASSR v 30–40 gg. *Voprosy sotsial'no-politicheskoĭ i sotsial'no-ėkonomicheskoĭ istorii Respubliki Komi XX veka*. Tr. In-ta jaz., lit. i istorii Komi NTs UrO RAN; Vyp. 61. Syktyvkar.

Kozlova, D. T. 2002. Sel'skie teatry i dukhovnoe vozrozhdenie sela. In *Sotsial'no-ėkonomicheskoe i dukhovnoe razvitie sela Respubliki Komi v XXI veke*: 146. Syktyvkar.

Kraĭnov, G. N. 1996. Natsional'no-osvoboditel'noe dvizhenie mariĭskogo naroda: istoriya i sovremennost'. *Probuzhdenie finno-ugorskogo Severa. Opyt Mariĭ Ėl* 1. Natsional'nye dvizheniya Mariĭ Ėl. Rossiĭskaya Akademiya Nauk. Tsentr po izucheniyu mezhnatsional'nykh otnoshenii Instituta Ėtnologii i Antropologii im. N. N. Miklukho-Maklaya. Moscow: Akademiya Nauk.

Krohn, Kaarle 1918. Kalevalankysymyksiä I–II. *Journal de la Société Finno-ougrienne* 35–6.

Kudryavtsev, Vladimir 2001. Kul'tovoe mesto i religioznaya praktika mari. In *Congressus Nonus Internationalis Fenno-Ugristarum 7.–13.8.2000 Tartu. Pars VII*. Redegit: T. Seilenthal. Tartu: Tartu University.

Kulemzin, V. M. 1976. *Shamanstvo vasyugansko-vakhovskikh Khantov (konets XIX – nachalo XX vekov)*. Iz istorii shamanstva. Tomsk: Izdatel'stvo Tomskogo Universiteta.

Kulemzin, V. M. 1984. *Chelovek i priroda v verovaniyakh Khantov*. Tomsk: Izdatel'stvo Tomskogo Universiteta.

Kulemzin, V. M., *et al.* 2000: authors' collective V. M. Kulemzin, N,V. Lukina, Timofeĭ Moldanov and Tat'yana Moldanova. *Mifologiya Khantov*. A.-L. Siikala, V. Napol'skikh and M. Hoppál (eds.), Ėntsiklopediya ural'skikh mifologiĭ 3. Tomsk: Izdatel'stvo Tomskogo Universiteta.

Kulemzin, V. M., *et al.* 2006: Vladislav M. Kulemzin, Nadezhda V. Lukina, Timofeĭ Moldanov, Tat'yana A. Moldanova, *Khanty Mythology*. The Encyclopaedia of Uralic Mythologies 2, ed. Anna-Leena Siikala, Vladimir Napol'skikh and Mihály Hoppál. Budapest and Helsinki: Akadémiai Kiadó and Finnish Literature Society.

Kulemzin, V. M., and N. V. Lukina 1977: *Vasyugansko-Vakhovskie Khanty v kontse XIX – nachale XX vv*. Tomsk: Izdatel'stvo Tomskogo Universiteta.

Kurkela, Vesa 1989. *Musiikkifolklorismi ja järjestökulttuuri. Kansanmusiikin ideologinen ja taiteellinen hyödyntäminen suomalaisissa musiikki- ja nuorisojärjestöissä*. Suomen Etnomusikologisen Seuran julkaisuja 3. Jyväskylä: Suomen Etnomusikologinen Seura.

Kuusi, Matti 1958: Omaistenvertailukertomus. *Kalevalaseuran vuosikirja* 38: 89–108.

Kuusi, Matti 1963: *Kirjoittamaton kirjallisuus. Suomen kirjallisuus I.* Keuruu: Finnish Literature Society and Otava.

Kuusi, Matti, Keith Bosley and Michael Branch 1977. *Finnish Folk Poetry: Epic.* Helsinki: Finnish Literature Society.

Kuutma, Kristin 2006. *Collaborative Representations. Interpretating the Creation of a Sámi Ethnography and a Seto Epic.* Folklore Fellows' Communications 289. Helsinki: Academia Scientiarum Fennica.

Laulajainen, Leena 1995. *Marilaiset, laulun ja uhritulien kansa.* Helsinki: Otava.

Lallukka, Seppo 1990. *The East Finnic Minorities in the Soviet Union. An Appraisal of Erosive Trends.* Annales Academiae Scientiarum Fennica, ser. B, tom 252. Helsinki: Suomalainen Tiedeakatemia.

Lallukka, Seppo 1998. Volgalais-permiläiset kansat ja venäläistymisen ongelma. Ison karhun jälkeläiset. In Pekka Hakamies (ed.), *Perinne ja etninen identiteetti yhteiskunnallisessa murroksessa*: 85–98. Helsinki: Finnish Literature Society.

Leach, E. R. 1982. Critical Introduction to M. I. Steblin-Kamenskii, *Myth*: 1–20. Ann Arbor: Karoma.

Leete, Art 1999a. An Outline of Descriptions of Ob-Ugrians and Samoyeds in the West-European and Russian Sources from the 11th through the 17th Centuries. *Pro Ethnologia* 8. Arctic Studies 3: 35–56. Tartu: Estonian National Museum.

Leete, Art 1999b. Ways of Describing Nenets and Khanty "Character" in Nineteenth-Century Russian Ethnographic Literature. *Folklore: Electronic Journal of Folklore* 12: 38–52.

Leete, Art 2000. *Põhjarahvad antiigist tänäpäevani: obiugrilaste ja neenetsite kirjelduste muutumine.* Eesti Rahva Muuseumi sari 3. Tartu: Estonian National Museum.

Lehtinen, Ildikó 1996. Kansanpuku identiteetin tunnuksena Baskirian marikylissä. In *Congressus Primus Historiae Fenno-Ugricae.* Historia Fenno-Ugrica I:1. Oulu.: Oulu University.

Lehtinen, Ildikó (ed.) 2002. Siberia. *Life on the Taiga and Tundra.* Helsinki: National Board of Antiquities.

Lehtisalo, T. 1923. Jurakkisamojedien pyhistä paikoista ja niiden haltioista. *Kalevalaseuran vuosikirja* 3: 192–226. Porvoo: Kalevalaseura.

Lehtisalo, T. 1924. *Entwurf einer Mythologie der Jurak-Samojeden.* Mémoires de la Société Finno-ougrienne 53. Helsinki.

Lehtisalo, T. 1933. *Tundralta ja taigasta: muistelmia puolen vuosisadan takaa.* Porvoo: WSOY.

Lehtisalo, T. 1947. *Juraksamojedische Volksdichtung.* Mémoires de la Société Finno-ougrienne 90. Helsinki.

Leikola, Anto 1991. *Saatesanat. Pehr Kalm, Matka Pohjois-Amerikkaan.* Helsinki: Finnish Literature Society.

Linde-Laursen, Anders 1995. *Det nationales natur. Studies i dansk-svenske relationer.* Lund: Historiska Media.

Lintrop, Aado 1993. *Udmurdi Rahvausund piirjooni.* Tartu: Keele ja Kirjanduse Instituut.

Lintrop, Aado 1998. Khanty Bear-feast Songs Collected by Wolfgang Steinitz. *Folklore. Electronic Journal of Folklore* 6: 1–17.

Linnekin, Jocelyn 1990. The Politics of Culture in the Pacific. In Jocelyn Linnekin and Lin Poyer (eds.), *Cultural Identity and Ethnicity in the Pacific*: 149–74. Honolulu: University of Hawaii Press.

Lisovskiy, Jurij, and Pavel Mikushev 2007. *Painting, Drawing*, ed. F. Butyreva. Syktyvkar: Art.

Lönnrot, Elias 1902. *Lönnrotin matkat I–II, vuosina 1828–1839, 1841–1844.* Helsinki: Finnish Literature Society.

Louheranta, Olavi 2006. *Siperiaa sanoiksi – Uralilaisuutta teoiksi. Kai Donner poliittisena organisaattorina sekä tiedemiehenä antropologian näkökulmasta.* Research Series in Anthropology, University of Helsinki. Helsinki: Helsinki University Press.

Luehrmann, Sonja Christine 2009. *Forms and Methods: Teaching Atheism and Religion in the Mari Republic, Russian Federation.* Deep Blue at the University of Michigan. Dissertations and Theses. Michigan.

Luke, Timothy W. 1996. Identity, Meaning and Globalization: Detraditionalization in Postmodern Space-time Comparison. In Paul Heelas, Scott Lash and Paul Morris (eds.), *Detraditionalization*: 109–33. Cambridge and Oxford: Blackwell.

Lukina, N. V., V. M. Kulemzin and F. M. Titorenko 1975: Khanti reki Agan (po materialam ekspedicii 1972 g.). *Iz istorii Sibiri.* Tomsk.

Marcus, George 1992. Past, Present and Emergent Identities: Requirements for Ethnographies of Late Twentieth-Century Modernity Worldwide. In Scott Lash and Jonathan Friedman, *Modernity and Identity*: 309–30. Oxford and Cambridge, Mass.: Blackwell.

Martynova E. P. 1995. Obshchectvennoe ustroistvo v XVII–XIX vv. In N. V. Lukina (ed.), *Istoriya i kul'tura Khantov*: 77–121. Tomsk: Izdatel'stvo TGU.

Martynova, E. P. 1998. *Ocherki istorii i kul'tury khantov.* Novye issledovaniya po ėtnologii i antropologii. Moscow: Rossiĭskaya Akademiya Nauk, Institut ėtnologii i antropologii im. N.N. Miklukho-Maklaya.

Mathisen, Stein Roar 2004. Ethnic Identities in Global and Local Discourses: Contested Narratives of Sámi Ethnic Heritage. In Jari Kupiainen, Erkki Sevänen and John A. Stotesbury (eds.), *Cultural Identity in Transition. Contemporary Conditions, Practices and Politics of a Global Phenomenon*: 141–57. Delhi: Atlantic Publishers & Distributions.

Merleau-Ponty, M. 1995. *Phenomenology of Perception*, trans. from French by Colin Smith. Routledge: London and New York.

Mikhaĭlovskiĭ, V. M. 1892. *Shamanstvo.* Izvestiya Imperatorskogo obshchestva lyubiteleĭ estestvoznaniya, antropologii i ėtnografii, T. XII. Moscow.

Mikushev, A. K. 1969. *Komi ėpicheskie pesni i ballady.* Leningrad: Nauka.

Mikushev, A. K. 1987. *Ėpos naroda komi.* Moscow: Nauka.

Mikushev, A. K., and P. I. Chistalëv 1966. *Komi narodnye pesni.* Vyp. 1. Vychegda and Sysola. Syktyvkar.

Mikushev, A. K., P. I. Chistalëv and Yu. G. Pochev 1971. *Komi narodnye pesni.* Vyp. 3.: Vym' and Udora. Syktyvkar.

Minniyakhmetova, T. G. 2000. *Kalendarnye obryady zakamskikh udmurtov.* Rossiĭskaya Akademiya Nauk, Ural'skoe otdelenie, Udmurtskiĭ institut istorii, yazyka i literatury. Izhevsk: UIIYaL UrO RAN.

Minniyakhmetova, T. G. 2001. Pominal'nye obryady zakamskikh udmurtov. In T. G. Vladykina (ed.), *Finno-Ugorskaya fol'kloristika na poroge novogo tysyacheletiya.* Materialy nauchnoĭ konferentsii (Mezhdunarodnaya letnyaya shkola. Glazov, 17–30 avgusta 2000 g.). Udmurtskiĭ gosudarstvennyĭ universitet. Udmurtskiĭ institut istorii, yazyka i literatury UrO RAN. Izhevsk: Udmurtskiĭ gosudarstvennyĭ universitet. Udmurtskiĭ institut istorii, yazyka i literatury UrO RAN.

Moldanov, Timofeĭ 1999. *Kartina mira v pesnopeniyakh medvezhikh igrishch severnykh khantov.* Tomsk: Izdatel'stvo Tomskogo universiteta.

Moldanov, Timofeĭ, and Tat'yana Moldanova 2000. *Bogi zemli Kazymskoĭ.* Red. N. V. Lukina. Tomsk: Izdatel'stvo Tomskogo universiteta.

Moldanova, Tat'yana 2001. *Arkhetipy v mire snovidenii khantov.* Tomsk: Izdatel'stvo Tomskogo universiteta.

Munkácsi, Bernát 1892–1921. *Vogul népköltési gyűjtemény* 1–4. Budapest: Hungarian Academy of Sciences.

Müller, J. B. 1720. *Leben und Gewohnheiten der Ostjaken.* Berlin.

Müller, Johan Bernard 1722: The Manners and Customs of Ostiaks. In Frederick C. Weber (ed.), *The Present State of Russia*. Vol. II: 37–92. London: Taylor, Innys, and Osborn.

Nagy, Gregory 2002. Can Myth be Saved? In Gregory Schrempp and William Hansen (eds.), *Myth, a New Symposium*: 240–8. Bloomington and Indianapolis: Indiana University Press.

Nalimov, V. V., and Ž. A. Drogalina 1995. *Real'nost' nereal'nogo. Veroyatnostnaya model' bessoznatel'nogo*. Mir ideĭ. Moscow: Mir ideĭ.

Napol'skikh, Vladimir 1989. The Dividing Bird-Myth in Northern Eurasia. In Mihály Hoppál and Juha Pentikäinen (eds.), *Uralic Mythology and Folklore*. Ethnologia Uralica 1: 105–13. Budapest and Helsinki Akadémiai Kiádo and Finnish Literature Society.

Napol'skikh, Vladimir 1992. Proto-Uralic World Picture: A Reconstruction. In Mihály Hoppál and Juha Pentikäinen, *Northern Religions and Shamanism*. Ethnologica Uralica 3: 3–20. Budapest.

Nenola, Aili 1992. Naisen ja miehen uskonto. In Katja Hyry ja Juha Pentikäinen (eds.), *Uskonnot maailmassa*: 361–71. Helsinki, Porvoo and Juva: Werner Söderström.

Nesanelis, D. A. 1992. *Traditsionnye formy dosuga sel'skogo naseleniya Komi kraya vo vtoroĭ polovine XIX – pervoĭ treti XX veka*. Avtoref. na soisk . uch. step. kand. ist. nauk. Syktyvkar.

Nesanelis, D. A. 1993. *Ot Rozhdestva Khristosa do Kreshcheniya: traditsionnye svyatochnye obychai i razvlecheniya v Komi derevne*. Èvolyutsiya i vzaimodeĭstvie kul'tur narodov Severo-Vostoka Evropeĭskoĭ chasti Rossii. Tr. In-ta yaz., lit. i istorii Komi NC UrO RAN; Vyp. 57. Syktyvkar.

Nesanelis, D. A. 1994. *Raskachaem my khodkuyu kachel': traditsionnye formy dosuga Komi kraya (vtoraya polovina XIX – pervaya tret' XX v.)*. Syktyvkar: Tsentr narodnogo tvorchestva Respubliki Komi.

Novitskiĭ, Grigoriĭ 1884: *Kratkoe opisanie o narode ostyachkom Grigoriya Novitskogo. Izdal Leonid Maĭkov*. Pamyatnik drevneĭ pis'mennosti i iskusstva 1884 g. St Petersburg: Izdal Leonid Maĭkov.

Ó Giolláin, Diarmuid 2000: *Locating Irish Folklore. Tradition, Modernity, Identity*. Cork: Cork University Press.

Olsen, Kjell 2004: Heritage, Religion and the Deficit of Meaning in Institutionalized Discourse. In Anna-Leena Siikala, Barbro Klein and Stein R. Mathisen (eds.), *Creating Diversities. Folklore, Religion and Politics of Heritage*. Studia Fennica Folkloristica 14: 31–42. Helsinki: Finnish Literature Society.

Olson, Laura J. 2004. *Performing Russia. Folk revival and Russian Identity*. New York and London: Routledge Curzon.

Onchykov, N. E. 1904. *Pechorskie byliny*. Zapiski IRGO. T. 30. St Petersburg.

Onyina, Szofia 2009: *Szinjai hanti társalgási szótár (nyelvtani vázlattal és szójegyzékkel)*. Budapesti Finnugor füzetek 20. ELTE Finnugor Tanszék. Budapest: ELTE Finnugor Tanszék.

Oracheva, Oksana 1999. The Ideology of Russian Nationalism. In Christopher Williams and Thanasis D. Sfikas (eds.), *Ethnicity and Nationalism in Russia, the CIS and the Baltic States*: 47–63. Aldershot, Brookfield, Singapore and Sydney: Ashgate.

Paasonen, H. 1903. Matkakertomuksia vuosilta 1900–1902. *Journal de la Société Finno-ougrienne* 21.

Paasonen. H. 1909. Die ursprünglichen Seelenvorstellungen bei den finnisch-ugrischen Völkern und die Benennungen der Seele in ihren Sprache. *Journal de la Société Finno-ougrienne* 26: 1–26.

Paasonen, H. 1980. *H. Paasonens südostjakische Textsammlungen*, 1–4, ed. Edith Vértes. Mémoires de la Société Finno-ougrienne 172–5. Helsinki.

Paden, William E. 1994 (1988). *Religious Worlds. The Comparative Study of Religion*. Boston, Mass.: Beacon Press.

Pápay, József 1905. *Osztják neköltési gyüjtemény* = Sammlung ostjakischer Volksdichtungen, auf Grund des Regulyschen Nachglasses und eigener Sammlungen. Dritte asiatische Forschungsreise des Grafen Eugen Zichy, 5. Budapest and Leipzig: Hornyánsky, Viktor, Karl W. Hiersemann.

Pápay, József 1913–18. Die ostjakischen Heldenlieder Regulys. *Journal de la Société Finno-ougrienne* 30: 36.

Patkanov, Serafin K. 1897. *Die Irtysch-Ostjaken und ihre Volkspoesie* 1. St Petersburg: L'Académie Imperiale.

Patkanov, Serafin K. 1900. *Die Irtysch-Ostjaken und ihre Volkspoesie* 2. St Petersburg: L'Académie Imperiale.

Pentikäinen, Juha 1995. *Saamelaiset. Pohjoisen kansan mytologia*. Suomalaisen Kirjallisuuden Seuran Toimituksia 595. Helsinki: Finnish Literature Society.

Pentikäinen, Juha 1998. *Shamans*. Tampere Museum Publications 45. Tampere: Tampere museums.

Perevalova, E. V. 2004. *Severnye Khanty: ètnicheskaya istoriya*. Seriya Panorama kul'tur Yamala. Programmy fundamental'nykh issledovanniǐ Prezidiuma RAN, "Ènokul'turnoe vzaimodeǐstvie v Evrazii". Ekaterinburg: RAN.

Piirainen, Timo 2002: The Sisyphean Mission: New National Identity in Post-Communist Russia. In Chris J. Chulos and Johannes Remy (eds.), *Imperial and National Identities in Pre-revolutionary, Soviet, and Post-Soviet Russia*: 151–73. Studia Historica 66. Helsinki: Finnish Literature Society.

Pimenova, K. V. 2009: The Emergence of a New Social Identity: Trajectories and Life Stories of Post-soviet Shamans in the Republic of Tuva. In Hugh Beach, Dmitri Funk and Lennard Sillanpää (eds.), *Post-soviet Transformations. Politics of Ethnicity and Resource Use in Russia*. Acta Universitatis Upsaliensis. Uppsala Studies in Cultural Anthropology 46. Västerås: Uppsala University.

Polyakov, I. S. 1877. *Pis'ma i Ochety o Puteschestvii v dolinu r. Obi*. Zapiski Imperatorskoǐ Akademii Nauka 30: prilozhenie 2. St Petersburg.

Polyanskiǐ, V. S. 1999. *Istoricheskaya pamjat' v ètnicheskom samosoznanii narodov*. Sotsiologicheskie issledovaniya 3. Moscow: Nauka.

Populenko, N. A. 2000. Narody kraǐnego severa Rossii vo vtoroǐ polovine 90-kh godov XXv. In *Èkonomika. Kultura. Politika. Obzor po materialam rossiǐskoǐ pressy*. Etnofor, informatsionniǐ byulleten'. Moscow: Stariǐ sad.

Powell, David E. 1994. The Religious Renaissance in the Soviet Union and its Successor States. In James R. Millar and Sharon L. Wolchik (eds.), *The Social Legacy of Communism*. Washington and Cambridge: Woodrow Wilston Center Press and Cambridge University Press.

Primiano, Leonard Norman 1995. Vernacular Religion and the Search for Method in Religious Life. *Western Folklore* 54.1: 37–56.

Prokhorov, Boris 1999: Russia's North since the Fall of the Soviet Union. In Aleksandr Pika (ed.), *Neotraditionalism in the Russian North. Indigenous Peoples and the Legacy of Perestroika*. Circumpolar Research Series 6. Seattle and London: University of Washington Press.

Prokof'eva, E. D. 1981. Materialy po shamanstvu sel'kupov. In *Problemy istorii obshchestvennogo soznaniya aborigenov Sibiri (po materialam vtoroǐ poloviny XIX – nachala XX v.)*: 42–68. Leningrad.

Propp, V. Ya. 1928: *Morfologiya skazki*. L. Voprosy poètiki . Gosudarstvennyǐ institut istorii iskusstv, vyp. XII. Leningrad.

Putilov, B. N. 2003. *Fol'klor i narodnaya kul'tura. In memoriam*. St Petersburg: Peterburgskoe Vostokovedenie.

Pyysiäinen, Ilkka, and Kimmo Ketola 1999. Rethinking "God": The Concept of "God" as a Category in the Comparative Religion. In Tore Ahlbäck (ed.), *Approaching Religion*. Scripta Instituti Donneriani Aboensis 17: 1. Åbo: Donner Institute.

Rabinow, Paul 1977. *Reflections on Fieldwork in Morocco*. Berkeley: University of California Press.

Rasin, Albert 1993. Der etnischen Nihilismus der Udmurten: das Wesen, die Grunde, dei Wege des Kampfes. In János Pusztay (ed.), *Die Wege der finnisch-ugrischen Völker zur politischen, kulturellen und sprachlichen Autonomie. Materialien eines internationales Symposions 15.-17. Oktober 1992 in Szombathely*. Specimina Sibirica 8. Szombathely: Savaria.

Ricoeur, Paul 1976. *Interpretation Theory. Discourse and the Surplus of Meaning*. Fox Worth: The Texas Christian University Press.

Rousseau, Jean Jaques 1993. *The Social Contract and Discourses*. Everyman. London: J. M. Dent.

Saar, Edgar 1998. On the Funeral Customs of the Northern Khanty in the Last Quarter of the 20th century. *Folklore, Electronic Journal of Folklore* 7: 31–7. Tartu.

Saler, Benson 2000 [1993]. *Conceptualizing Religion: Immanent Anthropologists, Transcendent Natives, and Unbounded Categories*. New York: Berghahn Books.

Salminen, Timo 2008. *Aatteen tiede. Suomalais-Ugrilainen Seura 1883–2008*. Helsinki: Finnish Literature Society.

Salo, Merja 2009. Hantin kielen historia ja tulevaisuus. *Idäntutkimus* 2: 55–69. Venäjän ja Itä-Euroopan Tutkimuksen Seura.

Salve, Kirsti 1998. Vepsäläisten kansallisesta identiteetistä. In Pekka Hakamies (ed.), *Ison karhun jälkeläiset. Perinne ja etninen identiteeti yhteiskunnallisessa murroksessa*: 119–40. Helsinki: Finnish Literature Society.

Sanukov, Xenofont 1993. Ethnic Revival Problems of Russia's Finno-Ugric Peoples. In *Die Wege der finnisch-ugrischen Völker zur politischen, Kulturellen und Sprachlichen Autonomie. Materialien eines Internationales Symposions 15.–17. Oktober 1992*. Specimina Sibirica 8, ed. János Pusztay. Szombathely: Savaria.

Sanukov, Xenofont 1996. Die Nationalbewebung der kleinen Völker der Mittleren Wolga (Mari, Mordwinen, Tschuwaschen, Udmurten). In Andreas Kappeler (ed.), *Regionalismus und Nationalismus in Russland*. Nationen und Nationalitäten in Osteuropa 4. Baden-Baden: Nomos.

Schmidt, Eva 1981. Trends in 20th Century Ob-Ugric Oral Tradition. In Lauri Honko and Vilmos Voigt (eds.), *Adaptation, Change, and Decline in Oral Literature*. Studia Fennica 26: 147–53. Helsinki: Finnish Literature Society.

Schmidt, Eva 1989: Bear Cult and Mythology of the Northern Ob-Ugrians. In Mihály Hoppál and Juha Pentikäinen (eds.), *Uralic Mythology and Folklore*. Ethnologia Uralica 1: 187–232. Budapest and Helsinki: Ethnographic Institute of the Hungarian Academy of Sciences and Finnish Literature Society.

Shils, Eward 1981. *Tradition*. London and Boston.: Faber and Faber.

Shutova, I. N. 2001. *Dokhristianskie kul'tovye pamyatniki v udmurtskoĭ religioznoĭ traditsii*. Rossiĭskaya Akademiya Nauk, Ural'skoe otdelenie, Udmurtskiĭ institut istorii, yazyka i literatury. Izhevsk: Udmurtskiĭ institut istorii, yazyka i literatury, UrO RAN.

Sihvo, Hannes 1973. *Karjalan kuva. Karelianismin taustaa ja vaiheita autonomian aikana*. Helsinki: Finnish Literature Society.

Siikala, Anna-Leena 1986. Variation in the Incantation and Mythical Thinking: The Scope of Comparative Research. *Journal of Folklore Research* 23: 187–204.

Siikala, Anna-Leena 1987 [1978]: *The Rite Technique of the Siberian Shaman*. Folklore Fellows' Communications 220. Helsinki: Academia Scientiarum Fennica.

Siikala, Anna-Leena 1992. *Interpreting Oral Narrative*. Folklore Fellows' Communications 245. Helsinki: Academia Scientiarum Fennica.

Siikala, Anna-Leena 1995: Mekrijärven Väinämöinen. In Jorma Aho and Laura Jetsu (eds.), *Mekrijärven Sissola, runojen ranta*. Suomalaisen Kirjallisuuden Seuran Toimituksia 626: 114–28. Helsinki: Finnish Literature Society.

Siikala, Anna-Leena 1998. Etninen uskonto ja identiteetti. Udmurttien uhrijuhlat traditiona. In Pekka Hakamies (ed.). *Ison karhun jälkeläiset. Perinne ja etninen identiteetti yhteiskunnallisessa murroksessa*: 194–216. Helsinki: Finnish Literature Society.

Siikala, Anna-Leena 2000a. From Sacrificial Rituals into National Festivals: Post-Soviet Transformations of Udmurt Tradition. In Pertti J. Anttonen *et al.* (eds.): *Folklore, Heritage Politics and Ethnic Diversity. A Festschrift for Barbro Klein*: 57–85. Botkyrka: Multicultural Centre.

Siikala, Anna-Leena 2000b. Generic Models, Entextualization and Creativity: Epic Tradition on the Southern Cook Islands. In Lauri Honko (ed.), *Textualization of Oral Epics*: 343–69. Berlin and New York: Mouton de Gruyter.

Siikala, Anna-Leena 2000c. Body, Performance, and Agency in Kalevala Rune-Singing. *Oral Tradition* 15/2: 255–78. Bloomington: Slavica.

Siikala, Anna-Leena 2000d. Variation and Genre in Practice: Strategies for Reproducing Oral History in the Southern Cook Islands. In Lauri Honko (ed.), *Thick Corpus, Organic Variation and Textuality in Oral Tradition*. Studia Fennica Folkloristica 7: 215–42. Helsinki: Finnish Literature Society.

Siikala, Anna-Leena 2002a. *Mythic Images and Shamanism. A Perspective into Kalevala Poetry*. Folklore Fellows' Communications 280. Helsinki: Academia Scientiarum Fennica.

Siikala, Anna-Leena 2002b. What Myths Tell about Past Finno-Ugric Modes of Thinking. In Anna-Leena Siikala (ed.), *Myth and Mentality. Studies in Folklore and Popular Thought*: 215–32. Studia Fennica Folkloristica 8. Helsinki: Finnish Literature Society.

Siikala, Anna-Leena, and Oleg Uljašev 2002: Henkien maisema. Pohjoishantien pyhät paikat ja niiden rituaalit. Siperia. In Ildikó Lehtinen (ed.), *Taigan ja tundran kansoja*: 155–85. Helsinki: Museovirasto.

Siikala, Anna-Leena, and Oleg Ulyashev 2003. Landscape of Spirits: Holy Places and Changing Rituals of the Northern Khanty. *Shaman. Journal of the International Society for Shamanic Research* 11.2: 149–78.

Siikala, Anna-Leena, and Jukka Siikala 2005. *Return to Culture. Tradition and Society in the Southern Cook Islands*. Folklore Fellows' Communications 287. Helsinki: Academia Scientiarum Fennica.

Simon, Gerhard 1991: *Nationalism and Policy toward the Nationalities in the Soviet Union. From Totalitarian Dictatorship to Post-Stalinist Society*, trans. Karen Forster und Oswald Forster. Westview Special Studies on the Soviet Union and Eastern Europe. Boulder, San Francisco and Oxford: Westview Press.

Slezkine, Yuri 1994. *Arctic Mirrors. Russia and the Small Peoples of the North*. Ithaca and London: Cornell University Press.

Sokolov Yu. M. 1926. *Ocherednye zadachi izucheniya russkogo fol'klora*. Khudozhestvennyĭ fol'klor: Organ fol'klornoĭ podsektsii literaturnoĭ sektsii Gosudarstvennoĭ akademii khudozhestvennykh nauk. Vyp. I. Moscow.

Sokolov Yu. M. 1931. *Fol'kloristika i literaturovedenie*. Pamyati P. N. Sakulina: Sbornik stateĭ. Moscow.

Sokolova, Z. P. 1971. Perezhitki religioznykh verovaniĭ u obskikh ugrov. Religioznye predstavleniya obryady narodov Sibiri v XIX – nachale XX veka. *Sbornik muzeya antropologii i ètnografii* 27: 211–38. Leningrad.

Sokolova, Z. P. 1975a (1974). Novye dannye o pogrebal'nom obr'yade severnykh khantov. *Polevye issledovaniya instituta ètnografiĭ* 1974: 165–74. Moscow.

Sokolova, Z. P. 1975b. Untersuchung der religiösen Vorstellungen der Hanti am Unterlauf des Ob. *Acta Ethnographica Academiae Scientiarum Hungaricae* 24: 385–413. Budapest.

Sokolova, Z. P. 1983. *Sotsialnaya organizatsiya khantov i mansi v XVIII–XIX vv. Problemy fratrii i roda*. Moscow: Izdatel'stvo Nauka.

Sokolova, Z. P. 1989. A Survey of the Ob-Ugrian Shamanism. In Mihály Hoppál and Otto von Sadovszky (eds.), *Shamanism, Past and Present*, Part I: 155–64. Budapest: ISTOR books.

Spain, Daphne 1992. *Gendered Spaces*. Chapel Hill and London: University of North Carolina Press.

Startsev, G. A. 1929. *Zyryane. Etnograficheskiĭ ocherk.* Natsionalnyĭ archiv Respubliki Komi. F. 710, Op. 1, D. 4. Syktyvkar.

Steinitz, W. 1938. Der Totemismus bei dem Ostjaken in Sibirien. *Ethnos* 3: 125–40.

Steinitz, W. 1939. *Ostjakische Volksdichtung und Erzählungen aus zwei Dialekten. 1. Teil. Grammatische Einleitungen und Texte mit Übersetzungen.* Tartu: Ōpetatud Eesti Selts.

Steinitz, Wolfgang 1950. *Ostjakische Grammatik und Chrestomathie mit Wörterverzeichnis.* Leipzig: Harrassowitz.

Steinitz, W. 1980. Das System der finnisch-ugrischen Verwandtschaftstermini. *Ostjakologische Arbeiten. Band IV. Ostjakische Volksdichtung und Erzählungen aus zwei Dialekten.* Beiträge zur Sprachwissenschaft und Ethnographie: 354–79. The Hague, Budapest, Berlin, Paris, New York: Mouton.

Stocking, George W., Jr 1992. *The Ethnographer's Magic and Other Essays in the History of Anthropology.* Madison: University of Wisconsin Press.

Stoner-Weiss, Kathryn 1997. *Local Heroes. The Political Economy of Russian Regional Governance.* Princeton: Princeton University Press.

Sugney, Oleg 2002. Press Coverage of the Problems of Russia's Numerically Small Arctic Peoples. In Thomas Køhler and Kathrin Wessendorf (eds.), *Towards a New Millennium. Ten Years of the Indigenous Movement in Russia.* IWGIA – Document 107. Copenhagen: International Work Shop for Indigenous Affairs.

Sundström, Olle 2008. *"Vildrenen är själv detsamma som en gud". "Gudar" och "andar" i Sovjetiska etnografers beskrivningar av samojediska världsåskådningar.* Nordliga Studier 1. Umeå: Umeå University.

Survo, Arno 2001. *Magian kieli. Neuvosto-Inkeri symbolisena periferiana.* Helsinki: Finnish Literature Society.

Suutari, Pekka 2010: Monitasoinen kenttä – musiikkitoiminnan muutoksen tutkimus Venäjän Karjalassa. In Jyrki Pöysä, Helmi Järviluoma and Sinikka Vakimo (eds.), *Vaeltavat metodit.* Kultaneito 8: 315–27. Joensuu: Suomen Kansantietouden Tutkijain Seura.

Tambiah, Stanley J. 1996. The Nation-State in Crisis and the Rise of Ethnonationalism. In Edwin N. Wilmsen and Patrick McAllister (eds.), *The Politics of Difference. Ethnic Premises in a World of Power*: 124–43. Chicago and London: Chicago University Press.

Tarkka, Lotte 2005. *Rajarahvaan laulu. Tutkimus Vuokkiniemen kalevalamittaisesta runokulttuurista 1821–1921.* Helsinki: Finnish Literature Society.

Tedlock, Dennis 1979. The Analogical Tradition and the Emergence of a Dialogical Anthropology. *Journal of Anthropological Research* 35: 387–400.

Tedlock, Dennis 1983. *The Spoken Word and the Work of Interpretation.* Philadelphia: University of Pennsylvania Press.

Tishkov, Valery Aleksandrovich 1997: *Ethnicity, Nationalism and Conflict in and after the Soviet Union: The Mind Aflame.* International Peace Research Institute, Oslo. United Nations Research Institute for Social Development. London, Thousand Oaks, New Delhi: Sage Publications.

Toĭdybekova, Lidiya 1997. *Mariĭskaya yazycheskaya vera i ėtnicheskoe samosoznanie.* Joensuu: Joensuun yliopisto, Karjalan tutkimuslaitos.

Toidybekova, Lidia 1998. Marien yhteisörukoukset. In Pekka Hakamies (ed.), *Ison karhun jälkeläiset. Perinne ja yhteisö yhteiskunnallisessa murroksessa*: 253–75. Helsinki: Finnish Literature Society.

Tuan, Yi-Fu 1989. *Space and Place. The Perspective of Experience*. Minneapolis: University of Minnesota Press.

Tuchkova, N. A., *et al.* 2004: authors' collective under N. A. Tuchkova: A. I. Kuznetsova, O. A. Kazakevich, N. A. Tuchkova, A. A. Kim-Maloni, S. B. Glushkov, A. V. Baĭdak. *Mifologiya Sel'kupov*, ed. V. V. Napol'skikh. Anna-Leena Siikala, Vladimir Napol'skikh and Mihály Hoppál (eds.), Ėntsiklopediya ural'skikh mifologiĭ 4. Tomsk: Tomskiĭ gosudarstvennyĭ pedagogicheskiĭ universitet, Tomskiĭ oblastnoĭ kraevedcheskiĭ muzeĭ, Moskocskiĭ gosudarstvennyĭ universitet, Institut jazykoznaniya RAN.

Tuchkova, N. A., *et al.* 2010: A. I. Kuznetsova, O. A. Kazakevich, N. A. Tuchkova, A. A. Kim-Maloni, S. B. Glushkov, A. V. Baĭdak, *Selkup Mythology*. The Encyclopaedia of Uralic Mythologies 4, ed. Anna-Leena Siikala, Vladimir Napol'skikh, Mihály Hoppál. Budapest and Helsinki: Akadémiai Kiadó and Finnish Literature Society.

Ugriculture, Contemporary Art of the Fenno-Ugrian Peoples 2000. Espoo: The Gallen-Kallela Museum.

Uotila, T. E. 1986. *Syrjanische Texte* B II, ed. and trans. Paula Kokkonen. Mémoires de la Société Finno-ougrienne B 193. Helsinki.

Urban, Greg 1996. *Metaphysical Community. The Interplay of the Senses and the Intellect*. Austin: University of Texas Press.

Vakhtin, Nikolaĭ 1993. *Korennoe naselenie kraĭnego severa Rossiĭskoĭ Federatsii*. St Petersburg: Izdatel'stvo Evropeĭskogo Doma.

van Gennep, Arnold 1960 [1909]. *The Rites of Passage*. London: Routledge and Univ. of Chicago Press.

Vasenkari, Maria, and Pekkala, Armi 2000. Dialogic Methodology. In Lauri Honko (ed.), *Thick Corpus, Organic Variation and Textuality in Oral Tradition*: 243–54. Studia Fennica Folkloristica 7. Helsinki: Finnish Literature Society.

Vdovin, A. I., V. Yu. Zorin and A. B. Nikonov 1998. *Russkiĭ narod v natsional'noĭ politike XX vek*. Moscow: Russkiĭ mir.

Vernant, Jean-Pierre 1992. *Mortals and Immortals. Collected Essays*. Princeton: Princeton University Press.

Vitebsky, Piers 1993. *Dialogues with the Dead: The Discussions of Mortality among the Sora of Eastern India*. Cambridge: Cambridge University Press.

Vladykin, V. E. 1991. *Religiozno-mifologicheskaya kartina mira udmurtov*. Avtoref. diss. na soisk. uch. step. d-ra ist. Moscow: Nauk.

Vladykin, V. E. 1996. *Religiozno-mifologicheskaya kartina mira udmurtov*. Izhevsk: Udmurtiya.

Voldina, T. B. 2000. Rodil'naya i pogrebal'no-pominal'naya obyadnost' kazymskikh hantov. In *Ėtnografiya narodov Zapadnoĭ Sibiri* (k yubilyu d.i.n. pfor. Zoi Petrovny Sokolovoĭ). Sibirskiĭ Ėtnograficheskiĭ sbornik. Vyp. 10. Moscow.

von Sadovszky, Otto, and Mihály Hoppál 1995. *Vogul Folklore Collected by Bernát Munkácsi*, selected and ed. Otto J. von Sadovszky and Mihály Hoppál. International Society for Trans-Oceanic Research (ISTOR) books 4. Budapest and Los Angeles: Akadémiai Kiadó and International Society for Trans-Oceanic Research.

Warshofsky Lapidus, Gail 1979. *Women in Soviet Society. Equality, Development and Social Change*. Berkeley, Los Angeles and London: University of California Press.

Weiner, James 1991. *The Empty Place. Poetry, Space, and Being among the Foi of Papua New Guinea*. Bloomington and Indianapolis: Indiana University Press.

Wichman, Yrjö 1892. *Tietoja votjaakkien mytoloogiasta: T. G. Aminoff-vainajan ja omien muistiinpanojen mukaan julkaissut Yrjö Wichmann*. Helsinki: Finnish Literature Society.

Willerslev, Rane 2007. *Soul Hunters. Hunting, Animism, and Personhood among the Siberian Yukaghirs*. Berkeley, Los Angeles and London: University of California Press.

Williams, Christopher 1999. The National Question and Nationalism in the Former USSR, 1917–91. In Christopher Williams and Thanasis D. Sfikas (eds.), *Ethnicity and Nationalism in Russia, the CIS, and the Baltic States*: 24–44. Aldershot, Brookfield, Singapore and Sydney: Ashgate.

Williams, Raymond 1977: *Marxism and Literature*. Oxford: Oxford University Press.

Yamal-Nenets Autonomous District, official site (http://www.adm.yanao.ru/145)

Yoder, Don 1974. Toward a Definition of Folk Religion. *Western Folklore* 33: 1, 2–15.

Manuscripts

Siikala diaries 2000 and 2001: Field notes on the Khanty culture, Shuryshkary, Tyumen Oblast', Russia in 2000 and 20001. The Department of Folklore Studies. Helsinki University.

Ulyashev diaries 2000 – 2004: Field notes on the Khanty culture, Shuryshkary, Tyumen Oblast', Russia in 2000–4. Komi Komi naucnyĭ tsentr, Syktyvkar.

Ulyashev, Oleg 2001, Pogrebal'no-pominal'nye obryady Shuryshkarskikh khantov. Rukopis' po polevym materialam. Komi nauchnyĭ tsentr, Syktyvkar.

Khanty words

The Khanty spoke three main dialects, the Northern, Southern and East-ern. Southern Khanty has all but disappeared; Eastern Khanty is spoken by around 3000 people, and Northern Khanty by around 10,000 (according to Merja Salo 2009: 58). Northern Khanty is divided into several subdia-lects. According to Salo, the best known of the Northern dialects is that of Kazym; fewer guides to the Shuryshkary dialect have been published. There are, furthermore, dialect differences within the Shuryshkary area: the dia-lect of the villages close to Salekhard differs in manners of speech from that spoken in the southern villages. The influence of Komi in Synya is felt for example in the reduction of short vowels. The Khanty words given below were noted down during field work or else derive from literature, where usages are very variable. Vladimir Napol'skikh helped us in writing of some words and gave their Latin names. Merja Salo has given valuable advice and checked the word list, giving more dialectical variants for words and Latin names for different species of birds, fish and animals.

a

Aj-Moś-χu   Little *Moś* Man

aj χălaś, aj χăʌaś   graveyard for small childen (Karjalainen 1948: 372a–b)

aj lut   small goose, possibly white-cheeked brent goose (*Branta leucopsis*)

Aj-lut-iki   White-Cheeked Brent-Goose Old Man

aki, akə   grandfather, elder brother of the father or the mother (Steinitz 1950: 135)

aŋki   mother

appa   storage bag for spirit dolls

ar, arə   song (< Iranian)

ar-moś, -mońś   epic poems telling of divine heroes and local spirits

as   big river, also the name of the River Ob' in both of the Ob-Ugric languages (Khanty
    as, aś, äs; Mansi *as, ās, äs, oås* meaning in some dialects also "sea")

As-iki   the Ob' Old Man (see *Small-Ob'-tōrəm*, Karjalainen 1918: 306)

As-kŭr, pal-kŭr-iki   elder brother of *Töχləŋ-iki*, the Winged Man

aś, aśi   father

ašịn   sanctified cloth given to a family by a protector spirit (V. N.)

atəm   bad, evil, ill

avət, ovat   high cape, bluff, former Khanty town, later used as a place of sacrifice
    (Karjalainen 1948: 18a–b)

b

budarka   (modern) fishing boat (Russian)

e

eʌ'əŋ   motley (parallel word to *χănšaŋ*, Steinitz 1950: 136)
ēriγ, jēri, ēri, ēru   song (Mansi)
etər   clear, light, cloudless
etər-iki   Old Man of the Sky

χ

χăʌtị, χăltị, χoltị   die
χăʌaś, χălaś   graveyard
χăʌa, χăla,   grave
χălev   gull (*Larus*) or some other white fishing bird, tern (*Sterninae*)
χălev-iki   Gull Old Man
χănši, χănšə   design, ornament, letter
χănšaŋ, χănšeŋ   multicoloured, decorated
χănšaŋ voj   motley beast; seal, possibly spotted seal (*Phoca larga*) or ringed seal (*Pusa hispida*, formerly *Phoca h.*)
χănti   Khanty (Northern Khanty), *kăntəγ* (Eastern Khanty)
χănti vasịt   Khanti ducks
χătʌ   sun, day
χătʌ-χănši, χătʌ-χănšə   design of the sun
χăttị   go, move forward (Karjalainen 1948: 363a–b)
χătʌop, -ʌup   oar (*ʌop, ʌup, tup* oar, Karjalainen 1948: 1078b–1079a)
χenši, χenśi   teal, common teal (*Anas crecca*), or possibly garganey (*Anas querquedula*)
χiʌi   grandchild, nephew, niece
χiń, kịń   illness, epidemic disease (Northern and Eastern Khanty, Karjalainen 1948: 320a), *χiń, χịń* epidemic disease, death (Northern Khanty, Honti 1982: 49), *χeń* Satan (Southern Khanty, Karjalainen 1948: 320a)
Xịń-iki, Xyn'iki, Hiń-iki   Master of the Lower World, god of illnesses
χot   conical tent, house
χotəŋ-imi   female home guardian
χŏn   breast, belly, "boat" in 40/50-day remembrance ceremony
χŏr   appearance, form, image
χŏtəŋ   swan, probably whooper swan, hooper (*Cygnus cygnus*)
Xul   Master of Lower World (old Ugrian)
χul, χut, χol, χoʌ   spruce (*Picea abies*) (Karjalainen 1948: 366a; in the Middle Ob' dialect area *l > t*)
χurəχ, χuləχ, χoləχ   raven (*Corvus corax*) (Karjalainen 1948: 300b)
χus, χos   star
χuśʌ, χuśl   dawn (Steinitz 1950: 139, Honti 1982: 49), *χońʌ, χuńl, χuńtl* dawn (Karjalainen 1948: 323b, Honti 1982: 49)
χŭl   fish
χŭl-vŏj   fish fat
χŭʌəm, χŭləm, χoləm   three
Xŭʌəm noχr   an island in Voĭkar

i

iki   old or mature man
il, iʌ   below, lower, down
Ilpi mŭv iki   Man under the Earth (Martynova 1998: 123)
il'l'a χătʌ   St Elijah's day

imi   old woman, wife, woman, female person (not a small girl)
Imi-χiʌi   Nephew of the Aunt
is   shadow, shadow soul, life, spirit; bear's blood
is-χŏr   shadow soul, shadow, ghost (of a person who is going to die soon) (Karjalainen
    1948: 88a)
ittərma, ŋittərma   death doll, forefather (< Nenets)

j

jaj   older brother, older or younger brother of father, stepfather (Steinitz 1980: 368;
    Honti 1982: 26)
jalań   wooden idol with pointed head
Jalań-iki   giant man-eater
jăm   good
jem, jeməŋ   holy (Eastern Khanty *jim*)
Jeməŋ-aŋki   Holy Mother, guards everything that grows
Jeməŋ-ńŏʌ   holy cape
jeməŋ ʌor, jeməŋ lor   holy lake
jeməŋ ura   holy storehouse of spirits
jeməŋ χănši   sacred embroidery
jeməŋ χot   sacred house, church (Eastern Khanty *jiməŋ kât*)
jernas   woman's dress (< Komi)
jevər   wolf
Jevri iki   Old Wolf, a spirit protector
jik, jiŋk   water
jik-ves   water monster
jir   sacrifice
jir jŭx   sacrificial tree
jox   people
jol, jolta-ko   witch, fortuneteller, a shaman (Eastern Khanty)
još   hand, arm
još-vŭs   window in a dead person's hut in graveyard
jŏχan, jogan, jugan   river
Jŏχan-iki   Old Man of the River
juχ, jŭχ   tree, wood
juš, jos   way

k

kaldanka   traditional boat made of boards
Kasəm   Kazym river (Karjalainen 1948: 437a)
Kasum-naj-imi, Kasum-naj   the Great Kazym Woman
Kăltaś, Kăltəś, Kăltaś-imi   female deity
Kăltəś-aŋki   wife of the supreme god
kăt, kat   two
Kăt-χul   Two Spruces, the name of an island
Kev-ńŏʌ   Stony Cape
kev pelak   "the stony side" referring to the Ural Mountains (which are called *Kev* in
    Khanty)
Kev-ur-χu-akem-iki   Stone Nenets Old Man
kevan   bottle (*kev* + *an*, "stony vessel")
Kun avət joχ   a group of the *Moś* phratry in Kunovat
Kur-iʌpi-iki, Kur-iĺpi-iki   Master of the Lower World, see *kur[t]*
kurt, kur'   village (< Komi)
Kuš avət joχ   name of a kin group

kŭl lit. *kul, kuľ,* a malevolent supernatural being, *kŭľ* (Synya), *kuľ* (Obdorsk) devil,
evil spirit (Honti 1982: 61), *kŏʌ'* forest or waterdevil (Kazym), *kŏľ, kuľ* devil, evil
spirit (Southern Khanty, Karjalainen 1948: 397a) (< Komi)

Kŭľ-iki, Kŭľ-ilpi-iki, Kŭl-ilpi-iki Master of the Lower World

kŭškar, kŭnškar, kŭnš, kŭš, kŏš, kus, kŏs nail

kŭr leg, foot

kŭrek northern pintail (*Anas acuta*) (< Komi)

kŭrəŋ χot sacred storehouse on four legs

kŭrəŋ lŏpas sacred storehouse on four legs

kŭštị voj "whistling beast, whistler"; hazel-grouse, hazelhen (*Tetrastes bonasia,*
formerly *Bonaso b.*)

Kŭtəp-Moś-χu Middle *Moś Man*

kŭvś, kŭvəś long male coat

l, ʌ

ʌaŋki, laŋki, taŋkə red squirrel (*Sciurus vulgaris*)

lapăs, lŏpas (sacred) store house

ʌarăś, larăś chest

ler, ʌer root, strand, fibre, worm

ʌiʌ, lil breathing soul

ʌiʌ χot a tiny chum made for the 40/50-day remembrance ritual for the soul

lipət, lipət leaf

ʌoʌmaχ wolverine (*Gulo gulo*), thief

ʌoŋ-vertị-imi a local spirit

ʌoŋχa, loŋχa spirit protector

ʌor, lor, lar lake, wide area more or less constantly flooding

Lor-naj a female spirit

Lor-paj a holy place

ʌov, lov, lav horse, mount

ʌovəŋ-χu, Lovəŋ-χo Man who sits on the Horse, a deity

ʌuχ, luχ, ʌuŋχ, lŏŋχ spirit, image of spirit (Honti 1982: 80–81), *tuŋ'χ, ʌoŋ'k, lŏŋ'k*
spirit, guardian spirit at home (Karjalainen 1948: 1065a–b) (*hlunk* Eastern Khanty,
Barkalaya 2002c)

ʌuχ ʌarăś a chest for spirits

ʌuχ χŏr image of spirit

lŭŋ, ʌŭŋ summer

lŭŋ-kŭtəp-χătʌ Midsummer's Day

lut, lunt, ʌont goose (*Anatidae*)

ľ

ľaktị, ľakstị spit, throw (Steinitz 1950: 164, Honti 1982: 90)

ľaksas soul of a kinsman born again in a child

ľaksum people related by reborn souls

m

maš-jŭχ the forks on both sides of the fire, on which the crossbar rests

măntị go

meŋk, mek forest spirit (Southern Khanty: man eater (not evil), very strong, Mansi:
mēŋkw, mēŋk devil, forest spirit) (< Iranian)

mir people, world (< Russian)

Mir-šawiti-χu, Mir sawittə-χu mythical ancestor and protector of *Moś* phratry,
seventh son of the supreme god (= Mansi *Mir-susne-χum*)

Moma-aŋki   Earth Mother
moś, mońś   folk tale
Moś   man (a heroic ancestor); phratry
Moś-χu, -χo   *Moś* man
Moś joχ   *Moś* people
Moś-ne   *Moś* woman
mŏχsəŋ   Siberian white fish (*Coregonus muksun*) (Yakut > Khanty > Russian)
mŭʌ-taχa   holy place of the house
mŭʌ śuŋ   holy corner of house
mŭv   earth, country
mŭv eʌ'əŋ voj   description of magpie: motley beast of the lower world, parallel line
   to the next
mŭv χănšəŋ voj   motley beast of the lower earth
mŭv-χot-pauʌ   earth village (*pauʌ* < Mansi *pāvəl* village)
mŭv-kertti-χu   "the man who goes round the earth" = *ʌovəŋ-χu*
mŭv-ler   earthworm
mŭv-vantti-χu   "the man who looks at the earth" = *ʌovəŋ-χu*

n

naχr   armour, an iron shirt (cf. *tăyər, ʌăyər, lăyar,* coat of mail, which should be made
   by a virgin in order to be hard, Karjalainen 1948: 1955b; Honti 1982: 75) (< Iranian)
nait   magician (*näjt-ku* magician in Eastern Khanty)
naj   fire, sun, sunny, light, but in a ritual connection woman, mistress according to
   Kulemzin 2006 ("female spirit", Steinitz 1950: 148)
Naj-aŋki   female deity, life-giver for people (Fire-Mother)
naŋk   larch (*Larix sibirica*)
ne (neŋ-)   woman, wife
nel'ma, ńel'ma   freshwater white salmon (*Stenodus leucichthys nelma*) (Russian)
niməl   skis covered in the skin of a reindeer's forefeet
nimləŋ juš   Milky Way, "the track of the skis"
noχr, noχər   cone of the Siberian cembra (its seed, in Khanty *sem,* is called in Russian
   orekh, "nut")
noχr-leti-ne   nutcracker (*Nucifraga caryocatactes*), (according to Karjalainen 1948:
   572b) Eurasian jay (*Garrulus glandarius*)
noχraś   Siberian cembra (*Pinus sibirica*)
nŏrəm   platform, bridge, shelf
nuj   broadcloth
nuj săχ   woman's dress
num   upper, top
Num-torəm   god of the sky
nupət   life given by God, age, century, epoch

ń

ńajt, ńajt-χum   magician (Mansi)
ńoʌ, ńuʌ, ńăl   cape, nose, bow of a boat

o

ort   spirit, spirit assistant
Ort-iki   Old Ort Man (Karjalainen 1918: 306)
Otšam-iki   a hero
Ovolaŋkur[t], -kur'   the Khanty name for Ovolyngort (*ov oləŋ kur',* "village [standing]
   on the mouth of a river")

ŏ

ŏχ, uχ   head, top
ŏχ pontị   "putting down [one's]head"; bow
ŏχsar, vŏχsar   fox (*Vulpes vulpes*)

p

paj   heap, stack, hill, island
păl, păʌ   ear
păl, păʌ   high
păləŋ, păʌəŋ   cloud
păləŋ-ŏχ-lipət   water flower (water lily)
păsan   table (< Komi)
păsəŋ   holy
pătlam χot   "dark house", a shamanic ritual
Päi-īka   Old Man of Thunder and Storm (Dem'yanka)
Pelym-tōrəm   (Karjalainen 1918: 306, spirit of Pelym)
poχər, puχər   island, islet of forest on a swamp
poχrəŋ joχ   people of islands (Steinitz 1950: 154, Honti 1982: 122)
Por joχ   *Por* people
porχa   an image of the deceased wrapped in his/her shirt
Por-ne   *Por* woman
por-ne-kuškar   medicine called "a nail of the forest woman"
pori, porləm   sacrifice
poriʌiti   sacrificial ritual
pos, pas   kin symbol (Russian *tamga*) (< Komi)
poslan joχ   people of ducts or channels
pottị, patta   freeze, ice up, frost up
potəm vöj   frozen fat
pŏχ   boy, son
pŏrton, pŏrtum   medicine
pŭʌəp   wooden cover of open fireplace
pŭt jŭχ   "cauldron tree", crossbar for cauldron above the fire

r

rut   relative, kin, family; kindred
rŭś   Russian (< Komi)
Rŭś iki   Russian man, a god of the Lower World
rŭś vasit   Russian ducks

s

savne   magpie (*Pica pica*)
săχ   shirt, women's coat made of fur or broadcloth (Russian *yagushka*)
săχ-kiŋenit   string of coat
săran rut   Komi
sevkel   fake plaits (*sev* plait, pigtail + *kel* string)
sir   kin (Eastern Khanty; Russian *rod*)
sojm, sojəm, sajəm   brook, waterhole, deep
Sorńi-iki   Golden Old Man
Sorńi-naj   Golden Woman, wife of the supreme god
Sorńi-ńoʌ   Golden Cape
Sorńi-pŏχ,   Golden Boy
sort, sor'   pike (*Esox lucius*)
Sort jugan joχ   a kin group, *Sort jugan* people, people of the Pike river

suŋ, śuŋ, sŏŋ   corner, angle
sŭv   pole, bar, stick, stake
sŭvsər   hunter's staff

ś

śak, saχ   hammer (*ś-* in Shuryshkary, *s-*in Obdorsk)
śak-voj   "hammer animal", a goose with red throat , possibly red-breasted goose
   (*Branta ruficollis*) (Honti 1982: 165: *śag-woj* the smallest goose, Russian *čekvoj*)
Śăńa joχ   Synya people (*Senja joχ* Perevalova 2004: 132), *Śəńa jŏɣan* (Obdorsk) Synya
   river (Karjalainen 1948: 913b)
śiśki   little bird
śohma   unclean, sin (the latter meaning according to Russian ideas; cf. Kazym *śomŋa*,
   Obdorsk *śămma* "uncleanliness, menstruation", Karjalainen 1948: 911a, Honti 1982:
   167)
śŏχəʌ, śŏχəl   open fireplace in the house corner covered by wooden cover
śuŋ   see *suŋ*

š

šar, sar   twist, tobacco for chewing
šepən, sepan   shaman
Šiẕiŋ-ʌor   name of a lake
šuməl, šoməʌ, soməl   stroke, mark, cut, hole
šumləŋ juχ   stick calendar (Voïkar)

t

tăχa, tăχi   place, area
tij, tăj   top, mouth, end, spring
tiləś   moon, month (< Komi)
toχtəŋ   loon (*Gavia arctica*)
Toχtəŋ-iki   Diver Old Man
tojpər, mojpər   bear (*Ursus arctos*), some kind of sacred animal (Honti 1982: 92)
Torəm, Turəm   the universe, God, god of sky, weather and air
Torəm-aśi, Torəm-father
Torəm-pŏχ   Son of *Torəm*
Torum-iki   Torum Old Man
tŏχəl   wing
Tŏχləŋ-iki   Winged Man
tŭt jŭχ   "fire tree", tree for pots over fire
Tŭt-imi   Old Fire Woman

u

uχəl, uχəʌ, oɣəʌ   sledge (in Eastern Khanty *uɣəʌ*)
uləm-is   dreaming soul
Un-moś-χu   Big *Moś* Man
un-voš   big town
upit šup uśʌa   a ritual for transferring the ʌiʌ soul in the 40/50-day remembrance
   ceremony
ur'   the god who watches every person
ur'-χo, -χu   uncle. In dictionaries: Synya *urt*, Obdorsk *ort* lord, owner, rich man,
   moon, month (Honti 1982: 18–19)
ura   hut for images of spirits, where the spirits of the dead are served
urt, uras uj   wandering soul
urt   hero, forfather's spirit, guardian spirit (Steinitz 1950: 164). Shuryshkary *urti* uncle,

mother's younger brother, cousin (Khanty-Russian dictionary). Kazym *orti* nephew (Honti 1982: 19)

ut, unt   forest

ut puχǝr   forest, cedar-tree islands among the swamps

ŭli, vŭli   reindeer (*Rangifer tarandus*)

ŭli leṭi voj   wolf (*Canis lupus*), lit. "reindeer-eating animal"

ŭli porṭi voj   "terrible mauling beast", protector spirit, euphemism for wolf, lit. "reindeer-biting animal"

ŭp   father-in-law, brother-in-law (Synya, Honti 1982: 15)

ŭs, vŭs   hole

ŭsǝŋ jŭχ   a tree full of holes, a shaman tree

v

verṭi   do, make, build

ves   mythical being living in rivers (Karjalainen 1948: 246a–247a)

ves-iki   mythical being living in rivers, like burbot (*Lota*)

veš, venš   face

veš lopǝs   mask in funeral ritual

voj, vaj   animal, snake

vŏj, vǎj   fat, grease, suet, butter, oil

vŏrŋa   crow (*Corvus corone*)

Vŏrŋa χǎtʌ   Crow Day, an important feast in early spring

vŭ-   see *ŭ-*

vŭjǝv   wigeon (*Anas penelope*)

Transliteration of Komi

Komi	Transliteration
А а	a
Я я	ja
Э э	e
Е е	je
И и, I i	i
Й й	j
О о	o
Ё ё	jo
Ö ö	ö
У у	u
Ю ю	ju
Ы ы	y
Б б	b
В в	v
Г г	g
Д д	d
Д' д'	ď
Ж ж	ž
З з	z
З' з'	ź
К к	k
Л л	l
М м	m
Н н	n
Н' н'	ń
П п	p
Р р	r
С с	s
С' с'	ś
Т т	t
Т' т'	ť
Ф ф	f
Х х	x
Ц ц	c
Ш ш	š
Щ щ	šč
Дж дж	dž
Дз дз	dź
Ч ч	ć
Тш тш	č

Index

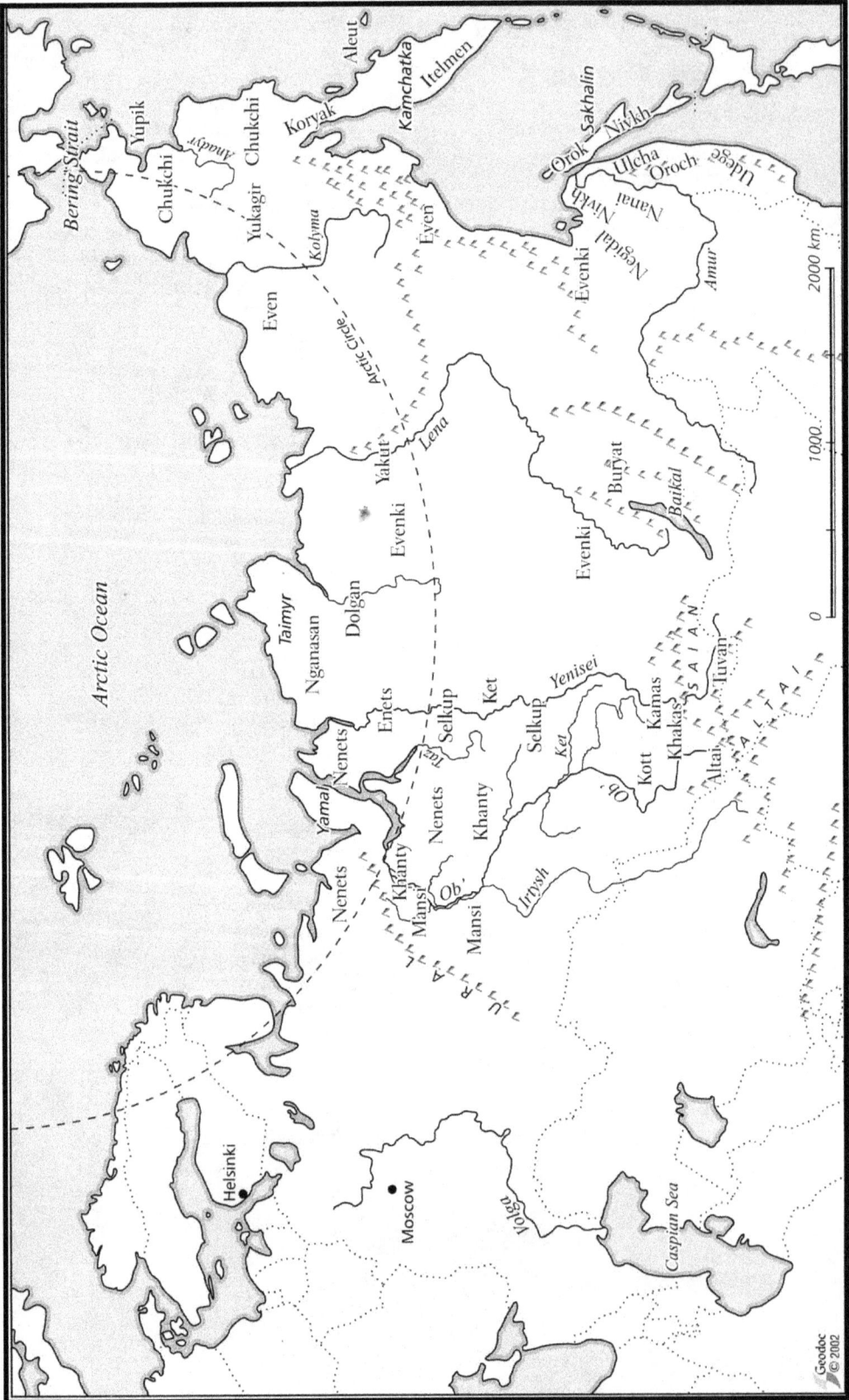

Map 1. Khanty groups and their neighbours in Western Siberia. Ildikó Lehtinen (ed.), Siberia. Life on the Taiga and Tundra. National Board of Antiquities. Helsinki, 2002, p. 22.

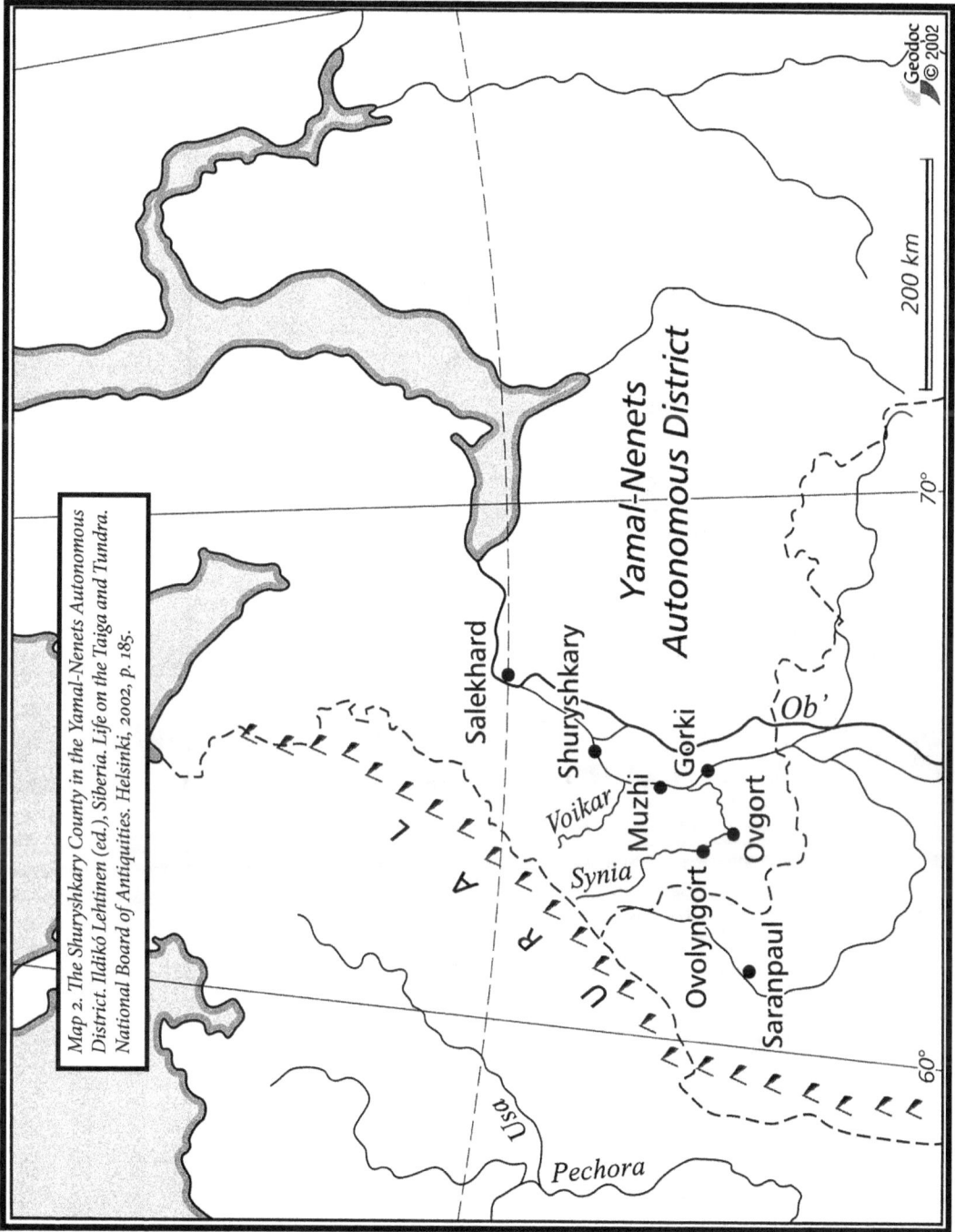

Map 2. The Shuryshkary County in the Yamal-Nenets Autonomous District. Ildikó Lehtinen (ed.), Siberia. Life on the Taiga and Tundra. National Board of Antiquities. Helsinki, 2002, p. 185.

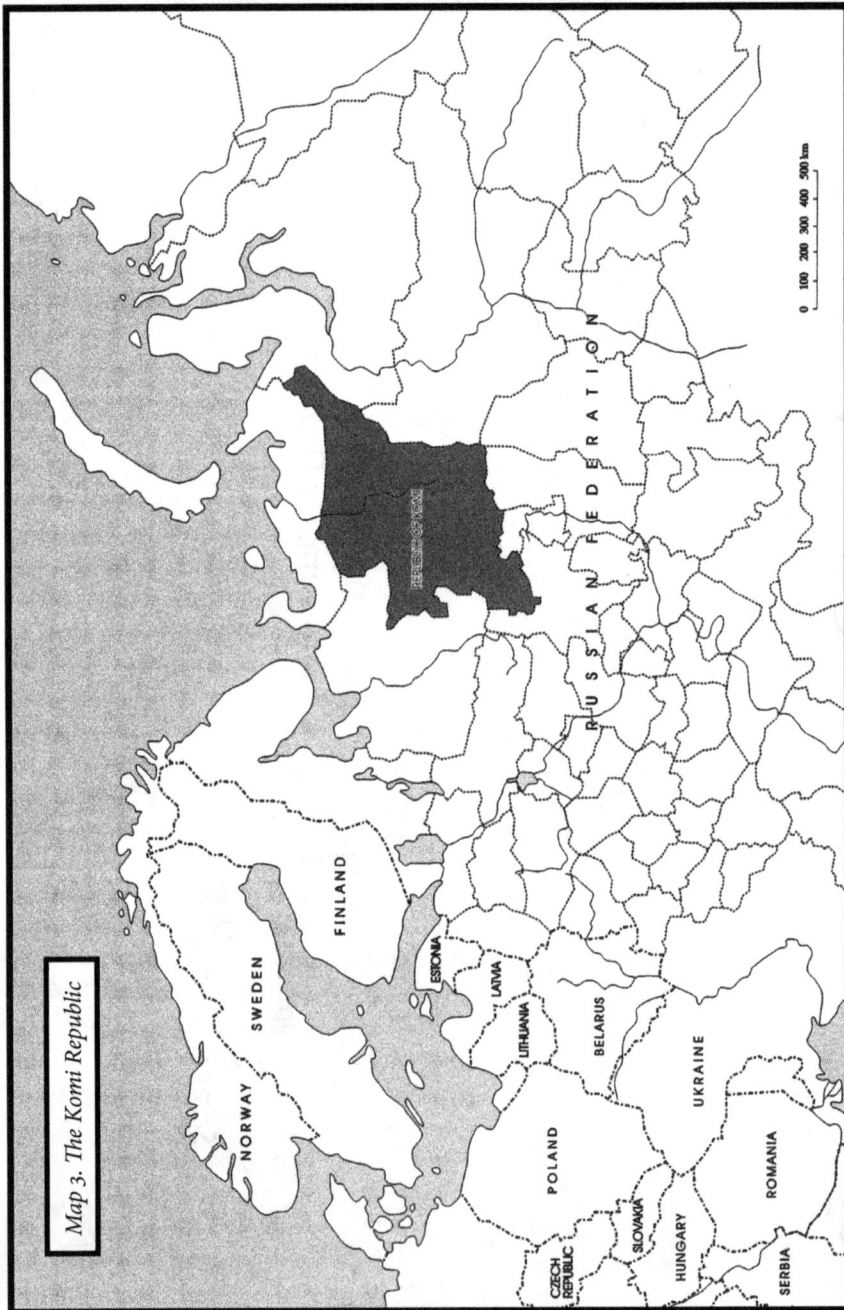

Map 3. The Komi Republic

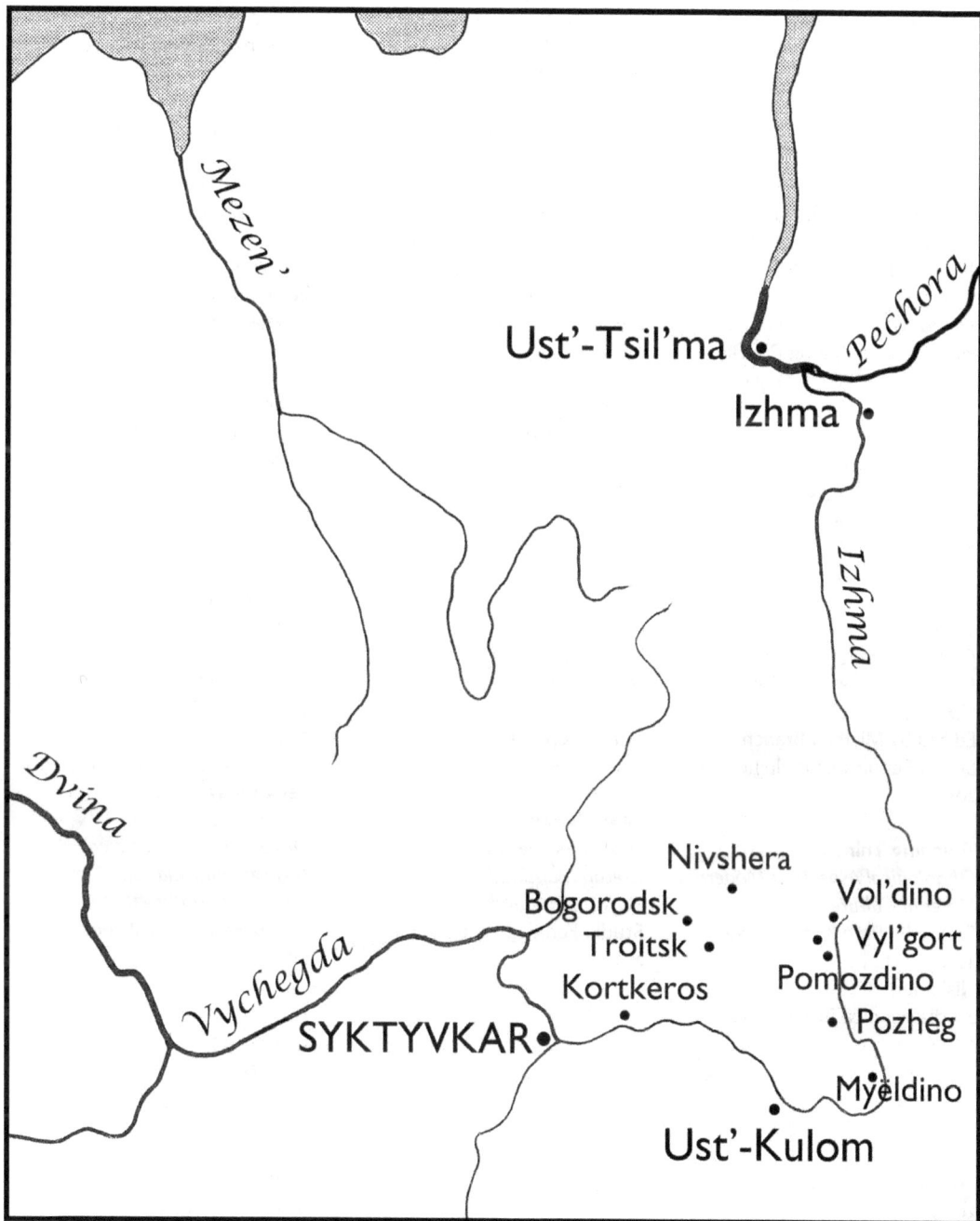

Map 4. *The field-work sites of the Upper Vychegda and Izhma areas*

Studia Fennica Ethnologica

Making and Breaking of Borders
*Ethnological Interpretations,
Presentations, Representations*
Edited by Teppo Korhonen,
Helena Ruotsala & Eeva
Uusitalo
Studia Fennica Ethnologica 7
2003

Memories of My Town
*The Identities of Town Dwellers
and their Places in Three Finnish
Towns*
Edited by Anna-Maria Åström,
Pirjo Korkiakangas & Pia Olsson
Studia Fennica Ethnologica 8
2004

Passages Westward
Edited by Maria Lähteenmäki &
Hanna Snellman
Studia Fennica Ethnologica 9
2006

Defining Self
*Essays on Emergent Identities in
Russia Seventeenth to Nineteenth
Centuries*
Edited by Michael Branch
Studia Fennica Ethnologica 10
2009

Touching Things
*Ethnological Aspects of Modern
Material Culture*
Edited by Pirjo Korkiakangas,
Tiina-Riitta Lappi & Heli
Niskanen
Studia Fennica Ethnologica 11
2009

Gendered Rural Spaces
Edited by Pia Olsson & Helena
Ruotsala
Studia Fennica Ethnologica 12
2009

Studia Fennica Folkloristica

Creating Diversities
*Folklore, Religion and the Politics
of Heritage*
Edited by Anna-Leena Siikala,
Barbro Klein & Stein R.
Mathisen
Studia Fennica Folkloristica 14
2004

PERTTI J. ANTTONEN
Tradition through Modernity
*Postmodernism and the Nation-
State in Folklore Scholarship*
Studia Fennica Folkloristica 15
2005

Narrating, Doing, Experiencing
Nordic Folkloristic Perspectives
Edited by Annikki Kaivola-
Bregenhøj, Barbro Klein
& Ulf Palmenfelt
Studia Fennica Folkloristica 16
2006

MÍCHÉAL BRIODY
**The Irish Folklore Commission
1935–1970**
History, Ideology, Methodology
Studia Fennica Folkloristica 17
2007

VENLA SYKÄRI
Words as Events
*Cretan Mantinádes in
Performance and Composition*
Studia Fennica Folkloristica 18
2011

Studia Fennica Historica

**Medieval History Writing and
Crusading Ideology**
Edited by Tuomas M. S.
Lehtonen & Kurt Villads Jensen
with Janne Malkki and Katja
Ritari
Studia Fennica Historica 9
2005

Moving in the USSR
*Western Anomalies and Northern
Wilderness*
Edited by Pekka Hakamies
Studia Fennica Historica 10
2005

DEREK FEWSTER
Visions of Past Glory
*Nationalism and the Construction
of Early Finnish History*
Studia Fennica Historica 11
2006

**Modernisation in Russia since
1900**
Edited by Markku Kangaspuro &
Jeremy Smith
Studia Fennica Historica 12
2006

SEIJA-RIITTA LAAKSO
Across the Oceans
*Development of Overseas
Business Information
Transmission 1815–1875*
Studia Fennica Historica 13
2007

Industry and Modernism
*Companies, Architecture and
Identity in the Nordic and Baltic
Countries during the High-
Industrial Period*
Edited by Anja Kervanto
Nevanlinna
Studia Fennica Historica 14
2007

Charlotta Wolff
Noble Conceptions of Politics in Eighteenth-Century Sweden (ca 1740–1790)
Studia Fennica Historica 15
2008

Sport, Recreation and Green Space in the European City
Edited by Peter Clark, Marjaana Niemi & Jari Niemelä
Studia Fennica Historica 16
2009

Rhetorics of Nordic Democracy
Edited by Jussi Kurunmäki & Johan Strang
Studia Fennica Historica 17
2010

Studia Fennica Anthropologica

On Foreign Ground
Moving between Countries and Categories
Edited by Minna Ruckenstein & Marie-Louise Karttunen
Studia Fennica Anthropologica 1
2007

Beyond the Horizon
Essays on Myth, History, Travel and Society
Edited by Clifford Sather & Timo Kaartinen
Studia Fennica Anthropologica 2
2008

Studia Fennica Linguistica

Minna Saarelma-Maunumaa
Edhina Ekogidho – Names as Links
The Encounter between African and European Anthroponymic Systems among the Ambo People in Namibia
Studia Fennica Linguistica 11
2003

Minimal Reference
The Use of Pronouns in Finnish and Estonian Discourse
Edited by Ritva Laury
Studia Fennica Linguistica 12
2005

Antti Leino
On Toponymic Constructions as an Alternative to Naming Patterns in Describing Finnish Lake Names
Studia Fennica Linguistica 13
2007

Talk in Interaction
Comparative Dimensions
Edited by Markku Haakana, Minna Laakso & Jan Lindström
Studia Fennica Linguistica 14
2009

Planning a New Standard Language
Finnic Minority Languages Meet the New Millennium
Edited by Helena Sulkala & Harri Mantila
Studia Fennica Linguistica 15
2010

Studia Fennica Litteraria

Changing Scenes
Encounters between European and Finnish Fin de Siècle
Edited by Pirjo Lyytikäinen
Studia Fennica Litteraria 1
2003

Women's Voices
Female Authors and Feminist Criticism in the Finnish Literary Tradition
Edited by Lea Rojola & Päivi Lappalainen
Studia Fennica Litteraria 2
2007

Metaliterary Layers in Finnish Literature
Edited by Samuli Hägg, Erkki Sevänen & Risto Turunen
Studia Fennica Litteraria 3
2009

Aino Kallas
Negotiations with Modernity
Edited by Leena Kurvet-Käosaar & Lea Rojola
Studia Fennica Litteraria 4
2011

The Emergence of Finnish Book and Reading Culture in the 1700s
Edited by Cecilia af Forselles & Tuija Laine
Studia Fennica Litteraria 5
2011

www.ingramcontent.com/pod-product-compliance
Lightning Source LLC
Chambersburg PA
CBHW081735270326
41932CB00020B/3279